PRELUDE

PRELUDE

A Journey of Growth, Song, and
Self-Discovery

Ron Boucher

MERIPOINT BOOKS | Williamsburg, Virginia

For permissions, contact:
Meripoint Books LLC
P.O. Box 1512
Williamsburg, VA 23185
meripointbooks.com

Author's Note: The people and events described in this work are drawn from memory and shaped by personal reflection. Every effort has been made to portray them truthfully according to the author's recollections. Some names and details have been changed to preserve the privacy of those involved. This story is not meant to pass judgment, but to understand the forces that shaped a life.

Photo credits: p 252, ©Beth Bergman, Saint of Bleeker Street, Nov. 1976 A-23 NYC Opera. Used with permission. p. 270, ©Beth Bergman, Otello Sept. 1979 A-5 Met Opera. Used with permission.

Library of Congress Cataloging-in-Publication Data
Boucher, Ron.
Prelude: a journey of growth, song, and self-discovery / Ron Boucher. — First edition.
     pages cm
Summary: "An autobiography chronicling the author's personal and musical journey, highlighting experiences that shaped his life and career as a singer"—Provided by the publisher.
ISBN 978-1-960808-15-8 (paperback) — ISBN 978-1-960808-16-5 (hardcover)
    1.   Boucher, Ron — Biography. 2. Singers — United States — Biography. I. Title.
ML420.B68 A3 2025
782.0092—dc23

Library of Congress Control Number: 2025944681

Printed in the United States of America
Williamsburg, Virginia
First Edition

Baskerville 11 pt

Dedication

To my beloved wife, Sandra,

Through every chapter of life, your unwavering support, boundless love, and enduring companionship have been my guiding light. Your resilience and grace have been the backdrop against which I've danced, stumbled, and found my way. As I pen these words, I am reminded of the countless moments we've shared—the challenges we've faced, the dreams we've woven, and the laughter that has carried us through.

This book is a testament to the profound impact you've had on my journey. Your presence has been the muse behind my words, the strength beneath my aspirations, and the warmth that has illuminated the darkest corners of our path. From the stages of our youth to the stages of life we continue to traverse, your love has been the melody that accompanies me every step.

May these pages reflect the depth of my gratitude and the breadth of my affection. Just as you've been the leading lady of my heart, may your essence shine through these lines, reminding me and the world of the extraordinary woman whose spirit has enriched my existence.

With all my love,

Ronnie

Contents

Preface: Overture to Life

Reality consists of one's personal perceptions. These perceptions embody the truths that shape one's journey throughout a lifetime. To recount my life, I must share my reality, the truths as I perceive them.

This narrative isn't an endeavor to critique or analyze the individuals I've chosen to write about. Passing judgment on their thought processes and choices isn't my intention. Yet, if this serves as a mirror reflecting the people who've crossed my path, then so be it.

Ultimately, this is my story—the way I've interpreted life's interactions and how they've influenced my responses to comparable situations and their outcomes. As I embark on this written voyage, my aim is to unravel the purpose and meaning behind these experiences, mend any wounds they've caused, and unearth a resolution that fosters a profound sense of self-love.

CHAPTER 1 THE PRELUDE

BABY, TAKE A BOW

Ron

The year was 1955, the golden age of the fine arts, but also an era of rock 'n' roll and rebellion. It was the time of the Baby Boomers, and I was ready to make my mark on a world in motion. During this time, my own journey began. The labor of childbirth commenced a daunting thirty-six hours before I made my entrance into the world. The story, frequently recounted by my mother, paints a terrifying picture of a childbirth process that nearly claimed her life. The guilt I might have carried if her sacrifice had led to her demise was unimaginable. At 8 pounds 2 ounces, it's as if, according to her, I possessed the power to decide life or death. Those agonizing hours of labor pains, guiding me through the birthing canal, the narrow passage an infant navigates like a snake through grass.

What began as nonchalant coaching from nurses and doctors evolved into cautious concern as complications arose. By 9 p.m. on March 6th, the situation demanded a life-threatening decision for both my parents. "Your child is stuck in the birth canal, and a cesarean section isn't feasible at this stage," the obstetrician explained.

In hindsight, why wasn't this option considered earlier? A practical solution to avert harm to both parties should have been apparent. A scalpel, an incision, and the task would be accomplished – a baby brought into the world! However, life's narratives are seldom so straightforward.

Since I seemed to have a say in the matter, I opted for a more dramatic resolution. There was nothing comedic about my birth. "We'll need to use a specialized serum derived from a bull. This will intensify contractions, hopefully aiding the baby's passage with forceps. Yet there's a risk Mrs. Boucher might hemorrhage, and we could lose the child. Given the potential danger, Mr. Boucher, we need your consent," the doctor informed my father, who had spent the last thirty-something hours in a designated room for expectant fathers.

This wasn't a Henny Youngman one-liner like "Take my wife...please!" It was profoundly serious.

The serum worked, thankfully, or I wouldn't be here narrating my tale. But the process wasn't complete. The doctors used forceps to gently reposition my body, guiding my skull into alignment. Thankfully, an infant's skull is malleable, allowing the plates to shift, aiding movement through the narrow passageway. The vaginal canal, perplexingly, narrows rather than widens, necessitating elasticity in the vaginal lips to facilitate passage. Nature's design also requires these lips to stretch further to accommodate a fetus' shoulders without tearing.

At 1:42 a.m., March 7th, my presence on this planet was officially registered by the attending nurse. I had triumphed. Was it a reason for celebration or resentment? This joyful couple, who anticipated a typical experience—hours of labor followed by slumber leading to a newborn—were now grappling with complicated feelings. How could they muster affection for this little one after enduring such an ordeal?

The birthing process was unkind to my skull. The result of the doctor's forcefulness was evident; my cranium appeared reshaped, accentuating my forehead and complemented by a full head of dark, spiky hair. As my father quipped, I was the missing link Darwin had been searching for. Did he consider swapping the bassinet for a tree, or perhaps sending me back for another attempt?

The decision was simpler by the third day, as my head assumed a more conventional form. The happy couple returned home to embark on their journey with *Ronnie*. Why "Ronnie" you ask? Knowing my father, it's likely my mother proposed the name, and his response was, "Sure, that's nice." Being of French-Canadian descent with the last name "Boucher," numerous relatives named Francois, Pierre, or Jacques, all harmonized well with the surname. Why did my mother choose that name? What dashing, dark-haired actor of the '50s silver screen might have influenced her choice? Cary Grant, Rock Hudson, Robert Mitchum, or Gene Kelly? None of the above. It was Ronald Reagan who held her fascination. Thus, my birth certificate read, "Ronald Bertrand Boucher."

And there you have it—the foretelling of my destiny played out in my birth process. From the start, my life was destined for challenges; accomplishments wouldn't come easily. Drama would be a constant companion, and I'd attain a modest level of notability, earning a small place in the community's recognition. Is this speculation, or could it be a glimpse into the future I hold?

Mom, Dad, Baby Ronnie

DAD: THE BALLAD OF FATHERHOOD

Roger Donat Boucher, born on January 19, 1930, was one of the thirteen children of Ulrich and Denise. He arrived as the eighth child in rapid succession.

After his birth, my grandmother experienced postpartum depression, prompting her to turn to her sister Eliza for help. Eliza, married to prosperous businessman Donat Boisvert, owner of an insurance business and multiple real estate holdings, offered to care for Roger until my grandmother recovered.

Dad

Eliza's two older daughters, Florence and Theresa, lavished attention on their new cousin. Unable to have more children of her own and with my grandmother already managing nine children and expecting another, Eliza proposed adopting Roger after three years of nurturing him. They assured my grandparents that my father would have unrestricted access to visit his birth family whenever he wished.

My grandparents, however, felt affronted and decided to take Roger back. An alternative offer was made by Roger's aunt and uncle that he could visit them at any time. Life at Eliza and Donat's home stood in stark contrast to his life with his biological family. With his aunt and uncle, he experienced nurturing, refinement, etiquette, respect, love, compassion, and a deep religious conviction. At home with his parents, survival was paramount, both physically and emotionally, amidst financial struggles and an absence of emotional support. According to my mother, his home life was traumatic with incidents of incest, moral decay, and a lack of mutual respect.

Roger must have grappled with his desire to be with his siblings, even if it meant accepting hand-me-downs, cramped living spaces, and lowered educational and vocational aspirations. Later, as Roger entered eighth grade, Eliza and Donat were ready to support his college education or even the opening of a pharmacy, should he choose to continue schooling. However, my father opted to follow in his older siblings' footsteps and enter the workforce. Over the years, I've sensed a certain resentment from his family due to his privileged treatment during his formative years, seen as receiving a metaphorical silver spoon. Despite his limited formal education, my mother helped him cultivate a suppressed sophistication. My dad possessed a sensitivity that went unappreciated and was often seen as a weakness by his family. Substantial differences between my paternal and maternal grandparents will become clearer in the later chapters of my life story.

With no clear career path or vocational plan, my father enlisted in the army during the Korean War and was stationed four years in Germany—a time he rarely discusses. Upon returning to the US, he courted and married my mother. Experiencing layoffs became a recurring pattern. With one child and another on the way, my mother urged him to take the civil service exam for the U.S. Postal Service. After several attempts and numerous novenas—series of prayers repeated nine times—he eventually succeeded. This opportunity prompted him to return to high school and earn a complete four-year diploma. He rose to become the President of the Postal Union, a position he held for ten years. He reached the rank of Postmaster during his final years in the postal service, retiring at sixty to Florida. After twenty-five years of retirement, he returned to Massachusetts, choosing to spend the remaining years living with Mom in a beautiful spacious home owned and occupied by my sister Carol.

My relationship with Dad remained consistently steady, emotionally unfaltering. Mom often conveys his pride in me through her communication. As my story unfolds, you'll notice that my connection with him lacks dramatic highs and lows, resembling instead the vast, sweeping plains of the Midwest. It is in deep contrast to my relationship with my mother, but in hindsight, a much-needed balance that may not have been appreciated and to this day is still not understood by me.

Mom: The Melody of Maternity

Mom

My mother, born on April 12th, 1933, in the south end of New Bedford to Hector and Alice Serra, was the second daughter. She arrived just one year and six days after her sister Doris.

Her schooling began at St. Anne's, nestled in the city's South End. Soon after, her family moved to a home on Coffin Avenue in the north end of New Bedford, leading her to transfer to St. Anthony's Elementary School.

New Bedford's reputation was intertwined with its cotton mills. My grandfather, Hector, was a loom fixer—a trade that secured his employment until his retirement. While money was scarce, both of my grandparents carried immense pride. From my grandmother, my mother inherited a sense of etiquette and a keen appreciation for quality, traits that remained with her throughout her life. Sociable by nature, my mother has always radiated a zest for life and is often immersed in laughter. According to my grandmother, my mom was always the center of attention making people laugh from the age of three. Her academic performance was above average, and she chose to pursue a clerical/secretarial career that served her well during her working years.

Upon completing high school, Mom worked two jobs. One was at the Sunbeam Baking Company, one-half block from her house and the second was a woman's clothing store on Acushnet Avenue called the Venetian Shop, contributing all her earnings to the household and receiving only a modest allowance. There was one exception—during the year leading up to her marriage-- she used her money to furnish essentials for her future home with her husband. Mom exhibited remarkable resilience in the face of financial challenges, always returning to work when necessary. My earliest memory of this was when I was in the third grade when she went to work at the Continental Screw Company from 2-9 p.m. Wherever she worked, she enjoyed herself, brought home captivating stories, and effortlessly made new friends.

Mom's presence has always been larger than life, infused with endless laughter, jokes, and a "joie de vivre" that remains her lifeline when life throws inevitable curveballs. While she has always possessed intelligence, her focus often gravitates towards social interactions, frequently with a drink in hand. Throughout their marriage, she has been the driving force, urging my father to venture beyond his comfort zone. Her ability to forge lifelong connections is evident in the friends she has collected over time.

A profound connection formed between my mother and me from the very beginning. From birth, my mother loved to make me laugh and I loved the attention she doted on me. Throughout my life, she was always there to stand up for me, when necessary, while also providing the support I needed to fight my own battles. Her friendships and active social life sometimes raised concerns about her family priorities, a sentiment often echoed by her mother and sister. Nevertheless, one thing you could always rely on was joy, celebrations, and a constant stream of entertainment, from which I was almost never excluded.

As I grew older, I began to feel like an integral part of her social circle, a privilege few other children in our group could claim. In the following chapters, I hope you'll gain insight into my mother's character, especially in contrast to my father's. It wasn't until my teenage years, during my journey of self-exploration, that I began to sense her efforts to keep me from straying too far from the ideals she had set. Our relationship often felt like a tug of war between love and frustration, but today, I deeply respect her strength and unwavering determination.

French Canadian Catholics: Hymns of Heritage

Allow me to share some genealogical background, painstakingly pieced together with the assistance of Ancestry.com and the diligent efforts of my father's sister-in-law. The roots of my lineage, both on my paternal and maternal sides, lead to French-Canadian ancestry that traces its origins back to France. These ancestors cultivated their families in the heart of French culture, centered around St. Anthony's Church in the North End of New Bedford, Massachusetts. This very town served as the backdrop for Herman Melville's timeless novel, *Moby Dick*. Though it must be noted, New Bedford later gained a different kind of notoriety when a pool table incident was sensationalized on CNN, sparking debates depending on one's political inclination—was it truth or fiction, fact, or fake news?

In the 1950s, a consequence of World War II was the United States' aspiration to unite its citizens under a common identity. During this time, many Americans who had returned home sought to shed their ethnic distinctions, no longer identifying themselves as French, Polish, or Italian. Nevertheless, a contingent remained resolute in preserving their heritage and native languages. This commitment to heritage found a steadfast supporter in St. Anthony's Parish, nestled in New Bedford's northern precinct. St. Anthony's exuded a vibrant presence and held a captivating grip on the community, reaching every parishioner. At the helm of this fervent preservation movement stood Reverend Monsignor Albert Bérubé. This esteemed clergyman reigned over St. Anthony of Padua Catholic Church, a magnificent architectural masterpiece hewn from red sandstone, its origins dating back to 1912. However, it was in 1952 that Monsignor Bérubé enlisted the expertise of Italian artist and architect, Guido Nincheri, to oversee the renovation, infusing it with renewed life.

Within our familial orbit, there were several who had answered the call to religious orders. Notably, my paternal grandfather's brother, Osias Boucher, shared a lifelong camaraderie with Albert Bérubé, tracing back to their childhood. There were also clerical connections through my maternal grandmother's sister, Aunt Josephine, a devoted nun, and her brother Hubert, known as Brother Edgar, as well as a cousin, Fr. Gerald Boisvert. Monsignor Albert Bérubé and my great uncle, Monsignor Osias Boucher, were kindred spirits, both friends and rivals. Their competitive journey had led them to serve as chaplains during World War I, a time that witnessed a wager on which of them would be the first to preside over their own diocese. Although my uncle claimed victory, Albert had the resources and support to transform St. Anthony's into a cherished masterpiece, where he continued his service until his passing in 1973.

The inauguration of the church coincided with my parents' impending wedding, a ceremony where my father's uncle had pledged to officiate. Yet, the specter of uncertainty loomed as his battle with cancer cast doubt on his ability to fulfill this promise. Monsignor Bérubé also envisioned his dedication ceremony as the pinnacle, the inaugural mass that would affirm his achievement. The challenge was to reconcile his desire to bestow this honor upon his lifelong friend with the knowledge that time was fleeting. Yielding to friendship's embrace as has been recorded, on September 7th, 1953, my parents exchanged vows, an event that could have been lifted from the cinematic enchantment of *The Sound of Music*. The processional march resounded as my mother made her entrance, the organ harmonizing Wagner's "Here Comes the Bride," accompanied by a chorus of voices. Adding to the visual tableau, the archways of the church illuminated sequentially as she passed beneath. Hearing these family stories left me wondering how fate could have led me anywhere other than the stage, bearing a name like Ronnie and having an inherent propensity for drama.

St. Anthony's played a pivotal role in shaping my childhood. While one might assume that my narrative would pivot towards the Catholic Church's priest scandal that has garnered public attention, my focus centers on the devoted Sisters of Christ. These women, who embraced lives of service, poverty, chastity, and obedience, laid the cornerstone for my intellectual development, psychological disposition, and understanding of faith. To me, the nun's habit emerged as a symbol of both virtue and duplicity, encapsulating a duality that I will expound upon as my story unfolds. As a young child, I stood awestruck in the presence of "God," as embodied by St. Anthony's gothic architectural marvels, statues in marble and plaster, resplendent stained-glass creations, frescoes, and paintings. The grandeur of this architectural triumph left an indelible imprint on my artistic sensibilities, a legacy that endures to this day.

We attended the "high" mass, a regal affair marked by music, pomp, and circumstance. The grand pipe organ, the largest on the eastern seaboard, and the celestial choir infused the proceedings with a transcendent quality. The strains of Bach cascading from the choir loft's balcony seemed to resonate with the heavens themselves. Occasionally, when the organ reached its zenith, the vibrations were felt through the pews, the sound on the cusp of shattering the imported Italian stained-glass windows. While other children may have found such rituals tedious, the church's ceremonies held a mesmerizing allure for me, captivating my attention far beyond what was typical for a child.

The weekly hour-long service fell short of satiating my hunger for connection. My aspirations were fulfilled around the age of eight, when a cardinal rule allowed young boys to become altar servers after reaching the age of reason, typically around third grade. While most boys busied themselves with superhero fantasies, I found contentment within the hallowed walls of the church. My earliest recollections of role play centered on my portrayal of revered clergy figures, particularly that of a priest. I often imagined the day when I could don a black cassock with a distinctive Nero-style collar, a white cardboard band tucked within to bridge the gap, and a black satin sash. I am confident my sister Renee could vouch for these memories as she patiently endured countless lengthy sermons during my dramatic reenactments.

I was always struck by the priest's ability to hold the congregation's attention, even in the face of yawns and drooping eyelids. During my reenactments, I went to great lengths to imbue realism into my performances. I distributed my version of the holy wafer, crafted from Sunbeam bread, a batter-whipped, white bleached flour product promoted with the tagline "Look ma, no holes." This flawless bread, flattened and

St. Anthony's Church

dried, became a makeshift representation of the Eucharist. To complete my portrayal, I donned my father's inherited maroon satin dressing gown, a cappa in the church's nomenclature, worn by celebrants during mass. This robe, inherited from his affluent uncle, served as my connection to the sacred rituals I so deeply admired.

My aspiration, or perhaps delusion, was rooted in the hope that one day I might receive a divine calling, a spiritual beckoning to join the revered men held in the highest esteem by the faithful. These were the men entrusted with the sanctity of the confessional, sworn to eternal secrecy regarding the sins confessed within its confines. The allure of St. Anthony's went beyond rituals; it was a symphony of sights and sounds, a procession that invoked images of coronations. Every Sunday's high mass commenced with the resounding pipes of the organ, the very foundations of the church resonating. The nuns, adorned in black habits with starched white bibs and distinctive silver hearts, were the first to enter, moving with precision. Upon reaching the front bench, a wooden clapper echoed. Together they knelt in unison, heads bowing in reverence before rising to proceed to their assigned seats.

Following the procession of the nuns and angelic altar boys, whose black cassocks and white surplices took on a crimson hue during special feasts, a small red cape with gold fringe completing their attire, a sense of privilege emanated from the sacristy near the altar. This sacred space allowed one to bask in proximity to the divine, albeit accompanied by the physical trials of kneeling on unpadded wooden kneelers, a contrast to the clergy's velvet cushions. In the entourage that followed, the deacon and sub-deacon walked ahead of the celebrant, their path unfolding from the vestibule in the church's eastern wing. Their procession, resplendent with pageantry, navigated down the side aisle before ascending the central one.

On notable occasions, the celebrant donned a regal gold shawl, a splendid cloak that enshrouded his hands as he held the Monstrance—a magnificent gold vessel cradling the consecrated Eucharist. Preceding him were two altar boys swinging incense burners like pendulums of a grandfather clock. The fragrant streams of smoke that unfurled signaled the congregation to genuflect as they passed by, making the sign of the cross. The protocol dictated that if the consecrated host was exposed beyond the tabernacle, genuflection required both knees. If contained within, one knee was sufficient.

In the realm of aesthetic appreciation, some children possess a heightened affinity for classical music. In my case this held true. The music, choir, and soloists within St. Anthony's sanctuary profoundly moved and inspired me. Just as Verdi's triumphant march in *Aida* conjured images of grandeur, Sundays unfurled with a similar splendor. The resonance of Wagner's compositions pervaded the church, echoing through its very foundations in what seemed like an effort to rouse even the departed.

The liturgy began with customary cadence: the Kyrie, the Gloria, dialogues exchanged between priest and choir loft. The offertory showcased the choir's harmonious offerings, succeeded by the Sanctus.

Communion held a special place in my heart, marked by a soloist's mellifluous rendition while the congregation approached for communion. The culminating recessional march stood as a mirrored reflection of the service's inception. The vestments worn by the clergy were akin to costumes deserving of a Tony Award.

Drawing from Pope Innocent III's twelfth-century codification, the church's use of five liturgical colors—violet, white, black, red, and green—aligned with the seasons: Advent, Christmas, Epiphany, Lent, and Easter and ordinary times. This chromatic symphony wove symbolism into the sacred calendar. A prime example emerged in Lent, distinguished by deep, rich purple hues that even shrouded the statues of saints. These colors shifted dramatically as Lent gave way to Easter, characterized by whites adorned with vibrant red accents that symbolized the radiant light of the risen Christ. The arrival of Easter lilies signaled the triumphant heralding of spring's return.

In the sacristy, a royal blue plush carpet created an air of regality. Centered above, a monumental sculpture of a dove stood as an emblem of the Holy Spirit, the third persona within the divine trinity. It was easy to imagine this avian effigy coming to life, soaring from its perch, which happened one day as a bat that had taken up residence behind the sculpture descended during mass. In a swift, unhesitating motion, the priest's arm dispatched the bat, which fell onto the altar before being brushed aside and onto the floor. With an air of nonchalance, the service continued, leaving the custodian to address the bat's fate.

I received a deep-rooted sense of cultural and religious identity that was shaped by my French-Canadian ancestry and the significant role of St. Anthony's Church in my life. The vivid memories of the church's rituals and the influence of religious figures instilled in me a profound appreciation for my heritage and spiritual traditions. My early aspirations to join the clergy, inspired by the solemnity and reverence of the religious ceremonies I witnessed, reflect how these experiences have influenced my sense of self. Additionally, I hope you see, as I do, the importance of preserving cultural traditions amidst socictal changes. These memories reinforce my commitment to maintain and honor my family's heritage as I continue with my story.

My Grandmother (a.k.a. Mémère Serra): A Lullaby for Mémère

St. Anthony's Church, with its magnificent splendor and captivating pageantry, left an enduring imprint on my fascination with the arts. Experiencing the vocal performances of the soloists at the church set a standard for the kind of auditory experience required in such a grand space. This understanding later equipped me with the skills needed to meet the vocal demands of operatic performances. Nonetheless, it was my grandmother who laid the foundation for my musical inclinations, even though I admit that her training was rather limited considering my strong affinity and talent for the arts.

Allow me to share a bit of background regarding my maternal grandparents, who held the roles of patriarch and matriarch within our family. Despite the occasional disagreements between my parents and my grandparents, both parties had their own distinct space for retreat. This balance of oversight allowed my parents the freedom to establish themselves as individuals and fostered a sense of family unity rarely found in modern homes. My grandparents provided stability for us grandchildren, affording my parents the space to work and build their lives.

Our family embodied a European lifestyle, with three generations coexisting under one roof. Although we lived within the same building, our home was divided into two floors. Known as tenement housing, a common architectural style in New England, these rectangular structures comprised two or three floors, each housing five rooms, one bathroom, and a small kitchen. In keeping with local tradition, one room, the "parlor," was reserved for formal occasions and was decorated for that purpose. In my grandmother's home, the parlor featured a magnificent oak floor adorned with an antique oriental carpet displaying a royal blue background and a

Alice Serra, Yvette, and Ronnie

resplendent medallion in deep reds, purples, and beige and gold accents. This carpet became my favorite and was an inheritance I cherished after my grandparents passed away. The parlor also contained Queen Anne-style furniture—a couch and two chairs upholstered in light grayish blue moray satin fabric that had faded over time to a silvery grey. Other elements included a two-tiered lamp table, an ornate console table adorned with a plastic floral arrangement and the wedding photos of my mother and her sister, a coffee table, and a knick-knack box holding delicate porcelain figurines.

As in many homes, the kitchen was the heart of our family. After my mother and her sister were married, my grandparents transformed a bedroom into an eat-in kitchen, installing two casement windows that opened out to the backyard. That kitchen, centered around a rectangular Formica table, became the stage for countless memories—some joyful, others painful.

My mother and her mother, Mémère Serra, both had culinary talents. While my mother could whip up impressive dishes that even made Julia Child envious, it was Mémère's cooking that always won the family's everyday vote. When it came to family meals, Mémère held the upper hand—especially since we came home for lunch, with our elementary school just two blocks away.

On Fridays, we observed the tradition of abstaining from meat year-round, not just during Lent. On alternating Fridays, Mémère would make her signature fish and chips—pan-fried sole with freshly cut, deep-fried potatoes—or a clam chowder so rich it could have earned accolades. On the other Fridays, my mother would send me to pick up fish and chips from a specialty store. The contrast was clear: while Mémère's dishes were homemade masterpieces, the store-bought version, wrapped in newspaper, was a distant second.

Sundays, however, were when a competition heated up between my grandmother and my father. Mémère's elaborate Sunday dinners were served promptly at noon after church, complete with a homemade dessert. My father, having worked as a cook in the army, began preparing his own Sunday meals, but his timing and consistency were unpredictable, and his meals often lacked the flair and flavor of Mémère's. His meats were plain, his vegetables came from cans, and dessert was nonexistent.

The competition between them became obvious when my grandmother decided to prepare the same dishes my father was planning—like pot roast —but his versions never quite measured up. While Mémère's roast came with fresh, seasoned vegetables and always ended with something spectacular like her angel food cake filled with Jell-O and strawberries, my father's meals were simpler, missing that special touch. Tensions between them escalated further when my mother couldn't resist her own mother's cooking, often eating at Mémère's table before sitting down for my father's meal.

The competition over meals, though seemingly about food, was a reflection of the deeper family dynamics at play—love, tradition, and loyalty, all intertwined with moments of tension. Mémère's presence in the kitchen symbolized stability and control, while my father's attempts to compete showed his desire to assert himself in the family.

In retrospect, these family meals were a subtle tension that shaped our family life.

Long Pond: Reflections on Water

In my experience, there is always an unspoken societal expectation for friends to follow similar life paths. For my mother and her friends, the relationships that were formed while attending St. Anthony High School solidified into lifelong bonds. After graduation, they all sought jobs, dated, and eventually committed to marriage. Between 1952 and 1953, all the girls—Yvette Serra, Pauline Meunier, Pauline Thomasette, Leola Picard, Pauline Marcoux, Georgette Bessette, Pauline Guilbeaut, Evelyn Bertrand, and Juliette Lapointe—became engaged and then married.

Following marriage, the focus shifted to starting families, resulting in the births of children between 1954 and 1955. The order children born to these mothers was Ronnie, Ricky, Sharon, Mark, Michael, Paul, Jeanne and Steve, Anne, and Douglas. Four of us, including myself, attended St. Anthony's Grammar School. Within this group of friends, there was an intriguing practice that I didn't fully understand—calling adult friends of my parents' "uncle" or "aunt," even when we weren't blood relations. This tradition might have been a cultural or regional norm, reflecting a deep level of familiarity and respect within the community.

An unusually close and inexplicable bond existed between my mother and one friend in particular, stemming as far back as grammar school. Neither my mother nor this friend had positive feelings toward the other's spouse. In fact, my mother might have openly disliked her friend's husband. Despite these complications, their friendship endured over time, which is a matter that, looking back, might warrant psychoanalysis to fully comprehend. Understanding the dynamics of this relationship is crucial because it appears that this connection had a substantial impact on the events that nearly shattered my self-esteem and self-confidence.

The girls and their first-borns

Experiencing peer bullying is one thing, but enduring the undermining of adults adds an entirely different layer of suffering. Upon reflection, it seemed that my mother's friend had the desire to be the most popular figure among her peers, a trait she passed down to her eldest son. I'm not entirely sure if this inclination was a product of genetics or learned social behavior, but it certainly felt foreign to my own nature.

Even at a young age, my perceptions were that being a property owner at a lakeside community conferred a certain stature, fostering a sense of self-importance and superiority that often led to insensitivity. For the less fortunate, adhering to the role of guest and following established protocols set by this friend granted others the privilege of accessing the community's privacy and amenities. This dynamic was evident in our social standing at the cottage.

At the time, my mother's friend's family was considered upper-middle-class, as her father owned a mechanic shop, a house, and land. She and her brother inherited the land near the lakefront in an area known for its summer cottages along the pond. It was here that I spent most of my summers—a place where I learned to assess relationships and develop my understanding of friendship's importance. It was also here that I honed the skill of survival.

To justify the indignation my family faced at the pond, one might have assumed we were guests at the Kennedy estate. The reality was that for many years, there was a converted old school bus on the property, containing only the driver's seat, which entertained countless children over time. Walking down the aisle of the bus, you would find a kitchen sink on the left, followed by a gas stove/oven, refrigerator, and storage cabinets. On the right was a small folding table and the escape door. The back of the bus featured four bunk beds and a toilet in the middle, separated by a cloth curtain for modesty.

Typically, at least six families were present at any given time at the lake. We played badminton, croquet and predominantly, horseshoes. During that era, gender roles were more clearly defined, with fathers returning from work, changing into swimming trunks, engaging in quick lakeside activities with their children, then heading back to the cottage to barbecue selected meats for the evening. They would enjoy beer and a few rounds of horseshoes.

Meanwhile, the women gathered indoors or around the picnic table to prepare a variety of salads to accompany steaks, chicken, hotdogs, or hamburgers. Afterward, they would clean up, wash dishes, and get the children ready for bed, as their exhausting day in the sun led to restful slumber. By the grace of God, my family returned home each evening, allowing me to either nestle into my grandmother's arms or find solace in my room, sometimes just staring at the picture of the Sacred Heart that hovered on the wall next to my bed.

Although I had other fathers to observe, the essential components for building a strong father-son bond seemed to be missing. Even as I grew older and began to grasp the concept of male bonding, I often felt lost. My father participated in activities like horseshoes and badminton, but something was always off. He never seemed to earn the respect that I thought he deserved, nor did he forge close friendships with the other men. It was as if he was present but not truly accepted, always a tolerated guest rather than an equal.

The motorboat that came with the cottage represented more than just a way to get around; for most men and boys, it was a symbol of masculinity and ego. For me, it added layers of confusion about what it meant to be a man. As a young boy, I naturally looked to my father for guidance through those early, awkward experiences that required a mix of strength, confidence, and reassurance. But with my father, I struggled to find that connection, that role model I longed for. He was there, but I often felt like I was navigating the path to manhood on my own.

We spent six to seven days a week at the Pond during the summer. My mother's friendship with her girlfriend carried an emotional attachment I couldn't fully grasp. From what I observed early on, their relationship seemed to function well when they were alone. However, when other guests arrived, my mother became the target of ridicule and insults. Despite this, her infectious "joie de vivre" always shone through, though it often provoked a negative reaction from her friend, who craved the spotlight. The most difficult part for me was seeing not only my mother insulted but also my father and myself drawn into the dynamic.

Like my mother's situation, my own social standing depended on whether I was alone with her friend's son, or if others were present. Given the close relationship between our mothers, it was expected that her son and I would naturally be friends, well at least that was the impression I got. And just like our mothers, we got along fine when it was just the two of us. But everything shifted when the other boys joined us. In their presence, I became the target of laughter, criticism, and even physical bullying— spitting, biting, and exclusion. Anyone who dared to show me kindness faced the same treatment. Even when I tried to make friends with boys from other cottages, something would always intervene, leaving me isolated once again.

As time passed, the dynamics—both physical and emotional—at the Pond changed, turning what should have been a place of summer fun into a living nightmare for me. Much like my mother's struggles with her own friendships, I found myself trapped in an unequal relationship, unable to escape the harsh judgment of others.

By the time I reached an age where I could reason through it all, I had lost the desire to be at the Pond altogether. The allure had faded, and I sought refuge in the comfort of my room and the nurturing environment my grandmother provided. Avoiding yet another summer marred by bullying seemed far more appealing than staying trapped in that toxic dynamic.

Canada: A French Rhapsody

In stark contrast to life at Long Pond, I found myself delighting, if only briefly, in the immersion of Canadian culture each summer. These visits meant connecting with numerous paternal and maternal relatives scattered around the Montreal region. Upon my arrival, an unexplainable sense of belonging enveloped me, a feeling of openness and acceptance of my emerging true self.

I happily anticipated spending time with Canadian relatives each summer. I felt a kinship with the culture, a sense of home, tranquility, and the freedom to explore and satiate my curiosity. Though my time in Canada was limited to just a week or two during each summer, a part of me wished we could move there permanently. It was in Canada that I witnessed both my parents being treated with the respect they deserved, warmly welcomed on every visit.

My fluency in French, my primary language, turned out to be a gift. It endeared me to many of the priests and nuns at St. Anthony's Church until they realized that I could understand every word they uttered in my vicinity.

There existed an enigmatic bond between my cousins and my real aunts and uncles, particularly the trio of brothers: Christian, Michelle, and Alain. Christian, the eldest, was the son of my uncle Roland and aunt

Dorothé. What struck me most was Christian's uncanny resemblance to Peter Fonda in *Easy Rider*. The brothers, separated by only two years, were, in my eyes, the kind of "bad boys" whose behavior would have been unacceptable to my mother and mémère. They enjoyed an independence that allowed them to come and go freely without consequence. Dating girlfriends and riding motorcycles were parts of their lives that my mother vehemently opposed even though she liked them. This was a fascinating paradox that served as a guidepost for my own journey.

Their sibling interactions often involved playful rough housing, and they included me comfortably in their teasing and wrestling. There was a marked distinction between these interactions and those with the boys at Long Pond. This contrast stemmed from genuine acceptance and the sense of being regarded as equals. For instance, on one occasion, they playfully tied me to a tree and left me there for about half an hour. At first, it was amusing, then it turned uncomfortable, and finally, it ended in tears. The significant difference lay in the aftermath of this escapade—my cousins and my aunt Dorothé gathered around to reassure me that it was all in jest. These experiences were cherished; they kindled in me a deep yearning and even a few prayers for a brother to share such camaraderie with.

Another profound aspect of my Canadian experiences was the impact they had on my perspective towards music and dance. In Canadian culture, these art forms were embraced, nurtured, and encouraged, with the talents of artists celebrated. All my Canadian relatives shared a love for music, singing, and dancing, without attaching any connotations of being "sissy" or "gay." In fact, my Canadian male relatives seemed remarkably secure in their masculinity, which they often displayed with brutal vigor on the hockey rink.

However, a particular incident highlighted the conflicts that arose from my mother's deeply held beliefs about sexuality. One evening at a chalet in the mountains of Quebec, my older cousins Jacques, Pierre, and Jeffre decided to put on a drag show and invited my father and me to join them. Their wives enthusiastically supported the idea, helping with clothing, hair, and makeup. They even invited me to participate. But while the atmosphere was lighthearted and fun for everyone else, my mother's reaction was starkly different. She made it clear that she disapproved, voicing her objections, and sending a strong message that this kind of behavior was unacceptable and, by implication, wrong. Her attitude cast a shadow over an otherwise joyful moment, making me acutely aware of the cultural and personal conflicts she imposed.

Sex and Canada: The Temptation Tango

In those years in New Bedford, sex, with the sole exception of marriage, was regarded as a deviant behavior condemned by the Church, and the origin of all things sinful. To be in communion with holiness and approved by God, one had to safeguard purity, striving to distance all sexual thoughts and actions from conscious awareness. In the eyes of the Church, boys' self-gratification constituted a perpetual sin, while premarital intercourse stood as a mortal transgression. Girls who used their bodies to allure boys were doomed to eternal damnation. The ethos at home further underscored these taboos; my grandparents slept apart, and my parents' unspoken physical relationship was a notion we avoided. To my sister and me, our mother took on the mantle of the Virgin Mary, and we emerged as products of immaculate conceptions.

In stark contrast, my Canadian relatives embraced a radically different perspective on sexuality compared to the norms prevailing in New Bedford. My first poignant encounter with this contrast came when our cousins Claudette and Jacques chose to spend their honeymoon at our house, a choice dictated by financial constraints. One morning, as Pépé Serra sat in his green recliner engrossed in the morning paper, and Mémère Serra and I were ensconced in a rocker reading a book, the bedroom door opened, and Cousin Jacques emerged. Tall and athletic in his early twenties, he strolled towards the bathroom wearing only white BVDs. With an air of self-assuredness and a smile. He was neither inhibited nor embarrassed, even in the presence of my grandparents. Soon after, his bride, only twenty-one years of age, emerged from their bedroom, adorned in a captivating white peignoir set complete with satin-heeled slippers. At five feet eight inches, she epitomized the classic measurements (36, 26, 36), her form accentuated by the soft fabric and her nipples subtly visible beneath the sheer silk—a visage reminiscent of Brigitte Bardot, the iconic French actress known for her sensuality.

As she closed the bathroom door behind her, my grandfather, in a cryptic tone inquired, "Ronnie, what do you think of that?"

I remained unresponsive, convinced this was one of those trick questions. I hadn't seen a thing, hadn't noticed a thing—just engrossed in my book. The perplexing element was the air of approval that seemed to fill the room. It defied conventional wisdom; surely, we were all on the brink of eternal damnation. This had to be sin incarnate, a manifestation of the devil's handiwork. Yet she was remarkably beautiful.

The following year we visited Claudette and Jacques, who had established their first home as a newlywed couple. Oddly, after the leisurely seven-hour drive to Montreal, my mother insisted on each of us taking a shower. I drew the short straw and found myself stepping into the bathroom, only to be confronted by a poster-sized image of a nude woman. Panic surged within me fearing impending retribution for gazing upon this poster— shame, anticipating an inappropriate response to the provocative image, and guilt, acknowledging a hidden gratification in what I had seen. I promptly exited the bathroom and rejoined my parents, deep in conversation with Claudette and Jacques. My mother urged me to take my shower. I stood paralyzed, incapable of offering a coherent explanation for my hesitation. Eventually, my father intervened and accompanied me to the bathroom, seeking to understand the source of my distress. I pointed at the door as I closed it behind us. "Daddy, look!" I said.

Remarkably, my father didn't manifest shock or embarrassment, nor did he avert my gaze or warn of impending blindness—the fate reserved for the act of masturbation. Instead, he calmly reassured me that everything was fine, urging me to complete my shower without further ado. As it turned out, Playboy centerfolds were commonplace in Canadian bathrooms, a phenomenon that men embraced. Nudity carried a natural connotation, be it a mother nursing her child or individuals disrobing to take a dip in the pool, regardless of the age or company present.

There was even one relative whose bathroom was positioned at the top of the stairs, entirely devoid of a door or curtain for privacy in sharp contrast to the fact that such activity was conducted behind a closed and locked door in our house. In Canada, premarital sex lacked the taboo or damned implications that haunted New Bedford. My Canadian cousins embodied a comfort with their bodies and a willingness to express their sexuality—though not promiscuously. It was yet another reason I felt drawn to Canada, even if I wasn't fully conscious of it at the time.

St. Anthony's School: Lessons in Harmony

St. Anthony's Elementary School was established in September of 1896, under the guidance of the Sisters of Holy Cross and Seven Dolors. In September of 1924, the building that would become the backdrop for many of my formative experiences was erected behind the church, with its primary entrance on Ashley Boulevard. In 1944, under the leadership of the then reigning Monsignor Victor O. Masse and his successor, Reverend Albert Berube, the high school was founded. The mission and commitment to the St. Anthony parishioners encompassed providing an education rooted in the moral principles of the Catholic faith and nurturing an understanding of the French language to preserve the Franco-American culture.

What stood out that year was my parents' decision to relocate from Cedar Grove Street to the second floor of my grandparents' house on Coffin Avenue, just two blocks from the school. For the first half of the year, I resided with my grandparents until our tenement was prepared. My grandmother's affectionate doting complemented the joy of the move, initiating my Catholic school education on a positive note. Or so I believed.

At the age of four, the concept of spending thirteen years within a single institution was far from my mind. My memories of kindergarten are few;

the classroom was nestled in the school's basement under the guidance of Mrs. Berger, a wife and mother in her early 50s residing on the same street as me. My perceptions of her was a woman who easily lost her patience. I neither cherished nor detested that year.

To offer you a deeper understanding of the person I am today, I will narrate my experiences in chronological order.

Chapter 2 Elementary School Years

Cursive Mastery: The Penmanship Sonata

My journey through education began at St. Anthony's school, a parochial institution deeply rooted in the traditions of discipline and faith. As a young child stepping into the halls of knowledge, I had little idea of the adventure that awaited me in the first grade.

One of the earliest lessons ingrained in us was the art of cursive writing following the meticulous guidelines of the Palmer Method. The classroom bustled with the concentration of young minds eager to master the curves and loops. Special paper adorned with precise lines and a dotted center guided our pens, ensuring every letter adhered to standards of size and angle. An additional sheet, slightly slanted, served as the silent assistant, hidden beneath the paper where our efforts took shape. Penmanship was an art form, an endeavor not to be taken lightly.

My grandmother, a paragon of elegant penmanship, was a steady guide in perfecting the craft. Every evening, her practiced hand graced the newspaper with beautiful loops and swirls, a testament to her dedication to this fading art.

Throughout the early days of autumn, Sister Raymond stood before us, demonstrating the finesse of the Palmer Method on the blackboard. Confidence radiated from her as she boasted about her own handwriting prowess.

Unbidden and without pause I chimed in, "Sister, my grandmother's handwriting is even better!"

The room seemed to hush, and Sister Raymond's face seemed to turn a shade of crimson beneath her habit. A swift exit followed, leaving behind a classroom filled with gasps and chuckles.

My world abruptly shifted as my ear was captured in Sister Raymond's unyielding grasp. Dragged from the room, I felt pain radiate through my body as fear and confusion gripped me. The polished wooden floors beneath my shoes threatened my balance as I was propelled down the corridor, the journey feeling both swift and interminable. My mind raced with terror, wondering where this ordeal would lead.

Finally deposited into an office, I found myself facing the principal. Moments passed in silence before she approached, her stern gaze unwavering. Wordlessly, she condemned me as an irreverent and disrespectful boy whose conduct would not be tolerated within the sanctified walls of St. Anthony's.

"Go home and tell your parents you are expelled," she commanded, her words echoing in my ears.

Stunned, I made my way home, my throbbing ear a constant reminder of the day's events. The scene that greeted me at my grandparents' home was one of bustling activity. Mom and grandma were deeply immersed in creating an abundance of fall apple pies, and the scent of fresh apples mingled with the anticipation of warmth and comfort. They were surprised at my early return and my reddened ear prompted concern and further inquiry. With practiced hands, my grandmother examined my forehead for signs of fever, while my mother, observing my reddened ear, pressed for answers. My response, parroting the principal's words, seemed to provoke more bewilderment.

"Expelled?"

My mother's disbelief morphed into determination, setting in motion a chain of events that would reveal her resolve and resourcefulness.

Hours later, my mother returned home, her laughter echoing through the house. She recounted her encounter with Sister Raymond, her expressive retelling captivating both Grandma and me. My mother had managed to pierce the strict veneer, asserting that my penmanship lessons were drawn from the wellspring of family expertise. In fact, my grandmother had contributed samples for the Palmer Method books, her mastery forming the foundation for my budding skills.

However, the principal's obstinacy persisted, and my mother resolved to escalate the matter. She invoked my dad's cousin, Fr. Boisvert, whose influence held sway within the church. With an unyielding spirit, my mother navigated the intricacies of authority, asserting that my voice deserved to be heard, and my education preserved.

The following day brought a seismic shift. My triumphant return to school marked a small victory over misunderstanding and an affirmation of my place within the institution. While the incident remained unspoken, the atmosphere slowly transformed, reflecting the evolving nature of communication, advocacy, and understanding.

The story of my first-grade trials is a reminder that, even within the rigid structure of parochial schooling, the voices of children and their advocates can bring about change. My mother stepped up, showing her fierce determination to protect her own. Yet, it left me puzzled as to why that same fierce defense didn't apply to her relationship with her girlfriend—or mine with her friend's son.

An Altar Boy's Journey: A Sacred Interlude

Skipping ahead to the third grade, a pivotal moment in my spiritual journey awaited—an opportunity to join the ranks of the revered altar boys. The "calling" often whispered in hushed tones, beckoned young boys to serve in the presence of God Himself. Finally, the time had come for me and my fellow third graders to heed this divine invitation.

Our motley crew, a cluster of curious young minds, assembled in the schoolyard. Our short-lived chaos was quickly tamed by two nuns with distinct personas. The venerable Sister Evelina, a petite, French-speaking figure with spectacles perched on her nose, exuded an air of weathered wisdom. She seemed like a character plucked from an old sitcom; her presence reminiscent of Granny from "The Beverly Hillbillies." Then there was Sister Paul Henry, a youthful nun brimming with vigor, ready to usher us into our new roles and impose order with a gentle yet firm touch.

Ronnie, the altar boy

The sacred realm of the altar boys awaited us in the church's basement—a cold, dimly lit chamber with creaking wooden floors and benches that lined the hall. The walls were adorned with green-painted cupboards, housing the altar boys' vestments, creating an atmosphere filled with eerie echoes. As I donned the prescribed vestments, the weight of responsibility settled on my shoulders. A black cassock and a red counterpart, each paired with white surplices and meticulously labeled with our names, were entrusted to us. The red cassock even boasted a crimson cape adorned with golden fringe, reserved for solemn occasions and feast days. My place in the vestment cabinet, a numbered haven, marked the beginning of my journey as an altar boy.

The path to mastering the intricate rituals was paved with Saturday morning practices, lasting an entire month. Despite grumbles from reluctant participants, I reveled in the sense of privilege that came with this duty. A divine aura surrounded us as we practiced the procession, the choreographed pace to the music, the synchronized genuflections that punctuated our sacred service. Under the watchful eye of the head altar boy and his wooden claque, we learned to stand and sit in harmony, the gestures becoming a silent language.

However, maintaining silence proved the ultimate test. Whispers would inevitably ripple through the ranks, the confined space nurturing secrecy until the eruption of an angry priest's reprimand shattered the stillness.

An impatient glance cast toward the nuns accompanied the priest's stern command, "Sister, control your boys!"

This silent battle of wills often surfaced during the meticulous preparations of Holy Week, beginning with the pomp of Palm Sunday. The church gleamed with vibrant colors, sunlight streaming through stained glass, casting a kaleidoscope of hues on the polished oak pews. The rich, melodic hymns filled the air, wrapping around me like a warm embrace. The scent of fresh palms lingered as I remember the tactile pleasure of weaving the supple palms into a cross, each movement steeped in tradition and reverence.

Holy Week's progression saw us through solemn rituals that left an indelible mark on my young consciousness. I vividly remember Thursday's foot-washing ceremony, an intimate act of humility that required us to discreetly shed our shoes and socks for a symbolic cleansing. As I sat there, watching the priest lean down, I couldn't help but feel a mix of reverence and discomfort. The priest's peculiar request for us to preemptively address any foot odor made me self-conscious about my own, adding a touch of humor to the gravity of the moment.

Good Friday's service unfolded like a poignant tableau, with the Stations of the Cross-inviting reflection and introspection. I was struck as I watched the priest consume the consecrated Eucharist, leaving the tabernacle empty—a profound symbol of sacrifice. As the church closed its doors for the solemn observance, I felt the weight of the moment pressing down on me. We altar boys were then drafted for intensive rehearsals in preparation for Easter Sunday, and I remember the nervous energy buzzing in the air.

The crescendo of these rituals reached its zenith with the Midnight Mass —a hauntingly beautiful affair shrouded in darkness, punctuated by the ethereal sound of unaccompanied Gregorian chants. I could feel the anticipation in my chest as we waited for the glorious eruption of light as all of the lights in the church were turned on, illuminating everything around us and filling my heart with a sense of hope and renewal.

As I reflect on those pivotal experiences, I realize that my path as an altar boy mirrored the dedication, precision, and discipline that would define my future pursuits. The stage of worship provided a theater for refining action, perfecting movement, and attuning to timing—a formative preparation for the world's grand stage that lay ahead.

Never on a Sunday: A Song of Resilience

On another Sunday morning, I found myself running a tad late. Most of the altar boys had already arrived, creating an atmosphere of bustling activity. I descended the wooden stairs of the church basement, headed straight for the cabinet where my vestments were kept. However, both of my white surplices were missing. I knew one was at home, being laundered, but where was the other? Rushing over to Sister Paul Henry, I informed her of the situation. We searched the cabinet together, examined those nearby, and even checked the name tags of the boys who were already dressed. Alas, it was nowhere to be found. With a hint of frustration, she handed me a replacement surplice, much too big for me, and sternly directed me to join the line of altar boys. I believed that was the end of it, but I was mistaken.

After the mass concluded, we returned to the church basement to hang up our vestments. Just as I finished hanging my cassock, Sister Paul Henry's cold and biting voice pierced the air, calling for me. She stood by the toilets, extending her hand and pointing in their direction. I opened the green-painted wooden door of a stall and peered inside.

To my shock, my surplice was submerged in the toilet, its name tag visible. I was instructed to retrieve it and give an explanation. Panic creeping in, I stammered, "Sister, I honestly have no idea."

"You can't explain how your garment ended up in the toilet?" she pressed.

"No, Sister, I swear, I truly don't know," I asserted emphatically.

Then came the words that cut through me, shaking the very core of my moral being. "You're a liar"

Those words echoed in my mind, reverberating like a sledgehammer blow. How could she think so ill of me? How could anyone believe I would desecrate something so sacred and precious?

Following the mass, I returned home, choosing not to share the incident with my family. Perhaps, by the time the bells rang for high mass the following Sunday, the incident would be forgotten. As the day unfolded, much like any other Sunday, Sister Paul Henry's accusation continued to resound in my ears, lingering even as I lay down to sleep.

The next morning, as I prepared breakfast, an uneasy feeling weighed me down. I left for school and the day progressed as usual, but I couldn't shake the sense that something was about to happen. Approaching three o'clock, fifteen minutes before dismissal, a knock sounded on my classroom door. A student entered, handing a note to Sister Genevieve, one of my third-grade teachers. She then approached me, informing me that Sister Paul Henry wanted to see me in the hallway. Dread coursed through my veins as I left the room, sensing that this encounter wouldn't bode well. The door closed behind me, and with every step I took, Sister Paul Henry's gaze seemed to grow taller and more ominous. Her voice was biting as she uttered,

"Why did you throw your surplice in the toilet?"

Fear gripped me, and as I neared her, she seemed to tower above, her demeanor menacing. In a degrading tone, she pressed, "Admit it, you little liar."

My eyes widened, my body trembled, and I uttered, "but Sister, I didn't throw it in the toilet, I swear."

The next thing I knew, her hand struck my face, and the sting seared through my skin. Tears streamed down my cheeks, muffled by Sister Paul Henry's grip as she taunted, "Stop crying, you little sissy."

Eventually, she released me, instructing me to return to my classroom.

As I retreated, she added, "Oh, and by the way, you'll write one hundred spelling words as punishment tonight."

The next day, I approached school with hesitancy, dreading what might transpire once again. The day progressed normally, though I was ever vigilant for the storm that could erupt at any moment. It was nearly three o'clock when another knock came at my classroom door. A student entered, delivering yet another note, and once again, I was summoned to the corridor by Sister Paul Henry. A sense of dread filled me as I left the classroom, the door closing behind me. As I approached her, she scowled. The words she spoke were hauntingly familiar.

Again, she canted, "Admit it, you little liar."

Her hand struck my face, leaving a sting and shaking me to my core. My cries echoed, silenced only by her grip. She mocked my tears, calling me a little sissy. Finally, she released me, instructing me to return to class.

Yet, before I left, she added, "You'll write another hundred spelling words as punishment."

My mother had taken a job to help with bills, working from 3-9 p.m. Grandma cared for us until my father returned from night school. She sensed something was wrong but couldn't pinpoint it. She was concerned about my well-being, and when I would fall asleep while trying to complete my homework, she would finish it for me. She shared her concerns with my mother, who heard the distressing tale of my daily torment at the hands of someone who should epitomize goodness and compassion. I sat with my mother on the couch, recounting the pain and degradation I faced each day.

"Mommy, I just didn't want you to think I did something bad," I said as tears flowed.

That afternoon, my mother allowed me to stay home. We sat together, and she comforted me, promising that things would improve. Around 2:30 p.m., she sent me downstairs to my grandmother's and set off on a mission. When she returned, I could see exhaustion etched on her face. Overhearing her conversation with my grandmother, I learned she had met with Sister Paul Henry. When my mother confronted the Sister with my firm denial, she received an unexpected response.

"Oh Mrs. Boucher, we know he didn't do it, because we found out who did. Besides, any child who can go that long without admitting to it had to be telling the truth," Sister Paul Henry revealed.

My mother was shocked by this revelation. As she recalls, she threatened to call the police and report Sister Paul Henry to Sister Jeanita, the Mother Superior and my mother's friend, if she ever touched me again. She recounted that the fear in Sister Paul Henry's eyes was visible; she knew my mother meant business.

No apology was offered, and life at school remained surreal. Was I supposed to forget? Wasn't forgiveness a principle Sister Paul Henry believed in? The months that followed were marked by difficulties in the subjects she taught, particularly spelling, English, and math. Having begun school at four years old, it was decided I would repeat the third grade. I was destined to face Sister Paul Henry once more.

A Re-run of Sorts: A Reprise of Memories

Repeating the third grade didn't turn out to be as bad as expected. While my relationship with Sister Paul Henry remained broken, as she simply chose to ignore me, the year brought about two significant changes. Sister Evelina, the nun previously in charge of the altar boys, was replaced by a gentle and kind nun named Sister Marie André. She liked me and looked out for my well-being, often offering a reassuring pat on the head. Little did I know she would later become my savior.

Remember my favorite antagonist at the pond? Well, as luck would have it, one of the most notable outcomes of repeating the third grade was that I now shared a class with him. His behavior created constant tension, and his mother would compare our academic performances, often focusing on her son's strength in math skills. However, my mother had me focus on my strengths, particularly my artistic talents. This underscored the importance of resilience and finding one's unique path to success, a lesson I believe I learned at this very young age.

The Performance that Never Happened: The Lost Overture

My maternal grandmother, who cherished me deeply, nurtured a love for music within me. Despite not having a piano, she introduced me to an unusual musical contraption called a Melodica—a device that required blowing into it while pressing keys on its side, producing a one-octave range of notes.

Alongside this contraption, she possessed a blue leather-bound book filled with French songs. Through her patient guidance, she imparted melodies that have etched themselves indelibly in my memory. Like most kids, I reveled in singing for an audience. Family weddings, grand affairs during my childhood, brought cousins from far and wide. Dressed in a mini-Frank

Sinatra style, I'd take the stage with the band's indulgence. Though people complimented my ability to carry a tune and found my performance adorable, they couldn't decipher the words I sang. Truth be told, I was often unfamiliar with the lyrics myself.

With Mémère Serra's encouragement, my artistic education began. My mother and Mémère decided to enroll me in Yvonne Green's Dance Studio. Mrs. Green, a stern and short blonde woman, carried an impeccable reputation, having been a skilled tapper in her prime. Perched above shops on Acushnet Avenue at Lund's Corner, her studio became a weekly destination for me. Monday evenings were dedicated to dance—a routine that necessitated dinner's punctual completion by 6:15. After a quick family meal, we'd rush to the studio. Ms. Carol and Ms. Diane were Mrs. Green's instructors. As I waited for my class to begin, I could hear Ms. Diane's voice piercing the air, calling out dance steps for her class. Her class concluded 15 minutes prior to mine. When her door opened, and she stepped from her dance room, it seemed like her abrasive manner was in contrast to Ms. Carol, who exuded a soft-spoken, patient demeanor— qualities that also stood in stark contrast to most of the nuns I'd encountered. Despite a ten-year age gap, she and my mom forged a lifelong friendship. Unwittingly, she set a standard for the kind of woman I'd later seek to fulfill my destiny. Yes, I developed an infatuation with my dance teacher.

Being the only boy in the class, a common occurrence even today, didn't bother me. In our hour together, we covered ballet, jazz, and tap. No traditional tights or ballet shoes for me; I'd just wear socks, shorts, and a T-shirt. Our weekly routine included an abbreviated ballet barre session— pliés, tendus from first, second, and fourth position (which were supposed to be fifths, but few bothered with such precision). Jazz followed with two exercises I despised: high kicks to the front, met with Ms. Carol's reminder to point my toes; then the clumsy back kicks, where reaching for your head while arching backward made you wobble unsteadily, resembling someone emerging from a dizzying playground ride. Tap was next—hastily swapping our shoes for ones with metal taps. Ms. Carol's taps produced a

Ronnie's Dance Recital

jingling sound when she moved, imbuing her tapping with a brighter resonance than ours, which landed with a dull thud on the wooden floors.

We spent the entire year preparing for a much-anticipated recital complete with elaborate costumes. Mrs. Green rejected catalogue costumes, instead entrusting moms to bring to life her original designs. My grandmother's sewing prowess shone as she executed my costumes to perfection. I'd reuse them for the community Halloween costume contest, invariably claiming first prize. The inaugural costume was sewn from pale blue satin, adorned with sequins that trailed along the pant legs and vest collar. Another version in black satin with gold sequins followed for a Spanish tap routine.

My favorite, however, was the ensemble for one of my ballet numbers—the Russian dance from "The Nutcracker." Mémère Serra truly outdid herself: white satin trousers with a deep burgundy sash, and gold spats resembling boots. The wide-legged pants ballooned where they tucked into the spats, while the top featured a Cossack-style tunic, its high collar trimmed with gold brocade. Completing the look was a tall white fur hat, also trimmed with the same gold brocade, towering at least twelve inches high on my head.

Ms. Carol informed my mother that I excelled, even surpassing the girls in my class. Onstage, I exuded a commanding presence, radiating passion and joy. This was the year St. Anthony decided to host a variety show showcasing talented students. Mrs. Green was appointed director and choreographer for the event. To participate, students had to audition and be recommended. Aware of my performing aspirations, Sister Marie André signed me up. Not only was I selected, but I was also assigned to perform my Russian dance, a piece I had performed in the previous June recital.

In the week preceding the show, we convened in the auditorium for a rehearsal. Before we began, the principal summoned me onto the stage, announcing to all present that I had been removed from the show, without an explanation or reason. Mrs. Green assumed I had committed an infraction, although she couldn't fathom what that might have been. She contacted my mother to relay the unsettling news. Returning home from school, my mother confronted me, inquiring why I'd been ousted from the show. My disappointment and hurt were obvious, and in true maternal fashion, she set out to seek answers from the convent. There, she met with the principal, inquiring about my perceived transgression. Mom recounted the scene.

Unmoved by my mother's persistence, the sister simply stated, "Nothing, Ronnie has done nothing wrong."

Now my mother was even more perplexed. "Nothing? I don't understand! Why remove him when he's talented and performing well, as Mrs. Green attested?"

The principal's tone shifted, adopting a condescending sweetness as she tucked her arms into her wide black sleeves. "My dear child, life teaches us many lessons. One of them is humility. Ronnie knows he's good, and we need to teach him the virtue of humility."

How does one argue against such a rationale? For the first time, my mother was left speechless. She returned home, defeated, and I, for the first time, experienced a deep disappointment—a sense that my mother's intervention couldn't alter the outcome. This was the one thing that ignited my passion, the one endeavor in which I felt confident and had already garnered recognition. The perplexity of why it had been taken away haunted me.

Over the four years in dance, my mother and Ms. Carol developed a close friendship. My mom even attended some of her art classes at Southeastern Massachusetts University (now the University of Massachusetts at Dartmouth). However, Carol's impending graduation marked the end of my weekly dance lessons. As she headed to the University of Mexico for her master's in textiles, my incentive to continue waned. Simultaneously, my mom's friend convinced my mother that pursuing dance would inevitably lead me to become gay. As a result, the following four years marked a pause in my performing arts education, affirming the challenging perceptions associated with boys pursuing careers in the arts.

Mass: A Priestly Serenade

In a twist of incentives, the boys were lured into serving mass with the promise of financial gain—a meager ten cents for weekday masses and twenty-five cents for weekend ones. A more substantial reward of twenty-five cents awaited those who served at the convent. The weekly server schedule was meticulously posted, but for reasons unknown, my name seemed to find itself omitted, looping through rotations without inclusion. The exclusion perplexed me, as the other priests commended my service, hailing me as dependable and reverent. A quiet whisper of a potential calling to the priesthood wafted through conversations, a notion I would have embraced if the decision were mine to make.

The culmination of my eager anticipation arrived—a momentous occasion that marked my initiation as a server. Enthusiastically attired in my altar boy vestments, I explored the vast room, absorbing every detail. An altar-like table stood against the far wall, donned with priestly vestments meticulously arranged for the upcoming mass. Nuns from the rectory undertook the task of preparing and restoring these sacred garments. The room bore a sense of grandeur, embellished with finely carved mahogany cabinets, velvet-covered kneelers, and a large porcelain sink. It was an exquisite European masterpiece, set to become a historical landmark, among the most magnificent churches in the world.

My senses were enveloped in this splendor, until the entrance of Father Chabot disrupted my reverie. Father Chabot, known for his rapid pace and expedited services, breezed in with an air of urgency. He was renowned for his brisk approach to mass, often vowing to "get through this today" at an impressive speed. His unique offertory ratio of $1/4$ water and the rest wine, or sometimes even bypassing water altogether, set him apart from the norm.

As Father Chabot dressed for the occasion, my initial enchantment gave way to an unfamiliar hand on my shoulder—a custodian beckoning me towards a closet. He handed me an ornate brass vessel containing incense and instructed me to follow suit. The brass blazed in the sunlight as I maneuvered the vessel over a candle-lit charcoal, releasing a pungent blend of frankincense, myrrh, spices, and fragrant woods. Though I was engulfed in a cloud of aromatic smoke, my reverence for the occasion demanded endurance.

Father Chabot then donned his priestly attire with practiced precision, a symphony of garments with the first vestment being the amice, a square piece of cloth with two cords attached that went around his neck and covered his collar. Next was an alb, a long white robe. The alb is a symbol of purity and as such is often used in baptisms. After this he put on a cincture, made of cord or rope and worn as a belt. Next, he put on a stole which is a long piece of cloth that is worn like a scarf over the neck that fell down the front of his chest, ending near his knees. The final vestment was the chasuble, a poncho style vestment that comes in liturgical colors; purple for Lent and Advent, green for ordinary time, red for Pentecost and white for Easter.

His gaze met mine, and his knowing smile acknowledged my fledgling status. With that, the custodian presented each of us with a vessel of incense, and Father Chabot motioned us into position. The sun's rays danced off the vessels, and I held my sacred role within my grasp.

Monsignor Bérubé, a vigilant figure in my life, singled me out as a server. Under his watchful eye, I embarked on the early morning masses, a devotion that demanded rising at the pre-dawn hour of 5:30 a.m. An old alarm clock, a relentless sentinel, catapulted me out of bed and into the morning chill. Fumbling in darkness, I completed my morning rituals and ventured into the quiet streets. Racing against time, I navigated through the shadows as my grandfather's gifted watch was a steady reminder of the urgency. At the rectory, I rang the buzzer to gain entry. Addressing the good sister in French seemed to transform her from grumpy nun to warm hostess.

Guided by the monsignor, we scuttled through the secret tunnel connecting the rectory to the church basement, a mix of darkness, creaky floors, and musty scents until we arrived at the door to the convent. The small chapel was within the convent, a setting reminiscent of a cinematic portrayal of a cloister. As we dressed in silence, Gregorian chants from the choir echoed off the chapel walls, a backdrop to our sacred preparation. With the monsignor leading, the service unfolded, and after its conclusion, I received his blessing along with a coveted quarter.

In the midst of the cloistered environment, some nuns seemed less than pleased by my presence, notably Sister Paul Henry who simply ignored me. After my mother's stern warning, she simply acted as if nothing had ever happened. Monsignor Bérubé, though stern, was a source of safety for me. His smile and recognition conveyed a sense of acceptance in an unfamiliar territory.

The Candles Burnt: A Candlelit Reflection

Renee and Ronnie: First Communion at St. Anthony's Church

The peril of finding comfort, security, and confidence is that it can sometimes breed complacency. Consequently, when the unexpected strikes, we're caught off guard, and the consequences can be far graver. In the company of Sister Genevieve and Sister Marie André, the caretakers of the altar boys who seemed to hold me in high regard, I had grown accustomed to the notion that this year would be a favorable one. They consistently treated me with extra care, particularly after I served mass at the convent for Monsignor. Notably, my grades experienced a significant upswing during that year.

Additionally, my mother had begun teaching CCD (Confraternity of Christian Doctrine)—catechism for kids attending public schools, often dubbed by the nuns as "the lost souls." Every Wednesday evening, my mother would arrive at 3 p.m. after school and remain until 5 p.m. I found myself deeply impressed by her transformation into a veritable schoolteacher. Watching her class proved both intriguing and amusing. But then again, that was characteristic of my mother. Give her any audience, regardless of age, and you could rest assured that amid the learning, hearty laughter would ensue. Humor was her forte. She had a knack for recounting biblical stories better than anyone I knew. Yet, her narratives didn't always align with those in the Bible; nevertheless, they proved to be quite entertaining. On occasion, characters from disparate tales would find themselves coexisting within a single story. I made efforts to clarify that Cain and Abel were not passengers on Noah's Ark and that Mary Magdalene despite her reputation, wasn't involved with the apostles. My mother's response would be a simple "Oh! That's different!"

The tranquility that the fourth grade brought was something I treasured. It ignited a heightened religious devotion, prompting me to establish a small altar in my room. Centered around a statue of the Blessed Virgin, my makeshift shrine also featured two vases filled with freshly cut flowers. Since May held special significance for Mary, I crafted beautiful arrangements using our lilacs. Each night before bed, I would recite the rosary, often accompanied by my mother and Mémère Serra. Additionally, I had developed a routine of visiting the church after lunch, prior to returning to school, to offer a brief prayer of gratitude and to steer clear of a particular bully in the schoolyard. Since my sister and I traveled to school together, albeit grudgingly on her part, I'd insist she accompany me. If the prayer was swift, she didn't seem to mind, eager to reach school and play before the bell rang.

A certain Wednesday, my mother arrived at school as usual for CCD teaching. I was hoping to spend the day with her. When we entered the school building, a somber-looking Fr. Folster awaited her at the top of the stairs. My mother must have sensed something was amiss. She turned to me, kissed me, and instructed me to head home, assuring that she would see me later.

I returned home and, as per my routine, began my homework in my grandmother's kitchen. Before long, the front door burst open. My mother was utterly livid, her demeanor resembling that of a possessed woman. Storming into the kitchen, her eyes ablaze with fury, she appeared mortified and betrayed. Before my grandmother and I could even inquire about the situation, my mother grabbed me by the hair, her free hand striking me repeatedly wherever it landed. Escaping her grip, I dove beneath the table, with my mother's hand still reaching out, attempting to maintain her hold. Both Grandma and I pleaded for an explanation. "What on earth could have happened?"

My mother's anger dissolved into tears. My grandmother coaxed her to sit down, urging her to calm down and recount the events. Tearfully, my mother shared that Fr. Folster intercepted her at school and led her into his office. He conveyed the events told to him by parishioners who claimed to have seen my sister and me playing with votive candles in the church and inadvertently setting a fire. Fortunately, the witness managed to douse the flames before any significant damage occurred.

Fr. Folster asked my mother to leave immediately, informing her that she could no longer teach CCD, that I had been expelled from school, and that my parents were henceforth banned from attending St. Anthony's Church.

My mother's gaze bore a mixture of disdain and pain. She looked at me like she didn't know who I was as her eyes pleaded for a rational explanation.

"But Mom, Renee and I didn't go to church this afternoon. Remember, we were watching TV with Mémère. Plus, we were running late, so we had to go straight to school," I pleaded, hopeful that she'd believe me. My grandmother swiftly corroborated my statement, confirming to my mother that indeed, that was what transpired.

Though it seemed profoundly cruel at the time, this turned out to be one of the most instructive experiences of my life. At 10, it seemed my mother would let me confront this challenge on my own.

"If you didn't do it, then you need to go see Fr. Folster right now, at the rectory, and explain exactly what you just told me!" My mother stated in a firm, cold tone.

Thus, I embarked on that walk of two blocks, which felt like the longest journey I had ever taken. My nerves kept my feet moving in a forward trajectory but my brain loudly repeated "turn back." Paranoia slowly crept in, as I imagined that everyone on the street was staring at the boy accused of setting fire to the church and nearly burning it down. Arriving at the rectory, I hesitated momentarily before ringing the doorbell. A nun answered the door, and my best attempt at requesting to meet Fr. Folster in French seemed to prompt smiles, briefly easing my tension. They weren't aware, it seemed, that I was the alleged arsonist responsible for the church fire.

The sound of heavy footsteps descending the stairs from the second floor intensified my heart's rhythm. Fr. Folster materialized before me, his tall figure casting a shadow. His athletic build was emphasized by his well-fitted black shirt and sharply creased trousers. His demeanor was serious as he closed the door behind us.

We sat, and before he could utter a word, I blurted out, "I didn't do it."

In response, he accused me of lying, reigniting the familiar sensation of having salt rubbed into a wound. Once again, I found myself branded a liar despite my innocence.

"No Father, seriously, I didn't do it because I wasn't at the church today, and neither was my sister!"

I implored earnestly. Fr. Folster rose from his seat, asserting that he would prove my falsehood. He grabbed my arm, leading me out of the rectory and toward the convent, traversing the schoolyard where students engaged in basketball and other activities stared at me. For every step he took, my legs struggled to match his pace. We rang the doorbell, and when Sister Marie André answered with a smile, a fleeting moment of relief washed over me. Her welcoming smile indicated that she must not have been informed that I was the arsonist who had set their church ablaze.

"Bonjour, Father," said Sister André, "May I help you?"

Father Folster spoke with a determination already anticipating the response. "Sister, would you please repeat what you told me this afternoon in front of Master Boucher?"

Sister André's eyes grew wide with a panic distorting her facial expression. "Oh, mon Dieu!" she blurted. "Mon père, my apologies. You have the wrong Boucher child, it was his cousin we were talking about."

Heavy silence filled the air. No words were spoken, creating an agonizing eternity. Fr. Folster thanked Sister André for clarifying the confusion, and she retreated into the convent. As the heavy wooden door closed behind her, Fr. Folster turned to me. My heart swelled with anticipation, hoping for a heartfelt apology and an embrace. Yet, the world had not turned upside down. He simply instructed me to return home.

The following day, I returned to school. In the schoolyard, Sister Marie André enveloped me in her arms and placed a kiss on my forehead. No words were exchanged regarding the incident. A knock on the door interrupted the conclusion of our morning prayers, summoning five boys to the principal's office. I was one of the chosen five.

We entered her office and were instructed to sit on the wooden chairs lining the wall. Puzzlement hung in the air; none of us understood the reason for being summoned. Eyes darted between us, seeking answers or indications of what was to come.

The principal entered, and our attention was drawn to the rope belt she was removing from her waist. An uneasy tension settled in the room. Some boys let out nervous laughter, while others squirmed uncomfortably in their seats. The principal commenced speaking, her words a blur as our focus remained on the rope she wielded. A chilling thought crossed my mind, *This can't be good.* Laughter gave way to fear, and unease was unmistakable.

The principal eventually broached the topic, "I understand that one of you boys set fire to the church yesterday."

A sigh of relief escaped me, thinking, thank goodness, she knows it wasn't me. We cleared that up yesterday. As my body relaxed, a sharp sting struck my side as the rope struck me. My cries of pain mingled with the fearful screams of my peers. The shrill sounds reverberated through the school building.

The principal's anger intensified, her gaze fixed on me as she charged, "Admit it, you little liar! Confess that you set fire to the church."

I attempted to deny the accusation, but another blow cut me short. With rope in hand, she again aimed for the third strike, when Sister André's voice resonated around the corner, imploring the principal to cease.

"Mon Dieu!" she gasped. "Reverend Mother, there's been a misunderstanding."

With that, she led the principal out of the room. Minutes later, the principal returned, dismissing everyone except me. Alone in the room, she instructed me not to share the incident with anyone, not even my parents, before sending me back to the classroom. Although the pain from her hand had subsided, the embarrassment and humiliation of being beaten in front of the other boys was mortifying.

Upon arriving home from school, I defied the directive and shared the experience with my parents. My parents wanted to put the incident behind us and chose not to pursue any action against the school. Life seemed to return to its usual rhythm, but my mother never resumed teaching CCD. Fr. Folster also kept his distance.

Sister Marie André later tried to explain the communication errors by saying that the confusion arose because only the last name "Boucher" was used, and I was frequently seen at church. This led people to quickly assume a connection, especially since the other Boucher also had a sister the same age as me. However, what remained baffling was how easily they jumped to this conclusion, ignoring my clean record. Meanwhile, a cousin

—the family's black sheep, with whom we had little contact—had developed a reputation as a perpetual troublemaker, making the mix-up even more perplexing.

This ordeal left an indelible mark—a conscious and subconscious fear of being wrongfully accused. When paired with cinematic and literary narratives brought to life by my overactive imagination, it birthed recurring nightmares. An even more intense emotional response is triggered when I'm accused of lying.

Three Times You're Out! The Baseball Ballad

Impossible! Not again. Sister Paul Henry was back to teaching the 5th grade? Couldn't the Vatican spare a few more nuns? It felt like either God was playing a malicious prank, or I had descended into hell, reliving my worst nightmare for all eternity. Seriously, come on!

September had arrived, marking the start of my 5th-grade year. The Red Sox were contending for the Pennant. In an unprecedented move, the school allowed our class to bring in a TV so we could watch the game. The rationale? Sister Paul Henry's brother was a Red Sox player. As the TV was set up, Sister Paul Henry rushed us to finish our assignments. She efficiently collected papers row by row, starting from the first, and handed them back to the students. The TV flickered to life, its picture distorted and fuzzy. Sister Paul Henry wrestled with the rabbit ear antenna, attempting to find the right angle for a clearer image. The class got into position; eyes glued to the screen.

Suddenly, Sister Paul Henry leaned close to my left ear and whispered, "Ronnie, take your library book and go read in the principal's office."

Without hesitation, I complied, never questioning her instructions. I never determined the reason I was banished from the classroom, secluded in isolation with the stern principal intermittently shooting disapproving glances my way. Perhaps being in her office was a constant reminder of her blunder, assuming she was even capable of remorse.

Strangely, I found myself unbothered by the situation as I was deeply engrossed in my book, *Marty the Martian*, a discovery from one of my Saturday visits to the Brooklawn Park library. Marty's space adventures whisked my mind away to distant realms, providing an escape from the harsh realities that the world had cruelly heaped upon me.

That year, I also discovered my knack for writing. In our English class, we were tasked with writing about our favorite TV show, and mine happened to be that year "It's About Time" with Imogene Coca and Joe E. Ross. To my surprise, we were required to read our compositions aloud to the class. I was the fifth student to present. I'm not certain if it was my delivery or the style of my composition, but my teacher couldn't contain her laughter. The more I read, the harder she laughed, and soon, the entire class was caught in a fit of uncontrollable laughter—a kind where you forget what you're laughing about but just can't stop! It was the first time I felt in control, accepted, and, if I may dare to say, even valued.

A Frosty Arrival and a New Bond: Caroling Confessions

December 23rd arrived, ushering in a holiday break that stretched blissfully until January 2nd. A snowstorm had swept in the night before, just as my mother went into labor and my father whisked her off to the hospital. When I woke, the world lay buried under a pristine three-foot blanket of snow—a magical setting for the arrival of a Christmas baby.

By lunchtime, there was still no news. Armed with my sled, I ventured into the frosty wonderland, relishing every moment of winter's enchantment. But my fun was cut short when my grandmother called me, her voice carrying an air of urgency that hinted at the day's unfolding miracle.

On the porch, she divulged the much-awaited news, "Your mom had the baby, and it's a…"

"I have a baby brother!"

My excitement outpaced the sentence, quelled only by my grandmother's correction, "No, it's a girl!"

Disbelief filled me. "No, I don't want it! Send it back!"

My declaration met my grandmother's horrified gaze, and she unleashed a torrent of reprimands in French. My protest over, I marched back inside, resentment for my new sister simmering beneath the surface.

Later that evening, my father gathered with us to share the news. "Your little sister was born just after 11 a.m. this morning," he said, his expression tinged with concern.

As his narrative unfolded, dread tightened its grip on me, and the joy for our newest family member dimmed. "Your sister was born with a dislocated hip and will be coming home in a brace," he explained, words echoing as though from a distance.

The phrase "dislocated hip" resonated while the rest slipped away. Guilt engulfed me, and my tears flowed uncontrollably.

"Daddy, this is my fault. I didn't mean it, I'm so sorry,"

I confessed amid sobs. My father, baffled by my self-imposed guilt, reassured me that my feelings were misplaced, but the weight of responsibility clung to me, determined.

My new sister, Carol Ann, entered our lives on Christmas morning. Amid the joy and chaos, the news of her dislocated hip faded into the background. Yet, beneath the surface, the gnawing guilt persisted, driving me to find ways to atone for my perceived transgression. She wore the "Freddy the Frog Splint," an X-shaped contraption that harnessed her dislocated hip, supporting it as it healed. Despite her predicament, Carol exuded happiness, perhaps relishing any reprieve from the brace.

My role expanded as I took on responsibilities usually reserved for parents. Bath times became a ritual, with my grandmother's assistance, converting our dining table into a makeshift bathing station. My father entrusted me with nighttime feedings and diaper changes, given my ability to wake easily. The nights echoed with Carol's soft coos as I held her in her brace. Her infectious giggles brought joy to our home.

Carol, Ronnie, and Renee

With winter's firm grip, we faced small challenges caring for Carol. Frozen cloth diapers hanging on the clothesline became my routine. Thawing occurred indoors as I warmed them on our Humphrey heater, the sizzle and steam loudly resonating throughout the apartment. Over time, I embraced my role as Carol's semi-caretaker, growing into the responsibilities that guilt and circumstances had thrust upon me. The bond that ultimately developed between us transcended guilt feelings, forging a deeper connection between my sister and me.

Sister Beatrice Millette: Songs of Sisterhood

Sister Beatrice, a formidable figure cloaked in black, radiated an aura of sternness that held sway over the entire student body. Her presence was synonymous with fear, her demeanor as unyielding as an army drill sergeant. For all the students, Sister Beatrice was a figure of dread, impervious to favoritism and merciless in her actions. Yet, a single day unraveled the established perception.

One day, a conversation I overheard completely changed how I viewed Sister Beatrice. It was around 1965, when nuns were allowed to return to their birth names. Before that, they had assumed new names upon entering the convent. I was home for my usual lunch when my maternal grandfather, pépère Serra, started up a conversation. "So, who are your teachers this year?" he asked between bites of his sandwich.

"Beatrice Millette," I replied casually.

He paused mid-chew, his eyes lighting up with recognition. "Beatrice Millette? Now, there's a name I haven't heard in years!"

"Why?" I asked, curiosity piqued.

"Well," he began with a chuckle, "I dated a Beatrice Millette once. Thought she was quite the catch—until I found out she smoked." He shook his head. "Couldn't stand it. I wouldn't date a woman who smoked. Always thought women smoking made a person seem... cheap."

I stared at him, stunned by the revelation. Sister Beatrice—*my teacher*—was his ex-flame? I tried to reconcile this image of her with the stern, devout woman I knew from school. The thought raced through my mind: what could I do with this bit of family history? Its potential significance and the possibilities for leverage were almost too much to process.

As the school year began, I found myself in Sister Beatrice's class, my attention split between my daily lessons and the mystery of her enigmatic past. My gaze seemed fixated on her, a Cheshire-like grin playing across my face, leaving her perplexed by the unfamiliar sight of me smiling. A palpable tension of curiosity lingered between us, as if we were both quietly studying one another, each trying to uncover the other's secrets.

As the day drew to a close, Sister Beatrice asked us to bow our heads in prayer. Afterward, the students began filing to the back of the classroom to retrieve their coats and bags from the closets.

As I joined them, I heard a familiar voice call my name, her tone tinged with a hint of mystery. "Master Boucher, would you please step out into the corridor?"

With my mind racing in bewilderment, I followed her into the school corridor. She closed the classroom door leaving it slightly ajar, a gesture implying this wasn't a grave matter. An odd sense of relief washed over me.

"Is there something wrong my child?" Her piercing gaze locked onto my face; her brows slightly furrowed as she questioned my unusual behavior. There was no escaping her scrutiny. I hesitated, feeling the weight of the moment.

"No, Sister, nothing is wrong," I replied, my tone calm but deliberate, trying to convey reassurance.

Her curiosity didn't waver, and I saw my chance. I took a breath, steadying myself. "Well, my grandfather wanted me to say hello."

Her head tilted slightly, intrigued. "Your grandfather?" she asked, her voice carrying a note of genuine interest.

"Not my dad's father—my mom's," I clarified, watching her eyes narrow in concentration.

"And his name?" she pressed, leaning forward ever so slightly.

"Hector! Hector Serra," I stated confidently, watching as her expression flickered with recognition. Her composed demeanor faltered, replaced by a mix of surprise and distant memory.

She blinked, as though piecing together a puzzle, and leaned back. "Go on," she urged, her voice softer now.

I chose my words carefully, recounting my grandfather's story: how they had dated long ago, how he'd admired her, but how their relationship ended because of her smoking habit. Her reaction was subtle but telling—her lips parted slightly, and her eyes seemed to glaze over, as though transported back to another time.

For a moment, she stood still, processing my words. Then, a wistful smile spread across her face, and she let out a soft chuckle. "Hector Serra…" she murmured, more to herself than to me. "That feels like a lifetime ago."

She began to speak, her voice now tinged with a rare vulnerability. "That was a very long time ago," she admitted, her tone balancing nostalgia and reflection.

I stayed silent, not wanting to interrupt the moment. Her usual air of authority seemed to soften as she looked at me, her gaze filled with something close to trust.

With a small, conspiratorial smile, she added, "Let's keep this between us, shall we? Our little secret." Her voice was firm but not unkind.

Eager to cement my place as her confidant, I nodded quickly. "Yes, Sister. I promise I won't say a word to anyone about this."

"Good," she said, her voice regaining its usual composure. But the hint of a smile lingered, a subtle reminder of the bridge we had just built between the past and the present.

With that exchange, an unspoken bond formed. Sister Beatrice's demeanor toward me softened, kindness infused in her interactions. The remainder of the year continued with a subtle undertone of affection, a secret shared between us, bridging the gap between stern teacher and me.

Childhood Adventures: The Friendship Fugue

My childhood was enriched by the company of a few local friends, each bringing their own unique quirks and interests to our group. Danny and

Richard were my closest companions from the neighborhood. And then, of course, there was the antagonist—a figure who added a touch of conflict to our otherwise harmonious circle.

Danny's family owned a local furniture store, and he had an older brother who was already dating and idolizing the Beatles. Danny's younger brother, the epitome of annoyance, often drove us to seek refuge elsewhere.

Then there was the freckled red-haired boy, whose interests shifted as he got involved in local baseball leagues, leaving me primarily with the antagonist as a playmate.

His cellar held treasures that every boy coveted. His father had meticulously crafted a grand wooden table upon which rested an elaborate Lionel train set, the ultimate of electric trains. This was not a simple circular track; it looped and rose in a figure-eight configuration with multiple cars, each serving a purpose. Watching the antagonist's command over the train, smokestack puffing and log cars loading and unloading, was an enchanting experience. But the excitement quickly faded, and boredom set in as my mind wandered.

Throughout the school year, we engaged in the quintessential games of boyhood. Army games took shape with the pretense of shooting yet always sparing our comrades and denying hits. Another favorite was our version of hide and seek, with the local post office's loading dock as the designated safe zone. The count of ten signaled the beginning, while the rest of us scattered, blending into the twilight. The challenge was to return to the safety of the loading dock without being tagged.

Like most boys, I found solace and escapism in these games. Climbing trees was a particular fascination, the act itself a dance with nature's elements. The thrill of scaling as high as the branches allowed was exhilarating, while the gentle sway of the wind was oddly soothing. The towering vantage point afforded a sense of achievement and control, a microcosm of risk and reward.

The beauty of my childhood lay in the simplicity of those moments—the pure joy of discovery and the bonds formed with friends. Through games, talks, and shared moments, I found my way through the maze of growing up. Those days were filled with a sense of freedom, unburdened by the weight of adult responsibilities, allowing me to embrace life with a carefree spirit.

Tears of Strength: The Friendship Fugue

In my experience, society expects men to embody stoicism, demanding that we suppress any outward signs of pain—whether physical or emotional. Tears, often viewed as a symbol of weakness, are something we're taught to avoid showing.

Nevertheless, it is my belief that a man who sheds genuine tears possesses a deeper consciousness and a stronger connection to humanity. This is my way of understanding why my eyes instinctively well up with uncontrollable tears, in my senior years. Or perhaps, it's an automatic response cultivated from years of watching soap operas.

It was always an unspoken understanding due to our extensive time together that although he was exasperating, my favorite antagonist held the title of my best friend. But then again, I had no basis on which to judge a healthy friendship. There were times when he and I shared peaceful moments together. We had sleepovers, enjoyed bike rides and exploring (my favorite activity), and sometimes just relaxed in front of the TV.

In the summer of '65, my parents made a surprising and, in hindsight, rather inspired decision: they invited my favorite antagonist to join us on a trip to the World's Fair in New York. You might think I'd have been upset or uneasy about it, but strangely, I wasn't.

That weekend, something remarkable happened—my antagonist transformed into my closest ally. He wasn't the troublemaker I knew from home; instead, he became a kindred spirit, someone I could laugh and explore with. I saw a side of him I never expected, and it changed how I viewed him forever.

For me, that weekend was pure magic. I was traveling, brimming with excitement to experience what felt like the East Coast's answer to Disneyland. Of course, this was before Disney World had come into existence, so to my young mind, the World's Fair was the pinnacle of wonder and possibility. It was a weekend of discovery, not just of the marvels at the Fair, but of the unexpected good in someone I thought I had all figured out.

It was a technicolor dream of the future! I remember being awestruck by General Motors' "Futurama II," a sprawling 3D animated exhibit showing life in the distant world of 2064. I marveled at American Telephone and Telegraph's groundbreaking "Picturephone" (imagine that—a phone where you could actually see the person you're talking to!), a towering dinosaur sculpture, and the Vatican Pavilion, where Michelangelo's *Pietà* was on display. Then there was the Carousel of Progress, a dizzying ride through technological wonders.

But my favorite memory? It came right around lunchtime. My mom's internal clock started ticking, and she needed food immediately, or else she'd faint—a well-documented phenomenon in our family. Unfortunately, every food line at the fair seemed to stretch on forever. Mom's urgency became apparent.

Then, she spotted it: a small Asian eatery with a blissfully short line. It was like watching someone in the desert crawl toward a mirage, her eyes locked on the oasis of food. We finally made it to the front, only to be greeted with a rather... unconventional menu: fried ants and grasshopper legs.

Well, that was the end of Mom's appetite—but the start of a laughing fit that lasted the rest of the day. I don't think any of us stopped giggling about her near-insect lunch experience.

Once we returned to the routine of summer and daily life, my favorite antagonist was back to his usual antics. Somehow there was heightened competition between us, owing to significant changes at Long Pond. The owner's association had vetoed the revamped school bus, leaving my mom's friend and her brother with the decision to either construct a cottage or sell the land. They chose to build.

That summer, after work each evening and all day on weekends, the fathers collaborated on building the cottage. It was a simple structure, featuring two bedrooms, an open kitchen and living area, and a small bathroom. The shower was installed outdoors.

Adept at construction, my dad contributed by working on the cottage during the day. As the fathers gathered after work, my dad headed back to work returning at midnight. Sometimes my dad would finish early and occasionally took the boys water skiing.

As I mentioned earlier, included with the cottage was a polished wooden motorboat, boasting a massive Mercury engine that propelled it with such force that it would surge into the air before crashing onto the water's surface with a resonant thud. My antagonist was always first in line, followed by his cousin Bobby and his siblings Donald, Mark, and Paul. I took my place at the back of the boat, signaling my dad whenever someone fell off their ski. With deft maneuvers, my dad directed the boat, propelling the boys at high speeds over the waves as they clung to the rope. After the adventure, we'd return to the cottage, where the mothers had begun preparation for dinner. And if you hadn't already noticed, I never got my chance to ski.

I waited for one of the boys to say, "Hey, Uncle Roger, what about Ronnie?"

But no such words were ever spoken. For some reason, I believed I wasn't supposed to expect the same treatment—as if there was some unspoken rule that altar boys weren't meant to ski, like a strange, sacrificial duty. This silent exclusion stung, creating a rift in my relationship with my father.

To make it worse, just after 5 p.m. the other fathers would arrive at the cottage, quickly trading their work clothes for bathing suits and rushing to the water, their sons in tow. One by one, the boys would take to the skis, trying new tricks and jumping the waves stirred up by the boats' sharp turns.

It wasn't long before the boys' skills evolved, enabling them to try advanced maneuvers like the slalom, a specialized single ski with two cups—one for the left foot in front and the other for the right foot in the back. Patiently, I waited my turn on the pier with the rest of the boys, though my turn seldom came. Only one dad extended an invitation—Bobby's father, Maurice. Still a novice compared to the other boys, I failed to hold the attention of the competitive men, who quickly grew bored with my simplistic wave-riding approach.

They even tried to knock me off by spinning the boat in tight circles, but I clung to the rope, determined not to be dislodged by the relentless waves. It always played out the same—after a few minutes, it was over, and we headed back to the cottage for dinner.

As the fathers cracked open beers and played horseshoes, the moms busied themselves setting the picnic table, while one of the dads took charge at the grill. The evening felt routine, almost ritualistic, but for me, each time it reopened the same wound.

By 9 p.m., it was time to go home, where I could retreat to my sanctuary—my refuge from the silent sting of exclusion, a place where I could tend to the emotional bruises that seemed to deepen with every visit.

It seemed as though my father's stance unintentionally gave the adversary the green light to ramp up mockery, insults, and bullying. That summer, it didn't take long before I felt that isolating myself was the only answer to avoid constant conflict. The last thing I wanted to do was to cause a situation that would prohibit my parents from going to the pond. So, I'd set off on long, quiet walks around Churchill Shores. The gravel roads crunched under my feet as I wandered past other summer cottages and friendly neighbors waving from their porches, young children running carelessly about. Sometimes, I'd sit alone beneath the towering pines, the scent of fresh sap filling the air, and listen to the wind rustling through the branches—searching for a moment of peace, even as everything inside me felt far from it. Despite my aversion to confrontation, dealing with the adversary seemed inevitable.

I yearned to stay at home with my grandmother, fervently pleading with my mother to forgo trips to the pond. However, my pleas fell on deaf ears.

One day at the cottage, in an effort to avoid my favorite adversary, I sought refuge in the neighbor's yard, settling onto a swing hanging by a rope from a massive pine tree. Swinging always brought a sense of liberation and flight, akin to spinning after coiling and releasing.

"Get off!" said a voice that cut through my solitude, shattering my brief moment of peace.

"I said, get off!" he repeated.

His insistence triggered a surge of emotion, a rising tide within me. But no, I had to retain control. Obedience and acceptance were expected, regardless of the harassment. I continued to swing, hoping he would eventually relent. With the swing's forward motion bringing me face-to-face with him, I suddenly felt a stinging slap across my face.

"I said, get off!!!"

Remembering Jesus' words, turn the other cheek, I did not comply. His words grew more demanding. Defiantly, I clung to the swing. Another slap followed.

"You're going to get off! This isn't your swing!"

It was a weak attempt to justify his actions. But those slaps ignited something I couldn't control. The buried emotions, stemming from countless encounters with Sister Paul Henry's daily hand against my cheek, surged forth like the legendary Kraken.

"I'm warning you, stop," I declared with such intensity that it should have signaled a change, evoking a sense of danger.

In sync with the third strike, an inner beast was finally unleashed. I released the rope, propelled forward, and landed on my adversary, toppling him. Control slipped away as my arms swung uncontrollably. Self-defense spiraled into rage. He bore the brunt of my anger, an anger initially reserved for Sister Paul Henry, Fr. Folster, and my school principal.

The adversary cried out, "Stop, you're crazy, stop!" Then, hands intervened, separating us, restoring sanity to the moment. Rage gave way to tears.

"He's crazy, he just kept hitting me," he muttered as he slinked back to the cottage, tears streaming.

Alone by the swing, there was no one to comfort me, no one to acknowledge the physical and emotional wounds I carried. Reality settled in, and I pondered the impending consequences.

Then, from the cottage porch, my dad's voice rang out, "Ronnie, go sit in the car."

Looking up at my father, I noticed an unfamiliar look, a departure from the usual disappointment. This one held a glint in his eyes, a smirk playing on his lips, an assertion of authority as he meted out my punishment of solitude in the car. In that moment he nodded in approval, a recognition that I had finally stood up for myself. It marked the first time I felt a true father-son connection, one of the most cherished and memorable moments of my childhood.

Though life took us on separate paths, our parents' connection kept my antagonist and me loosely aware of each other over the years. But it wasn't until a few years ago that we finally came face to face again. I studied his face, searching for the boy I once knew behind the eyes of a man who now seemed uneasy in my presence. Seizing the moment, I brought up the memories of our childhood—the taunts, the rivalry—but to my surprise, he couldn't recall a single one. Affirming statements made by psychologists say that "bullies" often forget the actions they take when engaging in victimization.

A rare opportunity arose as both his mother and my father were facing their final days. I brought my mom to visit her lifelong friend for a final goodbye, and during our time there, he arrived. The encounter reignited every bitter memory I've recounted—the smug behavior, the disrespectful attitude—it all came rushing back, and my frustration boiled over.

But then, just days later, at my father's wake, there he was again. This time, he stood before me with that familiar charm, his bright smile lighting up his blue eyes. For a moment, it was disarming. "Stop that!" I scolded myself. "You're confusing me—you're supposed to be the villain of my story."

And yet, there he stood, undeniably human. As much as I wanted to reduce him to what I had built in my mind, I couldn't deny the truth: he was himself, and I was me—flawed, complicated, and perhaps not so different after all.

Refuge in Chopin: A Harmony in Friendship

It was around the 5th grade, a friendship blossomed with another classmate, David Langevin. He was a fair-haired, blue-eyed boy who carried the burden of a speech impediment due to partial deafness, a result of a traumatic incident when he was just four years old. As a result, David was distinguishable by the conspicuous, oversized hearing aids that adorned both his ears, rendering him the target of unkind ridicule because of his speech. However, an extraordinary bond began to form between us, one that was tightly woven through our mutual love for music. David, despite the formidable challenge of his hearing impairment, emerged as a prodigious pianist.

During that particular summer, I was given an invitation to visit him in his new home near the New Bedford airport on Old Fall River Road. It was a small cottage nestled on a spacious plot of land.

Upon arrival, I had the honor of meeting his father, whose blindness was unmistakable, evident through the dark glasses that veiled his sightless eyes, and the guide stick he held by his side. Despite this, he possessed an extraordinary awareness of his surroundings.

Our initial encounter was somewhat disrupted by Mrs. Langevin, a straightforward and assertive woman, who promptly declared, "House rules! No moving any furniture that might pose a tripping hazard for my husband. We can't afford any accidents. Also, David must dedicate two hours daily to practicing the piano. So, if you're present during his practice time, you can either listen or go home."

It was surprising how swiftly the Langevin family warmed up to me.

Nevertheless, Mrs. Langevin did once cast a curious eye in my direction and quip, "Kid, you're a bit weird!"

When I sought further explanation, she chuckled, "I was convinced you'd head for the door when David had to practice. Yet, here you are, enjoying that Chopin stuff!"

The truth was, I relished the music deeply and secretly yearned to master it myself.

During this period, I was first introduced to the concept of a savant. Mr. Langevin had a penchant for music, and he would often enjoy concerts on television.

One afternoon, as we had our lunch, Liberace appeared on the screen, exuberantly performing Chopin's renowned Polonaise. After the dazzling performance, David, without any sheet music, stood up, walked over to the piano, and began to re-create the piece from memory.

Not knowing what to expect, I sat there casually, anticipating some loose variation of the music. But my low expectations were shattered the moment Chopin's melody filled the living room, each note echoing with precision and beauty.

Up to this point, I had a natural knack for most things I tried—like ice skating. I put on skates, stepped onto the ice, and glided with ease. So, I truly believed that David's approach to playing the piano wasn't anything extraordinary. From my perspective, it seemed simple: you listen to the music and somehow, instinctively, your fingers translate it into sound.

But when I tried, I placed my fingers on the keys and produced a jarring dissonance that startled even the cat. It was a humbling failure.

Later that summer, I was fortunate enough to accompany David to a lesson with Professor DeCosta, a distinguished pianist who resided in South Dartmouth. Professor DeCosta's home was a spectacular waterfront mansion adorned with antiques and graced by the presence of two grand pianos that faced each other majestically in the heart of his expansive living room. Under the professor's tutelage, David immersed himself into musical exercises and diligently honed the piece he was mastering. The experience stirred a profound longing within me, one that made me acutely aware of how much I missed the discipline, dedication, and passion that I had once embraced in my dance lessons.

A few weeks later, my sister Renee and I, found ourselves in the company of the Langevin family while our parents were away in Canada for a week. David had a sister, Gail, who was the same age as Renee.

This time, we all ventured to David's lesson at Professor DeCosta's home. While Renee, Gail, and Mrs. Langevin chose to bask on the beach, I opted to remain and immerse myself in the lesson. It was on this occasion that Professor DeCosta made an intriguing discovery about David. The professor introduced a new piece of music and requested David to play it. David, however, asked if the professor would perform it first and, moving away from the piano bench, he watched.

The professor hesitated momentarily, briefly seated himself, then swiftly rose and remarked, "David, I want to hear you play it first."

David, with his fingers resting on the keys, gazed at the music before him, seized by an immobilizing panic that colored his face a deep shade of red.

With encouraging words, the professor coaxed, "Go ahead, David, give it a try!"

Yet, David remained motionless, his distress intensifying. In a moment of frustration, the professor lightly tapped his own forehead and conceded, "How could I have been so foolish not to recognize that you can't read the music!"

This left me perplexed, for it seemed that David had been looking at the music while he played... or had he?

Thankfully, the issue was detected early in David's musical education, allowing the professor to introduce the necessary corrections. It didn't take long before David acquired a prowess in reading sheet music.

Influenced by the captivating legacy of Liberace, David's extraordinary journey began in his early years when he earned a prestigious invitation to partake in the annual Liberace Competition, an accolade that not only enriched his musical abilities but also bestowed upon him a generous scholarship to the illustrious Julliard School of Music. He pursued his passion, achieving a bachelor's degree in music and obtaining a teaching certification from Southeastern Massachusetts University of Music. Subsequently, he earned a master's degree in music education from the esteemed New England Conservatory.

As the symphony of his life unfolded, David's melodious journey transcended boundaries, eventually guiding him from the shores of New Bedford to the sun-kissed state of Florida.

David and I reunited during one of my visits to Florida. As we reminisced about our childhood experiences, I was intrigued to find that we both remembered the same events. I've often noticed that even among parents or siblings, discussions about the past can reveal vastly different perspectives. It was satisfying to feel as though we had both lived through those moments together.

There was a sparkle of joy in David's eyes as he excitedly shared his news. Just a few years prior, at the tender age of fifty-six, his life took a harmonious turn as he embraced the joys of matrimony and welcomed a bundle of joy into his world, a son, also named David. I vividly remember the exhilaration resonating in his voice and the profound pride that radiated from his heart as he embarked on the cherished path of fatherhood, a sentiment I wholeheartedly shared with him. I was only too thrilled to also share the joys and challenges I had been faced with but the rewards coming with a supportive and loving wife and the joy of watching my two wonderful children explore their own artistic talents and creativity.

Over the years, David and I sustained our friendship. He accompanied me several times on the iconic organ when I sang at St. Anthony's Church and often entertained the idea of collaborating on a project if I ever relocated to Florida. This was a dream we held onto. Sadly, in 2023, David fell victim to COVID-19, leaving behind cherished memories of our remarkable friendship.

Therapy and Play-doh: The Healing Harmony

The pre-puberty years of the 1960s were a time of constant comparison, where behaviors were scrutinized to ensure they aligned with societal expectations. The community played a role in reinforcing conformity, keeping everyone metaphorically penned in the same space.

My antagonist's mother seemed to be ever creative in her provocations, by taking up new tactics to unsettle my mother. One day, she dropped her latest, questioning my masculinity.

"Yvette, you know, if you don't do something, Ronnie might turn out... well, you know, queer!"

There it was—the seed planted, designed to stir anxiety and prompt parents to examine their child's every move. From that moment, behaviors would be dissected, signs searched for, and amateur judgments passed on something as complex as one's sexuality. And the prescribed solution to such perceived "problems"? Therapy, of course!

I was referred to a psychiatrist named Dr. Platt, who for reasons unbeknownst to me then referred me to another psychiatrist, Dr. Solomon. The office was small, illuminated brightly, a desk flanked by two chairs. I wasn't entirely certain why I was there but given that everyone addressed him as "doctor" I presumed something was amiss with me. Strangely I felt perfectly fine. No cold, no fever.

As the office door swung open, Dr. Solomon clad in a white lab coat breezed past me, swiftly blurting out, "So, you must be Ronnie?"

On his desk sat a bowl of peanuts, of which he offered me some. I politely declined. Amidst the interrogation, what etched itself most vividly in my memory was that he was munching on peanuts, spitting out the skins, some of which flew in my direction. The visit was brief and aside from the curious spitting unremarkable.

During my second visit I was administered the infamous "Ink Blot Test" also known as the "Rorschach" test. Psychiatrists use this to assess their patients' personality traits and emotional states.

Holding a card, Dr. Solomon asked, "What do you see?"

This was a breeze. "A butterfly!" I exclaimed.

Flipping to another card, he posed the same question.

"Birds, obviously," I replied. I mean, it couldn't be any more apparent! Card after card followed.

"Clouds—beautiful clouds!" I continued.

Each image conjured a sense of beauty. As swiftly as the session began it concluded, and I never crossed paths with Dr. Solomon again.

However, the journey through psychological therapy persisted. I was referred to Dr. Michael, a child psychology specialist. His office was more akin to a playground, filled with an array of toys, arts, and crafts. I perched on the chair facing his desk. As he began to inquire, my gaze darted around the room, exploring every nook.

"Feel free to play with anything in the room!"

He granted me permission to immerse myself into the array of options. Playdoh! That's where it all began. The Playdoh became the vessel that unlocked the floodgates. Kneading, squeezing, and rolling the dough between my fingers seemed to release a torrent of thoughts, emotions, and feelings much like a babbling creek. Dr. Michael quickly concluded that my parents should reassess their friendships and spend less time at the cottage. If they did head to the pond, I, for the first time, would be granted a choice. Naturally, I chose not to go. Initially, I spent my time with my grandmother, but as summer lingered on boredom and a touch of melancholy set in. My therapist encouraged my father to find activities that would foster interaction between us—quality father-son time.

First on the list was tennis. After dinner, as dusk descended, my father and I would head to the courts at Brooklawn Park. Yet, wielding a racket and striking a ball proved as fruitless as my attempts at baseball. I was akin to the proverbial Charlie Brown, the one nobody particularly wanted on their team. Dad ended up chasing the ball more than making any meaningful hits. After the third session, he relented, and we never returned to the tennis courts. Our next endeavor was basketball. A hoop was procured and installed in the driveway, though the space was rarely devoid of parked cars. Truth be told, I can't even recollect whether my dad ever engaged in a game of hoops with me.

I believed there was still hope, at least that is what my therapist told me.

YMCA: The Fitness Fanfare

It was the first summer free from the having to go to the pond. My parents found an alternative activity for me at the YMCA which was located in downtown New Bedford. This marked my first venture into solo public city bus and with each coin I dropped into the meter, it came to life with a rhythmic churn. I was enrolled in swimming lessons by my parents and arrived among a group of unfamiliar boys. I found myself following their lead, as I had no idea where to go or what to expect.

In a quick flurry, I was in a room filled with metal cabinets for stowing our clothes. Boys of all ages shed their garments until they stood fully naked. Despite having my swimsuit ready, one of the older boys casually informed me that bathing suits were prohibited. There we were, exposed and vulnerable, entirely nude. Surprisingly, the atmosphere felt normal, a sensation of utter naturalness and liberation. This experience sharply contrasted with the teachings of the church. My initial assumption was that the church's teachings were concerned only with glimpsing the naked form of a girl or woman. However, that notion quickly faded as we queued up to enter the pool, its expanse divided into multiple lanes.

Swimming instructions boiled down to "jump in, swim to the other end of the pool, and return." As I glided through the water with each elegant breaststroke, I savored a profound sense of liberty and independence. It was a pure depiction of innocence. This was also the first instance I didn't fear having my head held underwater by other boys or engaging in water games that usually concluded with the impending sensation of being submerged.

That summer at the YMCA was wonderful, an eagerly anticipated time. Regrettably, there wasn't much opportunity to form friendships. The routine was structured: you arrived, participated in your lesson, showered, and promptly departed, leaving little room for bonding. When my lesson concluded, I would head to the nearby post office, just a few blocks away, and wait for my father on the loading dock to finish work before we headed home together in painful silence.

The Bonds of Friendship: The Wondrous Witch Waltz

In the intricate web of my mother's friendships among twelve friends, the Paulines seemed to be entwined like a complex puzzle. Pauline Meunier became Pauline Gadbois, Pauline Guilbeault transformed into Pauline Boisvert; Pauline Thomasette evolved into Pauline Rusick; and Pauline Marcoux transitioned into Pauline Bastille. The distinctions between maiden and married names are often blurred, adding to the confusion.

One of my mom's friends in particular was a blend of complexity and contradiction. On the one hand, she radiated vivacity and thrived in the company of friends, but there was another side to her I didn't fully understand at the time. Her concept of masculinity seemed tied to physical appearance, something I noticed in her husband: tall, trim and muscular with rugged facial features, crew cut—like the image of the *Marlboro Man* on the cigarette commercial. I never fit that mold. As the tensions escalated between her son and me, in my young mind, I could imagine her as the wicked witch from *The Wizard of Oz*, not because of anything she said outright, but because I sensed a disapproval I couldn't name. Even at this youthful age, it appeared to me that there was both an unhealthy rivalry between the two mothers, rooted in their own childhood experiences, and an intangible bond.

In stark contrast was my friend Steve's mother, Pauline Boisvert. To me, she was the embodiment of a saint, the good witch Glinda. Her friendship with my mom began in high school, fostered by a teacher's advice for my mom to make new friends. It wasn't until the 5th grade that I developed my own relationship with Pauline's family—Jeanne, Steve, Cathy, David, and eventually Danny. The memories of our visits were filled with genuine laughter and warmth, a stark contrast to the emotional turmoil of the adversary saga.

Steve's mom suggested to my mom that I join him in their Boy Scout troop. Those Wednesday nights were my favorites that year, though my recollection of the actual activities during Boy Scouts is rather hazy. What truly stuck with me were the moments that followed our weekly meetings. Steve's family owned one of the first color TVs in our neighborhood. Once our meetings concluded, we'd rush back to his house to catch Lost in Space while awaiting my parents to come and pick me up. Life at their house felt remarkably distinct from ours.

Steve's father, Leo, had been my dad's childhood best friend. My perception of Leo was that of an opinionated, authoritative figure. Most evenings, as far as I can remember, he'd be seated in his recliner after a long day running his construction business, a beer in hand, his substantial belly protruding, issuing orders to whoever happened to be nearby. Jeanne, his eldest daughter, was a year older than Steve and me. She possessed remarkable intelligence and a sharp wit that she could wield like a weapon if you crossed her—a skill I wished I had mastered earlier in life. Cathy, on the other hand, was the quintessential girl next door. Her disposition was sweet, caring, and compassionate, embodying the spirit of a Suzy Homemaker. She was the type of girl you wanted to date and be friends with at the same time. Then there was David, at that time, just old enough to be the pesky little brother we often tried to evade. Then came Danny just before my mom had my sister Carol. Both were beautiful children and both mom and Pauline had them secretly betrothed at the age of three.

However, the most significant detail, while unrelated to my relationship with Steve and his family, was the fact that they had an in-ground swimming pool that I was welcome to use anytime. The pool provided an alternative to the pond, both for my mother and me. With the arrival of summer and a bicycle that granted me independence, my visits to Steve's house increased. Yet, this newfound independence didn't come without its consequences. The more we distanced ourselves from the pond, the more tension seemed to arise between Mom and her friend.

One day, just a few weeks into the summer, my antagonist showed up at Steve's house on his bicycle.

"Hi! Is Ron here?" he asked, as though he didn't already know I was there. What was this? Why was he acting like he was my friend? But again, like the cottage, this wasn't my house. It was clear he was angling for an invitation to swim. His intentions were obvious, especially since he was already wearing his swimming trunks—a detail Jeanne was quick to point out. Despite his transparent motives, Steve's mom's graciousness shone through, and she welcomed him to join us in the pool. However, being the savvy observer she was, she sensed the underlying motives behind his actions and subtly came up with an excuse that he had to return home. Her maneuver worked perfectly; he never returned. Meanwhile, Steve had no interest in the cottage, his trains, or any other enticements meant to lure my friends away from our time together.

There was a sense of tranquility that enveloped me like a warm blanket on a cold snowy day—a feeling of acceptance, where I could wake up and anticipate a regular day with my friend, free from the emotional turmoil I had endured every summer for as long as I could remember. This family consistently showed me true friendship. While Steve and I may have differed in our interests, his mom steadfastly served as a guiding light of perspective throughout my life.

Adventures in DC: The Capital Concerto

As the president of the U.S. Postal Workers Union, my dad usually attended the annual conferences with my mom. However, because of my two-year-old sister, Carol, mom wasn't able to attend the 1968 conference in Washington D.C. So, she suggested my dad take me along; to have some of that father and son bonding that the therapist had recommended. It was August. The weather was warm, especially in D.C. Upon arriving at the hotel, my dad promptly called my mom to let her know we had arrived safely. Since it was late, we went to bed immediately. Just before my dad turned off the lights, I saw him slip his wallet into his shoe and stuff his sock on top of it.

"Daddy, why did you do that?" I asked curiously.

He explained that if anyone were to come into the room while we were sleeping, that would be the last place a burglar would check. Strangely enough, that gave me a sense of security, but with my dad right there next to me, I already felt safe.

The next morning, we were up early. My dad mentioned that the hotel hosting the conference provided breakfast. A few blocks away was the exquisite Mayflower Hotel. A buffet breakfast was set up in the foyer of the conference rooms, complete with my favorite Danish pastries and donuts. Of course, my dad insisted I eat the eggs and sausages first. There was also a gift shop in the lobby, and I asked if I could look. My father joined me, glanced around the shop, grabbed a $1.00 booklet of D.C., and made a quick purchase. I would have preferred the souvenir book with all the stunning pictures of the historical places in D.C., but it was priced at $5.00. We returned upstairs to the conference rooms, and my dad settled me into a chair, handed me the booklet, and instructed me not to move. Obediently, I sat there quietly and began to read.

The booklet mostly contained advertisements for Washington restaurants and stores, so I flipped through the pages rapidly. When I reached the center of the booklet, there was a pull-out tourist map of the city, featuring highlighted attractions and a prominent star marking "you are here." After calculating the distance, I realized I was just a few blocks from the White House. My sense of adventure intensified.

At 10 a.m., there was a short break. Still seated in my chair, My dad came out to check on me and introduced me to some of his colleagues. Dressed in a suit, the men joked about me resembling a budding politician want-to-be. Truth be told, if there were a pianist present, I might have burst into song like the shoeshine man in a rendition of "Mr. Bojangles" as they did in Shirley Temple movies.

Before my dad returned for his next meeting, he instructed me to be patient as this session would be longer. At noon, he would take me to lunch.

My adventurous spirit was in full gear, and realizing I had a two-hour window, I decided to embark on my first solo sightseeing escapade. Consulting my map, I set off toward my next destination. And I made it! There I was, standing in front of the White House. A group of people were gathering for a tour, and I somehow ended up with the group. Considering I was dressed nicely, no one questioned who I might be with. We toured through various rooms, with the guide providing historical insights about past presidents, first ladies, and the decor. When the tour concluded, I had a mere ten minutes to return to my seat at the Mayflower. I hurried, dealing with many pedestrian obstacles that made my journey more challenging. Finally, I made it to the hotel, rushed up the stairs, and sat in my seat, taking a deep breath just as the doors to the conference room swung open and attendees streamed out. There I was, and my father's expression was a mixture of relief and happiness.

"You must be hungry," he said as he grabbed my hand.

We went to a forgettable lunch spot, and I found myself amidst adults discussing business, relegated to the role of a child seen but not heard. We returned for the afternoon session, which began at 1 p.m. My dad sat me in my chair and walked away, presuming I wouldn't move. As the conference room doors closed, I returned to my map, plotting my next adventure.

The Washington Monument was just a few more blocks from the White House. Building on my successful morning escapade, I decided to attempt another solo sightseeing mission. Out the door, around the corner, and up the street, I dashed toward this iconic landmark. On a slight hill, I encountered another group of tourists waiting for entry. My plan worked again; the attendant just assumed I was someone's child. Swept into the limited number of people at a time, we ascended the 897 steps to the top, revealing a breathtaking view of the National Mall, the White House, and the Capitol Building. The descent was far easier than the ascent. Back outside, I pondered whether to set out on yet another adventure. As I strolled down the street, analyzing the map, I noticed a taxi driver keeping pace with me.

"Hey, little boy!" the cab driver shouted. "Are you sightseeing?"

I replied cordially, "Yes."

"Why don't you hop in? I can show you something really special!"

My instincts, trained to be wary of strangers, kicked in. I quickly devised a plan: since this was a one-way street, I could reverse course and lose him. And it worked. Once I regained my bearings, I promptly returned to the hotel. As I climbed the stairs, I spotted my father looking for me. He didn't seem to panic, just concerned.

"Where were you?" he asked.

I swiftly responded, mustering as much courage as I could, "I had to go to the bathroom and was looking for one."

That was true. My father gave me a knowing look and said, "Oh, come on, I was heading there too."

For the remainder of that afternoon, I sat quietly in my corner, akin to Cinderella, in my own little chair. When my father emerged at the end of the meeting, his colleagues joined us for dinner. Another evening where there was no one for me to converse with. Over dinner, I went over my memories of the White House rooms, the paintings, the colors, and the allure of the forbidden. On our way back from the restaurant, I noticed some windows along the way were opaque at my eye level. Curiosity got the better of me, and I attempted to jump up and stand on the ledge to see inside.

My father quickly pulled me away, remarking snappily, "You don't need to see in there!"

One of his colleagues, resembling Dean Martin, chimed in, "Oh, come on, Roger. He's going to have to see them sometime!"

With that, the colleague lifted me onto his shoulder. Now with an unobstructed view into the bar, I saw women dancing on the bar without their tops on. It was a brief sight as I was quickly brought down from the man's shoulders. My dad bid his colleagues goodnight, and we began our walk back to the hotel.

Recognizing it was too early for bed, my father decided to reward my good behavior. We returned to the hotel, got into his car, and drove around the White House before pulling up to the curb. We got out and walked up to the gate.

"Ronnie, this is the White House, where the President of the United States lives. I'm sorry we didn't have time during the day to take any tours," my dad said.

I couldn't believe my ears. Did he think I was naive?

"Not to be disrespectful, Dad, but I actually went and saw the inside of the buildings," I blurted out, unable to contain myself.

My father gave me an odd look but didn't inquire further about where I had gotten such details about the White House. Instead, we hopped back into the car and drove off, finding ourselves in front of the Washington Monument.

My father started to say, "Ronnie, this is the Wash..."

"Yes, I know, it's the Washington Monument. It has 897 steps, and when you reach the top, you can see all of D.C. The Monument, White House, and the Capitol Building are all in a row."

Back in the car, we drove to the next destination. Finally, it was something I hadn't seen. We arrived at the Lincoln Memorial, that massive marble tribute symbolizing honesty and freedom. We climbed the stairs and with each step the marble Lincoln statue grew larger and larger. There was an overwhelming sense of power and stability felt in its presence.

The return to the hotel was a quiet one, which was normal for my father and me as we had little to say to each other, unlike my mother and me. When we arrived, he called my mom to bid her goodnight and tell her how the day had gone. She wanted to speak to me, and I couldn't wait to share my adventures. My father sat there, listened, and began to worry that my imagination was a tad too vivid.

Taking back the phone, my mother said, "Roger, I thought you said he only saw the outside of the buildings?"

My father was emphatic that I couldn't have ventured from the hotel.

"I think he actually went and saw those things," my mother responded, finding more logic in that scenario. But my father dismissed the whole thing, saying,

"Let's get some sleep because tomorrow my meetings are at the Capitol Building."

The next morning, after a quick breakfast at the hotel, we headed over to the Capitol. We were early and managed to get a brief tour of the Rotunda with its vaulted ceilings and impressive dome in the center. As the meeting was about to begin, my dad seated me in a chair outside the room with strict instructions not to leave the area. However, boredom got the best of me, and like any curious child with the tendency to wonder, I began to explore the halls.

At one point, I came across a door with the sign, *Senator Edward Kennedy*. I was captivated, realizing it was Ted Kennedy's office. Being from Massachusetts, everyone knew about the Kennedy family, and the tragedy of President Kennedy's assassination in November of 1963 was still raw in everyone's heart. As I innocently peer through the open doorway, Mr. Kennedy's secretary greeted me warmly.

"Good morning, young man. Don't you look dapper!"

I replied with a gracious, "Thank you."

"So, what brings you here?" she inquired with a warm smile.

"My dad is in a meeting, and I have to wait for him," I replied. As I said this, a statuesque man in a black suit holding a manila folder emerged from an adjacent office.

"Well, who do we have here?" he asked with a smile.

"I'm Ronnie Boucher. My dad is the president of the post office," I added with a slight embellishment, "and he's in a meeting down the hall."

"Well hello Ronnie, I'm Senator Kennedy!"

At first I worried I might be in trouble, but Senator Kennedy's warm smile put me at ease.

"Look at you, all dressed up like a little gentleman. Would you like to come sit in my office? How about some ginger ale?" the Senator said as he escorted me into his office.

Senator Kennedy was charming and genuinely interested in getting to know me. He asked where I was from, what grade I was entering in a few weeks, whether I was excited to go back to school, and whether I was a good student, among other things. I basked in the attention and felt profoundly important. When the Senator asked about my time in D.C., I didn't mention my independent sightseeing adventures. Instead, I shared my reflections on the moments of solitude I experienced while waiting for my father during his various meetings throughout the day.

Apparently, as I was chatting with the senator, my dad popped his head out of his meeting to check on me, only to find my seat empty. Growing increasingly panicked, he began calling my name. Since it was August and the House and Senate weren't in session, many of the office doors were shut. As he passed the first open door, which happened to be Senator Kennedy's office, he spotted the secretary at her desk.

"Excuse me, have you seen a little boy in a suit wandering around?" he asked.

"Oh, you mean Ronnie. Is he your son?" she responded. "He's inside with Senator Kennedy. You can go in."

My father felt mortified, to say the least. Embarrassed, he entered the office, already apologizing. The Senator shook my dad's hand, exchanged pleasantries, and inquired,

"So, I hear you've been busy, and Ronnie hasn't had much fun." Then he dropped a surprising question. "What are you doing tonight at 5 p.m.?"

My dad was taken aback seemingly embarrassed that I had invoked this invitation.

Almost stumbling he blurted, "Um…Nothing. My meeting will be over about then," he answered still in disbelief that the Senator has proposed an invitation to a function that he was attending.

"Perfect. Meet me here at 5 p.m. There's a reception for John McCormick, our Speaker of the House. I think there will be other children there for Ronnie to play with."

My father felt that the Senator's command left him with little choice.

Roger, Senator Ted Kennedy, and Ronnie

Unfamiliar with D.C., we arrived in Senator Kennedy's limo at a secure garage entrance to a hotel. As we made our way to the ballroom where the reception was in full swing, I was struck by the size of the room. Tables draped in white cloth were laden with food, while servers moved gracefully among the guests, balancing trays of hors d'oeuvres. Senator Kennedy was immediately surrounded by greeters, exchanging the expected handshakes with ease. Taking a moment, Senator Kennedy informed me that he had something special for me. We headed to a corner of the room where a waiter held a pineapple adorned with shrimp on toothpicks.

"I heard you're a fan of shrimp cocktail, Ronnie. So, I ordered this for you. Eat as many as you'd like," he said with genuine delight as he saw my eyes widen with excitement. A few of the other children that were there quickly came over and I gladly shared with them.

I relished being the center of attention for the next hour. At the Senator's insistence, we had our picture taken together, followed by another picture with Senator McCormick and later one in front of the Capitol. However, the picture with Senator Kennedy is the one I cherish the most, a token of his kindness in making a young boy feel exceptional.

The Bullies: The Wounded Blues

The "sous sol" classroom, as it was called in French, occupied a space beneath the church but in a loft area just above where the altar boy's garments were stored. This makeshift classroom was seldom utilized, and it was overseen by none other than Sister Evelina, the very same nun from my altar boy days. She held the key to this domain and was now my teacher in the mornings. Sister Evelina, who had limited English proficiency, awarded me brownie points for conversing with her in French. Her tenure at St. Anthony's was substantial, and on the first day of class, she proudly revealed that she had taught both my mother and her sister. With this revelation came the expectation that my academic performance would match or even surpass theirs. She even went as far as to share that she had enjoyed teaching my mother but held a different sentiment for her sister.

The school year commenced without any hiccups. Things were progressing smoothly, and I began to lower my guard. Sister Evelina's favoritism toward me was obvious, and I found myself becoming the obvious teacher's pet. I couldn't deny that I relished this change in dynamics. A nun who treated me kindly, who made me feel valued and important, who had confidence in my abilities, and who treated me with genuine respect — this promised to be an exceptional year.

Most students overlooked the fact that much of Sister Evelina's French discourse was directed squarely at me. This petite figure, possessing the command of a military general, offered an unexpected amusement when witnessing her yank another student from their seat, grabbing their ear in the process. There were two unfortunate souls on her radar: John and Paul. John embodied a character straight out of an Oliver Twist movie — infrequent baths, greenish teeth, ragged and crumpled clothes, disheveled hair, and an unmistakable "defiant to the world" attitude. Paul, often seen as John' companion, was an oversized sixth grader whose intellectual capacity seemed to fall far from the triple-digit range. The special attention and favor that Sister Evelina bestowed upon me began to grate on John. Powerless to take on a nun physically, he opted to focus his frustrations on me.

For reasons unbeknownst to us, my sister and I had developed a habit of taking the avenue route home for lunch and the boulevard route for the end of the school day. On a particularly sunny day, as I strolled homeward without my sister, when I noticed the presence of John and Paul—no, not the apostles—trailing me. It struck me as odd, as they lived below the avenue and should have taken a different path. Despite their odd choice, I continued, unaware of the impending encounter.

As I moved along, the two boys were closing in on me at an alarming rate. Their taunts began in a sing-song chant: "Teacher's pet... teacher's pet." Brushing off the name-calling, I suddenly felt a searing pain as a hand seized a fistful of my hair, yanking me backward and halting my progress. Before I could react, I found myself ensnared in a wrestling arm hold executed by John. The pungent scent of his body wafted into the air, a detail I couldn't help but point out amidst the chaos. My retort earned me a knuckle noogie to the head—a painful, though tolerable, torture technique involving aggressive knuckle-rubbing against the skull. With my head locked under John's arm and my posterior positioned for an imminent kick from master Paul, I realized I was in serious trouble.

Surely someone would intervene, I thought, as we were right on the bustling avenue, where foot traffic from various stores was a common sight. Summoning all the vocal strength I could muster; I began to shout for help.

"Hey! Leave that boy alone!" a voice rang out from nearby, as a concerned passerby hastened toward us.

In the wake of this intervention, John released his grip, and I seized the chance to make a frantic dash for home.

I chose to keep the encounter to myself, opting not to share it with my mother or grandmother. Instead, I quietly slipped into our established lunchtime routine of enjoying a meal and watching mémère Serra's beloved soap opera, *Love of Life*. I had the timing down to a science. As soon as the show concluded, I had a five-minute window to return to school before the bell signaled line formation. The next day, I hoped that John and Paul had gotten their fill of testosterone-fueled aggression and that my sprint home for lunch would be a peaceful interlude. Alas, it was not to be. My anticipation of an uneventful lunchtime was quickly shattered. In response, I swiftly devised a strategy to navigate the situation.

Oddly enough, Sister Evelina had established a peculiar ritual of releasing us from class in small groups and in alphabetical order. With my last name beginning with a "B" and John's with a "P," this arrangement granted me a fleeting advantage of a minute or two head start. One could almost imagine the scene from the movie *Forrest Gump*, with the command to "Run, Forrest, run!" encapsulating the urgency that fueled my escape once I exited the classroom door. My plan was taking shape; I was managing to create a significant lead that kept them at bay. However, as the weeks progressed, Sister Evelina became increasingly efficient in her dismissal routine. This heightened efficiency brought about too many uncomfortable close calls.

Being an altar boy, I had mastered the intricate paths that crisscrossed the church. This knowledge granted me an advantage when I sought to evade John and Paul. After our class ended, as the boys rushed to the door, I chose an alternative route. Instead of joining them outside in the school yard, I descended the stairs into the altar boy's vestibule. Navigating this obscure passage, I emerged beneath the church, near the Bullard Street stairwell. This tactic allowed me to remain concealed until I was confident that the boys had departed in pursuit of me. Their chase had evolved into a spirited game of cat and mouse.

During this period, my strategy proved effective. I managed to avoid John and Paul for several weeks. Yet, fate had other plans. Sister Evelina somehow uncovered my secret exit through the church and promptly prohibited me from utilizing that route. Although she inquired about my reasons, I couldn't disclose the fact that her cherished pupil was harboring a streak of cowardice. Thus, I resumed my routine departure, adhering to the original schedule.

My newfound diversion had only exacerbated John's animosity, intensifying his determination to catch up with me once and for all. "Faggot! I'll kill you mother fucker!" yelled John.

Why had I chosen to wait until I was ensnared and vulnerable before I raised the alarm? My voice pierced the air, carrying a plea for help laden with desperation, as my little legs pumped furiously to escape the clutches of my pursuers. Regrettably, the bustling avenue appeared devoid of any potential saviors that day. The usually crowded streets seemed to have conspired against me, leaving me alone in my struggle.

On that occasion, John's hand snatched my hair, yanking me to a sudden stop. The impact of my skull against the unforgiving cement sent a jolt of pain through me. Then, a new agony seared through me as I experienced the full force of his shoe against my ribs. The blunt force left me momentarily breathless, and my cries for help were abruptly stifled. As I rose off the ground another blow followed, landing on my backside and causing my body to stiffen in response.

In the blink of an eye, John had seized my hands, wrenching them above my head and pinning them to the ground. Meanwhile, John positioned himself strategically, his weight immobilizing my pelvis and rendering my legs powerless to resist.

"I got you now you little faggot, mother fucker!"

Abruptly, a repugnant wetness splattered across my face. The sensation registered, and I couldn't believe my senses. Had John, in his malice, spat on me? My mind raced, contemplating what horror might follow this vile act. Was I to be subjected to further suffering? My thoughts spiraled into a frenzy of impending doom. Would lashes be lashed upon my back, metaphorical thorns pressed into my skull? How much more torment could I endure before my body surrendered? The notion of death danced at the fringes of my mind, an ironic escape from the cruelty I was experiencing.

Then, as if scripted, the universe provided a fortuitous distraction. At the precise moment, my mind whispered, *That's it... die,* John's fist collided with the side of my face. I seized the opportunity, orchestrating a masterful performance of feigned unconsciousness. My body crumpled dramatically, a convincing display of a young soul succumbing to the trials imposed upon it. The effect was profound; shock and fear seized the boys, their bravado crumbling like a paper castle before a storm.

"Oh shit! Let's get the fuck out of here!"

The urgency in John's voice betrayed his alarm, and without hesitation, the two assailants beat a hasty retreat, leaving me in a heap on the ground. It was over—well, not just that moment, but it was all over. My resolve solidified in that moment, an unbreakable oath to myself. I could endure no more of this torment. School held no more appeal; it was a chapter I was ready to close. Slowly, I gathered myself from the pavement, a body bearing the physical imprints of cruelty endured.

My mother was clearly concerned, and her scolding words dissolved into gasps of shock as she took in my battered appearance—torn clothes, disheveled hair, a portrait of turmoil etched on my face. Physically and emotionally shattered, I sought refuge in her embrace, releasing a torrent of tears that had been dammed up during weeks of enduring the unrelenting fear of torment.

The hours that followed brought relief. I was granted a reprieve from the school environment, allowed to remain at home. My mother changed her own attire and made her way to the school, her purpose was clear: to confront Sister Evelina, to unearth the truth of the matter, to protect her child. The meeting took place, the words exchanged—an assurance that I would be allowed to depart a full five minutes before the rest of the class, ensuring my safe passage home. Additionally, John's parent contact information was secured.

With these provisions, my mother's efforts were geared toward a resolution. Yet, when she returned, her fingers nimbly danced over the rotary dial of our telephone. The call to John's mother held no pretense, the urgency of her tone carrying the weight of a serious matter. She outlined what her son endured by John, the relentless cruelty that had persisted for weeks. The response: a flippant dismissal, the all too familiar refrain of "boys will be boys," punctuated by the suggestion that I should be the one to fend off my assailants.

My mother's reaction was swift, the resolve in her voice unwavering.

"If your son ever touches my son again," she declared, "not only will I report him to the police, but I will also contact my attorney."

The call ended, the line severed, and at that moment, it was over—not just the immediate ordeal, but the entire affair. The remainder of the school year was marked by a simple alteration in my routine: I was granted an early exit, a precautionary measure, and the two tormentors seemed to vanish into the ether, as if their malevolence had never taken root.

These events provoked a cascade of moral dilemmas, unearthing the internal conflict that arises when faced with abuse. The question lingered: when confronted by bullies, was it acceptable to stand one's ground and defend oneself? This quandary was amplified when the source of torment lay in the hands of individuals cloaked in authority—clergy, close family friends—or if the cultural expectations of resilience contradicted the basic principles of justice and dignity. Over time, these experiences contributed to a transformation within me—a determination to demand respect and a readiness to fight for it when the situation demanded, a realization that empowerment was the key to breaking the cycle of submission.

Sister Oliriènne: A Dark Serenade

Starting in seventh grade felt like I'd undergone a rite of passage. The school year kicked off splendidly. I made new friends, like Michael DiPaulo, a friendly Italian from a close-knit family, and David LaPlante, the school heartthrob who had every girl smitten. You know the type – the dark hair, a slight wave with that single curl cascading onto the forehead, an almost Superman-esque look. He possessed the quintessential athlete's physique and seemed to skip the awkward puberty phase. David embodied flawlessness. Adored by nuns and students alike, he graciously welcomed me into his circle. David's mother, reminiscent of my mémère Serra, emanated a strong French-Canadian aura. Her thick accent and maternal appearance reminded me of my grandmother. As the youngest, David's siblings were already in high school.

Our teacher that year was Sister Oliriènne, a round woman likely in her 50s or 60s – nuns' ages were often hard to decipher. Most seemed to age overnight. The schoolyard adhered to gender divisions. The boys enjoyed the larger section, providing ample space for various games. Sister Oliriènne, enjoying the company of boys, would often watch games and cheer them on. With a jovial sense of humor, she even laughed when she was the subject of their jokes.

One day, we gathered in a circle, and someone mentioned that Sister Oliriènne resembled an Oreo cookie. The comparison wasn't far-fetched – her rotund figure clad in black and white attire. Suddenly, a boy began chanting "Oreo, Oreo," *Wizard of Oz* style. More boys joined the procession, circling Sister Oliriènne as the chant grew louder. Like a Busby

Berkeley movie, the line divided, creating two circles that revolved around her. She stood gleefully in the center, arms raised in the air reminiscent of Julie Andrews on the mountaintop in *The Sound of Music*. The rhythmic chanting was interrupted by the bell's sound. Reluctantly, the boys dispersed, heading to their classrooms as the school day began.

The good sisters often displayed prejudices against students of non-French descent. This bias was particularly evident that year, targeting a newcomer from a wealthy Portuguese family named Susan. I believe she and her family had recently relocated from New York City to New Bedford. She exuded an alluring difference. Unlike other girls at St. Anthony's School, she had straight hair with bangs that partially covered her eyes – the cut was almost helmet-like, tracing her ears and nape. Her eyes sported heavy mascara on the upper lid, and she wore a light shade of rose-pink lipstick. Heart-shaped earrings dangled from her pierced ears. Susan's appearance channeled a 60s Goldie Hawn vibe that she confidently owned. In a class of camisole-clad girls, Susan bucked the trend, her white blouse revealing a bra embracing her already developed breasts. The nuns often used rulers to measure skirt hems, which were allowed a mere two inches above the knee. Most girls would surreptitiously roll up their skirts to match the contemporary 60s style. However, Susan's skirts, tailored to be at least eight inches above the knee, defied convention and highlighted her Twiggy-like legs. She was independent, outspoken, and indifferent to others' opinions.

"Mademoiselle Susan," Sister Oliriènne's voice pierced the classroom's chatter.

"Viens ici," beckoning Susan to approach her desk.

Although she didn't understand the French words, Susan recognized her name. Sister repeated,

"Mademoiselle Susan, viens ici."

Seated next to Susan, I was her linguistic guide, translating her command to "come here." Susan rose slowly, moving to the front where Sister Oliriènne's desk rested on a wooden riser. Sister grabbed a ruler, brandishing it like a dagger aimed at Susan. Then, seizing Susan's arm, she pulled her onto the platform. With ruler in hand, Sister measured Susan's skirt hem, finding it significantly higher than the mandated two-inch limit. Sister assumed it was merely rolled up. However, as she tugged the skirt, it was evident that the alteration was intentional. The entire class gasped as Susan stood there, mortified, and tearful, her mascara leaving black streaks down her face.

As Sister Olirиènne prepared to modify the hemline, she asserted that "good girls" shouldn't flaunt their bodies. She also expressed disdain for the sight of the back of knees, deeming them unsightly. All the while, my focus was on Susan's humiliation, my heart aching in sympathy. Suddenly, Sister Olirиènne's critique shifted to Susan's bangs, which she considered too long. She attempted to push them away from Susan's eyes. Susan, her arms flailing like someone swatting away a fly, protested,

"Get your hands off me, leave me alone!"

Yet, Sister Olirиènne persisted, grabbing Susan's hair, and lifting the scissors, poised to alter her hairstyle. Shocked and instinctively defensive, Susan thrust her arms forward, inadvertently pushing Sister Olirиènne backward. The Sister stumbled and fell into her chair, which then rolled off the platform, depositing her onto the floor. As she lay there, legs elevated, revealing her black hosiery covering her plump calves, the classroom was stunned. Some boys rushed to help her. As her chair was restored to the platform, Sister Olirиènne quickly reclaimed her place, returning to Susan. Grasping Susan's right ear, she led her out of the classroom and down the corridor to the principal's office. That was the last time we saw Susan. She was expelled and I was told she ended up in a public school. It would be a while before anyone dared challenge St. Anthony's dress code again.

For me, this incident awakened an appreciation for qualities I found attractive in a woman: independence, self-assuredness, and feistiness—traits that would later become important in my relationships.

The First School Dance: A Young Waltz

Seventh grade brought with it the introduction to a new world of social dancing, an area where boys and girls navigated unfamiliar steps in preparation for the highly anticipated school dance, a prelude to the Thanksgiving break. As the event approached, a buzz of excitement filled the air, with boys carefully choosing their dates and girls hoping to be asked by their desired dance partner. The mothers, too, engaged in a covert rivalry for chaperone roles, masking their motives under the pretense of vigilance or control. Both my mom and Pauline found themselves enlisted.

In this whirlwind of anticipation, Pauline's son was the first to secure his dance partner, sparking a familiar wave of pressure from my mom to follow suit. I, however, was discerning in my choice. I sought not just popularity, but someone genuine and kind. Denise Milloux, a brunette residing atop Massé's Pharmacy, caught my eye. Her reputation and family background spoke of decency, making the decision straightforward. One day in the schoolyard, I approached her, asking her to accompany me to the dance. She graciously accepted, setting our plans in motion. Our interactions were minimal until the day of the dance itself.

The evening's venue was a small room above Bouchard's tavern, an enchanting space lovingly decorated by the mothers, who reminisced about their own school dances. While girls busied themselves with beauty parlor visits and primping, the boys embraced their typical Saturday pursuits. A feast reminiscent of a classic movie scene unfolded: mémère Serra's baked beans, hot dogs, and delectable black molasses bread. As the hour drew nearer, I prepared. Shower, toothbrush, hair neatly combed—these tasks marked the beginning of my transformation. The product "Wildroot" had replaced the once rigid "Odell," striking a balance between style and comfort. My attire, beginning with BVDs and a T-shirt, culminated in a freshly shined pair of shoes, a product of my mother's meticulous care. As the last step, my dad handed me a wrist corsage, intended for Denise. With a farewell, he sent me off into the night.

By the time I arrived at the Milloux's apartment, night had fallen. I had never been there before and climbed the narrow, poorly lit staircase, knocking on the door when I reached the top. Mr. Milloux, a tall, thin man with the look of a businessman, wearing half-glasses and holding a newspaper, answered.

"You must be Ronnie!" he said, his voice firm but with a twinkle in his eye. "Denise will be right out. Have a seat." He gestured to the couch and settled back into his stuffed chair, returning to his paper.

Mrs. Milloux soon entered the room, and I quickly stood, offering my hand. She reciprocated with a warm handshake and a few cordial words of welcome. Moments later, Denise emerged from her bedroom. Her hair was mostly the same as usual, except for a curled section pulled back. She wore a simple dress and black patent-leather pumps with a small heel—a girl's rite of passage, at least from a boy's point of view. She smiled as her parents beamed at their daughter, their beautiful creation.

I handed her the box, which she opened with a dignified eagerness. Smiling, she accepted it graciously. Her mother helped slip the bracelet onto her wrist. Instead of a coat, Mrs. Milloux brought over a cape, draping it gently over her daughter's shoulders.

With Denise on my arm, we made our grand entrance greeted with the usual adolescent school dance behavior of whistles and applauds. The boys congregated on one side of the room avoiding the expectation of dancing with the girls, and the girls on the other scrutinizing each other's outfits and with sudden bursts of giggles. However, it wasn't long before the mothers intervened, encouraging boys and girls to dance together.

With the music setting the rhythm, I took Denise's hand and led her onto the dance floor. My familiarity with dancing, learned from my mom, proved invaluable. It was a simple foxtrot with a side together, side together, back step, which Denise seemed equally adept at doing. But most of the boys and girls did the proverbial rocking from side to side, keeping approved distances. Not that any of us would have thought to do otherwise, at that time. Denise's father arrived to retrieve her, relieving me of the responsibility of walking her home.

As I drifted into sleep, I relished the experience—a successful first date, the joy of dancing with a girl, and the comfort that came with my newfound popularity. I remembered my mom's stories about her and her friends attending their high school dances at the Lincoln Park ballroom. The night was a reminder of how relationships can be simple and enjoyable, leaving me with a contented sense of accomplishment. As for my favorite antagonist, he seemed to have taken the role of the wallflower, a stark contrast to his usual prominence.

The Infamous Incident A Relative Anthem

It had been a year since I had joined the Boy Scouts with my friend Steve. Meetings were held in St. Mary's School cafeteria. I had eagerly anticipated Boy Scout Camp that summer, even though my friend Steve had dropped out after the school year ended. I liked a few of the guys and decided to stick with it. Camp Cachalot, nestled within the Narragansett wildlife preserve, featured platform tents accommodating around four beds each. While the outhouse left much to be desired, the allure of the woods provided a preferable alternative.

The night before departing for camp, we attended a family celebration at the home of one of my father's relatives. The evening held the charm of a beautiful summer night, with many uncles, aunts, and cousins in attendance. It was a sweltering summer evening and very few people had air-conditioning. With the house bustling, we children spent most of our time outdoors.

One of the guests was affectionately referred to as "Uncle." Throughout the evening, he engaged us in a playful game of pretend monsters, bringing laughter to the younger children and prompting shrieks of delight. Their cheerful cries echoed as they scampered back indoors, a sign that the game effectively wore them out. This led some parents to depart for the night.

One of my cousins and I were outside when Uncle joined us. She excused herself and headed indoors, leaving me alone with him.

Standing around 5 feet 8 inches tall, he had dark hair, full lips, and a slender build. His gaze was intense, seeming to pierce right through me, despite the smile on his lips. He greeted me with a teasing remark about my growth since he last saw me, playfully ruffling my hair. His tone carried a sense of challenge, a typical form of interaction seen among fathers and sons, uncles and nephews.

The playful banter slowly transitioned into physical interactions. I found myself in a playful headlock, expecting discomfort but instead experiencing a light and harmless exchange. I hopped onto his back, something I had seen with other fathers and uncles horsing around at the cottage. What began as innocent fun shifted subtly as he carried me toward the back of the house and into the woods. Nighttime had fallen and as we walked behind the trees the darkness was even more apparent and so was my growing sense of unease. My heart raced, and I attempted to free my hands from his grasp, hoping to be released. Instead, he maintained a firm hold, continuing to move forward with his rocking side to side motion which cause friction rubbing my crotch on his buttocks. with each sway. The motion inadvertently led to our bodies brushing against each other.

Fear prompted me to try and break free from his hold. As I struggled for him to let go, in a quick maneuver, he flipped me around. He was now behind me. Panic surged as his body pressed against mine in a way that set off alarm bells. My mind raced, and I realized that this situation was taking an unsettling turn.

In a flurry of unease, I was transported back to fourth grade, a vivid memory of an assembly in the school auditorium. A towering movie screen occupied most of the stage, flanked by police officers at a lectern on the floor. Their words resonated with urgency, impressing upon us the gravity of interacting with strangers. To underscore their message, they screened harrowing crime scene images, displaying the tragic outcomes that could befall young children who ventured into the unknown. Among the images, one in particular had seared itself into my mind—an image of a boy, akin to my own age, lying vulnerable in the cold woods, discovered a week after his life had been brutally extinguished.

But could this truly be a comparable situation? Could this man, an adult figure in my life, harbor such darkness? My rational mind strained against these troubling thoughts, struggling to reconcile the inconceivable scenario that I was facing. His grasp around me felt like strangulation.

The notion that a relative could be capable of such a sinister act seemed implausible. Yet, rational thinking struggled to find a foothold in the grip of overwhelming fear. My heart pounded in my chest, its rhythm matching the surge of blood that coursed through my veins. But to my alarm, the escalation of my fear ignited a perverse exhilaration in this man.

I felt an oppressive pounding in my head, the combined effects of anxiety and heightened blood flow. Paralyzed by fear, my every move felt labored and sluggish, a stark contrast to my uncle's growing excitement. The tumultuous emotions I displayed only seemed to fuel his disturbing enthusiasm, pushing the encounter further into what was unthinkable.

His breath was hot against my ear, a raspy symphony of excitement that seemed to synchronize with the pounding in my chest. My breath came in rapid gasps, a result of hyperventilation that left me feeling lightheaded and dizzy, my body growing weak and unsteady under the weight of fear. My pleas to be released were muffled by his hand, which was clamped over my mouth with a vice-like grip, stifling my cries.

In the midst of this harrowing ordeal, his actions escalated. The belt came undone with a quick and deliberate motion, followed by the sound of a zipper being lowered. A wave of humiliation washed over me as my pants pooled at my ankles, leaving me exposed and vulnerable. His hand, intrusive and violating, ventured inside my underwear, its touch both alien and repugnant.

The touch on my penis sent shockwaves through me, a complex mix of sensation that overrode my senses. His fingers manipulated and squeezed, evoking a physical response that I couldn't control. And all the while, I could feel his erection pressing insistently against my buttocks, a disturbing reminder of the grotesque reality of the situation.

As his breathing grew heavier and more urgent, his whispered words slithered into my ear like poison.

"Oh, you like this don't you?"

The words were laced with a sickening mix of arousal and taunting, leaving me torn between the confusing surge of physical sensations and the profound revulsion I felt at his touch.

In that moment, my mind was a battlefield of conflicting emotions. Desire and aversion clashed in a chaotic dance, leaving me utterly bewildered. It was a maelstrom of sensation and cognition, a cacophony of fear, confusion, and an unfamiliar awakening that I couldn't comprehend.

His lips brushed against my ear, carrying with them the sound of deep, rhythmic breathing reminiscent of the pulsating tempo of Carmina Burana. As panic began to tighten its grip on me, dizziness swirled in, weakening my very frame.

Tension coiled within me as he started to manipulate and caress me, his own arousal pressing against my backside.

Amidst his ragged breaths, he again murmured, "You enjoy this, don't you?"

This marked the precipice of a chilling realization; his intentions were horrifyingly clear. I was on the brink of an unthinkable fate—assault, potentially murder, followed by abandonment in the depths of the woods. It was a harrowing prospect—the silence of the outdoors held no witnesses, no one to recount the horrors that would unfold. In the house, he would easily blend with his family, cloaked in their innocent revelry. Those minutes of his absence would pass unnoticed, unaccounted for. But there I was still standing with my pants around my ankles, immobilized. Panic surged; my options seemed futile. Just as he began to lower my underpants, an unexpected interruption shattered the moment. A figure emerged on the back porch—it was his wife.

"Sweetheart... Honey!" she called.

His response was swift, a vice-like grip clamping over my mouth, anchoring me to him with unyielding strength. He waited; his actions were pregnant with tension. Again, her voice pierced the night, her calls growing more desperate. "Hey, where are you?"

A desperate plea rose within me—a silent entreaty for someone, anyone, to come searching for me. My parents, a friend—anyone who might disrupt this nightmare. And then, the sound of the screen door closing, sealing her return indoors where the revelry masked any potential cries for help. Darkness swallowed her presence, and the yard stood empty, devoid even of the children.

Yet, in that charged moment, a twist of fate granted me a reprieve. His advances ceased; my underpants remained intact. His grip released me, and in a frenzy, he adjusted his own clothing. Swiftly, I pulled up my pants, a surge of readiness coursing through me. The window of opportunity opened, but his grip seized me once more. His eyes gleamed with malice; his voice laced with cruelty.

"Perhaps give it a moment. You wouldn't want them to spot that erection."

His assumption faltered; such a reaction eluded me. As swiftly as desperation could muster, I broke free, sprinting across the yard, ascending the stairs to the refuge of the house. Nausea gripped me, and my body trembled as I sought out my father amidst the crowd. Found in a rare conversation with distant relatives, I implored, "Dad, I'm not feeling well. Please, I want to go home."

But my plea fell on distracted ears; my urgency was overshadowed.

"Yeah, soon, we'll leave soon."

Meanwhile, Uncle remained a lurking presence, his search for me evident. I was convinced that he would try to ensnare me once more, to drag me back to that ominous spot. I had to devise a means of self-preservation. With him inside, I approached a cousin, stationed at the front of the house. With veiled words, I warned her of Uncle's treacherous intent. But her skepticism clouded her understanding; my truth seemed a fabrication. Her dismissal was swift, and she retreated into the house, her silence an intense barrier.

I did everything I could to avoid being in the same place as Uncle. If he was inside, I made sure to stay outside. But if, on the rare occasion he managed to catch me and drag me back to that tree—the one that had witnessed my trauma—I had a plan. I placed a stick at its base, a small, desperate gesture to reclaim a sense of control, thinking it might somehow help if I found myself there against my will.

Still, I couldn't shake the uneasy certainty that he would return. My vigilance was constant, and when the moment came, I seized it. As he approached, I circled around to the front of the house, my heart pounding, and slipped inside before he could stop me.

 Once more, I approached my father, determined to convey the urgency of my need to leave, this time claiming the impending camp departure required my immediate attention. But fate was unkind; Uncle entered the house. It was a signal for me to retreat once more. My head spun; heart raced—there he was again. Racing to the opposite side of the house, I tried a different approach, beseeching my mother. Sensing the validity of my plea, she offered a solution.

"Roger, take Ronnie home and come back!"

Her decision was an irrefutable directive my father couldn't dismiss.

And so, we departed, the Chrysler a vessel of escape. Home offered me safety and my room, a haven. Stripped of my clothes, I donned pajamas, seeking comfort in familiarity. But rest eluded me; despite being emotionally and physically spent, my mind was a torrent of replayed horrors. Why? How could Uncle do this? The question echoed, a ceaseless loop of desperate attempts to rationalize the senselessness. I yearned to banish the memories, to find solace at summer camp among friends, to leave the darkness behind.

The following morning, my dad accompanied me to the bus stop, where a gathering of boys stood with backpacks and camping gear. Parents bid farewell with hugs and kisses as each of us boarded the bus. The company of my friends was a welcome distraction, a bulwark against the darkness that sought to resurface. Upon arriving at the camp, we unloaded our gear, our camp leader distributing tents and designating locations. As a unit, we carried our equipment and marched in disciplined formation to our assigned campsite. Once there, we claimed our sleeping arrangements, setting up sleeping bags atop comfortable mattresses. These tents came equipped with raised platforms to shield us from inclement conditions.

By the time we had settled in, it was time to gather at the dining hall for lunch. Amid the camaraderie, rules and regulations were outlined for us to follow. Our meal consisted of hearty chicken noodle soup and bologna sandwiches. Post-lunch, we returned to our tents, changing into our swimwear in anticipation of the afternoon's activities. Swimming was first on the agenda. Scouts were tested based on their swimming proficiency— beginners confined within a roped-off area, intermediates restricted to buoys, and advanced swimmers permitted to venture out to a raft a short distance from the shore. Thanks to my strong swimming skills, I was designated an advanced swimmer, affording me opportunities for canoeing and rowing with a partner. The afternoon progressed swiftly, a whirlwind of aquatic enjoyment. The sound of the whistle marked the end of our activities, prompting us to return to the shore and then back to our campsite in preparation for evening activities.

Once back, we formed a single file, ready for an outdoor shower before donning our uniforms. Dinner was a formal affair, all of us dressed in full Boy Scout uniforms, proudly wearing sashes—adorned with merit badges. Each badge represented and accomplishment – whether it be helping an elderly woman cross the street, mastering complex knots, or surviving a solo weekend in the woods. In formation, we marched toward the camp's central gathering area. The sight was awe-inspiring, each troop forming a circle around the flagpole, the American flag billowing in the gentle summer breeze sweeping in from Cape Cod's eastern coast.

"Attention! Salute!" commanded one of the leaders.

As the order echoed, we raised our right arms in a military-style salute, our postures rigid and steady. Two scouts approached the flagpole with deliberate grace, commencing the solemn act of lowering the flag. However, as the flag descended, a sudden disorientation overcame me. My head spun, nausea surged, and my vision blurred. Desperately, I attempted to fixate on the flag, but before I knew it, I collapsed to the ground.

When I regained consciousness, I found myself inside a tent, a nurse gently placing a cold towel on my forehead. Her voice was calm as she said,

"There you are! How are you feeling?"

Confusion gripped me, and panic began to swell.

"What just happened? Where am I?" I stammered out the words, my fear overriding any sense of understanding.

The nurse inquired if I wanted to wait until morning, allowing a night's rest to gauge my condition. But I was resolute—I wanted to go home. Mr. Carter, one of our scout leaders, offered to drive me back. Upon arrival, I found my parents absent, having hired a babysitter for my sisters Renee and Carol. In my parents' absence, popcorn had been made, a humble offering that awakened my appetite, having missed dinner earlier. When my parents eventually returned from their evening out, they were surprised by my presence at home. My mother's concern was visible as the sitter relayed Mr. Carter's account of the events that had transpired. With the hour growing late, we all retired for the night.

The following morning, my mother reached out to my pediatrician, Dr. Schwartz. His primary concern was the possibility of a petit mal seizure, a type of epilepsy. During the appointment, Dr. Schwartz conducted a thorough examination, examining every detail and posing numerous questions. He reassured my mother that if a recurrence were to happen, she should bring me back. Otherwise, he speculated that the incident might have been triggered by excessive sun exposure during that afternoon.

We returned home and my mother began preparing dinner while I sat on our big orange vinyl-covered chair reading a book.

"Hey mom! What does molest mean?" I asked, very innocently to avoid any suspicions.

My mother, comfortable answering any questions I had, simply responded that it was a sexual attack on another person, usually an adult, on a child. I was all ears and continued my questions.

"So, what like happens?"

My mother took a few minutes and then said, "A man might look for a situation that he can get a young boy or girl alone. With a boy, he might pretend to want to wrestle and then…"

Before my mother could even finish her explanation, I abruptly dropped my book and leapt out of my seat. Confronting her by the stove, I burst out, "Mommy, that's what happened to me!" Tears streamed down my face uncontrollably as I sought refuge in my mother's comforting hold.

She held me tightly, her face now level with mine. In a firm tone she asked, "Are you sure he did this to you? Did he hurt you? Oh my God, is this why you fainted?"

Her grip on me was so strong that it was almost suffocating, but in that moment, it felt like the only anchor grounding me. I recounted every detail of the unsettling encounter.

My mother stood there in a stunned silence, her mind racing to plan the next steps. However, time slipped away unnoticed. Before we knew it evening had fallen, and my father was returning home. As he entered the door, he could immediately sense the distress in the room with both my mother and me clinging to each other. He settled into his green rocking chair near the telephone, listening as my mother detailed what had transpired.

A wave of determination filled her voice as she told him, "He's not making this up! You need to do something about this!"

Yet, my father, typically composed and non-reactive, remained silent. Inside, I had already envisioned what I wanted—for my father to confront that man, to make him pay for his actions. I wanted him to understand that he couldn't escape the consequences of hurting someone, especially someone who couldn't defend themselves. Without a word, my father picked up the phone and began dialing.

"Who are you calling?" My mom asked.

His response was simple, "Someone who needs to know."

As the receiver crackled, my mother, I, and my father huddled around, straining to hear the conversation on the other end. The words that came through were harsh, a tirade of denial and accusation.

"He's a little liar, a liar! Tell him to shut his mouth and never concoct such stories again. You and your wife had better keep this to yourselves. Don't you dare believe the lies of your deceitful child."

My father hung up the phone, a mixture of disbelief and astonishment etched across his face. The room fell silent, tension and uncertainty thick in the air. I anticipated some sort of action, the eruption of a storm to wash away the wrong that had been done.

Breaking the stillness, my father asked, "Is dinner ready?"

The words hit me like a ton of bricks. No, this wasn't supposed to be the response. This wasn't justice. I wanted him to go and confront the darkness, to protect me, to make things right.

My mother's anger flared; disappointment outlined on her face as she confronted my father. "So, you're just going to let it go? You're not going to do anything?"

In response, my father's calm explanation followed, a finality that left no room for argument. It was enough; we knew the truth. But he felt powerless, for it would be my word against Uncle, and with the family's affection for him, belief would naturally lean in his favor. Especially when the family matriarch herself deemed me a little liar. And just like that, the matter was closed, shut away in silence, never to be discussed again.

According to Sigmund Freud's structural model of the psyche, the id, ego, and the super-ego function as distinct, interacting mediators within the psychic apparatus. These constructs provide a theoretical framework for understanding the activities and interactions that shape a person's mental life. Amidst this complex backdrop, I found myself grappling with an immense ordeal, a stolen innocence that left me isolated and alone. My mind swarmed with unanswered questions, and a visceral turmoil gnawed at my core. What had transpired within me? Why had this transgression occurred? Why had I been targeted? Amid these queries loomed "that" unspoken question: Could my mother's friend have been right? Was I, in fact, grappling with my sexuality? Could this be why I was singled out?

Encased in silence, I found myself bereft of a support system to navigate the aftermath of the trauma that had ravaged both my physical body, despite not being subjected to rape, and the fragile contours of my emotional psyche. Within this turmoil, the triad of id, ego, and super-ego within my psyche roared into overdrive, with the primal id seizing the reins. In the shadows of the unspeakable, Uncle had stolen something vital from me—my innocence. More profoundly, he'd done so without my consent, without affording me the readiness to confront such a violation. The impact of such an occurrence knows no gender-based discrimination; its ramifications span across all individuals. From that day onward, I was irrevocably altered—haunted by fear, plagued by inner conflict between morality and the primal sexual urges that surged within me, requiring vigilant containment at any cost.

In the aftermath of sexual abuse, survivors often find themselves navigating two distinct trajectories. The first is a perilous descent into sexual promiscuity, while the second involves a deliberate sublimation of any form of sexual activity with others. Whether my decision was a conscious one or born from the depths of my subconscious, I gravitated towards the latter path. This resolute stance remained my steadfast choice until the age of twenty-one.

To draw a parallel to the emotions I had come to bear, I'm reminded of the biblical tale of Adam and Eve, who grappled with profound shame after committing the original sin. Their response was to cover their nakedness. Similarly, I found myself undergoing a transformation. I could no longer view the human body as I once did, as when a line of boys readied themselves to swim at the YMCA.

That heightened awareness became more apparent shortly after. During that summer, our cousin Pierre and his wife Louise came to visit, and they expressed a desire to visit Horseneck Beach, one of Massachusetts' coastal beaches known for its popularity among surfers. This was my first encounter with the ocean, public sandy beaches, and vast dunes. The journey to the beach was longer than our trips to Long Pond. As we approached, we passed an entrance sign where an attendant collected a parking fee. Joining many other vehicles in a sprawling parking lot, the heat made the pavement squish underfoot as we gathered our belongings. We then followed a path that wound through the dunes, the intense sunlight forcing us to squint in its blinding glare.

Walking through those dunes felt like traversing a desert, and suddenly, like a mirage materializing before us, there it was—the vast expanse of the beautiful blue ocean. With no time to spare, my sister and I quickly kicked off our shoes and threw our shirts onto the sand. Running eagerly towards the water's edge, we were met by waves towering over six feet high. Within inches of entering the water, our footing became precarious as the waves crashed forcefully against our legs. The water was cold, carrying the distinct taste of salt. Despite the initial shock, there was an undeniable power and tranquility in the experience, a sense of healing that permeated the atmosphere.

The sense of tranquility abruptly shattered at the end of our stay. On that day, my dad, cousin Pierre, and I headed to a building at the beach to shower and change into dry clothes. Inside, there loomed a vast room adorned with more than two dozen shower heads, where men were showering in their nakedness. For the first time, I was acutely aware of the nudity surrounding me. As my dad and Pierre conversed under the water, they remained oblivious to my state of mind. I stood there frozen, much like a deer caught in headlights, as the water cascaded over my body.

In that moment, I couldn't help but notice the men of diverse ages, sizes, and body types, each engaged in the mundane act of cleansing themselves. I stood immobilized, incapable of movement, as if held in the grip of an invisible force. An adrenaline surge coursed through me, and in the recesses of my mind, I could almost hear the sinister breathing of Uncle echoing once again, accompanied by that familiar sickening feeling deep within my gut.

Abruptly, my father's voice pierced through the haze. "Ronnie, hurry up!" he said.

The spell that had kept me motionless was broken, and I managed to dry off and hastily dress myself. The uneasiness remained, exacerbated by the fact that I had to sit in the back seat during the ride home. Once more, I found myself isolated, left to wrestle with these feelings in solitude. There were no therapists to turn to, and I was burdened by a profound sense of disgust, reminiscent of Adam and Eve's awareness of their own nakedness and shame.

Suicide: The Incomplete Symphony

At that point in time, I'm uncertain if I truly comprehended the concept of suicide. What I did feel, however, was an overwhelming sense of isolation, even in the presence of others. Each passing day dragged me deeper into an abyss, as if I were gradually submerging myself in a pool of desperate thoughts. I lacked the perspective then to recognize that my encounter with Uncle and its subsequent aftermath were the very roots of my current state of torment.

On that Saturday, my thoughts swirled and clashed, an impenetrable storm of emotions that defied comprehension. I sat on my bed, grappling desperately for a way to capture the turmoil within me... "I want to die!" The words burst forth, a stark revelation of my inner torment. It was as though a blinding flash of clarity had pierced the chaos, presenting the solution to my predicament.

The next step was to determine how. My father's razor blades were a possibility, nestled within the bathroom medicine cabinet. Yet, that method involved inflicting physical pain on my body, a notion I recoiled from entirely. Needles frightened me; the idea of cutting my wrists was anathema. Pills, perhaps? The medicine closet held a near-empty bottle of Bayer Aspirin, far from a viable option.

Returning to my bed, I scoured my surroundings for an avenue that promised minimal pain, a swift conclusion. And then, my gaze fell upon my robe, draped at the foot of my bed, its sash suspended by two small loops. "That's it! I'll hang myself." However, an obstacle stood in my way. The highest point I could anchor the sash to be the knob on my bed's headboard. But standing a mere four feet from the ground, it presented a challenge.

Methodically, I secured the sash to the knob, then retreated to close my bedroom door, looking for solitude. To clarify the setting, our apartment's layout featured three bedrooms branching off from the living room's right side. My room was the first upon entering the apartment, adjacent to the galley kitchen and followed by the bathroom. My closet was shared with my father, and the family's laundry basket rested in my room—turning it into a well-traveled space.

Returning to my bed, I fashioned a slip knot at the opposite end of the sash. I sat on the floor, tears streaming down my face. This, I convinced myself, was the only solution left. With the noose draped around my neck, I pulled to tighten it, my mind racing. Experimentally, I shifted my position, hoping to ascertain if I would be positioned low enough for it to work. But this proved futile—awkward and unfeasible. Frustration welled within me as I attempted to remove the sash from my neck. The world around me faded as I faded into unconsciousness, my fall to the side tightening the noose around my throat, restricting my airway. It was working, I felt myself slipping away. The sound of my own blood pulsating filled my head as my room dissolved, replaced by a beckoning white light. This was it, the moment of passing.

"Goodbye, cruel world!" I whispered.

Suddenly, a voice broke through the quiet, a voice that sliced through the moment's stillness.

"Ronnie, what are you doing?"

The words resonated more loudly this time; my father's presence now tangible before me.

"Ronnie!"

I returned to reality, gasping for breath, my eyes fluttering open to the sight of my father's perplexed expression. Filled with embarrassment, I swiftly untangled the sash from around my neck.

"What on earth are you doing?" My father's voice was quick and concerned.

My response, murmured through tears, escaped me: "I was committing suicide."

Anticipating an outpouring of affection, the reassurance that I was loved and cherished, akin to the scenes in a Lassie episode when Timmy is swept into his mother's embrace, I was met with a different reaction. My father settled on the edge of my bed and, rather than an embrace, offered a straightforward assessment.

"You know what your problem is? You think too much. If you think things are tough now, you'd better follow through, because life only gets harder as you grow older. It's time for lunch! Come and eat; your mother has set the table."

I stood, following him to the living room, where my family was gathered around the table. Renee sat across from me, Carol content in her highchair, and my parents were positioned nearby. The gravity of the situation seemed poised for understanding, for empathy.

But when my mother inquired, "So, what was going on in there?" the response cut through solemnity.

"Ronnie was trying to hang himself!" my father said.

My mother's response, hardly one of empathy, was simple. "Well, that was silly."

Renee added her own brand of commentary. "Well, that was really dumb, and they call me a ta-ta head." She continued, "Oh Ronnie, you always have to be so dramatic."

Laughter erupted; the incident was seen as absurd from their perspective. It was, in a way, a scene right out of *Leave it to Beaver*. After lunch, as Renee and I washed the dishes, I felt an aversion to that robe.

My father's words echoed prominently in my mind, "You think too much."

In that moment, I realized the truth of his observation. I spent an inordinate amount of time within my own thoughts, a tendency that I had never truly recognized before. While I couldn't have known it then, those words would serve as the advice I needed, a foundation to navigate the forthcoming months, and a philosophy I would cling to on my path to adulthood.

Sister Rita: The Sister's Sonata

I hadn't managed to break free from the endless nightmares that tormented me, a cruel reminder of my experience with Uncle. Those nightmares would twist my stomach into knots, often leading me to my grandmother's kitchen at 3 a.m. Her struggle with a digestive ailment caused bouts of loud belching that resonated through the ceiling of her kitchen, just below my room. These sounds, particularly pronounced in the open windows of summer, disrupted my sleep. Unable to rest, I would descend the stairs to join her, seeking solace. She would prepare me a comforting glass of warm milk and produce her stash of Nabisco wafer cookies. After an hour or so, we would return to our respective beds, the night's disruption behind us.

And now, here I stood on the precipice of my final year before high school. St. Anthony's Elementary School claimed the first two floors of the building, with the high school occupying the third. Despite being in the same building, rarely… were the moments when we encountered the high school students, for our schedules were distinct. Curiosity once led me to stealthily ascend to the third floor, eager to catch a glimpse of what lay ahead. Peeking into classrooms, I observed desks of a larger scale, and in one room, hefty tables with black tops that I later learned were designated for chemistry experiments.

We eagerly anticipated the transition to the upper school—an excitement that ran through all.

It wasn't just another first day of school as an intangible difference hung in the air. An unexplained uncertainty niggled at me, though I attempted to push it aside as I arrived at the schoolyard. We were all dressed in our finest attire. I wore one of my new shirts, paired with my first-ever rope tie —an intricate string with metal accents and a clasp that secured it at the neckline, where a conventional tie's knot would rest. My Farah pants, a recent purchase from Star Store, and Bostonian shoes from Cherry & Webb completed the ensemble. Mom's approving smile as I left that morning only solidified my own belief that I looked rather dashing.

I reached the schoolyard early, and the atmosphere buzzed with excitement as we greeted one another. Conversations should have revolved around our summer exploits and the ever-present question of romantic interests. Strangely, though, our discussions focused on the approaching high school year and the looming entrance exam. Attending St. Anthony's Grammar School was widely assumed to be the precursor to St. Anthony's High School. However, it wasn't a guarantee; passing the entrance exam was a requirement, and it served as their method for filtering out the undeserving candidates.

When the bell rang, a sister holding a list of names assigned us to our homerooms—an annual tradition. My name was called first, placing me at the forefront of the class. The rest followed, row by row. Just as we were about to enter the school, Sister Rita approached me.

"Mr. Boucher, you will be in my homeroom this year," she stated, her voice holding a note of concern.

Truth be told, the specific class didn't matter much; I had friends in both sections, and there was limited social interaction during class time. Recess was when we were all together. Sister Rita arranged our seating in alphabetical order. However, in this class, I wasn't first in the alphabet. Regardless, she insisted I take the first seat in the first row. Furthermore, I was bestowed with the role of door attendant—assigned to anticipate arrivals, opening the door, and repeating the process for departures. This endeavor proved futile, as only a few ever bothered to knock, resulting in my often being too slow to reach the door. Each time I missed someone's entrance; Sister Rita's glares of disapproval were piercing.

Sister Rita's fixation on me seemed unrelenting, marked by a barrage of criticisms that poured forth incessantly. Despite excelling in three of my best subjects—Religion, English, and Science—a peculiar downturn in my grades began to occur. Strangely, Sister Rita never allowed me to review my test papers to understand where I had gone wrong. Before the entire class, she lambasted my compositions as juvenile and my science performance as failing. In the weeks that followed, my every action was under scrutiny, be it participating in group activities during recess or abstaining. While there were no overt instances of abuse, her attacks were deliberate and systematically eroded my self-esteem. Her motive was always unclear, with no apparent cause or reasoning. Even my peers questioned why she singled me out for such persistent scrutiny. I grew more resolute to mend whatever was causing this daily anguish. I became an exemplary student, intensifying my studies, paying meticulous attention to areas she had criticized. But the harder I tried to improve; the harsher Sister Rita's responses became.

One morning, as the school day commenced, the principal entered our classroom. By some stroke of luck, I managed to reach the door in time to open it. As I settled into my seat, I noticed Sister Rita casting a look of utter disdain my way. The principal announced a school contest for the best slogan to promote staying in school—an important cause in an era where eighth-grade dropouts were still common. When the principal left, I once again rushed to open the door, earning yet another glare of annoyance from Sister Rita.

My confidence soared; I was certain my creative talents could conjure up something at least worthy of a runner-up prize. Given the entire period to craft my entry, I delved into profound contemplation. However, my attempts were marred by hesitation, much like a writer at a typewriter, typing a few lines and then ripping the paper from the carriage, starting anew with another thought. Time was slipping away, and with the period over, I hastily scribbled another slogan on the back of my paper. I was the last to submit my entries, and Sister Rita was already poised to move on, not reading any submissions but placing them neatly on her desk, away from her new focus.

The following morning, Sr. Rita stood at her desk like a buzzard in waiting for the next kill. She placed all the entries in the center of her desk, preparing to read them aloud. As the class listened, most of the slogans missed the mark, failing to comprehend the essence of a slogan's concise message. When she reached mine, she first read it to herself, a menacing grin creeping onto her face.

"Would you like to hear what Mr. Boucher has come up with?" she inquired, taking pleasure in her words.

She read the slogan aloud, "Don't be a fool, stay in school," punctuating it with a malevolent chuckle and commenting, "This is what you took the whole class period to write?"

I quickly interjected, "No Sister, there's another one on the back!"

With a swift motion, she flipped the paper over, revealing my second slogan. "Be A Wiseman, Follow the Star of Education!" Her tone shifted from mockery to an almost pleasant timbre, as if trying to suppress her recognition that this was a commendable effort. My classmates seemed to concur, erupting into applause that incited an uncontrollable fury within Sister Rita. She seized my paper, tore it into pieces, and cast it into the metal garbage can beside her desk just as the noon dismissal bell chimed.

Frozen at my desk, I remained. I knew that second slogan was a winner, combining biblical allusion—apt for a Catholic school—and a call to pursue education.

The culmination of events, capped by Sister Rita's callous response to my slogan, felt like the last straw that finally broke the camel's back. The pain and disillusionment rendered me speechless, and I walked home in a daze, my emotions swirling like a tempest within.

It was a Friday afternoon, and upon arriving home, my mother had prepared dinner—a dish of frozen French fries that I found unappetizing, accompanied by a crabmeat salad soaked in mayonnaise and decidedly not to my taste. We ate while watching a rerun of the *Dick Van Dyke Show*.

My sister left for school shortly after lunch. I lingered behind, caught in my own thoughts. Standing before the Humphrey gas heater that provided warmth to our apartment, I sought to replace the inner chill with the soothing heat radiating from the device. My gaze drifted to my mother, who was busy at the sink, washing dishes. She turned, noticing my prolonged presence, and admonished,

"Hurry up, Ronnie, you need to get back to school."

I remained frozen in place, feeling my complexion paling as if drained of all color. In a sudden rush, I collapsed onto the carpeted floor. Tears streamed uncontrollably down my cheeks, and my body quivered with an overwhelming torrent of emotions. It was as if I was experiencing an emotional breakdown. My mother's worry escalated as she watched me in this state. Was it a health emergency? Did I need a doctor? What was happening to me? She had witnessed my distress before, but only once had she seen me succumb to such depths of despair. Could this be another episode akin to the one with Sister Paul Henry, she wondered?

This time, however, I struggled to put my turmoil into words. Unable to provide a definitive explanation, my mother allowed me to stay home and directed me to my room, urging me to rest. As she hastened to complete her chores and prepare herself for yet another visit to the convent, my mother was caught in a mixture of concern and uncertainty. At the stroke of three, my mother arrived at the school, resolved and prepared for a confrontation with Sister Rita.

Upon my mother's return home from the convent, she maintained a silence about the conversation. She instructed me to remain in our apartment while she went downstairs to make some phone calls from my grandparent's phone. When my father arrived home, they quickly had dinner before leaving again, stating that they had an appointment to attend. Hours passed, and upon their return, my mother revealed the decision that would reshape my schooling. As of Monday, I was to begin attending St. Kilian's grammar school.

A few weeks later, my mother finally shared her encounter with Sister Rita. When she arrived, she was greeted her at the door by a Sister.

"I'm Mrs. Boucher, Ronnie Boucher's mother, and I would like to speak with Sister Rita," she declared firmly.

She was directed to a small, secluded room. Its heavy door was designed to safeguard any confidential conversations.

Inside, my mother settled herself, contemplating how to broach the topic. Why did she find herself in this position again, defending her son? Was I a completely different person at school compared to the one at home?

The door swung open, and Sister Rita entered, taking a seat across from my mother.

"Why have you come, Mrs. Boucher?" inquired Sister Rita, her question carrying a mix of curiosity and defiance.

Surely, she must have some inkling of the reason, my mother thought. Gathering her thoughts, my mother began, "Sister, my son collapsed just before it was time for him to return to school. He told me he couldn't bear another day with you. Has Ron done something wrong?"

Her plea was laced with concern and a desire for clarity.

Sister Rita's expression took on a chilling aspect, reminiscent of those sinister German gestapo officers portrayed in movies.

"Why, Mrs. Boucher, Ronnie, has done nothing wrong. Ronnie is perfect!" she retorted with a biting tone.

Frustration welled up within my mother.

"Then what is the issue, Sister? My son didn't collapse for no reason. I need an explanation," she insisted.

"Mrs. Boucher, Ronnie isn't a normal boy! I assure you; I will change your son into a normal boy, a boy who curses and plays like the other boys."

Sister Rita continued to list her contentions from my attire to my manners, all being impeccable, as if she needed a way to rationalize her behavior. A note of disdain still lingered in her voice.

"I don't care how long it takes. If I don't succeed this year, I will continue next year, as I'm being transferred to the high school."

The tension in the room escalated.

"You're mad! I'm taking Ronnie out of this school," my mother declared, her fury now intense and her patience exhausted.

Sister Rita seemed unfazed, even offering a parting shot.

"Where is he going to go? Public school?"

Her tone carried a condescending undertone, as if public education was inferior to the standards of a Catholic institution. My mother, not deigning to reply, picked up her purse and made her way to the door. Just as she was about to exit, Sister Rita's voice stopped her.

"One last thing, Mrs. Boucher."

My mother paused, her hand resting on the doorknob, waiting.

"If you're considering transferring Ronnie to another Catholic school, keep in mind that I will need to fill out a recommendation form. I assure you; no one will want a damaged, unstable, and troublesome student."

With that, my mother departed the convent, her mind racing to determine the best course of action. One thing was certain: come Monday morning, I would not be setting foot in that school.

St. Kilian's was an Irish Catholic school managed by the Sisters of Mercy. The catalyst for this change was my aunt Doris, my mother's sister, who, upon learning of my struggles, suggested that my parents consult with Fr. Norton, a priest at St. Kilian's. Fr. Norton, upon hearing the circumstances, advised my parents to meet with the principal of St. Kilian's. After detailing the situation, the principal was convinced that my parents had good reason to request my transfer, notwithstanding a probationary arrangement. If any issues arose, I would have to leave the school.

For me, the uncertainty of transitioning to a new school was a much more appealing prospect than enduring Sister Rita's oppressive regime. A new day was dawning, one that held the promise of a fresh start.

Sister Mariana: The Renewal Rhapsody

Arriving early for my first day at St. Kilian's, I couldn't help but mull over the concept of probation. What did it entail? What criteria did I need to meet to stay and what actions could lead to my dismissal? As I entered the school yard, it was notably less populated compared to St. Anthony's and none of the eighth graders seemed to be around. I inquired with one of the nuns about my destination, and she directed me to the principal's office for check-in.

While I received a warm greeting, the principal made it clear she would be keeping a watchful eye on me, with the expectation for me to integrate successfully. *Fit in?* I pondered. That was an elusive concept for me, and I was almost convinced that this new endeavor was bound to fail. I'd end up in public school. After all, Pauline Boisvert's children were thriving there, how bad could it really be?

November 1st had arrived, and the rhythm of the school year had taken hold, forming friendships and routines. As I stepped into the classroom, a distinct difference was immediately apparent. The room had a more relaxed atmosphere, with plastic desks and chairs that could be easily moved—unlike the bolted-down, cast-iron desks with polished wooden tops at St. Anthony's. While the girls still wore uniform skirts of varying lengths, the boys no longer wore the neckties I was so used to seeing at St. Anthony's.

Sister Marianna, a Lebanese woman with a distinctive Mediterranean nose and a cascade of dark, curly hair, stood before us, her short veil sitting mid-scalp. The Sisters of Mercy had adopted a modified habit, featuring knee-length skirts paired with simple blouses, sweaters, or blazers.

As I hesitated at the doorway, pondering where to sit, Sister Marianna greeted me with warmth, introducing me to the class. The students flashed smiles and friendly gestures, and one boy, fully bearded and named Aaron, stood out. Lebanese like a few others, he was also the class president. Textbooks were handed to me, and our academic day commenced with math. Not being my favorite subject, I was much more focused on all the new students and was forming assessments on who I would approach first to spark up a conversation during recess. We had only been in class for around thirty minutes when unexpectedly, Sister Marianna halted the lesson, exclaiming,

"Alright, enough of that. Let's have some singing!"

Desks were swiftly pushed against the walls, and students assembled in a semi-circle. A chorus of voices rose, accompanied by Sister Marianna's guitar. Aaron joined in, his voice blending with the others.

"Sons of God, hear his holy name…"

The singing resonated throughout the room. My heart fluttered in exhilaration. Not only had I discovered a wonderful new school, but I found myself in a paradise of music. At any moment, I half-expected the principal to stride in, declaring, "Ronnie Boucher, you don't belong here. You should be in public school." But that moment never arrived. No crushing disappointment, no dashed hopes, only the bell signaling lunchtime.

I hurried home, brimming with excitement, eager to share my day with my mom and mémère Serra, who awaited with hopeful anticipation. As I told my story, their shoulders relaxed, dropping about two inches from their ears. The rest of the year flowed smoothly…well almost!

An invitation to join the basketball team marked another milestone. During a game, my Charlie Brown syndrome appeared. The ball was in my hands, and the path to the hoop lay clear ahead. The crowd's cheers surged; adrenaline coursed through me. I scored! Yet, the teams froze in bewilderment. I had inadvertently shot a basket for the opposing team, leading to our loss. The embarrassment was profound. Dread filled me as I faced the locker room, convinced of the impending punishment. I was mistaken. While some expressed frustration over the defeat, no blame was directed at me. No insults, no belittlement.

Aaron, stepping into the shower, offered words of reassurance, "Hey bud, don't worry about it. These things happen."

Monday brought no mention of the mishap. As the school year neared its close, a variety show was organized. Sister Marianna approached me, asking if I'd be comfortable with a solo performance. Instantly, I agreed, though disbelief lingered. Could this be a trick? The thought of a solo seemed incredulous. She requested "I Am a Rock" by Paul Simon. I spent weeks rehearsing. The culmination of my efforts was a gratifying performance where applause and cheers greeted me. Had the curse that haunted me for years finally lifted?

Sister Maureen Francis: The Teaching Tango

January 2nd signaled that the holidays were over, and I was eager to show off my Christmas gift, a guitar that I had started learning to play over the break. This instrument was a vessel for a new form of self-expression I was excited to explore. Aaron and Sister Marianna were happy to help me learn some basic guitar chords.

"C, A minor, F, and G7—that's all you need for most of the songs we play," Aaron reassured me.

True to his word, I was strumming these chords within a week, and with pride, I joined Aaron and Sister Marianna to form a trio. This musical outlet opened a new world for me.

Another surprise awaited on the first day of school after the holidays. The desk in front of me, always empty until now, was suddenly occupied by a girl with striking strawberry blond hair. Karen Langford had a bouncy personality, a great smile framed by petite teeth, and freckles. She had just recuperated from a severe bout of mononucleosis. She looked fantastic. And the attraction was clear, at least from my side.

You know you're smitten when you begin doing inexplicable, foolish things in the presence of the opposite sex. Well, I certainly did something foolish. For reasons that eluded rationality, I picked up my ruler from the desk and held it against her back. Truly, I had no idea why. To my surprise, one of the boys saw this bizarre action and burst into laughter, as if it were the height of coolness. However, amidst my observation of his reaction, I failed to notice that Karen had turned around, catching sight of the ruler.

And then, with a swift motion, her small hand connected with a resounding smack on my left cheek, leaving me utterly stunned.

Witnessing the spectacle, laughter echoed, and I, overwhelmed by embarrassment, sought refuge beneath my desk. Attempting to explain myself proved futile; she refused to listen. Despite her apparent anger, a faint smirk played on her lips. In my mind, this was the moment they would use to expel me from St. Kilian. Yet, astonishingly, no further repercussions arose from the incident.

The preparations for the high school entrance exams were underway. With St. Anthony's High School off the table, I still had a couple of options to consider. St. Kilian, lacking a high school program, left us with a choice between Bishop Stang, a college prep school under the tutelage of the Sisters of Mercy Holy Name, located in the south end of New Bedford; and Bishop Connolly, an all-boys' institution overseen by Jesuit priests, revered for their educational prowess within the Catholic Church.

One Sunday afternoon, my parents and I explored Bishop Connolly during their open house event. The priest guiding us took note, especially when my mother mentioned my initial interest in the clergy. Indeed, that interest had faded ever since a certain girl had slapped me in the face. Nonetheless, after forging connections with friends applying to Bishop Stang, I decided to follow suit.

Mock entrance exams came and went, and I consistently scored within the top ten percent. Greg Assad, James Azar, Dawn Bruce, Stephen Butts, Christine David, Robert Gaumont, Richard Holtkamp, Karen Langford, George Patisteas, Karen Wojtkuski, and I all aimed for Bishop Stang. Our academic standings ranged from average to above average, leading everyone to assume that our acceptance was a given.

Weeks passed after the entrance exams, and excitement grew as we anxiously awaited our acceptance or rejection letters by mail. Fr. Norton, who also taught at Bishop Stang, provided a heads-up that we should expect news imminently. In the end, all applicants received their letters except for me. I had to endure two more days of suspense, only to find a rejection letter in my hands. Yes, I stood as the sole individual denied acceptance. My peers rallied behind me, fervently believing an error had occurred.

In consultation with Fr. Norton, my mother and Aunt Doris deemed the situation perplexing and implored him to investigate further. Something didn't add up in the rejection letter. Fr. Norton agreed.

Given my academic and entrance exam scores that he had seen, he initiated a conversation with Sister Maureen Francis, the principal at Bishop Stang, inquiring about the rationale behind my rejection. With evident reluctance, Sister Maureen disclosed St. Anthony's transcripts, as that had been my primary institution prior to St. Kilian.

I later learned from my mother that Fr. Norton was shocked upon reading Sister Rita's scathing report. Fr. Norton said that Sister Rita's evaluation portrayed something severely amiss with me, and St. Anthony's was the only Catholic school equipped to manage such a problem student. He convinced Sister Maureen to grant me an interview.

After our initial discussion, she expressed the need to see my third-quarter grades and fourth-quarter interims before contemplating a reversal of her decision. Upon our second meeting, after she had received my exceptional 4th quarter interim grades, I was certain that Sister Maureen would reevaluate her stance. Yet, my optimism was misplaced; she insisted on waiting for my final grades.

On the morning of Friday, June 13th, with our eighth-grade graduation ceremony slated for 1 p.m. at St. Kilian's church, I was scheduled to meet Sister Maureen at 10 a.m. This time, my parents were to accompany me. We waited anxiously in her office while she concluded her business with her secretary, Mrs. Barker, in the front office. At last, Sister Maureen entered, greeting us with a smile and well wishes. She opened her folder, glancing at my final grades delivered by Fr. Norton.

"Well, young man, I can honestly say I've never encountered someone so resolute about attending this high school. I eagerly await the contributions you'll make to our institution, and I'm certain you won't disappoint me."

Struggling to maintain my composure, I joyously exclaimed, "Thank you, oh my God, thank you so much."

In tandem with my elation, tears streamed uncontrollably down my face, inducing a chain reaction with my mom, dad, and Mrs. Barker, who stood at the doorway, also wiping their eyes. Even Sister Maureen reached into her pocket for a handkerchief dabbing it softly under her eyes.

I returned to school just in time for graduation rehearsal, which was being held in St. Kilian's church. Fr. Norton paused, and the entire class turned watching me make my way down the aisle as the students sat with anticipation of my response. Fr. Norton broke the silence and said, "Ronnie, do you have any news?"

In that moment, with a gut-wrenching release of all the worry, frustration, and anger I'd been holding inside, everything changed as I announced my acceptance into Bishop Stang. The entire class erupted into cheers, and for the first time in my life, I truly felt the overwhelming support and camaraderie of my peers. I realized just how much I appreciated them for standing by me.

Those few months at St. Kilian's provided the healing of deep-seated wounds, although the scars remained, and reality dictated that wounds could reopen. That night, I lay in bed gazing at the religious icon of the Sacred Heart hanging on the wall beside me.

As my eyes lingered on the image of Christ, I softly murmured, "Must suffering be a prerequisite for experiencing happiness?" I cherished the triumph, and sleep overtook me in an embrace of contentment.

CHAPTER 3 THE HIGH SCHOOL YEARS

Bishop Stang: The Pontiff's Overture

Ronnie in uniform

Fortunately, I could now shift my focus toward a new beginning: high school. This experience had been the culmination of a year's anticipation and preparation.

The checklist was meticulously ticked off: a pristine blazer adorned with the school emblem, charcoal gray wool pants, a crisply starched white shirt with a smart collar, the school clip-on necktie, coordinated black socks and fresh shoes, all secured by a black belt. My book bag was packed and ready, marking my readiness for the upcoming four-year journey.

Public transportation to Bishop Stang wasn't available, and it was a brisk twenty-minute drive. My friend Steve lived in St. Mary's Parish, and since many students from the parish commuted to Stang, the church had arranged for a bus. I was told that if there were available seats, I could secure one for just $5.00 a month. I caught the bus at Nash Road, just a mile away. This translated to a brisk fifteen-minute walk or a ten-minute sprint from my house. Being one of the last to board, the bus was typically full, so I usually found myself standing near the bus driver in the stairwell. The driver was gracious, often flashing his lights to signal his acknowledgment of my approach and patiently waiting until I arrived.

That second day, as the bus doors swung open, a sense of relief washed over me; my tumultuous past might finally be behind me. Stepping out into the parking lot, it felt as if I were Judy Garland stepping into the vibrant

Land of Oz. A quick survey of my surroundings filled me with energy and excitement. As I looked around for familiar faces from St. Kilian's, my attention shifted toward the influx of cars streaming into the parking lot. Dozens of cars converged in rapid succession. Some were parents dropping off their kids, while others parked. Seniors could purchase a parking pass for the year, granting them the privilege of driving to school – a symbol of independence that I aspired to achieve.

I was intrigued by the seniors who were already scouting the first-year students, anticipating initiation day, a day when we newcomers would experience good-natured jests, a rite known as hazing but in a milder form. This being a Catholic school, my expectation was that any hazing would come from the nuns.

What I was witnessing was akin to a scene in a movie where, amidst a crowd, one person stands out and the camera zooms in. Picture a car pulling into a parking spot, and a guy emerges, jacket slung over his shoulder, shirt casually open to reveal his chest, and his sandy blond surfer hair cascading down to his chin. He radiates charm. A throng of senior girls flocked to him as he made his way to his male companions. It felt like a moment out of *Bye, Bye, Birdie*, reminiscent of Conrad Birdie's charisma. Who was this individual? Amid the buzz of excitement from the crowd, I caught snippets of conversation about an event from the summer.

"Oh my God! You went to Woodstock?" exclaimed one of the girls.

And so, welcome to 1969: a year filled with the sounds of The Beatles, Rolling Stones, Led Zeppelin, The Who, King Crimson, Chicago, Jimi Hendrix, The Doors, Santana, Simon & Garfunkel. My exposure to these artists came through the cafeteria's jukebox during lunch. Prior to this, my musical world consisted of Frank Sinatra, Perry Como, Julie Andrews, Bing Crosby, and the easy listening station that my mom played on Saturdays while orchestrating household chores. My bubble had burst, exposing me to a reality beyond my limited musical tastes. I was no longer confined to my sheltered environment, but a part of the world between the hippie era and the emerging disco scene. Yet, within the confines of my high school, marijuana and LSD were distant concepts, a subculture that didn't infiltrate my social sphere.

The orientation was behind us, and we had our class schedules in hand. I couldn't recall my homeroom teacher's name, but I vividly remembered the girl who sat in front of me: Corliss. She was a stunning blonde with a vivacious personality. Shortly after school started, she secured the position of head cheerleader for the junior varsity team, perhaps setting her sights on the football players, particularly Michael Bastille, a son of another Pauline. Michael embodied the All-American sports stereotype: handsome, athletic, and self-assured. Although we weren't close friends like our moms, we always treated each other with respect. I recalled a moment when he intervened to stop some football players from harassing me during gym class.

My first class of the year was P.E. with Mr. Millot. He also doubled as my French teacher and coached the junior varsity football team. After morning rituals, we headed to the gym for P.E. Mr. Millot distributed the gym uniforms, consisting of sweatshirts, sweatpants, gym shorts, and Bishop Stang T-shirts. Each of us was responsible for our socks, sneakers, and jock strap. The locker room awaited, a realm of expected adolescent antics, where some boys reveled in their physical development while others remained behind. The bell marked the transition to the next class.

Warm weather gave way to colder temperatures around November, moving gym class indoors – a change that suited me just fine. Running around the track was challenging; I was more of a sprinter and long-distance running wasn't my forte. Other boys shared this struggle, trailing behind me.

During the initial weeks, Mr. Millot evaluated our athletic abilities and recommended sports for boys who hadn't yet chosen a team. No recommendations came my way, a fact I didn't mind. Joining any of those teams seemed like an imposition. By the time it grew colder, gym class had shifted indoors permanently. The fear of jock antics in the showers had been exaggerated, and a group of us delayed our entrance to avoid the more developed boys. While there were inevitable towel slaps and taunts, the camaraderie among the less mature boys provided solace.

With my first weeks of high school underway, I felt a new chapter in my life truly unfolding. The uncertainty and anxiety of the past year had given way to a cautious optimism. High school was no longer just an idea I had been preparing for, it was my present reality, full of new experiences, challenges, and opportunities. From the friendships beginning to form to the small triumphs in navigating this new world, I felt the weight of transition lift. High school wasn't just a place—it was the beginning of my journey toward independence. Still fragile yet eager, I couldn't help but wonder what would come next beyond the classroom walls.

Sister Marie Gurry: The Chorus Ensemble

Entering the expansive room with its towering twenty-foot-high ceilings, wooden risers jutting out from the walls, a sleek black baby grand piano, and tympani drums tucked in the corner, I felt a surge of excitement. This was the beginning of an experience that I instinctively knew would leave a lasting imprint on my life.

"Welcome, students. I am Sister Marie Gurry, your chorus teacher," declared Sister Marie as she stood before us.

She was a woman of about five feet three inches, and her hair seemed prematurely gray in comparison to her youthful face. After evaluating our vocal ranges, she assigned me to the Tenor I section, the highest male register. Just like my experience with Sister Marianna, I felt as if I had stepped into a realm of pure bliss. I wished for longer and more frequent classes with Sister Marie, who led Chorus I with a mix of excitement and expertise. The Chorus I class comprised both talented freshmen like me and sophomores, while the juniors and seniors belonged to Chorus II.

Sister Marie would throw open all the windows, regardless of the chill outside, and initiate our vocal warm-ups. After around fifteen minutes, the windows would be shut, and the sheet music for the day's practice would be handed out. Among these selections was the timeless Hallelujah Chorus from Handel's Messiah, a piece I held close to my heart. Our preparations were geared towards the annual Christmas Concert, a collaborative effort with our school orchestra and various soloists. As the concert date drew near, we held combined rehearsals that brought Chorus I and Chorus II together. The resulting blend of voices and dynamic harmonies transported me back to the days of the choir at St. Anthony's Church.

We had all invested considerable effort and energy, pouring hours into rehearsals, perfecting harmonies, and mastering every note. Finally, the day arrived, bringing with it a mix of excitement and nerves. If this was what team spirit felt like, I was an enthusiastic participant, proud to be part of something larger than myself. For the concert, we didn't don choir robes; instead, the boys wore dark suits, white shirts, and ties, while the girls donned black dresses. In the chorus room, we conducted a comprehensive warm-up session. I could sense a touch of nervousness in Sister Marie's demeanor. Adrenaline surged through me as the gymnasium doors swung open. As we ascended the risers on the left side of the stage, the auditorium came into view, brimming with an enthusiastic audience. The orchestra was positioned in front of the stage, and the musicians were tuning their instruments. Sister Maureen Francis, the Principal, took to the stage to deliver her opening remarks before signaling the concert to begin.

The concert exceeded all my expectations and desires. However, it was one of the soloists who would profoundly impact my journey and solidify my path as a singer. A senior named Denise Morency took the stage with a presence marked by unparalleled ease and confidence. As she stood there, I was unaware of what she was about to sing—oddly enough, I had never heard this particular song at St. Anthony's. The orchestra commenced the introduction to Albert Hay Malotte's rendition of the Lord's Prayer. Denise's voice emanated from deep within her being, soft and barely audible above the orchestral accompaniment. Through the initial section of the piece, occasional crescendos hinted at the immense vocal potential she possessed.

Then it happened—the moment when music and vocals merge into an enrapturing climax, and her voice soared to a fortissimo. She filled the entire auditorium with her vocals, reaching a crescendo on the word "forever," only to taper off with a swift decrescendo leading to the final "Amen." Even before her final note, the audience sprang to their feet in a standing ovation. Tears welled up in my eyes as I watched her humbly accept the resounding applause from the audience, the chorus, and the orchestra. The applause seemed unending.

In that moment, I had an epiphany—I knew what kind of singer I aspired to become. Her performance had shown me the path I wanted to follow, and I was resolved that she would be the one to guide me. The details elude me, but I somehow became her student, and I've since sung the Lord's Prayer numerous times, including at St. Anthony's Church. Each rendition carries with it a sense of gratitude for her profound inspiration and influence on my musical journey.

Academics: A Scholar's Aria

Mathematics had always posed challenges for me, but something changed when I encountered Algebra. Sister Agnes possessed a teaching style that just seemed to click with me, and this newfound understanding was reflected in my grades—never dipping below 90.

Similarly, Mr. Millot, who taught French, connected with me due to our shared French-Canadian background. This rapport translated into high scores in his class. Following lunch, I had history with Mr. Grant, a subject that often coincided with my afternoon nap time. Mr. Grant's soothing voice and my seat by the window, combined with a tendency to hit the snooze button, made history class an uphill battle—less because of the subject's difficulty and more due to my recurrent dozing. Another class, Typing I, on the other hand, was a breeze. I had already mastered typing since the fifth grade, guided by my mother who was a typing teacher herself. Under her tutelage, I practiced exercises like "jjj (space) fff (space)," eventually achieving a typing speed of 65 words per minute by high school. This skill didn't go unnoticed, and Sister Sheila informed Mrs. Barker, the office administrator. This resulted in my being excused from study hall and assigned to office duties during free periods, a position I retained until graduation.

Religion class posed a different challenge. Father Norton, who had also been my teacher at St. Kilian's, proved to be a blessing in disguise. By this time, I was already straying from the doctrines of the Catholic Church, influenced in part by my aunt Doris. She had introduced me to the works of Edgar Cayce, known as the Sleeping Prophet, who claimed to access a dream realm where all subconscious minds are interconnected. Cayce's perspectives on creation intrigued me. Thus, when Father Norton delved into Genesis, I was all too eager to discuss the Cayce version, much to his apparent exasperation. Nonetheless, my enthusiasm to share this alternative view led to an emotional reaction from a fellow student who vehemently opposed any ideas challenging Catholic beliefs. I relished a good debate and defended the Cayce version not as dogma, but as a plausible theory. The students' distress escalated to tears, prompting Father Norton to ask me to leave the classroom and spend the remainder of the period in the chapel. He assured me we would revisit the matter later.

Understanding that my aunt Doris had introduced me to the Cayce material, Father Norton decided that independent study would be the most suitable approach to my religious education at Stang. He never declared me wrong or that Cayce's visions were false. Instead, he fostered an environment that allowed me to arrive at my own conclusions, encouraging independent thinking along the way.

Brigadoon: A Highland Dance

January arrived, marking the time for auditions for the spring musical. Sister Marie had encouraged me to audition, so a group of us gathered to try out for *Brigadoon*. Although I was uncertain of what to expect, I didn't hesitate. Assembled in the chorus room, a man introduced himself as Gerald Morrissey, exuding an all-American midwestern cowboy aura. He provided us with an overview of *Brigadoon*. The abundance of talent in the room overwhelmed me. One by one, the voices of both guys and girls captivated me, leaving me wondering how Mr. Morrissey would manage to allocate roles among such skillful performers.

Dance auditions followed. Cheryl Grenier, a vivacious young lady with short blond hair, led the dance portion. She had an infectious energy that was hard to ignore. During the auditions, she focused on me, even using me as a model to demonstrate the dance steps to others, inflating my ego. Fortunately, my skill as a jumper, crucial in Scottish dance, became apparent.

As is customary, auditions were held on a Saturday morning, with the cast list scheduled to be posted the following Friday. When the day arrived, we clustered around the chorus room door, anxiously scanning the list for our names. There it was—my name was among those listed in the chorus.

About three weeks before the show's debut, an unexpected cast meeting was convened. Gathered in a classroom, Mr. Morrissey, visibly perturbed, informed us that the actor assigned to the role of Harry Beaton had withdrawn due to his aversion to wearing a kilt. In response, Mr. Morrissey inquired if anyone else had reservations about donning a kilt. When no objections were raised, he voiced his need for an actor who could act. This role didn't involve singing but a special sword dance. With no prior musical theater experience, I hesitated to volunteer. However, Barbara, a friend, took matters into her own hands and raised my hand. Recognizing my gesture, Mr. Morrissey engaged me with a Scottish accent,

"What's your name, young lad?" he asked, evoking giggles from the others. "So, you believe you can tackle the role of Harry Beaton?" he continued with his brogue.

"I can certainly try, sir," I responded, rolling my 'r's as he did.

He instructed me to meet him backstage in fifteen minutes, handing me the script labeled "Harry Beaton." *Did that truly just happen?* As a freshman, I was stepping into the shoes of a senior! I resolved to approach this opportunity earnestly, devoting my entire weekend to studying the script. By the time of my first rehearsal, I had memorized all my lines, impressing Mr. Morrissey.

Every available moment was consumed by this role. Ms. Grenier now faced the task of choreographing a sword dance for me. Although I had the steps down, I had an irrational fear of cutting my feet on the real swords. A week before the show, I was still fixated on my feet. Mr. Morrissey warned me that if I continued to look down, he would assign the dance to another student – a girl with some dance experience. Insulted and determined, I intensified my efforts.

The music began, and I executed the dance steps within the crisscross of swords while intently gazing at Ms. Cheryl, who gave me a look of approval from her position on the floor. I executed the steps without a single touch of the swords, eliciting thunderous applause from the cast as the music concluded.

Then I overheard Mr. Morrissey commenting to Ms. Grenier, "But if only he could act."

With a week left until the show, aware that I couldn't rectify my acting shortcomings, I vowed to give my best performance.

Opening night arrived, and the auditorium was filled. Backstage, I anxiously reviewed my lines and the dance routine. The overture played, and the curtain rose. My entrance was imminent, and just before I stepped onto the stage, my first line escaped me. As I hesitated, someone bumped into me from behind, propelling me onto the stage. It was too late to retreat; I found myself standing in front of the audience. My lines flowed as practiced, and the curtain descended after the first act. Mr. Morrissey appeared backstage, encouraging everyone to maintain their high standard.

"Places, everyone!" the call came, summoning us for the second act.

This was my significant moment, featuring a solo and a dramatic death scene. I was too focused to be nervous. As the lights dimmed around the chorus, I positioned myself center stage, starting the dance routine. Each step played in my head, maintaining the serious demeanor required by the character. The applause that erupted when the music concluded was heartwarming. The scene continued, preventing me from dwelling in the applause. As the fight scene unfolded, I reached the moment when I fell upon Charlie's knife and met my demise. I lay motionless on the floor until my fellow actors lifted me on their shoulders and carried me offstage. Curtain bows offered a final chance to bask in the audience's approval. Positioned center stage, the applause and cheers crescendo, offering me my first taste of an addictive sensation. I had completed my first show. Ms. Grenier was the first to congratulate me, followed by my parents and Mr. Morrissey.

"Where on earth did that come from?" he questioned.

"What do you mean?" I asked, uncertain if his words were praise or critique.

"That was incredible! Why didn't you show me you could act like that?" he asked with a broad smile. He turned toward my parents and said, "Mr. and Mrs. Boucher, I'm looking forward to working with your son for the next three years. He's immensely talented."

The weeks following the show's conclusion proved challenging. Each morning, I found myself needing to leave school by 10 a.m., feeling sick and distressed. By the second week I remained unwell and deeply despondent, akin to mourning a loss. By the third week, with no improvement in sight, my mom took me to see my pediatrician, Dr. Schwartz. He was a doctor who listened intently to his patients and even made house calls. He inquired about my well-being and the circumstances leading to my malaise. As I recounted the play, my performance, and the rehearsals, he explained to my mother that I was suffering from separation anxiety. He theorized that the all-consuming nature of the play had left a void when it abruptly ended, akin to losing a part of myself. Though I didn't fully grasp his explanation, the next day marked a shift, and things returned to normal. Well, somewhat.

With the musical no longer consuming my time, I found myself with excessive leisure hours. But soon after, Ms. Grenier extended an invitation that would shape my future. Believing in my capabilities, she asked if I wanted to pursue professional dance. I accepted eagerly. This marked the beginning of a lifelong friendship.

Everything Was Beautiful at the Ballet: A Dream Sequence

My youngest sister Carol possessed a posture and hip alignment that dancers would envy. The six months she spent in that splint had rewarded her with impeccable posture and a turnout that many dancers strive for, often dedicating a lifetime to achieving.

Recognizing her potential, Mémère Serra, Mom, and I decided that Carol, at the tender age of three, should embark on taking dance lessons. I enthusiastically took on the role of her guide, escorting her downtown to Miss Cheryl's studio. I might have even surpassed the usual tendencies of a stage mom. I was resolute in ensuring that Carol wouldn't resemble one of those bewildered three-year-olds stumbling on stage. I was determined to avoid the laughter of the audience when they witnessed youngsters who had no grasp of their actions. My sister was going to be the next Shirley Temple, and for nine months, we sang and danced to "Baby Take a Bow."

Yet, there was an ulterior motive driving my eagerness to accompany her every Saturday. It was an opportunity to spend more time at the studio, alongside Miss Cheryl, with whom I had developed a certain fascination. Yes, hormones had started coursing through me, and inexplicably, she ignited something within me. One might call it a romantic awakening that blossomed into innocent flirtations.

One Saturday, as I brought my little sister to her dance lesson, Cheryl proposed an unexpected opportunity. She asked if I would be interested in dancing in an opera. Without a moment's hesitation, I responded, "Yes!"

"Great! Rehearsals start tomorrow," she announced, concluding with a firm, "be here at 8 a.m."

The next morning, I prepared myself, and Dad and I left the house in our usual silence. As we neared the car, he tossed the car keys in my direction, saying, "You drive!" Having obtained my learner's permit a few months prior like most boys in their sophomore year, my father remained visibly uneasy with me behind the wheel. However, I also sensed a hint of pride in finally having the opportunity to teach me something. Well, in a manner of speaking. Pèpé had let me drive since I was fourteen. My grandfather, devoid of any nerves, having been a special police officer and acquainted with all the cops, didn't harbor concerns.

Filled with unwavering confidence, I assumed the driver's seat, started the car, shifted into drive, and began moving forward when my father abruptly yelled, "Stop!" Then after meticulously explaining all the driving rules, we continued our journey downtown. Progress was smooth, especially with minimal traffic on a Sunday morning in the New Bedford business district, which was deserted.

Approaching a right turn onto Union Street, two police officers had just exited a coffee shop, breakfast in hand. As my father spotted them, he barked, "the cops!"

Startled, I instinctively jammed on the brakes, screeching to a halt. This drew the officers' attention, and one of them approached our car. I rolled down the window.

"Good morning, is there a problem?"

My father, embarrassed now, swiftly answered, "No officer, I was just teaching my son how to drive. He just got his permit."

The police officer nodded in understanding, recognizing this as one of those father-and-son rites of passage. "Have a good morning and drive safely," he said, waving us off before returning to his vehicle.

Soon, my father and I were engaged in a blame-shifting contest, with me squarely implicating him as the reason the officer approached us. Fortunately, we were a mere two blocks away from the studio, allowing me to end my driving lesson for the day, and make it to rehearsal.

Upon my arrival, a couple of other dancers were already present, and Cheryl warmly welcomed me. She instructed us to head to the barre for a brief warm-up session. It had been a while since I engaged in such activities, not since my lessons with Ms. Carol at Mrs. Green's studio. After the warm-up, we plunged into learning the choreography. I had no inkling of what production I was preparing for or where it would be staged. The movements mirrored those I had learned in my Russian Dance from *The Nutcracker*, where I had been assigned a solo section. I adapted seamlessly, as if I had been doing this all my life—an old soul in a young body. Could I have been Nijinsky in a previous life?

Several weekends of rehearsals later, we were informed that the upcoming rehearsal would take place with an orchestra at the theater, located at the newly constructed Southeastern Massachusetts University in North Dartmouth, near my high school. The auditorium's architecture, designed by Paul Randolph, then dean of Yale's School of Art and Architecture, was aesthetically modern, with its cold gray stone, pronounced grooves, and balcony boxes that projected into the auditorium. The stage dwarfed anything I had previously performed on. I was determined to make a favorable impression.

It was then that I learned I was participating in Gian Carlo Menotti's operas, *Amahl and the Night Visitors* and the modern opera *Help! Help! The Globolinks*. The choreography for the latter was absurdly peculiar and perilous. Clad in green tube costumes with diminutive arms, we resembled Christmas trees. The headpiece consisted of a plastic bucket with the front cut out to enable sight and breathing. The green fabric cascaded from top to bottom, stretched over three hoops from small to large, creating the effect. The intimidating part was that I could barely see through the material, and I had to descend a rope ladder from the highest patron box, which felt like the height of a 10-meter (33-foot) diving platform. From there, I had to make my way to the stage, and once the music reached a particular point, we moved in all directions, appearing confused and disoriented until a designated musical cue signaled the conclusion.

Performing in *Amahl and the Night Visitors* was a distinct experience from any of my previous productions. I relished the resonance of the men's voices, particularly the deep basso. The man with the resonant bass voice was slight in build, yet his voice exceeded his physique – an aspect I would later learn to be common. However, what struck me most was the young boy portraying Amahl. Claude, son of famed opera singer Jacqueline Bazinet and conductor Josef Cobert, possessed a head of blond curls and a soprano voice that rivaled his mother's. At approximately twelve years old, he displayed a captivating unchanged male soprano voice. His acting skills were also remarkable, charming the audience. If Menotti had witnessed Claude's performance, he would have cast him in multiple productions, given his exceptional talent. The experience proved addictive, drawing me into the world of professionals, stoking a desire to learn and improve.

Meanwhile, back at Stang, Mr. Morrissey extended an offer for me to participate in a fall school drama, *The Lark*, written by playwright Jean Anouilh, depicting Joan of Arc's trial. I portrayed the character Monsieur de la Tremouille. In hindsight, I must not have been particularly drawn to dramatic plays at the time. Mr. Morrissey sensed my lack of engagement and focus. A group of us had gotten into trouble by visiting McDonald's while fully dressed in our costumes. It was during this escapade that I learned some crucial theater rules. Rule #25: Never leave the theater in costume or makeup.

At some point during the production, Mr. Morrissey became aware of my involvement in another show and, for reasons unbeknownst to me, seemed displeased about it. However, since my participation didn't conflict with his production, he couldn't voice any objections. Nevertheless, I detected a shift in his attitude towards me. A perceptible distance had arisen, and I keenly felt its presence.

One Moment in Time: An Isolated Note

Once again, spring had arrived, and Mr. Morrissey was preparing for the musical *Guys and Dolls*. I still hadn't amassed a collection of musical theater knowledge, so without familiarity with the script or score, I lacked a clear expectation of which role might interest me. The cast list was posted, and my name listed as "Ron Boucher (see me)." Mr. Morrissey explained that due to the lack of a suitable role, he intended to spotlight my dancing skills during the second act overture section of the song, "Luck Be a Lady Tonight," which commenced as the curtain ascended.

Each day, instead of having lunch, I'd grab my cassette tape recorder and head to the stage, switching on the work lights. With the curtain drawn, I'd rehearse the choreography repeatedly, meticulously going through each step—grand battements, lunges, and cheneé turns.

This period coincided with a time of rapid growth for me. An excruciating and overwhelming growth spurt propelled me from a height of five feet to an additional eight inches within six months. A back brace that encircled my shoulders offered partial relief from the spasms that wracked my back. Another temporary solution was my sister Renee walking on my back. Furthermore, my calves would spasm during the night, forcing me to spring out of bed, fearing that the residual soreness would render me incapable of dancing again.

With just a brief cameo role, I found myself exempt from attending rehearsals. Only two weeks remained until the show, when Mr. Morrissey requested to see the dance.

I placed my little cassette recorder on the edge of the stage and pressed play as Mr. Morrissey took his seat in the audience. The music for the second act overture began, and I launched into the dance segment of "**Luck Be A Lady Tonight**," with everything I had. Kicking my legs high like a Rockette, my breathing steady, energy surging, I nailed every step of the choreography. For two months, I had spent my lunch breaks secretly practicing behind the curtain, preparing for this exact moment. Mr. Morrissey watched intently, and I danced not just for him, but for his approval—as if my very future hinged on it.

A few intense minutes later, it was over. He stood, paused, and said, 'That was very good. I can see you worked very hard on the dance.'

Then, without another word, he turned and left.

However, a few days later, he informed Sister Marie that he had decided not to include the number in the show. This was a crushing blow. I had poured my heart and soul into perfecting the dance, striving to make it both polished and impressive. Even Ms. Cheryl had expressed her approval of its quality. While nursing my disappointment in my room, the phone rang.

In full voice my mother called out, "Ronnie, it's Cheryl. She wants to speak with you."

I bolted for the phone, eager to hear what Cheryl had to say. Cheryl told me that the opera company I performed for in *Amahl and the Night Visitors* was staging *Die Fledermaus*, and a renowned dancer from New York was coming to choreograph. However, this opportunity wasn't guaranteed; I would need to audition in two weeks. This announcement effectively shifted my focus away from the disappointment I had just experienced at school. What I couldn't foresee was how this upcoming event would set me on a life-altering journey—both in terms of my career and my romantic pursuits.

On a brisk Saturday morning, I arrived at Cheryl's studio, joining a group of boys attending the audition. Seated on a bench in the hallway, just at the foot of the stairs, I watched as a young, diminutive dancer entered. She was dressed in a black V-neck leotard and skirt, her thick chestnut hair pulled back into a bun, partially covered by a scarf. A crochet black shawl draped her shoulders. As she ascended the stairs, she glanced at me and smiled. An aura enveloped her, a captivating and electrifying presence that sent shivers down my spine. This sensation was foreign and perplexing, yet oddly alluring and consuming. But this was a professional audition, and my focus needed to be unwavering.

Ms. Cheryl, also dressed ready to audition, stood in front of the wall of mirrors. With an air of excitement and awe she said, "Everyone, I'd like to introduce Ms. Sandra Balestracci. A professional ballerina and soloist at Radio City Music Hall in New York City, Ms. Sandra is originally from New Bedford and has graciously agreed to choreograph for us."

I stood in a state of sheer awe, fixated on this breathtakingly exquisite woman. Her beauty transcended mere facial features—her perfectly proportioned cheekbones, captivating blue eyes rimmed with dark lashes, and softly defined lips. Her petite, curving torso was accentuated by delicate wrists and ankles peeking out from under her cropped tights. The leotard she wore left her breasts unsupported, allowing their natural shape to define her body's proportions. The deep V-cut of her leotard plunged down her back, revealing the intricate details of her trapezius, rhomboids, and latissimus dorsi muscles. The cut ended just above the start of her buttocks, which were gently curved like a pear. Her legs were in perfect harmony with her upper torso, showcasing an athletic definition that was subtle yet captivating. The allure I felt wasn't confined to the external—it stirred a clear, undeniable physical response within me. It was a fusion of the captivating charm of iconic screen actresses like Sophia Loren, Leslie Caron, and Natalie Wood.

Like most dance auditions, this one began with the traditional barre exercises—a series of combinations designed to warm up joints, ligaments, and promote body alignment. As we progressed from movement to movement, I suddenly felt her hands on my shoulders, gently coaxing them downward to release tension. Then, she moved on, placing her hand on my stomach and guiding it inward, simultaneously instructing me to lift my lower spine. Although my recollection of the warmup is a bit clouded, in clear focus are each time that she touched me and gave me an erection… I meant correction. With each interaction, my fascination with this goddess, this embodiment of dance, grew stronger. My observation might sound overly effusive, but it's important to understand that I was fifteen years old —a young adolescent male ignited by surging hormones. My id was eager to relive scenes from Franco Zeffirelli's Romeo and Juliet, yet my experience with "that uncle" had prompted my super ego to quell and temper these impulses. This internal conflict would persist until I reached the age of twenty-one. The coarse, aggressive nature of my adolescent id would be suppressed, replaced by the courteous, respectful behavior expected of a gentleman—a transformation designed to ensure women felt comfortable and safe, far from any realm of sexual pursuit.

As we were summoned to the center to execute a few combinations, my sense of purpose was rekindled. Another dancer, a tall, young blond man named Paul, seemed to have captured her attention. He possessed the attributes often referred to as "the beautiful people" by my paternal grandmother—tall, blond, and blue-eyed. I suspected Paul was a former student of Sandra's, as were some of the girls auditioning. Just as the audition was ending, Ms. Balestracci turned to the boys and announced,

"Alright, boys, we're going to do a simple shoulder lift."

Paul was chosen as her partner for the demonstration.

"Hold me at the waist like this, and when I plié, assemblé, and jump, place me on your shoulder."

In an instant, she was elevated onto Paul's shoulder.

Several of the boys struggled with the coordination required for the lift. When it was my turn, she fixed her gaze on me and asked, "Are you sure you're strong enough for this?"

She positioned herself in front of me, placing my hands on her waist. Fueled by confidence and determination, I stood behind her, catching a whiff of her perfume and the scent of hairspray. Her body emitted warmth, contrasting with my own nervous perspiration. Plié, assemblé, and suddenly she was soaring above my shoulders. In an instant, she tensed up and descended awkwardly to the floor. Swiftly turning to me, she uttered,

"Oh, my goodness, I'm sorry, I didn't anticipate your strength. Let's try again, this time just lift me to your shoulder."

Once more, she executed a plié, assemblé, and ascended to rest on my shoulder. As I observed her reflection in the mirror, it was evident that she was satisfied. The touch of her thigh muscles, covered by black tights, brushed against the side of my face, and I hesitated to lower her.

"Thank you, everyone," she announced, gliding down my front, "that was an exceptional audition. I will inform Ms. Cheryl of my selection, and we'll commence rehearsals next weekend."

And with that it concluded, and she departed.

Upon returning home, my mother took a single look at me and exclaimed,

"Oh my God, who is she?"

I naturally responded that it was Sandra Balestracci. Her response grounded me.

"Come back to reality, she's a celebrity and too old for you. She went to school with your first dance teacher, Carol. You're chasing after the impossible," she said.

Yet, a guy can always dream, can't he?

A few days after the audition, Cheryl reached out to me with the news I'd been waiting for—she had chosen me, along with Paul and another boy, for the production. I was thrilled, especially at the thought of working with Ms. Sandra again. That anticipation carried me back to the studio, where we dedicated about four intense hours to mastering the choreography. As she wrapped up, Ms. Sandra told us Cheryl would take over rehearsals, and she would return in two weeks to check on our progress.

A week later, Cheryl contacted me again. This time, her message carried an unexpected twist: both Paul and the other boy had dropped out, leaving me as the only male performer. I was surprised but not discouraged. I knew it meant more responsibility—and more opportunity.

When Ms. Sandra returned the following week, it was time to re-choreograph, focusing on the lifts. Having no other choice, Ms. Sandra used me as her demonstration partner. Every move we rehearsed felt like a lesson carved in precision, and I took every chance to absorb her choreography. She didn't seem bothered by my eagerness; if anything, her amused smile hinted that she knew exactly how much I craved her attention.

Sandra Balestracci

As the rehearsal progressed, the time came to try the lifts with the girls. While I executed the movements with confidence, the girls seemed nervous. They were far from matching Ms. Sandra's grace. The contrast was stark, but I knew these were complex moves not easily mastered.

The rehearsals stretched on, and those moments with Ms. Sandra stayed with me, etching themselves into my memory. It wasn't just the choreography—it was the way she carried herself, her demand for precision, and the way she pushed me to be better without saying a word. By the time we reached the performance, the hours of practice had paid off. The show was a success, and I had proven myself not just as a dancer, but as a reliable performer within the professional community.

Turning Point: A Revolving Toccata

My desire to sing remained strong, even though opportunities had become rare since my departure from St. Kilian's and Sister Marianna's guidance. Because I continued to attend St. Anthony's Church, I approached the music director, Mr. Labens, with the hope of joining his choir. However, he swiftly dismissed me, insisting I was too young.

During this period, I had the pleasure of knowing a girl named Gina Despres, who, like me, was in search of singing opportunities. The Despres family owned and operated Norman's Meat Market on the Boulevard, a place that was well-known throughout New Bedford. Much like our own family, The Despres resided on the first floor of a tenement building, with the butcher shop adjacent to their home.

Gina had long, medium brown, straight, and silky hair, which she often gracefully flicked back—a gesture that Cher was well known for. Her sense of humor was as sharp as my mother's, and the two of them got along almost too well. At times, I felt like the oddball in the room.

But what truly set Gina apart was her voice, which landed her the leading role in two of the high school musicals. To capture its essence, I'd have to draw inspiration from the iconic musicals and their leading ladies. The first comparison is the character, Polly Brown, played by Julie Andrews in *The Boyfriend*—light, charming, and brimming with personality. But the performance that forever sticks in my memory was Gina's portrayal of Fanny Brice in *Funny Girl*. Though it's nearly impossible to compare any singer to the legendary Barbra Streisand, Gina's rendition had the kind of raw talent that made people believe she had a real shot at a Broadway career. Her voice wasn't just impressive—it was unforgettable.

By intertwining Gina's voice with these leading ladies, I began to see that she wasn't just another aspiring performer. She had something special, something that connected her to the greats, and I wasn't the only one who thought so.

Together we formed a duo, assembling a repertoire of contemporary church music. With me on melody and guitar, and Gina harmonizing, we were a pair eager to perform. The challenge was finding a venue to showcase our music. I decided to approach Monsignor Berube, requesting permission to sing during a mass when Mr. Labens wasn't playing. This proposition, however, contradicted Monsignor's traditional inclinations. Considering his dedication to preserving French culture and language, my suggestion of contemporary music and a guitar was quite the departure. It was a long shot, but I felt compelled to try. As he pondered my request, I anticipated his refusal, envisioning him uttering "No, not in my church" or denouncing our chosen music as "the devil's music." But then he surprised me.

"Let's give this a try. You can sing at the 8:30 a.m. mass on Sundays," he said pausing before continuing, "and only once a month."

Ecstasy mixed with reality surged through me. On one hand, I was thrilled at the prospect, yet I knew this mass was sparsely attended. Typically led by Fr. Chabot, the 20-minute service catered to those, like my grandfather, adhering to the bare minimum of Catholic obligation.

The day arrived for our first performance, only two weeks after receiving Monsignor's approval. Naturally, my mother rallied her friends, ensuring their presence at the mass. Gina's extended family lent their support as well, filling a couple of rows. Our stage was set at the front of the church, just inches from the communion rail. Two microphones were positioned, one to share for vocals and another for the guitar. After a sound check, we retreated to the vestibule to await the moment when the priest would signal for us and the altar boys to enter. Finally, the time arrived. We took our designated seats in the group of pews reserved for the altar boys during the high mass.

At the offertory, we stepped forward, prepared to perform our first song. As there was no applause in this setting, smiles and nods of approval validated our efforts. The second song, slated for communion, was allowed to last only as long as it took the priest to serve the congregation. Performing the second song, I relaxed slightly and surveyed the church. My eyes fell on Monsignor Berube, who appeared solemn. However, the smiles radiating across the congregation offered ample confirmation of our success. After the mass concluded, Monsignor approached us. In that moment, my heart sank, fully expecting him to refuse or to declare that our music had no place in his church. The silence felt heavy, and I braced myself for the worst. But then, to our astonishment, his stern expression softened, and instead of delivering the blow I feared, he smiled. 'I'm looking forward to your next performance,' he said, leaving us momentarily speechless. The relief was substantial, and what I thought would be the end turned out to be a new beginning. The following month couldn't arrive soon enough. Gina and I practiced new songs, gravitating toward a style akin to Simon and Garfunkel, aligning more with contemporary folk. That morning, I noticed a significantly larger crowd dispersed throughout the church.

Before the mass began, I approached the microphone and asked those seated toward the back to move forward, an audacious request met with compliance. Following the mass, Monsignor conveyed his decision to increase our appearances to twice a month. By the third month, he suggested that we sing at the 9:30 mass, which boasted a slightly larger attendance. Word had spread, prompting most attendees from the 8:30 mass to transition. In this short span, Gina and I had garnered a devoted following, earning a reputation as the modern-day Sonny and Cher of our local church.

As Gina and I spent more time together, we decided to officially label our connection, and she became my first true girlfriend. Our time was filled with laughter; she had a marvelous sense of humor. She enjoyed coming to my house, though I couldn't help but feel she sometimes preferred the company of my mother over spending time alone with me. Her parents were easygoing and granted us a degree of independence, due to Gina's watchful older brothers.

Gina particularly idolized her brother Tom, a member of a rock band, FEUD, which had gained popularity in the greater Boston/New England area. With long, sandy brown hair, he embodied a Jim Morrison-esque aura. His band was steadily gaining popularity throughout the state. Although most rock enthusiasts reveled in the piercing wail of steel-string guitars, I was captivated by the vocals. One rehearsal evening, Tom sang "MacArthur's Park" by Jimmy Webb, reminiscent of Freddy Mercury's rendition released years later. It was on this night that Gina divulged her aspirations, expressing a desire to pursue a musical path distinct from church and musical theater.

During the summer of '72, Gina's parents invited us to accompany them to a drive-in movie theater in North Dartmouth. I had been to this movie theater with my parents several times before. It was the kind of place where families brought their young kids to see films like *The Nutty Professor*—or something so boring that we'd inevitably doze off.

Gina and I were unaware of the film that was playing, but we understood that drive-ins often provided a venue for couples to indulge in romantic interludes. Gina jokingly cautioned her parents not to embarrass her by engaging in make-out sessions while we were in the back seat.

"You can always get out of the car," her mother retorted.

The movie was *Klute*, starring Jane Fonda and Donald Sutherland. Notably, it was considered daring at the time, holding an "R" rating. As the film's intensity grew, Gina and I heeded her parents' advice, migrating to an open spot next to our car.

On the grass, away from prying eyes, my thoughts were to initiate our first intense make-out session. Despite the persistent urging of my id, that primal part of me that clamored for more, my super ego maintained its stronghold, reigning in my intent. This internal tug-of-war between desires and moral boundaries would persist. Looking back, it was the interplay of these forces, combined with subsequent events, that gradually strained our relationship. As time went on, I grew more at ease with the notion of our connection remaining platonic. The bond we shared through our musical collaboration played a significant role in sustaining our identity as friends.

About a year and a half into our musical journey, Gina's enthusiasm began to fade. She decided to sit out during one of our performances, giving me my first taste of the solo spotlight. In that moment, I realized the potential I had to become a soloist. Coupled with the inspiration of working with Sandra, this set new goals and ambitions in motion. It became clear that it was time for me to move on from our partnership and pursue a new path.

Fr. Rob & Sister Ruth: The Ecclesiastical Duet

That year, a new priest named Fr. Rob joined the parish. A young, vibrant personality, he was genuine and calm. Monsignor assigned him to the 9:30 mass. One Sunday, Fr. Rob approached me, proposing the idea of teaching CCD (Confraternity of Christian Doctrine) classes. A vacancy had emerged due to the illness of a 2nd-grade class teacher, and he wondered if I'd be interested in filling in. I was taken aback. Was he serious, or testing me? If I said yes, would a coalition of nuns rise against me? With my mother's background in teaching CCD, I agreed, comforted by her assurance that she would help me craft lesson plans.

My first attempt was successful enough that Fr. Rob invited me to continue the following year, elevating me to teach the 3rd grade class where I was again tasked with imparting the expected Christian doctrine to these young souls. These children, attending public schools, were deemed by some to be on a path to damnation, deprived of a proper Catholic education. This meant that they were missing the spiritual enrichment that came with being in a Catholic institution. But I was about to challenge one of the long-standing traditions of the faith and the rite of passage from innocence to the age of reason. "Bless me, Father, for I have never sinned."

The first half of the year proceeded smoothly. I followed the provided curriculum while adding my own touch of music, much like Sister Marianna had done. The last fifteen minutes of each class were spent singing, and it seemed to work like a charm. My class attendance was nearly perfect every week, and parents were excitedly bringing their children to my class just to meet this charismatic teacher named Mr. Ron, who had sparked a newfound interest in religion. Every so often, Fr. Rob and Sister Ruth, the principal of St. Anthony's Elementary School, would observe my class. I interpreted their presence as an indication of their approval as they offered no criticisms.

As the second semester began, Fr. Rob requested that I meet with him one day early. I anticipated that he had some concerns, yet I wasn't expecting what followed. He informed me that I was to prepare my students for their first confession and first communion. I was prepared to fulfill my responsibilities, but as the days went by, I started to grapple with the idea of teaching seven-year-olds to confess their sins. I delved into Exodus, Chapter 20 of the Bible, carefully reviewing each commandment. Upon reflection, I found it difficult to interpret some of these commandments for such young minds:

1. You shall have no other gods. *This didn't seem relevant to a seven-year-old.*
2. You shall not make idols. *Unlikely that children that age were creating idols. Unless a child had fashioned an altar with their Barbie doll or G.I. Joe, and knelt to pray before it, it was likely not relevant either.*
3. You shall not misuse the name of the Lord. *It wasn't common for seven-year-olds to go around saying "God damn it!"*

4. Remember the Sabbath, keep it holy. *Attendance at church really depended on parents.*
5. Honor your father and mother. *Child tantrums were unlikely to result in eternal damnation.*
6. You shall not murder. *Extremely unlikely behavior for seven-year-olds.*
7. You shall not commit adultery. *Clearly irrelevant.*
8. You shall not steal. *Tricky, but it could be complicated in certain scenarios.*
9. You shall not lie. *Common confession material but nuanced for children.*
10. You shall not covet. *Age-appropriate understanding of this concept was questionable.*

After considering this, I decided to speak to Fr. Rob before class. I explained that I couldn't comfortably prepare my students for their first confession, outlining my rationale. To my amazement, he agreed. My students proceeded to make their first communion without the traditional first confession. I had deviated from church norms and yet remained a CCD teacher without any consequences or excommunication.

Meanwhile, my sister Renee was still attending St. Anthony's School. Rumors were circulating about Fr. Rob and Sister Ruth, who were frequently seen together during and after school. Fr. Rob, also the school chaplain, had occupied an office next to Sister Ruth's. However, he unexpectedly moved in with Sister Ruth, leaving his old office vacant. As my sister Renee noted, they were often seen holding hands during basketball games and public outings. Intrigued by these accounts, I started to piece together their relationship.

One day, after one of my classes, I approached the principal's office to find the door ajar. Knocking twice with no response, I pushed the door open, curious about the commotion coming from the adjacent storage room. Knocking again and calling out, "hello," the giggling inside suddenly stopped. Fr. Rob's head emerged from the doorway, followed by his shirtless upper body, revealing his surprise at seeing me.

Sister Ruth, in a girlish tone, began, "Rob, you can't go out there like..."

Her sentence broke off as she noticed me. I closed the door behind me, and they both assumed positions, reminiscent of students caught in mischief. My mind raced with possibilities. Should I chastise them, like the disciplinary actions of my past? Fr. Rob, quickly regaining his composure, put his shirt back on, while Sister Ruth stood behind him, her hand on his shoulder. I asked them to sit down. The gravity of the situation filled the room.

I felt compelled to speak candidly. I reiterated the rumors that were circulating among the students and community, the public display of affection for one another. Continuing the escapade would only bring about anxiety and despair. I had hoped that they could just remember that God's blessings are not limited by societal norms. I could see that their love for one another was genuine.

I left the room abruptly, half-expecting a lightning bolt to strike me down any moment. Surprisingly, Fr. Rob and Sister Ruth waited until the summer to renounce their religious lives, marry, and leave behind their roles in the parish. The parishioners shunned them, leading them to find solace in another church, where their past was unknown.

This was my first opportunity to display my open-mindedness rather than hastily passing judgment or condemnation. As I left the room, I couldn't help but wonder who I had become at that moment. I had just granted adults the freedom to openly express their love for one another, even though it defied traditional norms, especially that of the Catholic church. Simultaneously, I couldn't ignore the prejudiced attitudes displayed by the parishioners, biases that often linger within communities. I recall a personal anecdote that I witnessed when my grandmother Boucher directed my mother not to allow my cousin into our house.

It was a typical summer afternoon, and I was lounging at home when the phone rang. My mother answered with her usual chipper, "Hello?"—the kind of voice that expects to hear a gossip update from one of her friends. But her smile faded quickly as she slid into the leather chair by the phone, resigned. It was Grandma Boucher, and whatever she was saying, my mother wasn't buying it. I could tell by the way she silently nodded, her eyes rolling like they had somewhere better to be.

No sooner had she hung up than the phone rang again. This time, it was my cousin Madaline, my mother's godchild.

"Hi, Madaline! How are you? Oh, of course, come right over. Twenty minutes? That'll be just fine."

Mom gently placed the receiver down and started straightening the already spotless house. The woman could've hosted royalty at any given moment without even fluffing a pillow.

Twenty minutes later, like clockwork, there was a knock at the door. Madaline walked in, baby carrier in hand, tears in her eyes.

"Aunty Yvette, didn't Grandma call you to forbid you from letting me in? None of the family will see me."

Mom smirked, that sly grin of defiance, and replied, "Oh, she did."

Madaline blinked, realization dawning. She knew this was a classic Yvette move. Defying Grandma was practically a sport in this house.

As we settled in, Madaline poured out her story—how she'd fallen in love with a Black man in New York, married him, and had a beautiful baby. Midway through recounting her tale of family drama, she paused, her face serious.

"Aunty," she asked, "do you think my baby looks very Black?"

All three of us turned to look at the baby, peacefully lying on a blanket on the carpet. Without missing a beat, my mother, ever the straight shooter, responded.

"Madaline, let me tell you something. Your baby *is* Black. No ifs, ands, or buts about it. But here's the important part—he's your baby, and you should be proud of him. You, your baby, and your husband are always welcome in my house," she said.

It was a defining moment, setting me on a path to consistently challenge and question norms when they conflicted with genuine feelings and desires. I embraced the role of a romantic, adopting the philosophy that authentic love deserves recognition and acceptance, irrespective of circumstances or societal expectations. In many ways, this experience foreshadowed my future as an advocate for the acceptance of love in all its forms.

Working Boy: The Uncovered Waltz

Spring always heralded an array of performing opportunities. While most high school students had their lives centered around school, I found myself juggling school, performing, and part-time jobs.

Since the age of thirteen, my father had arranged a job for me during the summers. My first job was at a local grocery store. I spent Saturdays stocking shelves and occasionally making deliveries. My inexperience with maneuvering a bicycle while carrying a loaded basket led to some challenges, especially uphill. The job had its downsides, particularly the unpleasant task of cleaning meat trays that emitted a repulsive stench once exposed to warmer air. Despite this, I was proud to earn money to contribute to my family and keep a small portion, actually $.50, for myself.

The following summer, I was now at age 14, working as a dishwasher/busboy at a restaurant called Mickey's Grille. This is where my grandfather had his breakfast every morning. I, as well as three other boys were hired as dishwashers. Our supervisor was a strange man with a dark personality. When he wasn't antagonizing us, he was peeling potatoes. He occasionally would lock one or two of us in the big freezer, which in summer was sometimes a blessing. That job ended when one day he pulled me into the freezer and exposed himself.

He gave me a sick disgusting look and said, "You want this!"

It wasn't a question; it was a command. His penis hung from his opened zipper with his hips thrusting forward. There was that feeling again, the adrenalin surge, that sense of perverted danger. Luckily, one of the other workers opened the door and he quickly dropped his apron. When I came home that night after work, I was feeling sick to my stomach, that unexplainable queasy feeling. Was this going to be the situation again when no one was going to believe me? Why did this happen to me again? My mom knew something was wrong and kept asking me. I finally told my parents, and she told me not to return.

For a couple of summers at the Ice Cream Parlor, we had a revolving door of teenage boys scooping, swirling, and—let's be honest—eating their weight in ice cream. The perk of unlimited frozen treats was thrilling. For about three days. After that, the mere sight of a sundae could trigger nausea.

When business picked up, the tile floors—coated in a fine mist of melted ice cream—became as treacherous as a skating rink. Even in sneakers, we found ourselves gliding, slipping, and executing unintentional pirouettes, all while desperately trying to stay upright.

In the fall of my junior year, I heard about an opening for an usher at the local movie theater, the State Theater, located in downtown New Bedford. This was a familiar world for me—both Mémère Serra and my mother had worked as ticket sales attendants at the Capitol Theater, just two blocks from our house on Acushnet Avenue.

One of the memorable figures from the Capitol was Nap, the usher/custodian. He was an older man with a nose that could've rivaled Jimmy Durante's, and he was particularly fond of my grandmother and mother. When the Capitol Theater eventually closed, Nap transitioned over to the State Theater, where I was about to begin.

The State Theater has an interesting history. It was a vaudeville establishment constructed in 1922, and within a year had transitioned into a movie theater. Its once resplendent interior cried out for repair. Backstage was a tattered area with dressing rooms resembling the aftermath of a bar brawl. Broken furniture, non-functional lights, and a pungent odor hung in the air. Yet, I envisioned a future where its former glory could be resurrected, where the community could once again relish live theater and music.

Unbeknownst to me at that time, my vision was destined to become a reality. In 1982, the theater reclaimed its original name, the Zeiterion Theatre. The restoration brought back its Georgian revival style splendor with marble columns and walls in shades of ivory and old rose, silk tapestries, gold leaf Grecian dancing figures, a solid gum wood orchestra rail, and a sparkling Czechoslovakian chandelier.

The State/Zeiterion Theater garnered fame for hosting world premieres, including the 1956 debut of *Moby Dick* starring Gregory Peck. My dad had the privilege of being Mr. Peck's personal driver during that time. I had known about my father's association with Mr. Peck, but I couldn't fathom why the story wasn't discussed more. This was a premiere event, and my father had direct access to a star like Mr. Peck. Surely, this position came with numerous perks that I personally would have exploited to the fullest.

It wasn't until much later that my mother shared the reason for her disdain whenever Mr. Peck's name was mentioned. My father had leveraged his association with Mr. Peck to introduce him to our family. The logical choice would have been my mother, a woman with the elegance and the physical attributes of a young Elizabeth Taylor, possessing wit, charm, and sophistication – qualities that would make for a delightful introduction. It should have been an exciting moment for a newly married man to present his beautiful wife and their adorable eighteen-month-old baby boy. Instead, my father chose to introduce Mr. Peck to my stern-faced grandmother. This choice, coupled with the fact that he didn't inform my mother beforehand, turned the encounter into a minefield. Grandma Boucher, always ready to incite irritation, relished the opportunity. In the face of rational questioning, my father remains silent, refusing to provide an explanation even to this day.

While working at the State Theatre, I was also juggling school, theater, and auditions. Our school was preparing for the musical *Kiss Me Kate*. Mr. Morrissey hadn't cast me in any role saying that he wanted to use my dance skills in this production. This allowed me to managed school and work. However, the arrival of a new choreographer, a young woman close to Ms. Cheryl's age, changed the course of the production.

When she discovered my dancing and singing prowess, she seemed elated. In fact, during rehearsals, she exclusively danced with me, virtually ignoring the other performers. She even convinced Mr. Morrissey to incorporate me into the "Too Darn Hot" number, alongside the two principal characters.

It didn't take me long to master the routine, and I felt my presence almost unnecessary. With my father's insistence that I work, I felt justified missing unnecessary rehearsals. Although Mr. Morrissey appeared unperturbed, the choreographer grew increasingly irritated by my absences. A week before the show's opening, she stormed into the State Theater, calling me to the lobby making a huge scene, raising her voice. There, in front of everyone, she demanded I leave work immediately and attend rehearsal. A Friday night with a full audience awaited, and her outrage knew no bounds.

The theater manager intervened, asking her to leave and subsequently turning to me, saying, "Ronnie, you've been an exceptional employee, and we appreciate your contributions. However, we cannot tolerate such incidents. You belong on the stage, so we're letting you go to chase your dreams."

This blunt revelation caught me off guard, clashing directly with my parents' expectations. My mother had always envisioned my sister Renee and me working in tandem. Since Renee aimed to become a dental hygienist from the start, my mother had pinned her hopes on me becoming a dentist. However, my ill-fated declaration that I'd rather be a doctor, specifically a pediatrician, created an unexpected stir. This single utterance transformed into my mother's incessant mantra: "My son! The doctor!" It marked the inception of an inner conflict that would grow into an arduous battle.

Meanwhile, at school, the choreographer had quietly replaced me in the show without a word. On opening night, I arrived to find one of the other boys in the chorus wearing my costume. Confused, I inquired, "Why are you in my costume?"

Clearly nervous, he stammered that I should discuss it with the choreographer. To me it seemed that she was standing in wait, plotting her attack and salivating at her ploy to humiliate me.

"Do you think you're so special that you can't be replaced? Well, you have been replaced!"

It felt as if her words dripped with rage; her eyes ablaze. As she continued, Mr. Morrissey walked in and questioned the situation. In tears, I recounted the events to him.

Infuriated, he declared, "Put on your costume and perform the show as rehearsed."

Then he turned to the choreographer, reminding her that it was his show, and she worked for him – and that such an incident wouldn't be repeated.

The "Too Darn Hot" number in the show proved pivotal. Although a trio, numerous comments after the show suggested I should have been in the center, given my advanced dancing and singing talents. Singing? Indeed, it was the first time my voice predominated over the others. People remarked it was as if I were performing a solo. My voice lessons had borne fruit. I was now sure that Mr. Morrissey would have to see me in a leading role next year.

Just before the beginning of summer, Ms. Cheryl extended an invitation for me to perform a tarantella dance at a private party. On a balmy June evening, Cheryl and I set out for the Kennedy estate in Hyannis Port, Cape Cod. Upon arrival, we were directed to the service entrance – a reminder that we were considered hired help—stripping us of any semblance of celebrity. Guided through the kitchen, we were led to a small bathroom to change. Given strict instructions not to mingle with the guests and to leave after our performance, we were essentially background figures. A sprawling tent dominated the estate, and a small grassy area was roped off for our performance, segregating us from the attendees. To me, performing at the

Kennedy estate was an immense honor. Our spirited number, accompanied by the clang of tambourines, sparked cheers and champagne toasts. As I prepared to bow, I noticed a man pushing his way to the front, Senator Edward Kennedy.

Without hesitation, I walked up to him, saying, "Senator, you may not remember me, as it's been a while. I'm Ronnie Boucher."

Searching his expression for recognition, I recounted our previous encounter, the party for Senator McCormick where I had been served a shrimp-covered pineapple. The spark of recognition finally came, and he acknowledged the event and remembered me. The woman who had earlier instructed us to leave the premises now clung to my arm, offering apologies to the Senator.

However, before she could finish, Senator Kennedy intervened, "Please, if you can, stay and enjoy some food and refreshments. There are plenty of people your age here."

Cheryl and I mingled with the guests, receiving compliments for our performance. We transformed from ingratiated hired help to guests of Ted Kennedy. When we returned to my house, we shared a parting kiss —one of those moments where you're unsure if it was warranted, desired, or simply a blip in time that prompts a casual "oops… oh well!"

Jay Dee Trio: A Threesome Tune

Bishop Stang's chapel, located on the first floor's west wing, was a peaceful haven for me. This lovely chapel served as a place for reflection and solace, and it was equipped with an electronic organ that I could use to practice songs I was working on. One day, while I was playing music that wasn't exactly religious, a junior named John entered the chapel. He was a guy with wavy brown hair that reached his shoulders. Curious about what I was doing, he joined me, and we started chatting. John mentioned he had a friend that played the drums and the accordion and was looking for a singer to collaborate with. His musical tastes leaned towards light pop, including artists like the Carpenters, Frank Sinatra, and Perry Como. I was all in. His father was also going to help us with booking gigs.

Our collaboration began with rehearsals, and John's father challenged us to put together a setlist of twenty-five songs in just a month to prove our dedication. We managed to meet this deadline, impressing John's father with our commitment. Soon after, John approached me at school and asked if I was available on Thursday nights. He informed me that we had a gig lined up at Thad's Steakhouse and Pub on Ashley Boulevard. This was an audition, as they were considering adding live music to their Thursday nights, which were typically slow. Our audition was a hit, and we were hired for a regular gig at the pub. Our success grew to the point that we were also asked to play on some Saturday nights.

During one of our pub performances, a wedding was taking place in the main dining room, featuring a seven-piece band led by Gill Ferro. During their break, Gill came down to the pub for a drink and stayed to listen to our music. Impressed with my singing, he invited me to join his group on stage for a song. Gill Ferro and his orchestra were well-known throughout the area, and his recognition of my talent helped spread the word about our group. This led to increased attendance on Thursday nights.

After about six months, John lost interest and decided not to continue with the group. His focus was on his new motorcycle, girls and his electric guitar aspiring him to music much more relevant to our age group. This was a fortunate turn of events for me, as it allowed me to focus more on my other community performances and opportunities.

College and the Job Market: A Career Concerto

As summer between my junior and senior years approached, I hadn't been actively looking for a new job after leaving the movie theater. There were hardly any performance opportunities during the summer, so I had no real excuse not to work. From my father's point of view, it seemed like everyone else had found jobs except for me. He wasn't having it. Frustrated, he accused me of being too picky and having unrealistic ambitions for a seventeen-year-old's job search. His view was simple: take any job, whether I liked it or not.

"You know, Mike Bastille got a job digging graves at the local cemetery... just saying," my father tried to convey subtly.

My father was right—I was quite particular about the kind of work I wanted. I enjoyed working in the school office and thought I could find a similar office job, rather than one involving manual labor. By mid-June, summer was already underway, and I still no job.

As my parents prepared for a trip to New Orleans, my father gave me an ultimatum before they left. "Find a job by the time I get back," he said exiting my room and then immediately returning to say, "or else."

Upon their return, my father stormed into my room and discovered a newspaper with a job listing circled. Reading it aloud, "Part-time assistant needed for Parts Department. Clerical skills required: typing, filing, ten-key adding machine. Experience necessary. Howard-Straffin Chrysler Plymouth Dealership."

He flung the paper at me as I sat on my bed and exclaimed, "Are you serious? Get realistic! You're just a kid without experience, and you're chasing a desk job."

Was this the kind of job I had been holding out for? His words stung, but I savored the spectacle of his rant until the perfect moment arrived.

"Dad, I got that job! I start on Monday!" I grinned, delivering the announcement.

My father's skepticism blinded him to the fact that I did indeed possess relevant experience. I could type sixty words per minute on a standard or electric typewriter, adeptly handle filing, and operate both a key punch machine and a mimeograph machine. I had been working in our school office since freshman year. Despite his doubt, my father still drove me to work that Monday and engaged Mr. Straffin, the owner of the dealership, in conversation. Mr. Straffin assured my father that he had rigorously tested my skills. While the parts department position was part-time, I'd be working full-time over the summer, with special assignments on the side, such as delivering new cars to Logan Airport in Boston.

At the start, the parts manager was not fond of me and seemed eager to find reasons to let me go. My sole responsibility was operating a ten-key adding machine, which I hadn't yet mastered. Adding up long columns of numbers was daunting.

My first week was a nightmare. Micky, the parts manager, would bark, "I need those numbers now, not next year!"

By the end of the week, I was at my wit's end. A service man once approached the counter for parts and asked, "Hey Micky, who's the kid?"

Micky, with a Humphrey Bogart demeanor, responded, "Yeah, can you believe it? The new boss wouldn't let me hire my own assistant. Instead of a blonde with big tits, I got *Leave It to Beaver*."

Leave It to Beaver? Comparing me to "The Beave?" If you're going to use a TV celebrity as a comparison, how about "The Fonz" from *Happy Days*, or Greg Brady from the *Brady Bunch*?

I was determined not to falter. Because it was summer, Mrs. Barker allowed me to borrow a ten-key adding machine from school for the weekend. I sought my mother's help, and she showed me how to use it, using specific fingers for each number. Sitting at our dining/living room table, within an hour, I was effortlessly adding columns at remarkable speed. I couldn't wait to display my newfound skills, hoping that Micky's harassment would finally cease. When the first order came in, Micky said to the service man,

"I'd better add this up or we'll be here all day," and promptly kicked me out of my chair to use the adding machine.

But as he made several errors, he was interrupted by a phone call, forcing him back to his desk. I swiftly regained my seat and began adding up the column. Micky dropped the phone on his desk and exclaimed, "Are you kidding me?"

Just as he did, I pressed the total button and handed him the calculated tape. As he scrutinized the numbers, he muttered, "Yeah, well let's see how many mistakes you made."

"None," I said confidently, watching him go over each number.

He was left dumbfounded as he declared, "No mistakes! How on earth did you go from using one finger on Friday to this in two days?"

I simply replied with an air of triumph, "Practice, just practice, Micky!"

The Calling: A Divine Hymn

Visiting Aunt Doris during that summer one evening, I was introduced to Jeff an older friend of my cousin Ken. Jeff was around twenty-one years old and of Italian descent, and he reminded me of the character Fr. Guido Sarducci from *Saturday Night Live*. My aunt suggested that Jeff and I had much in common, especially our interest in music, and encouraged us to spend time together.

At the beginning of the school year, I had a meeting with Fr. Norton to discuss my plans for an independent study project to fulfill my religion credit requirement. We settled on a research project that involved comparing several major world religions. However, Fr. Norton also brought up another topic during our conversation. He recalled that there had been a period when I had seriously considered a religious calling. Recognizing this, he recommended that I explore that possibility further. Bishop Stang was introducing a new course called "career exploration" for graduating seniors, where students would select a profession, find a business sponsor, and intern in that field during class time. Fr. Norton proposed that I should use this opportunity to shadow the life of a priest, spending time at the rectory and observing the priestly lifestyle. It was a unique suggestion, and I began to contemplate the idea.

Fr. Norton referred me to a local church to explore career options, and before long, I found myself back in a familiar setting—playing guitar and singing in a church environment. Around this time, my friendship with Jeff started to grow as we spent more time together.

In contrast, my relationships at school felt different—more superficial. I could never quite connect with anyone the way other guys seemed to, never experiencing that camaraderie or sense of brotherhood. I was constantly afraid of being rejected, mocked, or bullied. I was different—philosophically curious, eager for knowledge, and open to new perspectives. I had a deep love for the arts, not just performing arts but fine arts as well.

Jeff seemed to understand all of this. He showed a genuine interest in helping me embrace these passions, and as time passed, our bond grew stronger. For the first time, I found someone I could trust. With only a few years between us, I felt like I finally had the older brother I had always longed for.

Metamorphosis: The Transformation Tango

Graduation Photo

In my senior year, I made the conscious decision to focus exclusively on being fully engaged in my school and with my classmates. The impending college applications, specifically for pre-med programs, meant that my plate was already full. Also, there were various musical commitments, including the Christmas Concert where I was slated to perform a solo with the choir and the spring musical which typically offered senior students leading roles. Balancing these commitments, my independent study project for religion class, my mentorship at the rectory, and the career exploration course were going to be challenging feats.

Apparently, my shadowing the life of a priest was not accepted by the principal to satisfy the requirements for a course credit. So, in addition I secured a student teacher position at St. Anthony's school. However, my expectations of teaching religion, English, or science were dashed when I was assigned to teach math. The challenge was that I wasn't particularly skilled in math myself. To succeed, I had to approach teaching from the perspective of a student, which surprisingly worked well. By the end of the semester, the grades of my students, who were initially struggling, had significantly improved.

Meanwhile, life at the rectory, where I spent time as part of my mentorship, was more enjoyable than I anticipated. The camaraderie among the other priests and myself was striking. We shared meals, played cards, watched movies, and engaged in meaningful conversations. At the same time, my friendship with Jeff grew stronger, as we discovered shared interests and a deepening connection. This was a new experience for me – having a genuine adult friend who treated me as an equal and could talk about anything.

The Christmas concert that year was a success. I secured a solo performance, singing "A Child of Hope." Although not on par with Denise's Lord's Prayer, it marked a significant achievement for me. The Alleluia portion of the concert included alumni, and one graduate remarked that I sounded like Aretha Franklin hitting those high notes. I wasn't sure if that was praise or criticism, but it left an impression.

Sister Marie encouraged me to audition for District Chorus, but I instinctively resisted the idea, as I had an aversion to competitive singing. However, I agreed to try. During practice, I struggled with blending my tenor melody with the other three parts. To address this, Sister Marie gave me a tape of just my part to practice with. This helped me learn my part and resist getting pulled into the sopranos' lines. At the audition, I sang with three unfamiliar students. Despite performing well, a judge advised that my singing was more suited for a solo, as blending in a four-part harmony was essential. I adjusted and made it into the chorus. My high scores led to an invitation to the All-State Competition in Springfield, Massachusetts.

Oklahoma vs. Miss America: The Pageant Polka

As it was my senior year, I was determined not to let anything deter me from achieving success in my pursuits. The school musical, *Oklahoma!* was a significant event, and I had my sights set on the role of Will Parker. Although I recognized that Mike Brassard was more likely to get the part of Curley due to his vocal abilities and physique, I believed Will Parker was tailor-made for me. I meticulously prepared for my audition by researching the libretto and score and chose to perform Will's song "Kansas City." With confidence and purpose, I sang my heart out during the audition, capturing the attention of the entire room. The applause that followed assured me that I had given a remarkable performance.

On a Friday, the tension mounted as students congregated, eagerly awaiting the posting of the cast list. Finally, Sister Marie affixed the list outside the chorus room door before vanishing. Navigating the crowd, I homed in on the character Will Parker. Beside it read "Fred Cabral." Wait, what? Excitement surged – had I been cast as Curly? My eyes darted to find Curly's name. Alas, as I suspected, Mike had clinched that role. So where did my name appear?

There, nestled in the chorus. A wave of bewilderment washed over me. Fred was a junior, and he had broken his leg – crutches were in his future for the show. Will Parker demanded a triple threat. Doubts gnawed at me. *Had I overestimated my abilities?* Yet, I wasn't alone in my astonishment; as those around me mirrored my incredulity. Or perhaps their empathy masked their true feelings?

Back home, I shared the news with my parents and then retreated to my room, skipping dinner to nurse my bruised ego. The play had demanded significant sacrifices, and this was the result. Choosing to be part of the school musical meant giving up the community performances I had been involved in, and now I was left with nothing.

There was a quiet hush throughout the house. My dad finished the dishes while my sister watched TV with my mother. The stillness was abruptly broken by the sharp ring of the phone, its sound echoing through the house.

"Ronnie, it's for you!" my mother called out. With hopeful anticipation, I dashed to the phone, yearning for Mr. Morrissey to inform me of a colossal mix-up. I would, in fact, be playing the role of Will Parker.

"Hello, this is Ron," I answered, my heart racing.

"Hi, I'm calling from the Miss. America Pageant Committee. We were given your name by the Miss New Bedford Pageant. We are holding auditions and looking for someone who can sing the theme song for this year's pageant. Can you come to Boston Sunday afternoon to audition?"

Without hesitation, I agreed, jotting down the address.

"What should I sing?" I inquired.

The man replied, "Choose something upbeat and popular. First, perform part of "Oh here she is Miss America," the song Burt Parks sings."

Having watched numerous Miss America pageants on Labor Day Weekend, I was well-acquainted with the song. Sunday afternoon, my father chauffeured me to Boston, an hour's journey from New Bedford.

As I entered the audition room, approximately ten men occupied the space. I stood out as notably younger. One by one, they sang the Miss America song, many with impressive opera-like vocal prowess. In this environment, I felt conspicuously out of place, my turn arriving towards the end. As I launched into "Oh here she is…Miss America," the room fell still. The selection committee, once busy shuffling papers and taking notes, paused mid-action, their eyes locked on me. The air seemed to shift, and I could feel their focus narrowing.

When I finished, there was a brief silence before one of them leaned forward and, almost as if it was inevitable, asked, "Would you mind singing another?" "Ron, what's your second number?"

A popular song with my band was "Going Out of My Head," showcasing my vocal range and pop sensibility. When I concluded, a voice piped up, "That's the voice we want."

Yet, a woman seated nearby interjected, "But he's wearing braces on his teeth."

The response was unequivocal. "So what? The microphone will conceal them." "Son, the job is yours," one of the judges declared. They turned to the other auditioners and expressed their gratitude for coming.

Unbelievable! I was about to perform for the upcoming Miss America, who, as it turned out, would be Terry Ann Meeuwsen in 1973.

After explaining the situation to Sister Marie and the school administration, it became apparent that my participation in the All-State Competition was at risk of being used as leverage to get me to recommit to do our musical. A series of confrontations and negotiations followed, including a heated exchange with Mr. Morrissey.

One evening, I found myself engrossed in a book, nestled in the chair next to the telephone, just as it decided to ring. Without hesitation, I lifted the receiver and uttered a polite "hello."

It was Mr. Morrissey, and his voice dripped with disdain as he said, "I understand you don't want to be in the musical!"

His call had caught me off guard, and an uneasy feeling began to settle in. It was apparent that an unpleasant confrontation was looming.

"Mr. Morrissey, I can't participate in the musical because…"

Before I could say more, Mr. Morrissey erupted into a tirade of insults. His voice was loud enough for my father, standing just a few feet away, to hear. Though the exact words were muffled, the harsh, abrasive tone left no doubt about their intent.

"You, ungrateful little son of a bitch! You think you're so talented? Well, let me enlighten you. You can't act, which is precisely why I never cast you in our previous productions. Your dancing skills are merely passable, I've witnessed far superior dancers, and your singing, well, it's far from remarkable. You're merely a big fish in a small pond. Mark my words, you won't go anywhere as a performer beyond high school."

Before he could continue, my father intervened having been listening to the conversation from his desk phone in the other room, his voice firm and unwavering.

"Mr. Morrissey, this is Ronnie's father. First and foremost, how dare you speak to my son in such a manner? If his talents are lacking, then why has he been working professionally since his sophomore year and been chosen by a New York City choreographer? Furthermore, for someone with what you term a *mediocre* voice, why was he recently selected to sing for Miss. America? Mr. Morrissey, I believe our conversation has reached its conclusion. Goodbye!"

 With those resolute words, my father abruptly hung up the phone. It was then that I realized I still held the receiver, and I promptly followed suit.

Upon my return to school the following day, I thought my father's words had put an end to the matter. However, Mr. Morrissey had more to say. It baffled me why, if he didn't view me as particularly talented, he was insistent on my participation in the show.

Around 10 a.m. that morning, a page over the intercom requested my presence in the office. Mrs. Barker informed me that sister Marie wanted to speak with me. She met me outside the chorus room, discreetly closing the door behind her.

"Ronnie, you should be aware that your decision not to participate in the musical has put your place in the All-State Competition at risk. Your actions are suggesting a lack of teamwork, and considering the school covers the cost to send you, we are contemplating canceling our sponsorship for your attendance. I strongly advise you to reconsider your stance on the musical."

It was a moment of unexpected pressure. They were using strong-arm tactics to intimidate me. I replied, "Sister Marie, I can't pass up the opportunity to perform for Miss America. The rehearsals and performances clash with the musical, and next year, I'll be focusing on college and my pre-med courses. This may be my last chance to perform at this level. I'm sorry, but my decision remains unchanged."

With that, I turned and headed back to class, aware that it was too early to claim victory in this battle.

That afternoon, I was paged once more. "Ronnie Boucher, please come to the principal's office."

Everyone knew I often helped with administrative tasks for the principal, so it wasn't an unusual summons. Sister Barbara had taken over as principal when Sister Maureen retired after my sophomore year, and their personalities were markedly different. Sister Maureen resembled Mother Abbess from *The Sound of Music*, while Sister Barbara had the demeanor of a stern warden in a women's penitentiary.

As I entered her office I asked, "Yes, Sister Barbara, is there something you need me to do?"

She motioned for me to take a seat in front of her desk.

"I've been informed that you declined a position in the musical's chorus because you believed you deserved a better part. Sister Marie also mentioned that I must decide your participation in the All-State competition, which your actions have jeopardized. You know, young man, that Bishop Stang must cover your expenses."

Considering my response carefully, I chose honesty. "Sister Barbara, yes, I was truly disappointed not to get the role of Will Parker. Anyone who witnessed my audition believed I was perfect for the part. However, my decision was primarily driven by the opportunity to sing for Miss America. With rehearsals and performances clashing with the musical, it's impossible for me to be in two places at once."

Her expression shifted, and she exclaimed, "Miss America! You're going to sing for Miss America?"

Terry Ann Meeuwsen, Miss America 1973

Her tone softened as she admitted she was unaware of the circumstances, and she assured me that my participation in the All-State Competition would not be affected by my commitment to Miss America.

The school musical went on without me. Jeff had encouraged me to be the bigger person, so I attended the dress rehearsal. It was bittersweet.

I chose to focus on the positive opportunities that had arisen. Singing for the Miss. America Pageant proved to be an unforgettable experience, and witnessing the reigning Miss America's performance left a lasting impression.

As the year progressed, I navigated the complexities of senior year, from prom to graduation preparations. My romantic life was a bit tumultuous, involving various individuals like Barbara, Liz, and Diane. Eventually, prom night arrived, and I attended with Diane, marking a memorable moment in my high school journey.

Graduation was a culmination of my four years at Bishop Stang. Looking back, it was a year filled with challenges, surprises, and personal growth. The disappointments and successes I experienced helped shape my determination to pursue a career in music and performance.

Unrequited Romance: The Love Lament

As my senior year drew to a close, I found myself spending more time at the rectory, captivated by the clergy's lifestyle, which proved quite different from the expected image of celibacy, poverty, and all the traditional trappings. Despite months passing by and beyond my church duties, my relationship with Jeff underwent a transformation swiftly evolving into a newfound level of comfort and closeness. As a freshly ordained adult, the concept of having a male confidant felt foreign and took time to adjust to. It marked the first instance where I could connect with someone on a peer level, rather than just admiring them as an adult figure. Jeff had become the big brother figure I had always wished for. Already surpassing my eighteenth birthday which had been in March, the need for independence grew stronger, and Jeff was instrumental in assisting me on that journey.

New Bedford sat at the mouth of Cape Cod, although most people considered the Cape to begin after the Bourne Bridge in Hyannis. The drive from New Bedford to Hyannis took only about thirty minutes. My parents seldom ventured to the Cape except when our Canadian relatives requested it. My father frequently grumbled about the Cape traffic, using it as his primary reason for avoiding the trip, despite the fact that we had beaches on our side of the bridge. He wasn't a fan of saltwater, either. My only reference to the Cape was through my Canadian cousin, Pierre, a charming womanizer with a penchant for cigars and an overly confident demeanor. He firmly believed that the flirtations he received from gay men in Provincetown were actually directed at my father, rather than himself. Apart from this, I had neither opinions nor observations about the Cape to form any kind of preference. However, all of that was about to change.

On a beautiful sunny day in early June, Jeff called me early in the morning. "Hey, want to go to the Cape today?" he asked.

This was something typically reserved for adults, and the invitation felt I had reached that milestone. Jeff arrived in his Volkswagen Beetle, much newer than the one I owned, and we set off for the Sagamore Bridge, the gateway to one of Massachusetts' most sought-after tourist destinations. Jeff drove while enjoying his pipe, the tobacco's scent reminiscent of that used by my grandfather Boucher. With the windows rolled down, the fresh salty air invigorated my senses with a sense of joie de vivre. Conversations during the drive were a blur as we headed to Marconi's Beach in Truro.

After parking the car, we made our way to the edge of a cliff offering an awe-inspiring panoramic view of the beach and ocean stretching out in both directions. An expansive wooden stairway led to the sandy beach below. What struck me was the sparse crowd, likely due to it being a weekday. Where were all the tourists my father always cited as the reason for avoiding the Cape? And yet, there I was, enveloped by the ocean, the sun, and the air, infusing new life into my body and novel thoughts into my mind. It was an exchange of energies that left me feeling exhilarated and in awe. Amidst this, a feeling of tranquility enveloped Jeff and me. We shared the vast space while remaining independent in our contemplations. The dynamic felt akin to my mom's relationship with my dance teacher Carol.

We returned in time for dinner. This day marked a form of liberation, but it also marked the point where my mother's concerns escalated. Tensions grew, fueled by my mother's perception that I was spending excessive time with Jeff, returning between ten and eleven in the evening instead of the usual 9 p.m. However, my mother's concerns were slightly diminished by her sister's assurance that Jeff frequently spent time at her home without any qualms about the time he and Ken shared.

Coincidentally, Jeff's mother was also visiting for a few days that summer. I suggested to my mom to invite them for dinner, an opportunity for my parents to meet Jeff and hopefully ease my mother's apprehensions.

"Dinner is served," announced my mother as we all convened at the dining room table. Jeff's mother hailed from Queens, NY, and her accent was unmistakable. Despite the cultural differences, the evening proceeded as expected. Around 9:30, Jeff and his mother bid their farewells and departed. I retired to my room for some reading, while my parents tackled the cleanup.

Suddenly, my mother appeared at my door and without preamble said, "I don't want you seeing Jeff anymore," and returned to her dishwashing.

What had just happened? We had all shared a wonderful evening, hadn't we? Had I missed something? Hurriedly following her to the kitchen, I reacted with a mix of panic and confusion.

"Where is this coming from? Jeff is my friend, why would you want me to end our friendship?"

A response came, one that left me utterly flabbergasted and at a loss for words. "I think he's gay."

Was this the famed "mother's intuition?" Jeff didn't fit the stereotypical portrayal of gay men. He lacked the effeminate traits and most importantly, after knowing him for months, I had never perceived any hint about his sexual orientation being gay. I felt a surge of anger toward my mom. Why would she conjure such a flimsy excuse to sever my friendship? Was she being possessive? Was she grappling with the idea of her child leaving the nest and reacting out of fear? Typically, I would heed my mother's wishes in situations like this. But this time was different; this time, I felt the need to assert myself and make my own choice. Now, however, doubts had been planted in my mind, causing a conflict within me.

The following evening, after work, I went straight to see Jeff, where he sat reading. It was evident that something was troubling me as I sank to the floor beside him, clutching my head. Jeff, offering consolation, asked, "I was about to tell you what a great dinner we had, and my mom loved your parents…but what's wrong?"

"My mom doesn't want me to be friends with you anymore...she thinks you're gay!"

Without another word, Jeff grasped my arm and went to the rectory. He summoned the priests to join us in the living room. After we were all seated, Jeff prompted me, "Go on, tell them what you told me."

I complied, stating, "My mom doesn't want me to be friends with Jeff, because she thinks he's gay."

I scrutinized their reactions, hoping to discern any validity in her claim. One of the priest's voices broke the silence.

"Ron, regrettably, there are people with narrow perspectives who make baseless assumptions. Unfortunately, one such assumption is about being gay. Your mother may be holding onto you and fearing to lose you."

By the end of the conversation, I felt empowered and encouraged to stand my ground and confront my mother. Returning home, she awaited me. I recounted my actions and what the priests had shared.

"I don't care what they said. I think he's gay, and you will steer clear of him," she asserted with unwavering conviction, overriding any input that supported my stance.

Despite my explanations, she refused to budge.

The following week proved challenging for our entire family. Jeff and I continued spending time together despite my mother's threats. Undeterred, by week two, she resorted to a different strategy. This time, she assumed a catatonic demeanor, neglecting household tasks, cooking minimally, and even delaying going to bed with my dad until the early hours of the morning. After two weeks of this melodramatic and almost comical performance, my father made a special trip home during his lunch break. He invited me to sit with him in the car. Instead of issuing an ultimatum, he calmly inquired, "Can you explain why you're standing firm on this issue?"

I presented all the reasons I had shared with my mother, withholding just one.

"Dad, there's a significant bond between Jeff and me, and I've never experienced a friendship like this. For the sake of argument, let's say Jeff is gay. I've been accused of being gay since I was very young. I don't believe I am, but shouldn't I have the chance, as an adult, to figure things out on my own? If it's not bothering me, why is it such a big concern for you guys?"

My dad replied, "Alright, I'll need to sort this out with your mother. You're on your own with this one."

I'm not sure if my father had a moment of enlightenment or was too distraught to argue with me. But my mother wasn't giving up. She managed to persuade my grandmother to take me on a trip to Montreal, embracing the notion "out of sight, out of mind."

The excursion was deemed a graduation gift, marking my first visit to Canada alone with my grandmother and without seeing relatives. She remembered my complaints about missing out on seeing Montreal due to my parents leaving me behind. Thus, she booked a five-night, six-day stay in Montreal through Paragon Tours. And so, off I went, engaging in typical sightseeing activities during the days and some evenings. We explored Old Montreal, visited L'Oratoire du Saint-Joseph du Mont-Royal, experienced the German Beer Gardens, took a side trip to Parliament in Toronto, attended a nightclub show at Café Conc, and visited Palais de Jardins where my cousin Guy Boucher's TV show was broadcast live. However, it being summer, the show was off-air.

On one of the free nights, as I read, my grandmother caught my attention and casually remarked, "I heard one of the young girls on the tour saying they'll be going disco dancing at the nightclub."

Without hesitation, I leapt out of my chair and exclaimed, "Altitude 737? Can I go?"

My grandmother, already preparing for bed, turned to me and playfully responded, "Get out of here. You don't want to hang out with an old lady like me."

Swiftly changing, I donned my new plaid bell-bottom low-rise pants that I'd just bought and paired them with a form-fitting button-front polyester shirt, left casually unbuttoned to about mid-chest. The disco was conveniently across the street from our hotel. That evening, I met two girls from the tour, and there it was again—the sense of freedom, independence, and the ability to explore at my own pace. I was reminded of my need for independence and the freedom to make my own choices. Throughout that week, I had no contact with Jeff, and the separation provided me with space to reflect on what truly mattered to me. The craving for independence and the liberty to make my own decisions were now at the forefront of my mind.

On a Saturday evening, we returned home. My parents were out with their friends, so I decided to visit Jeff. Upon arrival, I found Jeff seated in a chair in the living room. We engaged in conversation about my vacation and various other topics.

While watching TV, Jeff decided to make some popcorn. Once it was ready, he joined me on the couch, placing the popcorn on my legs. We continued watching TV, indulging in popcorn, and occasionally Jeff would rub my feet when not reaching for the popcorn. After finishing the bowl, he moved it to the coffee table, and the foot rub began to extend to my legs.

At first, I tried not to read too much into it, recalling instances of family members exchanging similar gestures. However, the sensation started to intensify as Jeff's rubbing evolved into a massage. I couldn't deny the comfort it brought, particularly to my tense calves. His strokes grew broader, his fingers grazing the edge of my underwear beneath my shorts, and my thoughts started to swirl.

Conflicting emotions arose as I battled the intoxicating, erotic, and stimulating sensations. I reminded myself of the assurances from Jeff, and the other priests, that he was not gay. But the sensation persisted, and my mind was divided. What was happening? Why did it feel both pleasurable and distressing?

Then it happened, his hand was suddenly on my crotch. I was frozen as his hands unzipped my shorts. More confusion and more inner conflict. My thoughts immediately raced back to the moment with Uncle. No, this couldn't possibly be happening. Yet, I found myself trapped in a state of suspended animation, powerless to control the unfolding situation. The drumming in my head grew louder and more intense as I laid there motionless while Jeff studied my facial expressions. Then, in an instant, realization struck me. My mother had been right all along. I had gone against her, put my family through turmoil, all to prove her wrong. Most of all, I had placed my trust in Jeff. As I began to stir, Jeff swiftly moved, pinning my hands down at my sides.

"Ron, stop!" he commanded, his tone carrying an undeniable seriousness.

Jeff had never shown physical force before, but his determination was crystal clear.

"Ron, look at me," he insisted urgently, his eyes locking onto mine, brimming with intensity.

I could sense he was about to lean in for a kiss. Summoning all my strength, I managed to push him off, causing him to fall to the floor. We both rose to our feet. I confronted Jeff with tears streaming down my cheeks.

"Jeff, how could you lie to me like that?" I choked out, my voice quivering with emotion.

Jeff's response was immediate, his voice filled with remorse. "I'm sorry, I was scared to tell you how I felt."

In that moment, I grabbed my car keys and headed for the door. Abruptly turning around, I faced Jeff once more.

"You know something, Jeff? If you had just been honest with me, we might have been able to salvage our friendship. But your deception shattered my trust. Don't ever call or reach out to me again."

With that final declaration, I turned and walked away, heading back home.

My mother was seated in the chair next to the telephone, with my father already having retired for the evening. I was determined not to give her the satisfaction of being right. My plan was to head straight to my room. However, the moment I laid eyes on her, sitting there with a calm demeanor, she glanced at me and softly remarked, "Jeff tried something tonight, didn't he?"

I didn't delve into specifics, but I acknowledged her intuition and then made my way to my room.

In the aftermath of my mother's suspicions about Jeff, the situation between my mother and me became tense. Jeff's attempts to maintain our friendship through notes and visits outside my house were met with mixed emotions on my part. One rainy night, I spotted Jeff standing in front of my house in the rain. Despite his persistence, I decided not to engage with him and let him stand there soaked.

This marked the end of our friendship, and I never saw Jeff again after that night. The experience further intensified my self-doubt about my own sexuality. With no one to confide in or discuss my feelings with, I was left to grapple with a range of emotions on my own. The internal struggle between notions of good and evil, right and wrong, love and perversion added to the complexities of my identity.

As time went on, I chose to bury these feelings and move forward, compartmentalizing this experience as something that was behind me. However, the lack of understanding and support during this critical period in my life left me with unresolved questions and an ongoing sense of isolation.

Once more, it was the magic of music that provided me with a lifeline, allowing me to immerse myself in its melodic embrace, to maintain my focus on what I could manage, and to stave off the encroaching darkness that threatened to engulf me. Fortunately, I had the privilege of lending my voice to various intimate gatherings, from joyous celebrations to somber farewells and most memorably, a theatrical performance that left an indelible mark on my heart.

It was a minstrel-themed variety show, and for the first time I was given the privilege of selecting my own song. I was drawn to the hauntingly beautiful melody "Maybe This Time," from the musical *Cabaret*. It was performed by Terry Ann Meeuwsen, the enchanting Miss America, during that notorious pageant, which coincided with the controversies surrounding my high school production of *Oklahoma!* This moment represented the perfect opportunity, a chance to let my soul intertwine with the music that had always whispered to me. The orchestra's enchanting overture gently caressed my senses as I stood alone in the spotlight, its radiance highlighting me at center stage.

Despite the song's theme of unrequited love, it was the poignant refrain, "maybe this time I'll win," that resonated with profound significance deep within my soul. Perhaps, in the intricate game of life, this time would be my victorious turn. As I approached the crescendo, each note building to its zenith, the audience rose as one, offering an ovation that transcended mere applause. It was a standing ovation.

In that singular moment, bathed in the warmth of their acknowledgment, I felt something I had long yearned for take root within me: the validation that I wasn't just another singer blending into the background. I was seen and not just seen but recognized as someone exceptional. The word "outstanding" echoed in my mind, wrapping around me like a long-awaited embrace, affirming that all the sacrifices, rehearsals, and self-doubt had led to this moment of undeniable worth. I had a voice that stood apart, one that demanded to be heard.

With the onset of college in the fall, the need to earn money became a priority. With plans to commute to college and pursue a pre-med track, I applied for a job at my local hospital, St. Luke's, and was offered a position delivering supplies to the hospital wards. During the interview, the department supervisor expressed concern about the temporary nature of my employment due to my plans for college in the fall. Following my father's advice, I assured him that I intended to take a year off to earn money for tuition and was hired for the job.

I quickly integrated into the hospital environment and formed positive relationships with my boss, co-workers, and ward clerks. Working alongside me was a co-worker named Nick, who was married, around age twenty-five, and shared my height. Nick had a muscular build, blond hair, and a confident demeanor. We each had large hand trucks with flatbeds that carried orders requested by the hospital wards. These orders were distributed evenly between us.

One challenge we faced was an incline that I had to navigate with my cart. While Nick effortlessly managed the incline, I struggled to push my cart up the slope. Despite the difficulty, I persevered and managed to overcome the obstacle, even though it felt like my muscles were growing stronger in the process.

This summer job not only provided me with valuable work experience and a source of income but also allowed me to interact with different aspects of the hospital environment. It was a steppingstone in my journey toward supporting my college education and gaining a deeper understanding of responsibility and hard work.

My summer wasn't devoid of performing opportunities either. Your Theatre, our local community performing group, had an illustrious list of alumni, including figures like Sandra and her friend and colleague, Arthur Faria. Among his Broadway credits were his choreography for the musical *Ain't Misbehaving* and his staging of the Lena Horne's show, *The Lady and Her Music*. I aspired to add my name to this list.

They were casting the show, *Little Mary Sunshine*, an old-fashioned musical that humorously parodied operettas, featuring six Indian/forest rangers who were thinly disguised as Mounties.

During the audition, I found myself among a group of people who already seemed familiar with each other. Despite being the newcomer, I was cast as one of the Indian/Forest Rangers. This marked my first experience of performing six shows a week for seven weeks. Everyone in the cast was dynamic, however, there was one performer who truly stood out, and her name was Trudy Miller. She played the role of Madame Ernestine von Liebedich, an over-the-hill opera singer with sweet memories of her home in Vienna, Austria. Trudy's comedic timing was impeccable, leaving the audience in stitches at every performance. I closely observed her delivery, how she engaged with the audience, and her ability to gauge the timing of her lines and audience responses. Through my interactions with her on stage, I learned the nuances of slapstick, from what was "too little" to "too much."

Unbeknownst to the cast, my parents and a group of my mother's friends attended one of the performances. At the end of the first act, Trudy came offstage and said, "Oh my God! That woman's laughter is infectious. We need to find out who she is and hire her to attend every performance."

While this was my only production with Your Theatre, it proved to be a profoundly educational experience. Trudy had excelled in her role and indirectly taught me a great deal about the art of comedy, knowledge that has served me well in my own performances and in my work as a director.

CHAPTER 4: THE COLLEGE YEARS

Juggling: The Life Jive

Commuting was rarely an issue, except for those days when my first class was scheduled for the early hour of 8 a.m. on Monday, Wednesday, and Friday. To compound matters, it was calculus, a subject I hadn't been allowed to take during my senior year of high school. However, both calculus and physics were prerequisites for the pre-med program. Beyond my courses and my full-time position at the hospital, I didn't take on any additional responsibilities or activities.

It took me some time to find my internal rhythm and cope with the solitude that came with it. The drive to campus in my Volkswagen Bug was especially bitter in winter emphasized by the lack of heat and the hole in the floorboard. But amidst the chill, I could lose myself to the melodies on the radio. During a certain period, they played a particular song every morning at around the same time. Minnie Riperton's hit track, "Loving You" was climbing the charts, highlighting her ability to hit a high note from another realm.

By the second semester, I felt prepared to add a performance to my schedule. A notice caught my eye for auditions of *The Roar of the Greasepaint—The Smell of the Crowd*, a show that was unfamiliar to me. The director was Rosemary Melli, a former New Yorker, who, in hindsight, proved to be an exceptional theater director.

For reasons unclear, I wasn't adequately prepared for the audition, and my lack of preparation was evident. To make matters worse, I decided to audition with a girl I had recently met. I selected the duet "Once in A Blue Moon" from the musical I had just finished at Your Theater. Although I thought I knew it well because of hearing all those performances we did, neither of us had practiced it much together.

It was a fiasco, and we were fully aware that we had botched it. We were dismissed with a curt "Thank you…Next!"

As I began my departure, I overheard a pianist in the adjoining room playing the music to "**The Impossible Dream**" from *Man of La Mancha*. It was a song I knew like the back of my hand. The door was open, so I entered the room as he continued to play. As I approached him, I could hear someone singing in the audition room that I had just left. As I stood next to the pianist I began to sing softly. Hearing my voice, the pianist gave me the go ahead to sing full out. He assured me that nobody would mind as there were multiple rehearsals going on at the same time.

As I belted out the song, Ms. Melli burst into the room, exclaiming loudly, "Oh my God! That voice is exactly what I'm searching for... Wait, was that you? Who was just singing 'The Impossible Dream'? That wasn't the same voice I just heard!"

After clarifying my mix-up, she asked me to start from the beginning and sing the song again. Then she said, "Your voice is precisely what I need for one of the lead roles, but you look so young, and you're wearing braces!"

Still trying to see if this could work, she followed with the acting portion of the audition. On top of that, I had to adopt a British accent. To my surprise, I excelled effortlessly, as if it was a skill carried over from a past life.

"When will your braces come off?" she inquired.

"Within the next two weeks," I replied promptly and confidently. My answer seemed to satisfy her.

She said, "Very well, I'll cast you as the character, 'Sir,' provided you get those braces off; otherwise, I'll have to recast your role."

I was dumbfounded. Just like that, I landed my first lead role in a musical since *Brigadoon*.

On the morning scheduled for my braces to be removed, the orthodontist's secretary called to inform us that the doctor had sustained a golf course injury, breaking his arm, and would be unavailable for some time. She provided no return date. I conveyed this situation to Ms. Melli, while assuring her that, if necessary, I would remove the braces myself—a promise I genuinely intended to fulfill. As a cautionary procedure they had me grow a mustache and beard.

During show week, I still had my braces on, which caused Ms. Melli considerable distress. Adding to her anxiety, she had inexplicably chosen to stage the show in a tent, which also served as a venue for a spring arts festival. During Thursday night's dress rehearsal, my silver bands glinted around my teeth under the theater lights, visible each time I smiled. By this point, she understood that she had lost the battle, regardless of my assurances about removing the braces myself. I contacted the orthodontist's office to inform them of my plan. In an unusual decision, my orthodontist allowed his assistant to remove all the brackets and bands. On opening night, my gleaming pearly whites were on display.

Roar of the Greasepaint

There were three scheduled performances: Friday and Saturday evenings, and a Sunday matinee. Yet, a Northeastern storm began brewing during the Saturday show. Over the evening, the winds grew stronger until they toppled the tent, forcing us to postpone the show by a week and granting us three more performances. The production was a tremendous success, and Ms. Melli expressed her anticipation of collaborating with me again, extolling my talents and remarkable voice, a sentiment that oddly felt familiar. However, what I hadn't anticipated was a review in the local paper: "New Bedford Man Shines in Lead Role of *Greasepaint*!" As relayed by Mrs. Barker from Stang, she had clipped out the review, which also included a still photograph of me alongside three other main characters and placed it on Mr. Morrissey's desk.

In response he quipped, "Beginner's luck! Must have been low on talent."

My First Love Song: A Solo of Sorts

Greasepaint holds a special place in my heart. Over time, I've had the privilege to sing numerous songs from both Sir and Cocky's selections during concerts, and I've even taken on the role of directing the show myself. Yet, it was during this very musical that I experienced my first genuine romance.

The ingenue role of The Girl was portrayed by Michelle, a captivating blonde with a curvaceous figure that was complemented by her striking blue eyes which seemed to dominate her features. Her voice, light and sweet with a soubrette quality, was truly enchanting. Envy took hold of me as I observed her performing the duet "My First Love Song" alongside Cocky. In her presence, a newfound romantic interest blossomed within, something far more grounded and achievable than the illusions I had previously harbored for Sandra.

However, there was a complication: Michelle was already in a relationship with someone else. It marked the first time I found myself in a situation where I had to compete for someone's affection. Despite this challenge,

Michelle remained receptive to my playful flirtations. Our interactions were characterized by a remarkable comfort, and as time passed, we found ourselves spending more time together. Eventually, fate intervened, leading to Michelle's breakup with her boyfriend and the commencement of our own romantic journey.

Our connection deepened as we discovered common roots in New Bedford. To my surprise, we also learned that our mothers had attended St. Anthony's High School together.

Although I knew that Michelle's mother had passed, our conversations never provided an occasion to expand on the details of her death until the significant day when she met my parents for the first time. My mother instinctively knew this was just not some pretty girl, but someone I had sincere feelings for. This made my mother's inquisitive nature kick into high gear.

"Tell me about your mother," my mother asked Michelle.

Michelle's voice was steady, soft, and calm as she began to tell us about her mother.

"She was a beautiful woman, blessed with an exquisite voice. She sang solos at St. Anthony's during high school and for a few years after graduating."

You could sense my mother searching her memory, as she had known all the soloists at St. Anthony's.

"What was your mother's maiden name?" she asked.

"Collette... Collette Bourque!"

Michelle's response sparked an eruption of excitement from my mother.

"Oh my God, I went to school with her! She was in my class, and she used to perform all the solos at St. Anthony's. We all thought she'd go to Hollywood, due to her talent and beauty."

My mother's curiosity did not extend to questioning the tragic circumstances surrounding Collette's passing, a subtle mercy I deeply appreciated.

Michelle, Ma Belle: The Love Ballad

Michelle and I epitomized the ideal couple, you know, the kind you see in Hallmark movies. Well, at least that was my perception, and I was resolutely convinced of our profound love. Our most cherished shared activity was singing in harmony, a testament to our shared passion for the performing arts and our incurable romantic inclinations.

One day, I found Michelle gazing at her mother's photograph on her bureau. The picture lacked a frame, resting casually on the surface. She confided in me that it was the sole remaining image she possessed of her mother, as her father had cast aside all mementos during his period of mourning.

Summoning my courage, I delicately inquired about the circumstances surrounding her mother's tragic suicide.

Michelle confided that her mother had been a beautiful woman with an extraordinary singing voice, often performing solos at the church. She even performed on the Ted Mack show, a platform that showcased emerging talents from the Boston scene. Her appearance opened another offer to pursue a career in Hollywood, but she chose married life and children instead.

After marrying, the newlyweds moved to a secluded house in the countryside. Collette became isolated. The pressures of raising two children without a creative outlet, along with her struggle with bipolar disorder, deepened her despondency. When Michelle was in high school, she discovered her mother's lifeless body in the bathtub, a victim of suicide.

Motivated by a desire to create a meaningful gesture for Michelle, I asked to borrow the photograph. Though hesitant, she relented under the condition that I would return it promptly.

Fueled by my desire to impress Michelle and feeling like Michelangelo, I was certain that I could capture the stillness of her mother that would pulsate with life. Using pastels that my aunt Doris had given me earlier, I was inspired and worked all week. After seeing the finished artwork, my mother and aunt decided to have the piece framed before I presented it to Michelle.

I brought it to her. As she unveiled the portrait, her breath caught in her throat. Tears welled in her eyes as she gently traced the features with trembling fingers. Without a word, she rushed downstairs, clutching the portrait, eager to show her grandmother the cherished gift.

Mrs. Bourque exclaimed in awe, "She seems alive! Those eyes, they track you! They possess the same captivating gaze as in haunted house tales."

It was true, when you walked from right to left or vice versa, the eyes seemed to follow you. Michelle loved the portrait and was anxious for her father to see it when he returned home that evening. She chose to place it on her father's bureau in his room, ensuring it would greet him upon his return.

That evening, returning from a date, Michelle's father was confronted with the portrait illuminated by moonlight. He emitted an unexpected scream which caused Michelle to spring from her bed, racing to his room to find him standing before the portrait in distress.

"What is this?" he uttered.

Michelle promptly explained that it was a gift from me, artwork I had created. For her father, the portrait was so unsettling that Michelle reluctantly stowed it away in her closet. It was years later she told me that it was only when she was married with a home of her own that she was able to display it.

Guy Boucher: The Meeting Minuet

My parents had accepted an invitation to attend my Aunt Anna's 80th birthday celebration in Montreal over the Labor Day holiday. My celebrity cousin Guy Boucher was hosting the party in his beautiful loft apartment in old Montreal.

It hadn't even been a full day after my parents left when the phone rang at my house. As I answered, an operator's voice came through, "Will you accept a collect call from Roger Boucher?"

We sometimes played a trick when we didn't want to pay for a call but wanted to send a message. In this case it could have been that my parents were simply letting me know that they had arrived safely. However, this time I had the feeling I should just accept the call.

"Hi Dad! What's up?"

"Would you like to come to Montreal to meet your cousin, Guy?" As it was a long-distance call, my father expected a quick 'yes' from me, but I hesitated.

"Hello! Are you there?" he continued.

I finally blurted out, "Can I bring Michelle?" My romantic inclinations were fully awake, and naturally, I wasn't going without my girlfriend. To my delight, my parents readily consented to her joining me.

With enthusiasm and excitement, Michelle and I set off for Canada in my army green Datsun B-210, a used car I'd obtained after my Volkswagen Bug gave out on my way to school one day. Armed with memories of landmarks, as there was no map to guide us, we began our pilgrimage.

We sang the entire musical score from the *Sound of Music* for seven hours, infusing the mountainous landscapes with melodies. Eventually, we reached the border without any major complications.

Presenting our birth certificates and my driver's license, we faced a brief interrogation from the border patrol. When asked about my purpose in Canada, I happily revealed that I was visiting my cousin, Guy Boucher.

"The Boucher on TV?" the guard asked.

I confirmed, and with that acknowledgment, he swiftly allowed us through the gate. We had successfully crossed the border and entered Canada. Our next destination was my cousin Claudette's house.

Unexpectedly, a detour sign led us onto an unfamiliar road. We drove through vast farmlands, without signs pointing us in the right direction. Back then, there were no cell phones to rely on.

At a crossroads by a church on the riverbank, realization struck me. "Michelle, the church! We're here!" Unbeknownst to us, we were just streets away from our intended destination.

After settling in, Claudette guided us to our room. My mother intervened, informing Claudette that Michelle and I would not be sharing a bed. Speaking in French, Claudette playfully teased my mother about being old-fashioned and overbearing, suggesting that she couldn't believe we weren't already intimate. The truth was, we weren't. It was a fact that left me disappointed, as I couldn't help but think that had we shared a bed, we might have taken that step during one of our nights in Canada.

Guy Boucher, my charismatic cousin, had become a celebrity. He began in musical theater, but he soon transitioned into commercial television. He even secured his own TV show, *Les Coqueluches*, a variety show which ran for an impressive seven years, broadcast from the Complexe Desjardins in Montreal on Radio Canada.

Standing tall at six feet and three inches, Guy possessed a personality larger than life. He excelled in acting, singing, and dancing. In my eyes, he was an idol. His achievements and his decade-long seniority gave me a wealth of inspiration to draw from. I sought to emulate him in every conceivable way—collecting his albums, analyzing his style, studying his vocal technique, and tracing the trajectory of his success. He undeniably

Guy Boucher

played a pivotal role in shaping my artistic path.

Our time in Canada typically revolved around my mother's side of the family, as most visits were spent with them. Unfortunately, due to work commitments, we rarely managed to see my dad's relatives, despite the mutual enjoyment of our interactions. However, this occasion would be different, as it marked the first time we were reunited with both sides of our family.

We arrived at an apartment on a charming cobblestone street and ascended to the fourth floor, an attic space within a sizable apartment building. Guy's apartment embodied the ideal of "open concept". The only visible walls were the ones enclosing the bathroom. The loft-style space featured a pool table on one side, while his couch doubled as the seat from his jeep, gracing the cover of his latest album, 'Ma Jolie Rose!' The entire floor sparkled with a high-gloss black finish, reflecting light like a mirror, and was beautifully adorned to celebrate his mother's birthday.

Throughout the evening, Guy played the role of the perfect host, ensuring all his guests were having a delightful time. In true showman fashion, he treated us to some songs, grabbing a straw hat and a cane to perform a choreographed routine to the theme song from *Mame*.

Although the performance was captivating, I couldn't help but hope for a live rendition instead of a lip-sync to a recording. Then the family turned to me for a song. I began singing one of Guy's earlier recordings, "Neige Goo Goo."

Laughing, Guy admitted he had forgotten the lyrics. However, he was impressed that I knew the song. The family, however, was eager to hear an English song that was uniquely me. I chose to sing the "Impossible Dream" a cappella, and the ensuing applause and compliments bolstered my spirits. Afterwards, Guy approached me and extended an invitation to appear on his show, "Boucher & Boucher."

When I found a moment alone with Guy, I confessed my aspiration to become "just like him." His expression shifted to a serious one. He acknowledged me as a "real singer" and revealed that his studio-produced voice differed from his public persona. Offering his support in any way possible, he assured me of his assistance, a promise I intended to hold him to.

Later, Michelle and I strolled around Guy's neighborhood, exploring the architectural wonders of Old Montreal. The romantic ambience of the surroundings echoed our feelings, and we were both fully immersed in the blissful moments.

The party was over, and it was time to return to New Bedford. Once again, our voices intertwined in song as we serenaded the miles away. As our journey progressed, our conversation gradually turned more serious, shifting from our future plans to the topic of our relationship.

In a moment of unfiltered emotion, I blurted out, "I want to marry you."

The atmosphere grew still as we both grappled with the weight of my words. Was it too soon? Had I caught her off guard? The pause felt like an eternity until she finally responded, affirming that she shared the same sentiment. However, she suggested that we should finish our education before taking that step.

The Turning Point: A Musical Menage

Ms. Melli had her eyes set on directing the musical *The Fantasticks*, envisioning me as the embodiment of the character, Matt. The audition for the musical seemed like a mere formality to me. Hearing the score, I secretly wished I had been chosen for the role of El Gallo, the charismatic villain. Michelle would have been a perfect fit for the role of Louisa, but she had decided to abstain from performing that year and didn't audition.

Among the hopefuls, there was another girl with a vocal prowess that could adequately portray Louisa yet lacked the necessary delicacy and vulnerability. Ms. Melli, however, was more focused on my portrayal. I was still clinging to my "Sir" persona, maintaining an air of a pompous British aristocrat.

After weeks of frustration, Ms. Melli halted a rehearsal one day and queried, "Ron, what's your major?"

I answered, "Pre-Med."

"And your upbringing, was it fairly normal?"

Confirming this, she continued her line of questioning, "Tell me about your girlfriend."

I hesitated, puzzled by the direction of her inquiry then answered, "Why? You know her! What do you want me to say?" I said.

"Tell me how you feel about her!"

As I described my emotions and feelings, Ms. Melli responded, "Good! Now, recite your opening lines using the same tonality and reflect on the sentiment you just used."

Her words struck me like lightning.

"There is this girl. I'm nearly twenty years old. I've studied biology. I know the way things are and yet, in spite of all my knowledge, there is this girl."

The room erupted in applause. It was genuine, unscripted emotion that Ms. Melli sought. This marked my first real acting lesson: she wanted the real me. This unleashed a cascade of emotions and repressed conflicts, erupting like a volcanic surge.

On opening night, as I readied myself for my opening lines and first song, my knees trembled uncontrollably. Fearing I might not be able to turn around and perform, I scrambled for a solution. Then, it came to me, *Dear God, if you guide me through this, I promise to honor my art. I will use the talents you've bestowed upon me and pursue a career in the arts, if that's the path you desire.*

With that whispered plea, I turned to the audience and delivered one of my finest performances. Although my goal afterwards was to fulfill that promise, the transition was complex.

The review of the show followed the familiar pattern: Mrs. Barker diligently cut out the article and placed it on Mr. Morrissey's desk. This time, however, there was no response from him.

During rehearsals and the show, Michelle and I found ourselves with limited time for each other. Michelle sat in the audience; her eyes fixed on me as the final notes of the performance echoed through the theater. It was then, as I kissed Louisa under the stage lights, that a decision began to form in her mind. She realized in that moment that life with an artist was far more turbulent than she had imagined. My world—filled with late-night rehearsals, long tours, and an endless string of women in different roles—was worlds apart from the stability she craved.

She dreamed of a husband who came home at 5 p.m., shared quiet family dinners, and spent weekends playing with the kids. The life I was living, however, was unpredictable, fleeting, and always in motion. As she watched me on stage, Michelle knew our paths were veering in different directions, even if I tried to deny it. Deep down, I felt too the truth of her feelings settling uncomfortably in my heart, though neither of us had yet spoken it aloud.

My next endeavor was a variety performance scheduled at the Bishop Stang auditorium. Directed by Gladys Balestracci, who was Sandra and JoAnn's mother, the show presented a unique challenge. First, JoAnn was pregnant and in her eighth month. We weren't sure she'd make it to full-term. The second concerned a Snoopy costume that was for one of my numbers, "Happiness" from *You're a Good Man, Charlie Brown.* I quickly discovered that singing live while wearing the Snoopy head was impossible, so we decided to record our songs instead.

Sandra arrived during show week to help her mother and made a few adjustments to Miss Cheryl's choreography, set to the tune of "Shaft." At the last minute, I was given an additional task: learning and singing "My Coloring Book," a song Barbra Streisand originally recorded. I took on the challenge, even though I only had a day to learn it by singing it backstage with a microphone.

Post-performance, to my surprise, I learned that Mr. Morrissey attended the show. Approaching me, he remarked, "Very nice show." He skillfully avoided giving me direct credit.

"I was particularly impressed with *that* person who sang 'Coloring Book.' *That* voice was incredible!" He said attempting to distance himself from acknowledging my involvement.

"Mr. Morrissey, *that* was me," I answered, fully expecting him to retract the compliment. However, he stood speechless, failing to respond but quickly steering the conversation elsewhere.

The next day, I drove Sandra to the airport. Her flight had been delayed by Cape Cod's infamous fog, giving us plenty of time to chat. As we talked, I shared that my parents had agreed to let me live in Boston, but only if I stayed on track as a pre-med student. Now that I was in the area, though, I was hoping to find more professional performing opportunities to support myself.

Sandra thought for a moment then recalled her agent in Boston, a man named Frank Soper, who ran Adams and Soper Talent Agency. While she made no promises, she encouraged me to reach out to him.

Sandra was now married to the renowned American industrial designer and graphic artist, Louis Nelson, and thriving as a ballet soloist performing at both Radio City Music Hall and the New York City Opera. Meanwhile, I was still grappling with my path, attending college. Our interactions continued to evoke a profound sense of satisfaction, leaving me wondering what this connection truly signified. The inexplicable chemistry between us remained profound. Neither of us was sure how to navigate this connection.

Boston: A Symphony

The prospect of complete independence, while theoretically exciting, also carried a certain intimidation. The University of Massachusetts, Boston Campus, located in Dorchester, was primarily a commuter college, lacking dormitories and consequently sorority or fraternity houses. By the time my junior year rolled around my parents had agreed to let me rent an apartment. I naturally assumed I'd be residing in Boston like most other students.

One Sunday, my parents decided to take two of my friends and me apartment hunting. Armed with a newspaper, a list of available housing from the college, and a map, we began our search.

The first apartment we looked at was housed in a typical brownstone building, with limited curbside appeal. What was once a stunning single-family residence had been divided into two apartments per floor. As we ascended the staircase, the environment shifted dramatically, reflecting a mix of cultures and generations. As we entered, the scent transformed from weed to urine and booze, akin to an old saloon. The odor brought back memories of my newspaper delivery days.

This particular building accommodated older men, many of whom were alcoholics. During the summer, they would leave their doors open to allow air circulation, releasing a stench of urine and aged alcohol. The apartment for rent occupied the first floor and was equally uninspiring, with peeling paint on the walls and ceilings, a solitary lightbulb dangling from the ceiling socket where a grand chandelier had hung once. Despite its current state, I could envision its potential after a thorough cleaning and fresh coat of paint. However, the experience was marred by the shrieking and door-slamming emanating from the unit above us. In a sudden change of course, my mother led us back to the car.

"Mom, this is just how students live!"

I tried to convince her that this was a viable option. After some discussions and light-hearted jokes about the apartment, my father pulled out a map and located the college.

"Okay, here's the college. Instead of looking on this side, let's consider the other side."

Dorchester and Quincy Bay separated the college from land. The first and closest area was North Quincy.

"Look, here's an apartment!" my dad said. "Studio apartment, off Wollaston Beach, swimming pool and tennis court, laundry facilities."

We drove past the campus and onto Quincy Shore Drive, a picturesque beachfront stretch. We arrived at a complex of four buildings encircling a pool. Each building boasted designated parking spots. The property manager, Mrs. Sullivan, a statuesque Jewish woman, took charge of our interaction. Following introductions, my mother took the reins, as was her custom when she wanted things done.

"Mrs. Sullivan, I understand you have a studio apartment available."

Without hesitation, Mrs. Sullivan grabbed a set of keys and guided us to see the apartment, describing the complex's ambiance, tranquility, amenities, and charm as we crossed the courtyard. The studio apartment was on the first floor. With no patio, it featured a window roughly the width of the apartment. The parquet floors were a light maple color, the walls a classic off-white, and there was a small corner kitchen and a standard-sized bathroom.

"The rent is $230 a month," Mrs. Sullivan stated.

"We'll take it! It's perfect for my son."

Mrs. Sullivan's expression underwent a swift transformation.

"Oh, I apologize, Mrs. Boucher, I wasn't aware you were looking for your son. I assume Ron is a student, and we do not rent to students. You should consider student housing so he can be around his peers. Our complex caters to Boston's business community."

If my mother had been wearing heels that day, you would have heard them puncturing the wood flooring as she stood her ground with unwavering conviction.

"Mrs. Sullivan, my son is no ordinary student and certainly is not attending college for leisure and socializing. Ron is a pre-med student and a performer with a beautiful voice. He doesn't want the distractions of being around other students. As his mother, I will rest much easier knowing he's in a secure and nurturing environment. Mrs. Sullivan, you must rent this apartment to us!"

Mrs. Sullivan's stance softened slightly as she pondered the proposal.

"What kind of music do you sing?"

Interrupting before I could respond, my mother chimed in,

"Ron sang for Miss America a couple of years ago, and he had the lead in the last two musicals he performed in."

Despite her reservations, Mrs. Sullivan took a leap of faith and decided to rent it to me. My parents signed a one-year lease. As of August 1st, 1975, my new residence was 1 Canton Road, North Quincy, Massachusetts.

My apartment was the first on the left upon entering the lobby. From the beginning of the summer, we had accumulated used furniture including two end tables, a coffee table, and an antique dry sink that used to house a washbasin and water pitcher. I lacquered all four pieces in black and adorned them with red/orange Chinese decals. I already owned a two-tiered organ gifted by my grandmother a few years earlier. Since it was a studio apartment, we decided to invest in a convertible couch as the sole new piece of furniture. Mom's stipulation was that the couch should only convert into a single bed, discouraging any sleepovers. Adjacent to the kitchen area, we found a small used round table and two chairs. To let my grandmother feel involved, we provided her with the measurements, and she sewed curtains that echoed the orange and red tones of the decals. In the center of the room sat a sizable sunburst round carpet.

Mrs. Sullivan was so impressed that she asked if she could occasionally show my apartment to prospective clients who wanted to see an example unit. Naturally, she'd seek my advance permission before doing so.

Shortly after moving in, I struck up a friendship with an elderly Jewish lady, Mrs. Sally Maisel, who resided in the apartment next to the lobby entrance. She became acquainted with me after overhearing my singing. Occasionally, she'd knock on my door, carrying a container of her homemade chicken soup. She'd always say, "Please don't let me interrupt your practice."

I'd offer, "Sally, would you like to sit, have a cup of tea, and listen while I practice?"

This, of course, was the modus operandi behind the chicken soup.

To incentivize me to visit home on weekends, my dad allowed me access to his charge account at a local grocery store. I could stock up on all the food I needed for the week. If I returned home on weekends, I had a week's worth of free groceries.

It didn't take long after the fall semester began for me to notice a cute blond in my Abnormal Psychology class. I mustered the courage to invite her over for dinner. She was one of those students who lived in the type of apartment my mother would never approve of in Boston. Consequently, her commute was in the opposite direction of mine. She insisted on using the Red Line and walking a few blocks to my complex. I went out of my way to create a romantic ambiance. Soft lighting, music, fresh-cut flowers adorned the table, and I had baked chicken roasting in the oven with sides of roasted potatoes and fresh string beans. I remember it distinctly because it was the only meal I could prepare at that time which met acceptable standards for company.

My expectations didn't quite match reality. Instead of being impressed with the apartment, she seemed irritated, thinking I might be a privileged rich kid receiving everything on a silver platter. She didn't realize that I had worked full-time for two years to save for these final years of college.

You know those dates where everything you say is misinterpreted, intentionally? This was one of them. She didn't even want to try my renowned angel food cake, a recipe my grandmother had taught me, featuring a center of strawberries and Jell-O topped with whipped cream and cling peaches. She grumbled about how students shouldn't be living like this, with a pool and tennis court at their disposal. What particularly irked her was that I paid less rent than she did for her apartment. She hadn't even finished her meal before she slammed down her fork, declared the whole thing a mistake, grabbed her backpack, and walked out. I ended up knocking on Sally's door, inviting my appreciative neighbor in for coffee, cake, and a little serenade.

Adams & Soper Agency: The Agents Aria

Soon after settling into my new apartment and establishing my school routine, I realized the need for some cash to cover my day-to-day expenses without relying on my parents. Following Sandra's suggestion, I looked up the Adams and Soper Talent Agency and hopped on the Red Line to Boylston Street. The agency's convenient location on the second floor above Carl Fischer Music made acquiring sheet music a breeze. Climbing the imposing stairwell, I reached a glass door at the landing, leading to their office. The room was a vast expanse adorned with headshots of performers, undoubtedly their clients. The photos exuded vintage charm, with only a few showcasing a contemporary look.

"Can I help you, young man?" The man behind the desk spoke with a cigar dangling from his fingers, barely raising his gaze.

"Are you Mr. Soper? I'm here to see Mr. Soper!" I said, trying to project a bit of confidence.

"No," he said. Then he pointed towards the other end of the room. "That's Mr. Soper!"

Making my way briskly, I reached his desk and was met by an old vaudevillian agent. His desk was buried under piles of papers, and metal file cabinets surrounded him like a fortress.

"What do you want?" he gruffly asked.

"I understand you hire singers, and I would like to—"

He cut me off with, "I don't need a singer, sorry kid!"

My enthusiasm deflated instantly. I thanked him and apologized for the assumption, ready to head for the door. Just as I was about to touch the doorknob, Mr. Soper asked, "Hey kid! Who the hell sent you here anyway?"

Despite my lingering disappointment, I turned and said, "Sandra Balestracci."

Now with my hand on the door I heard, "Sandra Balestracci? My Sandy? How do you know my Sandy? Come here, kid, sit down!"

I settled into a seat in front of his desk, watching as his face lit up with an obvious fondness for Sandra.

"Let me tell you about my Sandy. That girl can dance!" He launched into a twenty-minute monologue about his Sandy, sharing booking stories and showing me publicity pictures.

"Mr. Soper, thank you for your time, but I have another appointment to attend," I said, attempting to excuse myself.

"So, kid, what are you doing on Monday around 7 p.m.?"

As I stood up to leave, I replied, "Nothing at the moment. I haven't received—"

He cut me off again. "Good. I want you to come to this address and bring two songs. Don't worry, the band can play anything you give them. All my singers must perform for my boys, and if they like you, I'll be your agent."

What just happened? This was an unexpected twist. It seemed his "Sandy" had left a profound impression, putting him in an exceptionally good mood. But what did he mean by "his boys"?

On Monday night, dressed in my notable white leisure suit, red and white polyester shirt, and white patent leather shoes, I located the address he had provided. For a moment, I wondered if I had the wrong address. Right before me was a Veterans Hospital. Surely Mr. Soper had given me the wrong address. However, I noticed the sign indicating the direction to the theater, and made my way. Once inside, I quickly surveyed the compact stage with seating accommodating around 150 people. The ten-piece band had already set up, and there was a comedian, a juggler, or a magician. Mr. Soper greeted me at the entrance, instructing me to hand my music to the pianist, who would go through it with me. He told me I would perform right after the comedian introduced me. The room buzzed with veterans and their family members. Wheelchairs lined the sides and back, occupied by men with a variety of injuries and emotional scars.

The show began with the comedian sharing jokes in the styles of George Burns, Groucho Marx, Milton Burl, Red Skelton, and others. I was too nervous to gauge the audience's response to his humor. There was applause and then the moment came.

"We have a new talent for you tonight. Ronnie Boucher is from New Bedford, sung for Miss America, and performed in musical theater shows. Let's give Ronnie a big hand!"

I entered as the applause waned and my song's intro began. An instinct I had developed at an early age was the ability to gauge the audience. The upbeat tempo connected instantly, and I could feel the audience's positive energy. The sound of rhythmic snapping filled the air. Before I could finish my last note, the applause started, and the show seamlessly transitioned to the next act.

I returned for my final number. My rendition of "The Impossible Dream" typically pleased the crowd. If people didn't remember my name, they referred to me as "the kid in the white suit with the big voice!" Once again, the audience exploded with applause. As I stepped off stage, Mr. Soper was waiting in the wings.

"My Sandy was right; you can sing Kid! But next time you perform for my boys, maybe consider a different up-tempo song. The first Wednesday of the month is payday, so come back in two weeks. If I have another gig for you, I'll give you a call."

The phone was ringing when I reached my apartment at around 10 p.m. It was my dad.

"So, how did it go? Where is this place, and what did Mr. Soper mean by *his boys*?"

Excitedly, I recounted that the performance was at a Veteran's Hospital with a theater where Mr. Soper entertained military veterans once a month —his boys. Evidently, Mr. Soper was also a vet himself, and he liked my singing and wanted to book me for gigs.

"And do you get paid?" my dad asked.

Reassuring him that I was getting paid, he sounded thrilled and relieved.

Now living in Boston, I seemed to have more time. I could focus on pursuing performing opportunities. U-Mass was staging the musical *Once Upon a Mattress*, and I landed the role of Sir Harry. The director had been a theater major and an alumnus. I invited Mr. Soper to the performance, and afterwards, he expressed interest in helping me secure roles in musicals.

Shortly afterward, I received a call from Mr. Soper.

"Hey Ronnie, it's Frank. I think I've got a spot for you in the cast of *A Funny Thing Happened on the Way to the Forum*, at a dinner theater in Nassau, New Hampshire. It's about an hour's drive from where you live."

I drove up to the theater for the audition on Saturday morning. Rehearsals were already underway, but they needed someone for the role of a Protean. The director felt I was a perfect fit and asked me to start immediately. During my visit, I spotted my college director, who now had the leading role of Hero. He was pleased that I had joined the cast, especially since I had a car, and he didn't.

On our drive back to Boston he asked in a perturbed tone, "How the hell did you manage to get an agent?"

The production ran for about three months, with performances on Thursdays, Fridays, Saturday matinees and evenings, and Sunday matinees. Comedian Jerry Vicchi played the role of Pseudolus. Jerry was a consummate professional—dedicated, reliable, and always on point with his lines and comic timing. For one Saturday evening performance, it was past sign-in time, and Jerry hadn't arrived. With the curtain set for 8 p.m. and already nearing 7:30 p.m., panic set in among the cast. What would we do without Jerry? No one could cover his role, and the director hadn't prepared for such an eventuality due to Jerry's consistent reliability. By 7:50, after several failed attempts to reach Jerry by phone, the director decided that he would have to inform the audience. Then, as the backstage door swung open, Jerry hurried in, requesting the show be delayed by ten minutes.

He turned to us, his fellow cast members, and said, "My friends, I apologize, but it's been a difficult day. My father passed away this afternoon."

Jerry assured us that he would go on with the performance—what his father would have wanted.

That night, I learned a profound lesson from Jerry. His comedic timing that evening was more impeccable and hilarious than ever before. It was so funny that I struggled to maintain my character, succumbing to laughter, as did the rest of the cast. Jerry's actions taught me the incredible resilience and professionalism a true artist can muster even when facing personal loss.

Little did I know that I would have to draw from that lesson in the years to come.

Radio City Music Hall: A NYC Harmony

During the festive Christmas season, I received an invitation from Gladys (Sandra's mother) to join her and Ms. Cheryl on a trip to New York City. The allure of NYC and the chance to see Sandra were an irresistible combination. As I ventured into the heart of the Big Apple, I fully embraced my inner tourist, reminiscent of Will Parker exploring the bustling streets of Kansas City in the musical *Oklahoma!*

Although I suppose I knew Sandra was married, that fact somehow wasn't fully registered. I was about to face this reality directly. At her building, we were warmly welcomed by the doorman who directed us to the elevators. After a brief ride, we emerged into a hallway that had the elegance of a high-end hotel.

As the grey metal door to their apartment opened, Sandra's warm smile invited us into a very contemporary interior furnished with furniture that Louis had designed. Louis, exuding charisma and reflecting a strong impression of success, greeted us.

Soon priorities took hold, and it was time to leave. Louis had to get back to work, and Sandra offered to give us a personal tour of the grandeur of Radio City Music Hall. Dressed for the brisk winter in NYC, Louis wore his long cashmere camel-colored coat. Sandra stepped out in a cropped fur jacket, gaucho pants, and high-heeled boots.

As we headed through the Lincoln Tower complex, there was a moment I mentally captured—like a Kodak still—Sandra holding on to Louis's arm, her head resting against it. One might have interpreted it as love, I on the other hand saw it as a sense of security. Louis was taking care of her; he was her pillar of strength. Together, they drew on that bond as they pursued their ambitions—he and she were driven with the passion of their careers.

Sandra set the bar for the kind of woman I hoped to be with one day, and Louis set the standard for the kind of man worthy of such a remarkable woman. Not knowing much about love, I assumed that someone like Sandra would only take me seriously if I had something substantial to offer. My drive for success was ignited that day, but my intentions were not focused in any way on being the "man" in Sandra's life. I felt honored, blessed, and satisfied with the connection we shared.

Arriving at the stage door on 50th street, everyone from the doorman onward recognized Sandra, treating her with the utmost respect, shown with the same nod you see in movies as noblemen pass by, and admiration, shown with smiles and warm greetings as we strolled down the corridors. She introduced us to her dressing room, the expansive main rehearsal hall, and finally the awe-inspiring stage.

The stage is a marvel of design, divided into three distinct sections, with a fourth area dedicated to the orchestra. Each section rests on hydraulic-powered elevators, allowing it to rise, fall, and transform at a moment's notice. This intricate layout and sophisticated technology allows for seamless set changes and breathtaking effects that have captivated audiences for years. The stage even features a rotating floor, adding yet another layer of versatility to the performances. Hidden beneath it all is a massive hydraulic system, powering the mesmerizing movements that brought every production to life.

Everyone was hustling in preparation for the show that was about to start. It was the annual Christmas show, which included the nostalgic Rockettes "Dance of the Soldiers" and the "Living Nativity" with live animals. Sandra escorted us quickly, and as I stepped onto the stage, I could picture myself performing on it, singing to the thousands who attended the multiple daily shows.

Back in her dressing room, Sandra prepared herself for rehearsal which was for the next production after the Christmas show ended. Returning to the stage, we were just in time for the Nativity scene. Positioning us in a non-invasive location, I was able to watch the incredible transitioning of motorized set pieces and elevated stage levels as sets and cast members rose and fell like the ocean waves in a turbulent sea storm.

Although the weekend was fleeting, the music hall had cast a spell on me —the heady mix of fascination and ambition that lingered long after I'd left its embrace. This wasn't just a hunger for career possibilities; it was a deep-seated drive, an obsession to reach the heights I'd glimpsed.

Back in college, life fell into a strict rhythm: early morning classes, preparation for taking my MCAT's, a seven-hour exam like that of college SAT's. That score would determine if I would be able to apply to McGill University in Montreal, a recommendation by my cousin, Dr. Yvone Boucher, Guy's brother. From Thursday to Sunday I was performing in *A Funny Thing Happened on the Way to the Forum*. When not on stage, I sat in the wings with my MCAT prep study guide, earning me the nick name "Doc." My visions of New York seemed sharper, like I was inching closer to that impossible dream I had set my sights on.

As luck would have it, my grandmother asked if I could drive her to New Jersey to visit my Aunt Ida—grandma's sister-in-law, whom I'd always liked. Aunt Ida had been widowed for years but had remained strong, supporting herself with a small business making wedding favors. I had fond memories of her, and on more than one occasion, she took me into New York City from Linden, taking the train to Penn Station, a quick 36-minute ride, give or take a few. It was a trip I could easily manage on my own. Grandma and Aunt Ida settled on a weekend for the visit, and as soon as plans were made, I called Sandra. I wanted to let her know I'd be in town and see if she'd be teaching while I was there.

There I was, back in the grand city of New York, and let's be honest—it wasn't just the city I was after, but the chance to see Sandra again. I casually mentioned to her that I was thinking of taking a ballet class, knowing full well that she'd be teaching at Carnegie Hall that evening. Of course, I didn't exactly have the right attire for such an endeavor. No problem, though! A quick detour to Capezio's on Broadway, and I was ready to commit to my little performance. There, I picked up my very first dance belt (a bit of a revelation, let me tell you), a pair of tights, and ballet slippers. Fully equipped and ready to fake it 'til I made it, I was all set to charm the ballet world—one pirouette at a time.

Just like my audition in New Bedford, Sandra remained steadfast in her role as a mentor, though my antics that evening nearly coaxed a smile from her. After class, we crossed the street from Carnegie Hall to a cozy café inside the Statler Hilton, where coffee and conversation flowed. She started with a question that seemed to hang in the air, tinged with both curiosity and concern.

"Ron, are you seriously committed to pursuing medical school?"

Her eyes searched mine with a quiet intensity. I didn't hesitate. "Honestly, medicine isn't my focus anymore. I want to perform. I can't deny it any longer."

Sandra's expression held no hint of approval or disapproval—only a simple acknowledgment, as if confirming something she'd long suspected. She paused, then began an honest assessment of my talents.

"Your dancing is commendable, but without disciplined training, you'd face fierce competition here. Many young men in New York are already far more advanced. But your voice… it's remarkable, though I'm not an expert on vocals."

Her words lingered in my mind, amplifying the pressure I felt to make a clear decision. I'd already secured early acceptance to McGill University's medical program, but if I let that go, I needed a viable path forward. Just as my thoughts were racing, Sandra offered a lifeline.

"I could reach out to a friend at Radio City and see if he'd be willing to meet with you. If he's interested, would you go?"

I couldn't hold back my excitement. "Absolutely—without question."

Her face softened, yet suddenly grew somber, as if something deeper had come to mind. She hesitated, studying her coffee, and then spoke in a calm tone that was almost surreal.

"Louis and I are separating."

Had I heard her right? Why was she telling me this now? I could hardly believe it, but her words hinted at something unspoken between us, a sense that perhaps we were bound by more than teacher and student. I wanted to explore this moment, to say something that might open that door. But my train departure was approaching, and I had a 23-block walk to Penn Station to get back to Aunt Ida's.

My entire trip to Aunt Ida's and again to New Bedford focused on two things; the possibility of performing in the Big Apple and the fact that Sandra's separation from Louis created a new dynamic between us. The question now was, which one was going to be my priority, Sandra or my career? Intellectually, I knew that unless Sandra saw that I was focused on my career, I could not earn favor with her.

My First Professional Headshot

True to her word, Sandra had arranged for me to audition for Will Irwin, the musical director at Radio City Music Hall. Aunt Ida was only too happy to host me once more, learning about my audition. I had been under the assumption that Sandra would be personally introducing me to Mr. Irwin. However, her own commitments with rehearsals at the NYC Opera kept her from accompanying me.

I reached the music hall half an hour before my scheduled audition, my mind wrestling with the choice of which song to perform for Mr. Irwin. I knew my selection had to be strategic, considering the caliber of singers I'd heard at Radio City—all possessing legitimately trained voices, not necessarily operatic, but strong and richly textured. When Mr. Irwin arrived, I was escorted to his office.

"Sandra mentioned you're quite the singer; I suppose we are about to find out if that's true. I've auditioned some pretty good singers," he remarked. I couldn't discern if he was attempting to unnerve me. His statement was slightly intimidating.

"So, young man, what will you impress me with?"

Retrieving the sheet music for "I'll Walk with God" from *The Student Prince* from my bag, I presented it to Mr. Irwin.

Placing the music on the piano, he commented, "Mario Lanza—do you think you can live up to his reputation with this song?"

Nodding in acknowledgement, I positioned myself by the piano. Mr. Irwin played the intro in rhythm; I drew my first breath and began to sing. As the melody flowed, I observed Mr. Irwin's expression shifting from mild curiosity to unmistakable surprise. As I crescendo to the final, resounding note, his eyebrows arched in astonishment. The moment of truth arrived.

"Ron, you possess an exceptionally beautiful voice, far more powerful than I anticipated given your slight frame. I expected a high lyric tenor, but instead, I was treated to the resonance of a baritone with the range of a tenor. Bravo! Very well sung, young man."

And then came the moment that would shape my future. "Are you available in July? I could use you for our summer run."

Mr. Irwin was simply casting his show and was impressed by my voice. Unbeknownst and irrelevant to him was the fact that I was a college student who, until very recently, had plans to attend medical school.

"Absolutely, Mr. Irwin!" I responded, fighting back my excitement and maintaining my composure.

He provided details about the contract, which would be finalized in the first week of June, with rehearsals to begin immediately thereafter.

That evening, I met Sandra again at the same café. She shared in my joy of the results of my audition, yet I could tell something weighed heavily on her mind. As we spoke, her words began to drift, growing faint and distant as my thoughts swirled with possibilities. In an instant, Pandora's Box had been flung open.

"So, you'll need a place to stay!" she interjected, snapping me back to the present. Do you know Bobby Amaral? He used to be one of my students at my New Bedford studio. He's here in New York. Let me reach out to him."

Could this strange turn of events truly be unfolding?

CHAPTER 5 NEW YORK

June is Bustin' Out: A Musical Jubilee

Significant decisions such as whether to go to medical school or pursue a career of uncertainty are accompanied by their own set of benefits and repercussions. One must weigh whether the benefits outweigh the consequences before cementing a choice. Nevertheless, the wheels had been set in motion with the decision to forego my career in medicine.

For me it was a non-painful long-distance phone call to the admission office. There was no hesitation, no second questioning if I was making the right decision. I was informed that my decline meant that I could not re-apply. I just assumed that my cousin Yvonne had something to do with my acceptance. The die was cast, guiding me southward to the vibrant expanse of the Big Apple—the place of aspirations and dreams, where I could truly be myself.

Mom resorted to old manipulations like those attempted in high school. My father just seemed to give up with a look of disgust. Despite the protests from my parents, they eventually relented and opted to accompany me to my new abode on the West Side of NYC.

A splendid Sunday morning marked the commencement of our four-hour drive from New Bedford. Uncharacteristically silent, my mother's lack of chatter during the drive enabled me to indulge in vivid fantasies about my impending future. Such moments of naivety indeed have their blessings, for had I foreseen the challenges, I might have instructed my parents to turn back and return me to New Bedford. My anticipation soared as we navigated the West End Highway and Riverside Drive. Upon our arrival, we located the building, nestled on the southern side of 98th Street between West End Avenue and Riverside—a central spot on the block.

The first obstacle emerged in the form of parking—a challenge in a city that seemed to thrive on such difficulties. Double-parking already had my father on edge, fearing his car might be towed, however, the situation left him no alternative.

The apartment, positioned slightly below street level on the first floor, greeted us with a black wrought-iron gate and a weathered brownstone façade that yearned for vigorous power washing, much like many parts of NYC during the 1970s. A few moments after ringing the doorbell, a petite girl with cropped, curly hair emerged.

"Hi, I'm Elaine, and you must be Ron, our new summer roommate!"

With this simple statement, she ushered us inside. A dim passageway unveiled a bedroom to the right, with a mattress sprawled on the floor and clothing strewn about. At the end, the dark corridor opened up to a spacious living room, revealing a large, barred window overlooking a small courtyard—a space that was both inaccessible and neglected. The kitchen area lined the left wall, its dark brown paint only minimally concealing the scuttling roaches along the sink's rear. Further along, past the living room and hugging the left perimeter of the dwelling, stretched a lengthy, narrow corridor leading to a bathroom and two bedrooms. My room lay sandwiched between the bathroom and the third bedroom.

"This is your bedroom!" Elaine spoke in a matter of fact tone.

The space was decidedly smaller than a college dormitory room. Adjacent to the door sat a twin bed, leaving a mere four feet to the window, which boasted a portable air conditioner, a feature that prevented its opening for a breath of fresh air—a redundancy in the tightly sealed spaces of NYC.

As we unloaded the car, my mother remained uncharacteristically quiet, while observing her surroundings. She restrained herself from her motherly impulse to whip out cleaning products and commence scrubbing. I was certain she was also considering staging a dramatic rescue mission, grabbing my suitcase and me by the arm and returning me to New Bedford. I was finally experiencing the quintessential college student living conditions Mom had prevented by finding the housing at the Quincy Commons Apartments while I attended U-Mass.

With my belongings now situated in my room, Elaine handed me a set of keys, and my parents and I ventured to Sandra's residence down West End Avenue. The distinction between the blocks was immediately evident as we approached Sandra's building—a high-rise apartment complex graced with a u-shaped driveway at its entrance. As we pulled up, a doorman named Karl, resplendent in his brown uniform, welcomed us, gallantly opening our car doors. He offered guidance to my father on where to park the vehicle, and with that settled, he buzzed Sandra's apartment.

"Miss Sandra, your guests have arrived!" Karl announced, pointing us toward the elevators with instructions to reach apartment 17E.

Reaching our destined floor, Sandra stood in the doorway of her apartment, greeting us with warmth. We stepped into her sunlit studio apartment, where the freshly painted eggshell walls reflected radiance against the chestnut parquet flooring. A single modular camel-brown leather couch, a remnant from her apartment with Louis, occupied the room, along with a butcher block maple finished table surrounded by five matching wicker-backed folding chairs. A galley kitchen extended to the left, featuring grey metal cabinets, while a sizable walk-in closet was positioned to the right. The entire width of the apartment encompassed six sets of windows draped with floor-to-ceiling panels of off-white transparent weave material. These curtains, suspended from ceiling to floor with silver metal rods, cast an ethereal glow over the space. The apartment followed an L-shaped layout, culminating in an alcove where a frameless queen-sized bed lay on the floor, flanked by a nightstand to the left. Two additional broad panels before the bed created a sense of partition, introducing a captivating boudoir element to the apartment. A petite bathroom, typical of NYC proportions, was situated just off the left side of the bed—an area my mother promptly requested permission to use. The apartment overlooked the complex's central courtyard, surrounded by the other structures constituting the Lincoln Towers.

This gleam of hope provided my parents some consolation. In their minds, if my path proved successful, I could eventually live in a similar fashion. Our visit with Sandra was relatively brief, as her rehearsal commitments beckoned. The conventional notion of a "nine-to-five" existence was nonexistent for performing artists. Following a dinner outing, my parents drove me back up to 98th Street before embarking on their journey back to New Bedford.

My mother's parting words lingered in the air: "I can't believe you're willing to embrace this lifestyle after everything you've had."

Freedom, independence, the allure of New York City—what more could one ask for? Returning to the apartment, my excitement compelled me to unpack and organize my meager belongings. Unable to find a place for my sunburst rug within my room, Elaine offered a spot on the bare living room floor.

Elaine, a vivacious singer and dancer, had an air of importance about her. She often highlighted her Jewish heritage, both in appearance and manner, concerned about how it might impact her artistic career. My understanding of religious, ethnic, and sexual identity was rudimentary at best. These notions had little bearing on my cognitive landscape. To me, everyone was an individual, evaluated on my personal interactions with them. This day marked my official entry into the grand city, and I had ample time to be exposed to new perspectives.

My other roommate, Harry, introduced himself upon his return home. In his mid-20s, he possessed sandy blond, chin-length, curly hair. An aspiring actor, he exuded a self-centered aura, displaying no interest in acknowledging my presence or acknowledging that we'd be sharing the apartment. He did, however, impart the rule of labeling food and the caveat that unlabeled items were free for anyone to consume. His girlfriend's arrival prompted their retreat into his room, which was swiftly followed by the same from Elaine and her boyfriend. The paper-thin walls left nothing to the imagination, each room's activities broadcast audibly. As everyone pursued their amorous passions, I sought my own distractions, yet without the comfort of television or radio to occupy my mind.

The subsequent morning saw Harry and the other man departing for work, leaving Elaine and me alone in the apartment. Clad in a silk nightgown, her presence evoked a casual sensuality enhanced by a flowing silk kimono robe. It was apparent that I was no longer a guest; the omission of a breakfast invitation underscored the point. She confided in me that she envied my entry into NYC with a prestigious position as a soloist at Radio City Music Hall. The phone rang, stationed oddly in my room, prompting Elaine to answer.

"That was my temp agency. They've assigned me a job starting at 1 p.m., so I must get ready!" She then hurried into the bathroom.

Meanwhile, I was scheduled to spend the day with Sandra. I met her at her apartment. She was already dressed in leotard and tights, a silk skirt draped over her, preparing her dance bag, placing ballet slippers and pointe shoes inside. We dashed out of her apartment and headed to a dance studio around 77th Street on Broadway, where she was attending a class with Finis Jung.

As I settled along the far wall near the door, Sandra joined the other dancers in performing pliés with an exquisite port de bras. Midway through, Finis halted the class, instructing everyone to observe Sandra as she executed her pliés with an unmatched expertise, dancing the exercise with her entire being. While I attributed her excellence to my infatuation, Mr. Jung's admiration could have been equally genuine, or perhaps she was truly exceptional.

After class, we headed down to Canal Street. Lost in the moment, I followed Sandra blindly, arriving at the 72nd subway station just as a train pulled in.

"This is the express. We can take it to Chambers Street and then walk to Canal."

Her familiarity with the city was apparent. Lost in my anticipation of spending time with Sandra, I barely noticed the discomfort in my feet that was beginning to settle in.

Back at Sandra's apartment, we settled in for a simple dinner—likely chicken and broccoli, a meal that felt healthy and modern before "Keto" was even a thing. We ate quickly, both electrified by what lay ahead. Sandra had just learned she'd be performing in the summer show, and the thought of sharing that world with her felt like something out of a dream. We had arranged to go to Radio City together to sign our contracts, a milestone that seemed almost unreal.

After dinner, we washed the dishes side by side, drying each one and stowing it carefully in the grey metal cabinets that lined her galley-style kitchenette. Sandra showed me a few of her city-living tricks: always keep the sink dry and seal open food packages in plastic bags to avoid roaches. There, in that tiny kitchen, even the most mundane tasks felt charged with anticipation. It was time for me to head back to my apartment, a walk to 98th Street, a thirty-block hike, that I used to reflect, absorb, and appreciate the luck that had been bestowed upon me.

The next morning Sandra received a phone call from Radio City Music Hall that changed everything. She called me immediately with the news.

"Ron, I just received a call from Radio City. They won't be signing any contracts this morning due to a potential Rockettes strike!"

She encouraged me to remain optimistic. The concept of a strike seemed temporary, a minor inconvenience that would be resolved within a day or two. After all, countless individuals depended on Radio City Music Hall for their livelihoods. A strike would be detrimental for everyone involved. But my debut at Radio City Music Hall couldn't be compromised, right?

"Ron, why don't you come by later for dinner?"

Although this affected both of us, Sandra still had income from teaching and many guesting opportunities. I, on the other hand, was—unexpectedly without work. The hope that this was just a temporary setback lingered in the air, even as doubt crept in. My conversation with my parents didn't yield any consolation. My mother, quick to seize on any sign, believed this to be a definitive signal.

"This is a message. You need to come back home. We'll find a way for you to go back to school. If only you had stuck to your plan of going to med school."

I ignored her words. My world had been shattered, and the possibility that she might be right only heightened the devastation.

Sandra overheard my conversations with my mother and sat me down offering her own advice and perspective on my situation.

"You have to decide now if you're in this for the long haul. If you are, then you have to chalk this up to one of those opportunities that didn't pan out because something better is waiting!" she said with conviction.

Something better? Better than Radio City Music Hall? Broadway, perhaps?

"You should get a copy of Backstage and start attending auditions," she advised. "So, when was the last time you took a ballet class?"

I admitted that my last class with her had been a few months earlier, and during that session, she pointed out that my form as a dancer was lacking —and that my skills had noticeably atrophied.

"I'm teaching at Carnegie Hall tomorrow at six if you want to come."

The next day, I spent hours poring over *Backstage*, focusing mainly on the audition section. In this business, being able to respond quickly to messages was essential. I had two options: an answering service, with 24-hour attendants who provided that personal, friendly touch, or a machine. Elaine preferred the service, while Sandra used a machine. I decided to go with the answering service. I still had my headshots and resumes from my time in Boston, which would have to suffice for now.

Summer's heat was in full swing when I arrived at Carnegie Hall where Sandra taught at the renowned Christine Neubert Children's Theater studios on the third floor. This institution provided training to young dancers from New York families, many of whom were involved in Broadway productions. During a conversation with Ms. Neubert, she introduced me to a young boy named Macaulay Culkin, later famous for his role in *Home Alone*, who was currently filming *The Nutcracker* movie with the New York City Ballet.

The boys, including me, changed in a communal bathroom shared by the suites on the floor. The tight quarters left us cheek to cheek as we rushed to dress. The other guys, more accustomed to the routine, quickly donned their attire. Still awkward with the intricacies of adjusting a dance belt, I struggled to find a comfortable fit.

"You might want to hurry a bit" a fellow dancer named Robert explained as he quickly was putting on his leg warmers.

"We have ten minutes before class, what's the rush?" I said, confused by his urgency.

His reply was sharp, "I know, but you want enough time to stretch before class."

Ah, stretching—the bane of my existence. My hamstrings were infamously tight, and my flexibility left much to be desired. However, I could jump and turn with unmatched prowess, and my charisma and stage presence were assets. I trusted Sandra's expertise to help me overcome my physical limitations and transform me into a professional dancer. Although my aspirations with Radio City Music Hall were put on hold, I now had time to pursue a long-held dream: partnering with the renowned Sandra Balestracci on stage.

To compensate for my, let's say, "unique" dance skills, I decided to lean into comedy. I channeled my inner Tim Conway, though, in truth, I looked far more like Lucy Ricardo in that episode where she disastrously attempts ballet. Like Lucy, flexibility was not my strong suit, and any stretch at the barre quickly turned into a full-body ordeal. I twisted, grimaced, and contorted myself into positions that barely resembled ballet, looking more like the Tin Man in the *Wizard of Oz* attempting to do yoga.

From the corner of my eye, I saw Sandra trying to keep her composure as the stern ballet mistress. But in the mirror, I caught the tiniest twitch at the corner of her mouth—a battle between laughter and professionalism. She quickly looked away, probably hoping I wouldn't notice, but the damage was done. For a brief, glorious moment, my accidental slapstick had cracked her serious ballet front.

Eager to improve my dance skills, I threw myself into as many classes as possible. With Sandra's teaching schedule inconsistent, due to her performance commitments, I sought out other instructors to fill the gaps. My short-term memory, however, posed a challenge—I relied heavily on others to guide me through sequences. But once I locked movements into my muscle memory, they stayed with me. I felt immense gratitude for the teachers who repeated their classes, giving me the chance to truly internalize the combination.

I managed to attend ballet classes three times a week at Neubert Ballet, learning from instructors including Steffan Hoff and a guest artist from Winnipeg Ballet who introduced me to "floor barre"—traditional ballet barre exercises performed lying on the floor, which was surprisingly effective for strengthening alignment. I also ventured into classes with David Howard and Willie Burmann at Steps on Broadway, but their styles didn't quite resonate with me.

Then Sandra introduced me to Mme. Darvash, a legendary Romanian teacher. From the moment I stepped into her class, I clicked with her approach—her focus on precision and artistry, which brought a whole new depth to my movements that felt almost *transformative.*

But it wasn't all smooth sailing. It wasn't long after I had began taking classes with Mme Darvash that I began working with the New York City Opera. After a full day of rehearsal, I was completely wiped. Once, I shuffled into Mme. Darvash's class, looking like a wet noodle in my pliés and tendus. She stopped the class mid-phrase, turned to me, and asked with that characteristic twinkle in her eye, "Ron, darling, are you tired?"

Not quite picking up on the unspoken message, I said, "Yes, Madame, we had a full—"

She interrupted me, waving her hand dramatically. "Oh, ok, Marie, give Ron his money back so he can go home and rest. He's a big opera star now!"

First of all, I'd never paid for class, so that was a bit of a mystery, but second —*message received*, loud and clear.

On another occasion, when I was dragging through class, Mme. Darvash would boost my energy by saying to the pianist, "Marie, play some opera music for Ron! He needs some inspiration!" And for some bizarre reason, it worked —my whole body would suddenly come to life.

Ron "Boucher"

Broadway Headshot by Alix Jeffry

The Millikin Breakfast Show: An Audition Aria

With substantially more classes under my dance belt, I felt much more prepared to audition as a dancer. *Backstage* listed the call for the *Milliken Breakfast Show*. I had heard many dancers discussing the audition, I knew this was an incredible opportunity. A few inquiries informed that Milliken, the textile giant, had been producing extravagant annual musicals for decades at the Waldorf-Astoria, launching each new season for their buyers and spending lavishly. From 1956 to 1980, the productions featured major stars including Ginger Rogers, Chita Rivera, Donald O'Connor, and Tommy Tune. The scale was Broadway-worthy and then some.

Excited but nervous, I arrived at the Shubert Theatre at noon where I had seen the musical *A Chorus Line* a few weeks prior. What greeted me was a line so long it felt like it had a life of its own, stretching from the stage entrance on West 44th, wrapping up 8th Avenue, around West 45th, and then curving back toward 7th. The plan was to admit 50 dancers at a time, so there was little to do but wait. Overhearing the other hopefuls chatting about Equity cards, I felt my heart sink. In my rush to audition, I'd overlooked that requirement entirely.

Just then, my mother's advice flashed through my mind: *Never wait in line.* Steering away from the queue, I positioned myself near the stage door, hoping to gather information about the audition's requirements for those without an Equity card. As the stage door swung open, I unexpectedly found myself swept up in the rush of dancers entering, and I was counted among the fifty selected participants. "Card!" the girl behind the desk demanded. Attempting to explain my situation, I barely got a word out before she instructed me to sign in and allowed me to proceed.

The fifty dancers were brought into a room and placed in one line. A man then walked down the line handpicking certain individuals and dismissing the rest.

"You, you, and you can go," the man said, respectfully dismissing the young hopeful candidates all vying for a change to first audition and then perform in this iconic industrial show.

"The rest of you stay and put your things over there," he said, pointing to a place in the wings on stage left.

To my surprise, I was one of the few who remained. Confused yet excited, I wondered why I'd been kept without a single dance move or note sung. The answer, as it turned out, was simple: typecasting. Chatting with someone who had been cut, he vented about auditions that left out important details—things like specific body types, hair colors, or ethnic traits that were often unspoken but crucial. For instance, the "ideal" Broadway look often meant being All-American: sandy hair, long legs, lean. Many young men in New York could slip effortlessly into this mold, often skimping on meals to stay lean enough.

As I thought about my own attributes—a lean build (check), slightly shorter legs in proportion to my long torso, and sandy blond hair (not)—it was clear I wasn't a perfect fit. But I quickly picked up on subtle hints hidden in casting calls. A listing that read "Dance Call: Men, 5'8"–6'2", blond hair, must be triple-threat" was a red flag that saved me from wasting time auditioning where I didn't match. Still, Sandra often reminded me that casting wasn't always rigid. She told me about an audition she'd had with Agnes de Mille for a revival of Oklahoma! at Lincoln Center. Though Sandra's dancing entranced de Mille, her assistant pointed out that Laurie was traditionally blonde. Despite the pushback, de Mille insisted on casting her, challenging the classic blond ingénue image.

Finally, my moment on stage arrived. As the lights blazed down, the audience faded from view, leaving only the buzz of anticipation. I felt the intensity of years of dedication, raw emotion, and sweat from all who had come before me, and I was determined to add my own voice to Broadway's story.

We were whittled down to thirty dancers, arranged in three lines of ten. I was placed in the third line. A woman onstage instructed us through a ballet combination, calling out a series of moves—tombé, pas de bourré, glissade, jeté, tour jete, cheneé across the floor. These steps were my strengths, and I felt a surge of confidence as I moved up to the second line —a small but hopeful sign. Halfway through, though, my foot hit a slight hole in the stage floor, causing me to stumble. I pushed forward, finishing the combination clumsily but determined. As the eliminations were announced, I braced myself for the inevitable cut.

"Would number 55 please stay and perform the combination again?" A voice spoke over the microphone.

That was me, number 55.

"Excuse me, it seemed you stumbled. Was there a problem?" the voice queried. The faceless voice echoed through the speakers that with the sound filled the theater.

"Yes, there's a crack in the floor, and my foot got caught..."

Before I could finish, a stagehand was directed to mark the floor with tape. Now at the forefront of the line, the voice requested,

"Again, please."

As we finished the combination, the man behind the voice appeared at the foot of the stage. Following a discussion with the dance mistress, he announced, "If we call your number, please stay for the jazz combo; if not, thank you for coming."

As numbers were called, I suddenly heard, "Number 55, would you please come to the front of the stage?"

The choreographer for the show was none other than the renowned Peter Gennaro, who later that year would choreograph *Annie*. He commented on the uniqueness of my dancing, noting that my upper body displayed skill while my lower half struggled to keep up. He recommended more technique lessons and inquired about my ballet instructor. Wanting to assure him of my commitment, I responded, "I'm primarily a singer, but I've started training with Sandra Balestracci."

His eyes brighten with recognition. "Oh, my goodness! Young man, if you study with Sandra all year, I will hire you for next year's show and please say hello for me!" He also suggested studying jazz at Luigi's, a directive I embraced. When I later shared my experience with Sandra, her surprise at the identity of the person I had auditioned for was evident. She revealed that Peter Gennaro had choreographed her *Charlie Chaplin Revue* at Radio City Music Hall, a production that had propelled her onto the front page of the Arts and Leisure section of the New York Times.

Day to Day Reality: A City Reel

My first humbling experience of living in New York City came when I ran out of clean clothes. Having zero concept of laundromats, I decided to improvise. In a stroke of genius, or desperation, I dumped all my clothes into the bathtub, added a hefty dose of soap, and filled it with water. Inspired by that classic Lucy episode where she stomps grapes, I hopped into the tub and used my feet as makeshift agitators, sloshing around for a good twenty minutes. Satisfied, I drained the tub, refilled it with fresh water, and rinsed everything by swishing my feet around some more, finally resorting to the handheld shower to finish the job.

After wringing out each piece with what little strength I had left, I arranged them on a drying rack in the middle of the living room. By the next day, everything was dry and ready for ironing, and I proudly declared myself set for another week. It was also the last time I attempted to play human washing machine.

When Sandra heard about my bathtub ballet, she nearly doubled over laughing and promptly invited me to bring my laundry over to her place. She revealed a hidden gem: her building's basement boasted about twenty washers and dryers, and around 10 p.m., the place was a ghost town. With Sandra's help, laundry night became a smooth, multi-machine affair instead of a tub-side adventure.

My finances were dwindling rapidly; I had been given only $500, with the expectation of earning money once I began working at Radio City Music Hall. Each time I left the apartment, I had to spend money on subways, food, jazz classes, and whatever else came up. By the end of the third week, panic set in as I realized I needed to earn money quickly. Rent was due in another week.

"Elaine, if you're not performing, how do you manage your expenses?" I asked, desperation clear in my voice.

"Oh, are you running low on funds?" she replied nonchalantly.

"Yes, I have about $100.00 left to my name."

"Well, the most popular job is, of course, waiting tables," Elaine said.

This immediately brought back memories of my one attempt at that kind of work when my dad had taken a job as a short-order cook at a local diner. I vowed never to be a waiter again.

Even though Elaine had mentioned her temp agency had called during a previous observation, I was still oblivious as what her job was about. "So, what do you do?" I asked, hoping for some spark of inspiration.

"Oh, I temp!" Elaine answered.

Having no idea what that meant, I eagerly awaited an explanation.

"I work for a temp agency that sends me out to offices as a receptionist or secretary. Can you type?"

Bingo! It seemed I had found a potential solution to my employment problem. "Yes, I can type 70 words per minute and handle most office tasks, except for shorthand."

Elaine was quite impressed and recommended that I visit her agency and sign up. She instructed me to go around 11 a.m., after the morning rush of sending workers to early clients. At the agency, I filled out the standard application with my job experience, followed by a typing test on an IBM Selectric typewriter. I was among five test-takers, anxiously awaiting the results.

As I sat in the waiting room, I watched the receptionist score the tests and call the first two applicants to her desk, only to reject them based on their timing scores and error counts. Anything under 40 words per minute was unacceptable, and three or more errors, regardless of speed, led to rejection.

As the third person was being called up to the reception desk, an interior door swung open, and a woman called out, "Ron Boucher!"

Nervously, I entered her office and sat facing her desk.

She glanced at my test and said, "Well, we have a little speed demon here. You typed 73 words per minute with only one error."

I was elated to learn that adrenaline had motivated my fingers after months of not typing.

Then, she made me a proposal. "You see, we're a rapidly growing company and we're looking for someone we can send out to new clients who can make a great first impression. However, if the assignment lasts a week, you must be able to commit to it. Can you do that?"

With no other job prospects on the horizon, I accepted the offer. My first week-long assignment was at Standard Chartered Bank near Wall Street. I counted up my cash and I had enough money to take the subway downtown, skip lunch and walk back home with a stop at Sandra's apartment in the hope of a free dinner. I dressed in polyester flared pants and a fitted open-collared shirt, but my journey began with a mishap as I stepped into dog feces. No shit!

Arriving in time, I found a tremendous contrast from the sweltering heat and the stifling subway ride to the frigid temperature of the office. I window shopped for the duration of my lunch hour, to distract me from focusing on my hunger pangs. At 5 p.m., I began my long trek back to 98th Street. I repeated this every day that week earning blisters on my feet that hurt so badly, I couldn't take class.

The following Wednesday was payday, when I collected my first paycheck. Because of the praises I had received for my services from the bank, the agency quickly sent me to my second assignment at Sunshine Biscuit Company, located on Park Avenue near the Pan Am building.

After that, week-long assignments took me to various businesses like Scali, Macabe, and Sloves, a mid-town law firm, as well as Touche and Ross, a CPA firm. There, I found myself tethered to a cubicle, where an executive would hand me tapes that needed to be transcribed and then retyped after meticulous edits. The grind was relentless, with scarcely a break from nine to five, except for that cherished hour of respite for lunch. Those sixty minutes were particularly enjoyable because the office was nestled in the heart of the bustling theater district.

Following this stint, I embarked on another week-long assignment with RCA on the Avenue of the Americas. Serendipitously, I had a connection within the company, Paul, a friend of the family who had made his mark at RCA. Paul, an aspiring composer, was primarily known for his compositions that found their way into elevator music. It was the year of the bicentennial, and Paul had penned a song titled "America Is." He had sought his boss's approval at RCA to produce a recording, having submitted a demo featuring a friend with a distinctively declining baritone voice that had already developed a wobble.

RCA, however, suggested using a younger voice. When Paul's boss learned that I was a singer and had been hired by Radio City Music Hall, he assumed I must have some talent. He recommended that we record a demo using one of the RCA studios. Collaborating with the pianist used for the original recording, I subtly increased the tempo and infused the song with my unique personal style. RCA was thrilled with the result, but Paul was anything but pleased. In fact, he vehemently rejected the recording, refusing to let RCA proceed with its production.

It remains unclear whether his objection stemmed from jealousy—perhaps he resented the notion that a young upstart from his hometown could stride into New York City and achieve success with a company he had faithfully served for 25 years, or if it were a genuine artistic disagreement regarding the interpretation of his musical composition. Regardless, the fallout from this episode had a lasting impact, creating a rift in our friendship and straining relations with my family. As my successes continued to mount, I felt that Paul's resentment grew deeper, distancing us even further.

Harmony and Heat: The City's Sensual Symphony

During my two months on 98th Street, my roommates indulged in their amorous escapades frequently, evenings, late nights, and early mornings. Their audible exclamations of ecstasy turned my living situation into an X-rated soap opera soundtrack. The influx of such intimate auditory experiences provoked a surge of stimulation in my primal instincts. My id was gaining the upper hand, keeping my desires in a heightened state of arousal for hours on end. I wondered, *was my manhood orchestrating this uprising, or was it merely lending its support to my id's insurrection?*

Over dinner one evening, Elaine and I pondered our respective jobs through the agency. She was astonished at my new role as the agency's front runner, acknowledging that the position and the significant increase from $10.75/hr to $17.50/hr would now provide the financial means to support myself without having to constantly scrutinize my daily spending. During our conversation, I coyly alluded to the impact of her passionate exploits, using vague terms.

" So, how have you been sleeping?" she asked.

"Well to be honest, it's a little frustrating to hear your boyfriend grunting 'Elaine, Elaine! Ah Elaine!' at my left ear and then Harry's girlfriend moaning his name to my right ear." I can't remember exactly what was said, but for some reason I must have given her a new perspective which revealed the status of my sexuality. To my surprise, her reaction was swift and direct.

"Oh my God! Are you still a virgin?" she asked.

Caught off guard, I fumbled, my attempt at denial almost faltering before it even began. "Well, yeah... I mean, how did you know?"

It turned out she had seen right through my twenty-one-year-old disguise.

"That's okay, I can change that for you," she said. Her response was casual yet electrifying.

In an instant, both my manhood and my id surged to the forefront of my thoughts, their suppressed desires breaking free.

"But not tonight, I just started my period," she added matter-of-factly. It was an unexpected caveat.

And just like that, anticipation enveloped me for the next week, each night becoming a canvas for imagined pleasures.

About a week later, it was around eight-thirty in the morning, and I was still lost in slumber when the phone suddenly rang, disrupting my restful state. I answered and a voice asked to speak to Elaine. Calling out to her, she came into my room with an apologetic tone, her voice hushed as she engaged in a business-related conversation. Initially, I tried to bury my head under the pillow, aiming to block out the noise and slip back into the tranquil realm of sleep.

Yet, as the conversation persisted, my efforts to retreat into dreamland proved futile. I sighed and shifted, feeling the mattress bounce as Elaine settled at the edge of the bed. The possibility of sleep now seemed distant, and so I turned, facing the ceiling, lost in my own thoughts while intentionally tuning out the irrelevant conversation.

The boundaries of my mind proved to be less steadfast than I'd hoped. My musings wandered, conjuring thoughts of Elaine and her boyfriend engaged in their intimate moments. The vivid images overwhelmed my self-control, and I could sense a newfound energy emanating from me. I had a distinct feeling that Elaine could somehow notice the charged undercurrent of my thoughts.

She was now sitting on the edge of my bed, my naked body covered loosely with a cotton bed sheet with my right leg exposed. As she continued her conversation, I felt her hand lightly touching my knee. Slowly stroking, her hand rose higher up my thigh until she came in full contact with a throbbing intensity just eager to burst. She abruptly ended her telephone conversation.

"Hey, listen, something has come up that I have to take care of. I'll call you back!"

My thoughts became verbal moans of ecstasy, escaping like a floodgate breached. Years of pent-up fantasies were suddenly unleashed, with my id finally assuming full control. It was a cathartic release that left me both exhilarated and stunned. Elaine, grasping the gravity of the moment and sensing my lingering unease, chose to address the situation with a renewed intensity. The momentary pause set the stage for a second, even more impassioned round.

As the encounter ended, an odd mixture of triumph and vulnerability washed over me. It was as if I had just validated my masculinity, a pumped-up peacock eager to flaunt its colors.

As we laid breathless, I was expecting there to be some kind of evaluation of my performance, something like: "Wow, you were wonderful!" Or "Damn, you are a hot lover!"

However, that triumphant feeling was soon met with a dose of reality, akin to Charlie Brown's fleeting moments of elation followed by Lucy yanking the football away.

"Do you ever think you could be gay? You would do well in this town!" she said.

Elaine's words landed like an unexpected curveball. Where on earth had that come from? How did my actions lead her to such an assumption? Confusion and concern knitted my brow as I confronted her, still standing naked while she emerged from the bathroom, wrapped in a towel.

"What did you mean by that? I just had sex with you, and that was your impression?"

My voice betrayed a mix of incredulity and insecurity, revealing the depth of my distress. Elaine met my gaze, her expression softening as she realized the unintended impact of her words.

"Oh, I'm sorry. I didn't mean to imply that I thought you were gay. It was just a random thought because you're cute, like a lot of the boys in the theater. This is a very gay-dominated industry, you know. The community is tight-knit, and if you're accepted, you'll do really well." Her attempt at reassurance left me torn between a sense of relief and lingering uncertainty.

Lincoln Towers: An Exquisite Tango

With a three-day holiday, Mom and Dad returned to New York City for the Fourth of July. The motive was quite obvious, Mom was perhaps hoping to find me miserable and eager to come back home. Yet, it was evident that I was thriving with money in my pocket, radiating a vitality they had never witnessed before. Their visit was brief, an overnight stay, graciously hosted by Sandra in her apartment. It comprised of a dinner, a bit of shopping for Mom, and then departure the following afternoon. As their visit concluded, I assumed things had gone well.

Mother had conducted herself surprisingly well during the visit, seemingly weighing all factors: my happiness, my strong attachment to Sandra, my stable finances, and my unyielding passion for performing. But her parting words carried an air of finality.

"If you're truly going to live in NYC, you're not staying in this apartment. Find a better place or you'll return home next month!" she said in a tone that left no room for negotiation, leaving me in no doubt that she meant every word.

With two mandates, Bobby scheduled to return from his summer stock gig on August 1st and the ultimatum decreed by my mother, the countdown to action had begun.

Sandra and I were almost inseparable that month, especially on weekends when I wasn't working. Spending so much time with her, I realized how centralized the Lincoln Tower's was to everything, banking, grocery store, restaurants, most of all work, all within a small radius. It was only natural that I inquired about apartment availability in the Towers and was met with a mixture of annoyance and surprise from Sandra, who explained that there was an extensive waiting list. But my mother's wisdom had taught me never to take things at face value.

The rental office was located in the building directly on the other side of the central courtyard, on the first floor. My hopes weren't high, but I asked about studio apartments. The expected response arrived: no availability for studio apartments, with a long waiting list, just as Sandra had told me. The subsequent weeks were spent scouring the Actor's Equity notice board and newspaper ads for roommate opportunities, but my heart wasn't in it. Time was slipping away.

One day, after work, I walked up Broadway and spotted a sign advertising available apartments at 10 West 66th Street, just east of Lincoln Center. It was a newly completed high-rise building that felt like a luxurious hotel with chandeliers and oriental rugs in the lobby. I approached the rental agent fully expecting the usual disappointment. Yet, to my surprise, she asked what size apartment I was seeking. When I requested a studio, her response was enthusiastic, offering to show me one. The studio apartment on the sixth floor was smaller than Sandra's but boasted high ceilings, maple parquet flooring, and a small kitchen. The rent was $425 per month, inclusive of utilities, with a move-in date of August 1st. However, a co-signer was required due to my lack of credit history.

I assumed this would not be a problem since it was my mother's insistence that I find a better apartment. "Look ma, no roaches!" On the other hand, my father took a bit more convincing since he wasn't thrilled about a) another trip to NYC just a couple of weeks after the last one, and b) he wasn't in favor a co-signing a lease that made him financially responsible if I couldn't afford to pay the rent. Nevertheless, my parents were scheduled to drive down to NYC after work on Friday evening. All was set and I would be moving to 10 West 66th Street. However, fate had a surprise in store.

On Friday afternoon, I had just had lunch with Sandra, and I left her near the entrance to her building. An inexplicable urge prompted me to pay a visit to the rental office once again. A woman named Janet, a warm and welcoming presence with a Dorothy Hamill haircut, greeted me with a friendly smile. Again, I asked if there were any apartments for rent. She confirmed the availability of one-bedroom apartments and noted that the rents were around $450 per month. When I expressed concern that it might be too much for me, she inquired about whether I would be living alone or could share the rent with a roommate.

"Well honey, why don't you consider a studio apartment? They run from $280 to $325."

This sparked my interest and kindled a sense of hope. I asked, "Well do you have any studio apartments available?" expecting a response of "not at this time."

However, her response was startling. "Yes, we do! Do you want to see it?"

My excitement couldn't be contained. She went to a rack searching for the key.

"Hey, did anyone see the key to apartment 28B in 180?" she called out.

"Yes, someone is looking at the apartment!" another woman said.

"Oh honey, you will have to wait until he comes back. Hopefully, he doesn't take it, and you will be able to go and take a look. Apartments go fast in these buildings."

After a mere five minutes, the man inspecting the apartment returned, visibly perturbed, unable to access the apartment due to an additional lock. Janet promptly informed him that maintenance had yet to remove this extra lock, which prevented his entry and would necessitate his return on Monday. Disappointed, he departed, and Janet expected me to follow suit.

However, I remained stationary. Observing my hesitation, Janet turned to me, her voice filled with empathy,

"Oh, sweetheart, did you hear that? You won't be able to view the apartment now; you'll have to come back on Monday."

Driven by a moment of desperation, I boldly inquired, "How much is the rent?"

She swiftly consulted her records. "It's $280.00 per month."

Without a moment's hesitation, I blurted out, "I'll take it!"

Remarkably, I had made this decision without even laying eyes on the apartment. My reasoning was simple: Sandra had a studio, so how different could it be?

Janet then approached Mr. Kern, the manager, to seek his approval for me to take the apartment sight unseen, and to my delight, he agreed. I swiftly made arrangements for my parents to co-sign the necessary paperwork the following morning, and just like that, the deal was sealed. I knew that my mother would be very pleased to know that I would be living in the same building as Sandra, that there would be someone to keep an eye on me. Frankly, I was too! A quick phone call to the rental office at 10 West 66th Street canceled the hold on that apartment, and as of Saturday morning at 10:00 am, I was a resident of 180 West End Avenue with a move-in date of August 1st, just one week away.

The moving process was orchestrated by my parents and their friends. By the time I returned from work, my apartment was set up and arranged by my mother, reflecting her determination to create a space for friends and guests in NYC. My apartment, though reversed from Sandra's layout, featured a walk-in closet and an incredible view. The stunning sight of city lights, the famous Ansonia Hotel and the Hudson River view which stretch all the way up to the George Washington Bridge played out in my windows, making each sunset an enchanting experience. The breathtaking panorama transformed my apartment into a magical space.

My mother quickly envisioned my apartment as her equivalent to Pauline's cottage at Long Pond, her way of holding the key to social engagement and popularity. However, one queen-sized bed (where my parents slept) and one convertible love seat (where I slept) was not sufficient to host another couple. So, The next day with my mother's insistence we purchased a new, queen-sized, Castro Convertible, striped rust, black and white couch, providing my parents with sleeping accommodations during their visits.

As soon as my parents left, I went to Sandra's expecting to spend the evening with her. When she opened the door and let me in, I immediately saw a man, small statured with a perpetual looking tan, sitting on the couch. He spoke with an undistinguishable accent.

"Hi Ron! This is Tony," Sandra said very nonchalantly.

Tony? Who the fuck is Tony!

During our introductory conversation, while Sandra was preparing to go out, shifting in and out of her bathroom, I learned that Tony was from Trinidad. He met Sandra while was having her Honda serviced. *Wait, what? Tony is her mechanic!* Tony was not a big celebrity, not a successful business executive, no one that I had assumed Sandra would even entertain having a relationship with.

"Ron, Tony and I are going out for dinner and then the movies." For a moment, my ego was shattered, but I quickly composed myself, hoping my feelings wouldn't be noticed by Sandra or Tony.

Since I had moved to New York, there had never been any indication of any other man in Sandra's life. I felt certain we were friends but also realized that our friendship had not yet established boundaries. The feelings of seeing her with Tony made me face the fact that I did have romantic and sexual feelings that I had been suppressing. After all, there was a significant age difference, and she had had other relationships and a marriage. Why would she be even interested in me other than as a friend? Yet, Tony was not only about my age, but he even resembled me in stature.

Returning to my apartment, my immature ego took control. I thought, *all right, two can play that game.* I called Elaine and asked her if she wanted to come over and help me christen my new place. I suppose I used Elaine, a petite, brunette ballerina, just as Sandra used Tony to replace me.

Not expecting to hear from Sandra that evening, she nevertheless called me. I couldn't have been happier to inform her that I had company.

She hesitated slightly before responding. "Oh, umm, I was just calling to see if you were taking class tomorrow?" I noted hesitancy before she continued. "So, who do you have over?

When I told her it was Elaine, she sounded surprised, then promptly ended the conversation.

"Oh… well, have a good evening!"

And there it was, the dynamics that began our relationship. I was the man she could call her friend, but, in a way, she didn't want me to have any other woman in my life, although she couldn't really say that if she didn't want our relationship to be romantic.

Unfortunately, Tony's presence was no momentary occurrence. His relationship with Sandra continued, and he became a fixture in our shared space. Tony, an amiable individual, displayed courteousness toward me, extending invitations whenever they planned outings. Their dynamic evoked something within me, unsettling my equilibrium.

La Boheme: Harmony and Dissonance

In mid-July, the agency called me in for another role. They wanted me to send me out as a temp project coordinator. They were now receiving requests for individuals to handle short-term projects. My first assignment was at Paramount Pictures, situated in the Gulf and Western building at Columbus Circle. Although the project lasted only a week and a half, I was highly recommended and moved up to Gulf and Western on the 40th floor, just one floor below the beautiful Top of the Park restaurant.

Two weeks into my project, an executive named Stuart, a sharp, well-dressed Jewish man with dark hair and an athletic aura, who seemed to be quite the ladies' man, called me into his office to discuss a proposition. Impressed by my coordination and organizational skills, he recommended that I become an independent contractor, and Gulf and Western would pay me directly what they were paying the agency. This marked my introduction to the world of independent contracting, allowing me to continue pursuing both my career in the arts and my business ventures simultaneously.

Many of the employees at Gulf and Western ate at the diner in the Mayfair hotel on Central Park West, the next block north of the GW building. What began as a solitude lunch session sitting at the counter alone with a book, quickly changed after a few days when the executives asked me to join them. During the general conversation about various topics Stuart looked at me.

"Several of us are heading to the beach this weekend. Want to join us?" he said.

This unexpected invitation marked my inaugural inclusion in a social endeavor. As I longed to be included, I eagerly accepted.

The weekend arrived, and I journeyed to the designated meeting point in a haze of anticipation. Reaching Penn Station via the subway, we began a series of transitions from train, busses, then ferry, ultimately leading to Fire Island. Stepping off the ferry, a large sign greeted us—bright colors and bold type, a clear invitation to Fire Island's lively, unabashed spirit. Around us, people embraced one another with laughter and flamboyant gestures, their conversations bubbling over with high energy and exuberance. The sharp suits and guarded expressions I knew from the office seemed to melt away, replaced by carefree bodies and colorful speedos, each movement and tone layered with a new openness.

Boom boxes pumped out disco beats that echoed along the sandy paths, mixing with the sound of glasses clinking and voices rising in chorus. Even the men I worked with, usually so buttoned-up, now laughed with an unfamiliar ease, their handshakes replaced with warm embraces and knowing glances. I watched, feeling the hum of the island pulse through me as I settled into the crowd, its energy drawing me in.

We wove through the thick green of the Pines, the scent of the sea growing sharper with each step, until the trees gave way to a stretch of pale sand meeting the Atlantic's sparkling blue. Dropping our bags on the beach, we shimmied out of our clothes down to speedos, blending in with the sun-bronzed bodies sprawled on towels.

As I was unfolding my towel, Stuart's voice cut through the beach chatter: "Here, you'll burn up without this," he said, holding out a bottle of sunscreen. Before I could answer, he was rubbing it across my shoulders, chatting with the ease with an old friend. His friends, too, seemed to know everyone here, sharing boisterous laughs and leaning close to greet locals with the kind of warm familiarity that put me instantly in the spotlight.

"New guy?" someone asked with a grin, eyes sweeping over me in appraisal. A few more glances and light touches followed, fingers trailing playfully along my arm or resting a little too long on my shoulder. Compliments mixed with teasing glances; I felt their eyes linger, curious, inviting, almost as if they were sizing up the "new boy on the block." I wasn't used to being at the center of attention like this, and it was both thrilling and just a little unnerving.

Amidst this attention, I realized a novel experience unfolding. For the first time, I was regarded as an attractive man, my non-blond hair and unconventional appearance no longer barriers to recognition. This newfound affirmation was a revelation, as the language and body dynamics of this setting presented a stark contrast to my past encounters. Even Stuart and the other executives displayed altered behaviors, their personas shifting within this unique community.

"Do any of your colleagues at the office know you're gay?" I asked.

"No, so let's keep it that way," Stuart responded.

My query seemed to have affected him, as he gradually shifted his attention to others. The remainder of the day passed with swimming, sleeping, and reading, and a self-inflicted limited social interaction. Finally, the ferry signaled the last opportunity to depart before the island's transformation into a hub of nocturnal revelries.

I returned to the city alone as Stuart and the others stayed behind. Silent contemplation accompanied my journey back. My reflection stared back from the darkened window, softened by the passing lights and shadows of the tunnels.

I leaned back, hands resting loosely on my lap, eyes unfocused yet fixed, feeling the weight of the day's discoveries settle in. The occasional screech of the train echoed the tangle of thoughts in my mind, while I tried to make sense of new realizations. Each stop brought a pause, the doors opening to nothing but empty platforms, mirroring the stillness within.

The next workday I learned that my project would be over by the week's end. The demeanor of Stuart and the executives was markedly distant, as though I had committed a wrongdoing. Though it stung, the feeling of rejection was fleeting. Redirecting my focus to work, my apartment, and Sandra, I maintained my stride.

My exposure to nightlife intensified when I discovered the Ice Palace and Studio 54, both epitomes of decadence. Welcomed without struggle, I marveled at my easy entrance, pondering the reasons for the bouncers' favor. Perhaps I resembled John Travolta, an inadvertent celebrity look-alike. Immersed in disco's rhythms, I unleashed my inhibitions, melding with the psychedelic ambiance. Amid gyrating bodies, the surge of sexual energy escalated, and anonymity granted liberation. Conversations were limited to first names only, each encounter ephemeral. By 3 a.m., I would find myself either at someone's apartment or hosting company in mine.

One night pushed me to question the extent of my experiences. Avoiding drugs or marijuana, my drink of choice was gin and tonic. As dawn broke,

I danced with an affluent older woman, a singular partner. Memories are hazy, but I recall waking up in luxurious sheets at the Plaza Hotel. My unfamiliar surroundings prompted a swift departure, my mind racing to bridge the gap between the nightclub and the hotel suite. As I retreated, it was evident that a moment of reckoning awaited.

New York State Theater: Overtures

Faced with the absence of a new project, I reconnected with my temp agency, which welcomed me back. I was assigned to an open-ended stay at Prince Carpentry. Their current major endeavor was the renovation of Avery Fisher Hall at Lincoln Center. My workstation was positioned behind a woman named Carol, with whom I found camaraderie in our shared love for music. Carol was also 10 years my senior, sharing the same birthday of March 7th. She was intelligent, held a Masters in Opera, and, much as I did, had a clear focus on her goals. Her interest in helping me develop my voice further was compelling, and I began weekly lessons. As the weeks progressed, sharing lunches and occasional dinners, she seemed to enjoy my sense of humor and my company. Our bond grew beyond friendship when an evening spent together took a more intimate turn, introducing a new facet to our relationship.

About mid-September, Carol's influence, though grounding, increased my yearning to be on stage. Frustration simmered beneath the surface, and during a dinner with Sandra, my mounting discontent spilled forth. Sandra urged patience, reminding me that opportunities required time. A week of venting to her finally bore fruit. Armed with connections at the New York City Opera, she approached a colleague named Jack on my behalf. This marked a significant step, potentially steering me toward my desired stage presence.

"Ron, I spoke with my friend Jack at the theater. He's head of the supernumeraries, the group of performers used as extras, like in movies. After I described your physical traits, he said he could use you. He has agreed to see you in his office at 5:30 p.m. tomorrow to try on a few costumes."

In anticipation, I hastily departed from work, giving myself ample time for the brisk walk from Prince Carpentry to Lincoln Center. The security desk recognized me, an assumed guest of Sandra's. With confidence, I informed him of my appointment with Jack and was swiftly directed towards my destination. While I had accompanied Sandra to the State Theater's rehearsal rooms on several occasions, my familiarity with the facility was limited. Stepping out of the elevator, my confusion grew; the circular hallway disoriented me. As I tentatively approached a partially open door, it swung wide to reveal a gentleman within, his surprise evident.

"Hi, I'm Ron Boucher. Sandra sent me!" eagerly introducing myself.

"You're late!" he chided, inviting me into a spacious rehearsal space with several men present.

"Please hand your music to the pianist!" the man instructed.

Now confused, I said: "Sing? I thought I was supposed to try on some costumes." He ignored my comment assuming I was just attempting a moment of humor. This unexpected scenario had caught me by surprise, but I always carried a binder of my music and my dance attire. The pianist's graciousness and the directive to sing something in English steadied my unease. I opted for "I'll Walk with God," a familiar choice.

"I wasn't expecting that from you," he marveled when I had finished, bestowing his Mazel tov.

Barely had I concluded when an announcement signaled the end of auditions.

"Gentlemen, I appreciate your presence here tonight. We're reaching a decision this evening, and we'll notify the selected individual by tomorrow."

With those words, we were dismissed.

Later that night, when Sandra returned home from the theater, she called me, clearly upset.

"Ron, how could you do that?"

Confused, I asked, "Do what?"

She responded with even more frustration. "Jack said you never showed up. I went out of my way to help you, and you stood him up!"

I was bewildered. "Sandra, I was there. I sang '"Walk with God,"' and then they told us they'd make their choice tonight after they released us!"

She thought I was losing my mind and abruptly hung up. She remained distant for the next week, so I kept my distance and spent more time with Carol.

I continued my assignment at Prince Carpentry and a week had gone by with no word. My daily ritual was to check in with my answering service just before noon.

"Good morning Ron, you had a call from the NYC Opera. They'd like to see you at 1 p.m. today."

Was this a callback? Turning to Carol I said, "Carol, I have a call back at the New York City Opera! Can I take a late lunch?"

She hesitated but understood the significance of this opportunity.

"Yes, but if you're not back by two o'clock, they'll have to move on."

It was a risk I was more than willing to take. With hopes raised, I navigated my lunch break, committed to seizing this chance. Returning to the State Theater, I entered a room steeped in familiarity from witnessing Sandra's rehearsals. There were two men seated at a table, one was a gentleman with a full head of curly grey hair much like mine who looked like he might be in his late fifties or early sixties. The other man I assessed was in his late sixties or early seventies, slender built with a serious expression, dressed in a black suit with an open-collared white shirt. A guy who resembled me, except for his curly blond hair, and an older woman

242

completed the group. Expecting to sing once more, I retrieved my sheet music.

"Oh, we've already heard your singing. We're considering each of you for a specific role in this opera and would like to work on a particular scene," one of the men at the table said. "In this scene, Maria has placed all her faith in Anina's healing abilities, hoping for a cure for her mute son. After months of silence, she implores her son to speak, and finally, he utters his first word, 'mama'."

A wooden bench was placed in the center of the room, and they instructed the other guy to go first. The woman delivered her line,

"Su bello mio, come on, say mama!"

Without hesitation, the guy responded with "mama," but the director shook his head disapprovingly.

"No, no, this is a crucial moment in the opera; take your time."

The woman repeated her line, and once again, the guy's response lacked the necessary emotion. The director still seemed unsatisfied.

Glancing at me he said, "Alright, would you please give it a try?"

I knelt beside the woman and she took my hand. An instant chemistry sparked as I gazed into her eyes.

"Su bello mio, come on, say mama!" she pleaded.

I pulled away slightly, turning my head. She gently tugged me back, turning my head to face her. She nodded, her eyes begging for the word she had so desperately prayed to hear. Drawing inspiration from the movie "The Miracle Worker," I reached deep within, producing the raspiest voice I could muster. Slowly, forcefully, and with great effort, I articulated the word, "Ma…ma."

The director leaped to his feet and exclaimed, "Bravo! Yes, yes, yes!"

As he sat down, the other gentleman spoke, "Maestro, we've never worked with this young man before. The other has performed with us several times. Are you sure about this choice?"

The director expressed complete confidence and dismissed the other boy.

The woman introduced herself, saying, "Hi, I'm Judith DeRosa. You were wonderful! I felt an incredible connection with you right away."

As I was leaving, I turned to Judith and asked, "Could you tell me who those two men are?"

She appeared surprised, almost thinking I was joking. "Seriously, you don't recognize them?"

I responded with a shake of my head.

"The man with the white curly hair is Julius Rudel, the conductor and NYC Opera Artistic Director, and the other is the composer and director, Gian Carlo Menotti."

Shocked, I exclaimed, "You mean the guy who wrote *Amahl*?" *Amahl and the Night Visitors* is the second opera that I did back in Boston.

The journey ahead required me to develop the skills of a true opera singer, skills I had yet to formally acquire. Carol, recognizing my need, stepped up as my mentor, sharing her vast knowledge. Her lessons were centered on vocal exercises to strengthen the vocal folds and refine the phonation of vowels. Beyond technique, Carol also provided valuable insights into the history of opera, helping me connect the repertoire of that season to its cultural and historical significance.

However, what I quickly discovered was that learning to be an opera singer through hands-on experience with seasoned professionals was a far different path than academic study focused solely on facts and theory. In New York, studying voice meant not only working on technique but also mastering a vast repertoire. Voice teachers in the city often specialized in one or the other—some focused-on technique, while others dedicated themselves to vocal repertoire—but you didn't work with just one. You needed both.

One coach I was introduced to was David, who would play a pivotal role in my training, offering valuable critique and guidance. David lived in a prewar building on 73rd Street. His enormous living room was painted a shocking fuchsia, and despite the vast space, it contained two grand pianos, each of which fit into one corner of the room, scarcely diminishing available space.

My first lesson with David, however, was anything but glamorous. It was, in fact, utterly humiliating.

"So, what would you like to sing for me?" David asked, his voice filled with excitement and anticipation. he was eager to hear what I, as a newcomer to the New York City Opera, could bring to the table. Feeling confident that I was about to impress him, I chose an Italian art song I had been working on with Carol—*Amarilli Mia Bella*. I tried to recall all the technical advice Carol had shared with me. I took my first breath, and the sound seemed to flow effortlessly as I moved through each phrase—until, suddenly, David stopped playing.

"Ron, you do indeed have a beautiful voice," he said, cutting me off mid-song. "But for opera, that's not enough. If you sing in Italian, you have to sound like you're Italian. If you sing in French, you need to sound like a Frenchman. Do you understand?"

He handed me a business card with a flourish.

"Here's an excellent Italian teacher," he continued. "I want you to work with him and prepare three tenor pieces from the Italian repertoire. When you come back, I want you to be sure of your pronunciation and be able to translate what you're singing. Do not schedule your next lesson until you've accomplished this. If you come back and haven't done the work, I will not continue teaching you."

And with that, my first lesson was over.

As I left David's apartment, a mix of confusion and frustration bubbled up inside me. *Why am I spending all this time on classical music when what I really want is to be on Broadway? Do I even want to be an opera singer? Do I even like opera?*

But the truth was, I loved a good challenge. I was working in an opera house, and although Broadway was my dream, that didn't seem to be coming together at the moment. Besides, the best part was that I'd soon be cast in an opera where Sandra would be performing as well. Now *that* was something to look forward to.

The moment I got back to my apartment, I called the number on the business card. "Is this Vincenzo? Hi, this is Ron Boucher, and I was referred to you by my coach, Da..." I was cut off mid-sentence.

"Yes, I just got off the phone with him, and he was hoping you'd call me! I understand you have a nice voice!"

Vincenzo turned out to be an exceptional teacher—native Italian, emerging opera singer, and, before long, a friend. He didn't waste any time getting to work. I wasn't allowed to sing the aria until I had perfected the phonetics. He was meticulous, and I quickly learned to appreciate his standards. To help me, Vincenzo invited me to his own coaching sessions, where he was preparing for a concert performance of Verdi's *Requiem* at St. John the Divine Cathedral.

His rendition of the main tenor aria, "Ingemisco", was stunning and gave me the motivation and inspiration I needed to really focus. It wasn't long before this piece became a signature part of my repertoire.

Two weeks later, I returned to David for my next lesson. I nervously set my music down on the piano, and David looked at the piece I'd chosen and grinned.

"Okay, no singing," he said, his tone playful but serious. "You must *say* the words."

He gestured for me to begin. "E'la solita storia del pastore. Il povero ragazzo voleva raccontarla, e s'addormi." The *r's* rolled off my tongue, the inflections perfect.

"That's enough," David said, holding up his hand. "Now, let's sing!"

Like football players in spring training, my typical week became a mix of intense practice and preparation. It consisted of one hour of technique lessons, one hour of coaching, an hour of Italian lessons, three ballet classes, and one jazz class. Through all of it, I bridged the language barrier, embracing Italian as an essential part of my operatic journey. Success in opera wasn't just about the voice; it was about *the language*, and I was learning fast that it was a prerequisite.

Art vs. Business: The Allegro

The start of rehearsals for *The Saint of Bleeker Street* was an intense and eye-opening experience. There were no formal introductions among the cast members, and I quickly realized that if I had been better versed in the opera world, I might have recognized many of the people around me. But as it was, I was a newcomer to the scene, both literally and figuratively.

As the rehearsals progressed, I found myself marveling at the exceptional voices surrounding me. Among the standout talents was Catherine Malfitano, the soprano cast as Annina, the saint. She embodied the essence of the Italian Catholic archetype—gracefully accepting divine suffering with both strength and humility. Diana Soviero, who played *Annina's* friend **Carmela**, possessed a similar vocal timbre to Catherine's, and over the years, their paths would often cross in overlapping roles. Diana's physicality, however, was more suited to the dramatic intensity of roles like Violetta in *La Traviata*. The role of Annina's brother, Michele, was portrayed by tenor Enrico Di Giuseppe, whose powerful, dramatic voice I admired greatly, wishing I could channel that same depth and resonance

247

The Saint of Bleeker Street
Catherine Malfitano, Judith DeRosa and Me
©Beth Bergman

into my own work. The opera was conducted by Stewart Kellogg, making his debut with the company, while Francis Rizzo directed, and Gian Carlo Menotti oversaw the entire production.

The entire ensemble gathered within the capacious rehearsal room on the fifth floor. Drawing from my past lessons, I adopted the strategy of observation, quietude, and learning from the best. In musical theater, we always had a read-through at the onset of rehearsals to give us continuity of who is who and what is happening in each scene as the show progresses. It helped us understand what was expected of the character we were portraying and how to develop that person. However, in this case my work on my character was done independently, anticipating that I had comprehended the expectations I was about to put into motion. We had been in rehearsal since 9 a.m. and there were many scenes that had been worked on but none of mine as I sat with Ms. DeRosa on the sidelines.

By 12 noon, a voice would call out, "Lunch!" signaling the end of the morning's work. The cast would rush out of the rehearsal room—some heading to the lunchroom downstairs, others to the deli on the corner of Broadway. As the afternoon wore on, I continued to sit quietly on the sidelines with Ms. DeRosa, waiting for my scene to be called. Finally, near the end of the day, Mr. Rizzo summoned Catherine, Judith, and me to work on Act One, Scene Two. Just as we were reaching the most intense moment of the scene, a voice cut through the air: "That's a wrap!" Within seconds, the room was empty. Some cast members were heading home for the night, others were off to perform in the evening's opera. And there I was, still walking around in a haze—confused, awestruck, anxious, and exhilarated all at once.

It wasn't until the end of the first week of rehearsal that I began to realize I hadn't received a contract. The lack of clarity about my status in the production began to unsettle me. I couldn't afford to work without pay; my finances were precarious, and I needed to know where I stood. The lavish setting of Lincoln Center seemed distant and surreal in light of my very real, everyday concerns.

I discussed the matter with Sandra, who suggested I reach out to her friend, Jack, who got back to me promptly. He explained that my role was considered supernumerary. I wouldn't be paid for rehearsals, but I would receive $10.00 per performance. He emphasized that many would envy the opportunity to perform with such a prestigious company. But that explanation didn't sit well with me. I discreetly asked other cast members about their contracts and pay, but this made them uncomfortable, and they quickly redirected me to management.

Jack's assessment was accurate, this was a rare and extraordinary opportunity. Still, I couldn't shake my discomfort. A few days later, I received a call from Jack, who was concerned about the questions I had been asking. He warned me that my inquiries had made other cast members uneasy. I listened, responding with a polite, but firm, "Yes, Sir."

Despite his warning, my instincts told me something wasn't right. The next morning, I took my score and headed to the American Guild of Musical Artists (AGMA) headquarters. I explained my situation to one of the staff, who, after listening to my concerns, said the AGMA president needed to address the matter. Fortunately, the president was available, and I was able to share my experience, including the verbal threat I had received.

The president listened attentively and agreed that, on the face of it, my role should be a contracted position, paying union wages. However, due to the opera's historical precedent dating back to the 1950s, the situation wasn't straightforward. He assured me that he would advocate on my behalf, but also asked whether I would be willing to stay with the company if the outcome didn't work in my favor. I expressed my gratitude for the opportunity and told him I would remain silent for now, still hoping for a positive resolution.

The final dress rehearsal was a blur. I donned my costume and took a few moments to familiarize myself with the stage. I marked my positions, took in the setting, and tried to calm my nerves. Suddenly, I heard a voice call out: "Rinaldo!" It was Menotti, who, with a twinkle in his eye, directed me to go back to makeup. "You look like you belong in GQ magazine," he said. "Go back and mess up your hair. You look too polished."

I returned to the makeup room, where Caroline, the makeup artist, did her best to make my curly hair look wild and unkempt. No matter what she did, it seemed to settle back into its natural state. Caroline then applied makeup to give the impression of dirt and wear. When I returned to the stage, Menotti was still not satisfied. "No, no… you still look too neat!" he said. He called Caroline over to inspect her work, and after a few more adjustments, he gave his approval.

The dress rehearsal began, and though my adrenaline was high, I felt surprisingly calm. I didn't have the usual jitters I would expect before a performance. This felt familiar to me—like musical theater, but on a grander scale. After the rehearsal, both Menotti and Francis came up to me to offer their congratulations. I left the stage, returned my costume to the makeup room, and went back to my apartment, reflecting on the surreal reality that I was about to make my debut at Lincoln Center with the New York City Opera.

On the morning of the opening night—Friday, October 29, 1976—I struggled to settle my nerves. My financial concerns had slipped into the background as my focus shifted entirely to delivering the best performance I could. Around 10 a.m., the phone rang. It was the AGMA president, with good news: he had successfully negotiated a contract for me, at an hourly rate of $25.50, with time-and-a-half for overtime, and $1,000 per performance. In addition, he had secured roles for me in multiple operas during the season, including *Carmen*, *La Bohème*, and *Cavalleria Rusticana*. Although I wouldn't secure another principal role, I would be working steadily and fairly compensated. This was a valuable lesson—especially given the financial strain I had felt in recent weeks. The president also informed me that my AGMA membership dues would be deducted from my first paycheck. He wished me luck, saying, "Bocca al lupo," an Italian expression meaning "Good luck."

While this was a huge relief, it was clear that management wasn't pleased with my inquiries. Still, I was relieved that I had secured the contract, and I looked forward to the opportunities that lay ahead.

Though Sandra and I didn't share a production that season, we often rehearsed at the same time, in different rooms. While I was working on *Boheme*, *Carmen*, *Cavalleria*, and *Bleeker Street*, she was involved in *La Belle Hélène*, *Rigoletto*, and *La Traviata*. It was a dream come true—being part of such a prestigious company, alongside talented professionals. But even as I reveled in this achievement, I remained aware of my novice status in this world, while those around me, like Sandra, were consummate professionals.

The Miracle of the Theater: Ritorna Vincitore

When I arrived at the theater that evening, I signed in at the front desk, then made my way to the makeup room on the second floor, where I had always been accustomed to going for my costume. I inquired about my costume from the makeup artist, Caroline.

In her characteristic flamboyance, she responded with a flourish, "Oh, darling, you're a big star now! Your dressing room is just across the hall."

True to her words, a room adorned with my name plaque awaited me, right across from the stairwell. Observing Sandra's dressing room on the third floor on several occasions had prepared me for this moment. It was clear to me that my own dressing room was a result of the negotiated contract by AGMA; had it not been for their intervention, this privilege might have eluded me.

A fellow cast member, Mr. Denson, who portrayed the main priest, visited my dressing room. His deep baritone voice resonated with sincerity as he congratulated me and expressed confidence in my burgeoning career.

"Places, everyone!" The phrase echoed with familiarity, yet this time, it carried the weight of a premiere. Positioned on the stage, I extended an outstretched hand for Judith, ready for the curtain to rise. Around me, whispers of bocca al lupo, that Italian phrase of well-wishing, resonated among cast members and stagehands. The moment was electric as the conductor took his position and the opera's overture commenced. While I had undergone this routine during dress rehearsal, this was authentic, the collective effort of every participant coalescing into a grand performance.

As the curtain ascended, Judith and I sprang into action. The lighting cast a night-like ambiance, bestowing an aura of shadow upon the characters on stage. Positioned downstage right, Judith and I prepared for Annina's entrance. The chorus swelled as she made her appearance. A chair was placed at center stage, with the Saint taking her seat. She appeared in a trance-like state, exuding an impression of agony. Our cue arrived when she collapsed, revealing bleeding stigmata in her hands. This phenomenon, the bleeding stigmata, was believed by Catholics to possess the power of miracles and cures. As the music reached its climactic zenith, Judith, portraying my mother, dragged me towards the Saint. Our coordination was essential—I had to provide convincing resistance to ensure Judith's hand contacted my mouth precisely as the music soared to its peak. The synchronization was impeccable, the Saint's blood now smeared on my lips and face. As we exited the stage, preparing for the next scene, we received accolades from the stage manager, and Mr. Menotti himself greeted me.

Then came the pivotal moment: The scene unfolded: Ms. Malfitano as Annina, seated on a bench before a chain-link fence. Maria Corona enters with her son, who was visibly reluctant and afraid of Annina after his interaction with her during her stigmata episode. Breaking free of Maria's hand, he runs to the chain-link fence and clings to it. Maria expresses her frustration to Annina at my continued silence. Annina beckons Maria to try once more. Waiting for my cue from Judith, she finally signals me over. With the violin music playing in sustained suspense, Maria beseeches, "Suo bello mio," pausing to seek Annina's affirmation, then "say 'mama'!" The gravity of the scene, the tension, and my gut-wrenching delivery of my first word, "mama," mirrored the poignancy of Helen Keller's breakthrough moment in "The Miracle Worker."

As the final curtain descended, I was prepared to retreat to my dressing room, eager to shed my costume. I hadn't even had to change to allow the moment to register when the stage manager intervened, reminding me of the curtain call. It was a whirlwind of bows, orchestrated by Judith, leading the principal characters back on stage for additional acknowledgments.

After the final bow, I agreed to join some of the cast members for a much-needed meal. As we were leaving the stage door, we encountered a group of individuals seeking autographs. The novelty of being asked for my autograph, given my perceived insignificance, was staggering. One enthusiast shared how my performance had outshone the 1952 production. Louis, a friend, quipped humorously about my ascent from contract to dressing room to autographs, playfully predicting I'd be a "divo" by the next day.

Normally I would have gone to see Sandra, but that evening, I returned to my apartment basking in the success I just had. All those years of ridicule, torment, belittling, and abuse seemed to have melted away like the snow when faced with the warmth of sunshine.

Retaliation and Redemption: The Revenge Rhapsody

It was thrilling to see NYC Opera bring *Bleeker Street* back to the spring repertoire for the 1977–78 season. The excitement grew with the news that one of the performances was set to be a special televised broadcast *Live from Lincoln Center* series in spring 1978. But in January, I learned that while the entire cast from '76 was being brought back, my role was the sole exception.

A call from Menotti himself informed me that he wasn't responsible for this, but he did ensure that I was included in the opera. As a member of AGMA, my role was downgraded to the insignificant young priest in the third act, and I participated in numerous chorus scenes. *Was this the result of my contact with AGMA?*

During this period, Mémère had been battling bone cancer for two years. It had now escalated, and she was swiftly deteriorating. Just a few days prior to the televised performance of *Saint of Bleeker Street*, I received a call on Monday morning, April 15th. My grandfather's trembling voice urgently implored me to come home, as the doctor had given my grandmother an estimate of hours to a couple of days. Explaining my contract and performance obligations was futile; the focus was solely on the imminent goodbye. My heart sank as I realized I needed to be with her. She was more than my grandmother; she was my mentor who had instilled faith in my potential and shared her limited musical knowledge during my formative years.

I called the NYC Opera management office to explain the situation, which brought forth a stern response. They understood but emphasized that choosing not to perform would constitute a contract breach and lead to immediate termination. It didn't take much contemplation to recognize that being with my grandmother was paramount. I arranged to leave for home and my parents to pick me up at the train station at 6 p.m. With bags packed and errands done, the phone rang again. This time, it was my grandmother's voice, weak but determined. She urged me not to worry, assuring me that she wouldn't pass before I arrived.

"Don't rush home, wait until Friday. See you then!" Her conviction resonated as the phone went silent.

There was a sigh of relief and the decision was made to remain in New York and perform as had been planned.

I couldn't help but anticipate minimal camera time for my relatively small role. However, to my surprise, I received substantial coverage. In a phone call directly after the performance, I learned that my grandmother's doctors and nurses had gathered in her room to watch the broadcast as they promised. It was abundantly clear that this event held immense significance for my grandmother, serving as the final item on her earthly to-do list before her departure from this world.

On Friday, as promised, I boarded the train to Rhode Island, met by my parents who drove me straight to the hospital. Walking into the hospital room, I was met by the sight of my grandmother sitting up, cheerful and vibrant. My aunt Doris and her family joined us—laughter, tears, prayers, and shared memories filling the room. It was an evening of togetherness, of mutual joy in her presence, and of unspoken understanding that her time was near.

The following day, my sister Renee was set to be the maid of honor at her friend's wedding. My grandmother knew about the event and requested we come dressed so she could see us in our formal outfits. Given how my grandmother had been the previous day, we believed we had more time so opted to attend the wedding and reception with my aunt Doris remaining in waiting.

Returning around 3 p.m., we found my grandmother unresponsive. I had the chance to sit with her, holding her hand, but no words were exchanged. She made sounds of discomfort, her breathing labored. Then, a moment of urgency came. She looked into my eyes, her gaze steady and intent, then beckoned me closer.

"I have one last request," she murmured, her voice soft but clear.

I leaned in, feeling the weight of the moment pressing around us.

"When my time comes," she continued, "I want you to sing at my funeral." Her eyes sparkled, a faint smile forming. "But not from the choir loft. I want you at the front of the church, where everyone can see and hear.

Her grin faded into a whisper, the unspoken words lingering in the quiet room.

I nodded, unable to speak. We were alone, and in that moment, a sacred promise passed between us.

We had just arrived home when the call came from my aunt Doris. "Mémère just died!" she announced. An eerie moment ensued as my father noticed that the clock in the center of our living room wall and his watch oddly stopped, marking the moment of her passing.

It was the morning of the funeral, and I still hadn't made my decision as to whether or not to sing as my grandmother had requested. The thought of maintaining an emotional connection without breaking down seemed impossible. However, my grandmother had been insistent, so I made the decision to keep my word. Mr. Labens, the organist from St. Anthony's, didn't offer any rehearsal. Fifteen minutes before the service, I met him in the choir loft and handed him my sheet music for the "Ave Maria" and the "Panis Angelicus". Although my grandmother wanted me to sing in the front of the church, it was easier for both Mr. Labens and I to perform from the loft. I felt my grandmother would be forgiving under the circumstances.

The service commenced with Mr. Lebens' accompaniment to the priest's traditional chants. before and while the covered casket was rolled up the aisle, Mr. Labens played the processional music. We reached the offertory, where I was to sing the "Ave Maria". Mr. Lebens pressed the keys of the grand organ, but no sound emerged from the massive pipes. He tried various stops and settings, but it was all in vain. He shut down and restarted the organ, but still, there was no sound. Grabbing my music, he said, "Come on!" We hurriedly descended the choir loft stairs and raced to the front of the church.

I stood in the same spot where I had sung with Gina, near the communion rail, where everyone could see me, fulfilling my grandmother's wishes. My father glanced at me and mouthed, "Oh my God!" My grandmother's last wishes had been granted. Mr. Labens was now stationed at the organ located in a hidden nook, on the side of the main alter. Unable to see me, he began to play without giving me a moment to dwell on my feelings about what I was about to do. I took a deep breath and let the first note fill the vast church. It wasn't the first time I felt an out-of-body experience. It was as if I were separated from myself, watching, and hearing my own voice. Somehow, I managed to get through the three verses of Schubert's beautiful composition.

In preparation for the second song, which I was to sing during communion, I retreated to the vestibule. One of my mom's friends, Lee, a former soloist for the church, came to offer moral support. I embraced her and let go completely, crying uncontrollably in her arms. I was convinced I couldn't do this again. Communion was rapidly approaching, and she began to encourage me to return to the sanctuary. I resisted, standing on the threshold. Suddenly, I felt a gentle push, moving me a few steps forward, then another. Finally gathering the courage, I stood ready to sing the *Panis Angelicus*. It was done. The first significant person in my life was gone, and I had shared with her one last time the gift she had given me.

Summer Interlude: A Warm Sonata

With summer rapidly approaching and the opera season ending in May, I found myself wondering how to stay financially afloat. Glancing through the audition section of *Backstage*, I decided to try my luck with summer stock. On impulse, I grabbed my jazz shoes, jazz pants, shirt, and my Broadway sheet music, which had been gathering dust, and headed to the studio where auditions were being held.

A small perk of joining AGMA was the automatic receipt of my Equity card, giving me access to those exclusive auditions reserved for union members—a door to a world of professional musical theater I hadn't yet stepped through.

"Hello, Mr. Boucher! What will you sing for us today?" one of the panelists asked, looking up from behind the audition table.

I handed my music to the pianist, and replied confidently, "I'm going to sing "Maybe This Time" from *Cabaret.*"

A small but unmistakable flicker of raised eyebrows passed among the panelists which made me cognizant that "Maybe This Time" was sung by a female character, which might have explained their surprise. The pianist played the intro, and I composed myself, breathing into the set tempo. I launched into the song, but my vibrato betrayed me, too fast for musical theater—a flaw that drew immediate looks of disapproval from the panel. Trying to compensate, I leaned into my operatic training, adjusting my resonance, though the effect likely came across as Plácido Domingo attempting pop.

The last note barely hung in the air when one of them responded crisply, "Thank you, Mr. Boucher, and best of luck with your opera career."

In that moment, my Broadway ambitions evaporated. I rationalized the incident, convincing myself that perhaps musical theater just wasn't meant for me.

When I shared the story of my disastrous audition with my parents over the phone, my father, always pragmatic and concerned about my summer plans, cut right to the point.

"So, Ronnie, what are your plans for the summer?"

"I'm not sure yet," I replied matter-of-factly. The fact was that I had no plans and no ambition. The reason being that Sandra and a Russian dancer, Misha, had already begun their summer tour, showing the world their amazing "One Hand Lift," and Carol was going to work in Italy and had sublet her apartment to a Julliard student, leaving me alone.

Snapping me back into the present, my dad's response was swift and convincing: "You're pretty skilled at cutting hair. Have you ever thought about getting your license?"

While I didn't always heed his advice, I decided this might be worth exploring. Thus began my enrollment at the Robert Fiance Hair School, a renowned institution in NYC. Despite my existing hairstyling abilities, I recognized gaps in my knowledge, particularly in areas like coloring and other aspects covered by the curriculum.

My adept cutting skills led to me becoming something of a teacher's pet, frequently chosen for demonstrations. However, there was competition for attention, courtesy of a figure named Mitchel. A Jewish boy, blond, slender, androgynous, with skin so pale it appeared translucent, Mitchel was openly gay, unreservedly sharing his sexual escapades with the class. He had a penchant for arriving late to the first class of the week, regaling us with tales of his weekend exploits on Fire Island. His notoriety as a "size queen," a term I needed explained, amused and intrigued many. What captivated me was his unabashed openness about his experiences and his ability to draw fascination from others, not to mention his summer gauze pants that did little to conceal his ever-ready state of arousal. With his uncanny resemblance to David Bowie, he carried an air of celebrity about him. Already working as an artist for fashion shows and magazines, his specialty was makeup. Over weeks, a mutual fascination developed. He was intrigued by my discipline, while I admired his free-spirited nature.

One day, a phone call during class changed my trajectory. Mitchel approached me upon his return.

"Are you free tonight? I need someone to do hair for a fashion show. Can you do it?" he asked.

Initially hesitant, I was swayed when he assured me it was easy. Around 6 p.m., we found ourselves at the Waldorf-Astoria Hotel where Mitchel introduced me to Betsy Johnson, the designer. Betsy briefed me on what she wanted and directed me to a room where the girls waited for their hair and makeup session. They were topless. Amid this unfamiliar scene, my instinct was to quietly observe. A table in the corner displayed lines of cocaine, indulged in by the girls and Mitchel during prep for the fashion show. Despite the atmosphere, I didn't partake. This was a stark contrast to Mitchel's weekend exploits involving various drugs and alcohol. My decision to abstain earned me a reputation for being a "tight-assed, goodie two-shoes." While I envied Mitchel's candidness and zest for life, they respected my decision.

Determined to indoctrinate me on another perspective of NYC nightlife, Mitchel formed a small group which included his roommate, who worked for "Don Kirshner's Rock Concert," an American television music variety show, along with her boyfriend. Also included in our caravan was another stylist, Jay and his girlfriend Claudia, and two girls, Lisa, and Michelle. Together we ventured into the city's nightlife, which began at 11 p.m. and finished with an early breakfast at a local diner. Thanks to Mitchel's connections, we gained entry to exclusive clubs like Studio 54, Limelight, and the Mudd Club. Discovering Mitchel and I weren't a couple, Mitchel's roommate showed an interest in me, and we briefly dated. Her ability to party deep into the night and function with a dose of cocaine in the morning fascinated me.

Under Mitchel's guidance, I honed my makeup skills and found opportunities to work on various fashion shows and magazine shoots. He introduced me to iconic fashion models: Esme, Jones, and Iman, as well as top modeling agencies; Ford, Wilhelmina, Elite, and IMG.

One memorable experience involved doing hair for a Cosmopolitan Magazine cover shoot. Again, Mitchel and I had our hands full in doing both makeup and hair. One of the models that I had exclusively worked on was selected for the cover. When the issue was released, I discovered that that Mitchel received credit for my work, causing a rift between us. We found ourselves, working more independently or working on a shoot with another makeup artist or hairstylist.

During this time, one of my fondest memories was working at Saks Fifth Avenue for Princess Marcella Borghese. One scorching summer afternoon, when the store was sparsely populated and Borghese was launching their new summer makeup line featuring earth-toned colors, a woman and a young girl strolled up the aisle. The woman sported tight white jeans, a form-fitting white jersey that highlighted her silhouette, vibrant red shoes, dark sunglasses, and bleached frosted hair with a soft medium brown underlay. Both casually perused the displays as they walked, but an increasing number of people gathered behind them, pointing and whispering. Within minutes, there were at least 25 people trailing her. As she neared me, we exchanged smiles, and when she came within a few feet, she lowered her sunglasses, revealing her unmistakable eyes.

"Ms. Taylor!" I blurted out in complete surprise. "You're not wearing any makeup. Would you like me to use Borghese's new summer line on you?"

She paused, glanced back at the growing crowd, and replied, laughing, "I think I'd better. I have an image to uphold! This is my stepdaughter, Mary."

For some reason, I felt compelled to explain my current role, mentioning that I was an opera singer with the NYC Opera. Elizabeth was polite and gracious, listening to my ramblings while I applied her makeup, almost seeming amused that we weren't discussing her career.

The crowd grew more intrusive, with some people even approaching her and others requesting her autograph, while her stepdaughter Mary tried to shield her.

"Is there a private area where we can finish this?" she asked.

We retreated to a back room where I had my supplies. The new makeup line complemented her hair color, and the smoky eye color with bronze highlights matched her skin tone beautifully. She was delighted and purchased two of every product I had used on her, along with some for Mary. As she leaned over to give me a quick appreciative kiss on the cheek, she tastefully slipped $200 into my jeans pocket. She then asked if there was a discreet exit. The store manager escorted her out of the building.

Employees from other makeup and perfume counters rushed to me, eager to know how it felt to do Elizabeth Taylor's makeup. I played it cool and eventually excused myself to take a break. I hurried to the nearest public phone and called my mother, who was working at City Hall.

"Mom, I just did Elizabeth Taylor!" Well, that didn't come out as I had intended. But before I could explain, mom echoed my statement to everyone in the office. "Ronnie just did Elizabeth Taylor!" After taking a deep breath, I explained in detail what had just happened.

The Met: The Opera House Melody

As September arrived, the thought of spending another six months in hairdressing school was beginning to wear thin. A cosmetology license was necessary for salon work, but I was content styling for fashion shoots, magazine covers, and doing makeup at upscale department stores. Meanwhile, my peers in the performing arts were back to their routines of classes, auditions, and survival jobs, while I sat through lectures on hair follicles and nail beds. Didn't they realize I had no intention of making a career of this? It was just a backup, an insurance policy for leaner times. I was destined for the stage, forever performing.

One Friday morning, I chose laundry over punctuality at hair school. As I stepped out of the elevator, my phone rang. Answering quickly, I heard an unrecognized voice on the other end: someone from the Metropolitan

Opera. They mentioned being impressed by my *Bleeker Street* performance in the NYC Opera broadcast and invited me for a meeting at the opera house later that day. Although I'd walked this short path for two years, this time felt different as I headed toward the stage door of the Metropolitan Opera, discreetly located beneath what would be 65th Street.

Passing through the secure door, I had no idea what to expect. At the front desk, I announced, "Hi, I'm Ron Boucher. I have an appointment—"

Before I could finish, a man nearby interjected, "Oh, are you Ron?"

He turned to the front desk attendant and said, "I know where he's going; I'll take him." With that, he whisked me through a locked door into the administrative offices, dressing rooms, and toward the main stage. His grip was firm, and once the door closed behind us, he leaned in and muttered, "You know, there are a lot of talented people who've been here for a while, so don't expect too much." But his attempt to intimidate me slid off, softened by my naive confidence.

He brought me to an office, where he introduced me to a warm, welcoming man who immediately complimented my performance from the NYC Opera broadcast. The company had noticed my look and talent, and they offered me a cameo role in their upcoming production of *Otello* for the opening night of the 1979–80 season—mirroring my position at NYC Opera. The man also noted that the first performance would be on opening night and would be televised on PBS as part of the *Live from Lincoln Center* series. I accepted without hesitation.

After notifying the school of this unexpected development, they generously accommodated my schedule. The administrator granted me flexibility providing that I make an effort to make an appearance from time to time. There was one stipulation. He asked for an autographed photo which I eventually provided him.

The energy at the Met hit me the moment I walked through the stage door —it was worlds apart from the nurturing environment of New York City Opera, which had always supported young artists. Here, the atmosphere

Otello
©Beth Bergman

was cutthroat, sharp with competition and whispers of backstage rivalries. Any attention I drew from principal singers or directors only seemed to intensify the tension.

Opening night, September 24, 1979, was surreal. Being part of a production with opera legends—Plácido Domingo as Otello, Gilda Cruz-Romo as Desdemona, and Sherrill Milnes as Iago—felt like stepping into a dream.

As the curtain rose, the town's people were gathering on the rocky shore, awaiting Otello's arrival, as the ship appeared in the distance. The stage lighting cast a dim glow, mimicking the dark of night, with only the flickering campfires providing warmth. I mingled with the townsfolk as the music swelled with anticipation. Director Kirk Browning had staged a courtship dance, our movements adding energy to the joyous atmosphere just before Otello's grand entrance.

As the Met chorus filled the stage, singing jubilantly, I navigated the uneven slope of the raked stage, adapting to the "rocky" terrain as Browning had instructed, bringing a folk-like quality to each step. And then—my solo. As I stood, simultaneously the chorus sank to the ground. The weight of the moment hit me: I was performing on the Metropolitan Opera stage, broadcast to the world, in front of a full house of over three thousand people. It was beyond real, an unforgettable moment suspended in time.

After the final curtain fell, I found myself backstage, basking in the warm compliments from fellow performers. Suddenly the stage manager, a man named Stanley, approached me.

"Ron, you were truly outstanding tonight. But be careful. There are people here who may not want you around," he said in a cautionary tone.

At that moment, I had no inkling of how vital his warning would turn out to be.

As the season unfolded, I had the privilege of working with Director John Dexter in his production of *The Abduction from the Seraglio*. The cast featured luminaries including Edda Moser, Norma Burrowes, Nicolai Gedda, Kurt Moll, Norbert Orth, and Werner Klemperer, renowned for his role as Colonel Klink in the TV series *Hogan's Heroes*.

Subsequently, another director, Bruce Donnell, a young man who had made his debut with the Met in 1975, expressed interest in having me in the production of Ponchielli's *La Gioconda*, which included Met legends Grace Bumbry (later replaced by Renata Scotto) in the title role, Mario Sereni as Barnaba, and Paul Plishka as Alvise. The most impressive, though, was Carlo Bergonzi, in the role of Enzo Grimaldo.

Abduction of Seraglio

During one performance, while Bergonzi was singing his celebrated aria "Cielo e Mar," Scotto stood beside me before our entrance in the gondola.

She grabbed my hand and asked, "Listen, is he going to do it tonight?"

I was utterly baffled and had no idea what she meant. However, a few moments into the aria, she turned to me, shook her head, and remarked, "No, not tonight."

She never elaborated on her comment, and this scenario played out in every performance except once when she posed the same question, and her response was, "Rinaldo, yes, I think he'll do it tonight!"

Indeed, Bergonzi received seven standing ovations. Afterward, turning to me, Scotto uttered words that have stayed with me forever, "It's moments like this that make retiring a very difficult decision."

Perhaps it was my innocence, youth, or my sincere thirst for knowledge, but many individuals took a keen interest in nurturing my career. They offered advice, coaching, and valuable networking opportunities.

Bruce and I remained friends even after "La Gioconda." One evening, he invited me to dinner. When I entered his apartment Bruce was already entertaining an older gentleman to whom I was introduced to as simply "Frank." Our conversation, as often happens with artists, gravitated toward the arts. Frank seemed to have a deep knowledge of the big screen. As he was leaving the dinner, he turned to me and said, "You should consider doing movies! I have a hunch you'd excel. I think I've become a pretty good judge over the years."

It was a parting comment. After he left, I turned to Bruce, "How does he know if I'd be good in film?" I asked.

He grinned mischievously and replied, "Oh! You have no idea who Frank is, do you?"

I admitted my ignorance, my curiosity growing.

"Ron, you just had dinner with Franco Zeffirelli."

I stood there in shock, realizing that I had spent an evening with the famous director of *Romeo and Juliet* who had just told me I had potential in film. Encouraged, I finally mustered the courage to ask Bruce if he believed my voice had the potential to make me a major opera artist.

His response was candid. "Ron, what I'm about to say has nothing to do with the quality of your voice or your vocal abilities. Personally, I believe your place is on Broadway, where you can fully utilize your multifaceted talents as a singer, actor, and dancer. Broadway would be a better fit for you."

I explained my struggles in getting work on Broadway, often hearing that my voice was too powerful or that I looked too Italian with my black Jew-fro hairstyle. At the time, I remained grateful for the blessings I had already received.

Broadway at Last! The Hip Hop Allegro

When Carol returned from Italy, we resumed our relationship, and my summer escapades with Mitchel and the gang had calmed my wild side. I came back down to reality. One evening Carol had invited her friends Jim Eiler and his partner, David Lyle, for dinner at her apartment. Their keen interest in my blossoming career, particularly given my youth and my association with the Metropolitan Opera, was evident. During conversation, the topic of my background as a dancer emerged. The two looked at each other without saying a word, both thinking the same thing. The silence broke with Jim speaking, revealing that they had secured a National Endowment grant for a national touring production in collaboration with a major symphony orchestra. They were seeking a talent to play the role of the White Rabbit in their production of "Alice in Wonderland." My interest was piqued, and Jim promptly provided me with crucial dates and his contact number, urging me to respond quickly.

Fate smiled upon me, as the tour dates fit seamlessly between seasons—just as they had for Sandra, who managed balancing shows at Radio City Music Hall with productions at New York City Opera. I was anxious, though, since I'd be away for three months. The hair salon agreed to continue honoring their commitment, as I did mine, stopping by as often as possible, even if just for an hour.

The next day, I headed to the West Village to audition. The process was rigorous. First, I demonstrated my musical abilities under the scrutiny of Gene Bargy, the composer and musical director, who guided me through complex musical passages. Then, Jim tested my acting skills, offering direction and refining each scene. Finally, I proved my dancing skills, showing I was more than capable of handling the choreography. To my elation, the verdict was swift.

"Young man, congratulations, you got the part!"

This was it, my first Actor's Equity contract, for a Broadway show/ National Tour! I could hardly believe it. All the years of work and dreaming had led to this moment, and now, Broadway was calling my name!

The Prince Street Players, founded in 1965 by Jim Eiler, initially occupied a loft on Prince Street in New York City. It evolved into a repertory company, expanding to include multiple touring companies performing in East Coast "Stock" theaters, on Broadway, and even on Network Television. A series of eleven children's musicals emerged, with four broadcasted as CBS-TV specials, one of which received an Emmy Award. I felt privileged to be a part of this remarkable company.

My debut performance took place at the prestigious Brooklyn Academy of Music, a revered venue on the Broadway circuit. For the second leg of our tour, the entire cast was whisked away to Minneapolis to perform alongside the Tri-State Symphony Orchestra. These destination performances had a certain charm; we'd give it our all onstage and then return home until the next engagement.

Our next performance was slated for the Kleinhans Music Hall in Albany, New York. Given the inclement weather, I opted to travel with the stage manager, who was responsible for transporting the scenery and props in a truck. This choice proved wise as we encountered heavy snowfall during our journey upstate. While our truck plowed through the snow with ease, we passed numerous stranded cars on the roadside. Our arrival at the hotel around 5 p.m. provided a brief respite, and I settled into my room.

The stage manager suggested a visit to the theater, and I readily agreed. The streets had already been cleared of snow, leaving behind towering mounds 10 to 15 feet high. Upon reaching the theater, I observed the stagehands and staff bustling about, preparing for the night's performance. The house manager extended an invitation to stay for the show, and I inquired about the performer.

"Who's performing?" I asked.

"Phyllis Diller," came the swift response.

My stage manager, weary from the snowy drive, was eager to get to his hotel and call it a night. If I stayed for the show, I'd be left to find my own way back. But Phyllis Diller was a beloved icon in my family—we'd watched every TV special, caught her as a guest on countless shows, and laughed through her appearances on comedy roasts. Missing her performance wasn't an option, no matter the circumstances.

Phyllis Diller's performance, as it turned out, defied my expectations. Much to my surprise, she showcased her prowess as a pianist, incorporating her musical talents throughout the concert. She seamlessly interjected her trademark comedic bits between musical pieces, delivering a truly remarkable performance.

With the stage manager gone, I had no ride back to the hotel, and walking in sub-zero temperatures was out of the question. With minimal rehearsal scheduled for the next day, I decided to mark out my dance steps on stage. As I leaped around, lost in my routine, Phyllis Diller emerged from her dressing room and joined me onstage.

"Oh, hello, Ms. Diller! I thoroughly enjoyed your performance, and I'm a huge fan," I stammered, momentarily stumbling in my dance.

"Are you a dancer?" she inquired about my activity, to which I explained that I was with the Prince Street Players, slated to perform at the theater the next day.

"Really!" now walking closer to me as her interest piqued.

"I've heard wonderful things about your company and have seen some of the productions on television. I wish I could see it, but I must leave in the morning for another show."

As she turned away, I impulsively asked, "Ms. Diller, I haven't eaten all day, and I'm famished. Would you like to join me?"

I expected a polite refusal, but to my astonishment, she replied, "That would be great! Do you know of a place?"

I shook my head, admitting my ignorance.

"Well, what hotel are you staying at?"

Luck was on my side once more; we were both lodged in the same hotel. She asked if I had transportation, and I explained that my stage manager had left, leaving me to my own devices.

"Then come with me! My limo is waiting!" she exclaimed.

Noting her full stage makeup, I offered to wait until she was ready. She quipped, "Honey, let me tell you something. If I were to take off my makeup, you might not want to have dinner with me!"

The evening kept getting better, and soon Ms. Diller and I were seated in the dining room, separated from the lobby by lush greenery. Around 10 p.m. the rest of the cast arrived. The actress playing Alice spotted us, and I introduced her to Phyllis. Her eyes widened, her face twisted in confused shock, and she quickly excused herself, claiming exhaustion, stumbling back to join the others at the check-in counter. Luckily, Phyllis's back was turned, but I could see the cast's astonishment as they learned who I was dining with and strained to catch glimpses through the decorative foliage.

My dinner with Ms. Diller was a whirlwind of laughter as she shared stories from her incredible career. The Phyllis on stage was exactly who she was offstage—genuine, sincere, and sharp-witted. When she complimented you, it was heartfelt. She wrapped up the evening by graciously picking up the tab, wishing me the best in my upcoming performances and my return to the Metropolitan Opera, and even planted a warm kiss on my cheek as we said goodbye.

The next morning, we headed to the theater, the freshly fallen snow glistening in the sun, radiating warmth like stage lights. Unlike at New York City Opera, I shared a dressing room with a few other men. Although no one mentioned my dinner with Ms. Diller, I applied my makeup and slipped into my costume, quietly replaying the night in my mind. The musicians struck up the overture, and we performed to a full house. After taking our bows, we packed up and headed back to NYC, the night with Phyllis lingering in my thoughts like a well-kept secret.

Next on our journey was a three-month stint in Florida, and while I was excited on some level, the prospect of extended time away from home, my refuge in the city, and living out of a suitcase initiated some trepidation. To prepare for the trip, I opened my first charge account at Macy's, and purchased a new wardrobe for the spring/summer season and a larger suitcase, as I didn't have one suitable for an extended stay.

As a newcomer to touring, I had no idea what to expect. Our journey began at LaGuardia Airport, and our destination was Sarasota. The dramatic shift in climate from thirty-two degrees at departure to a scorching and humid eighty-seven degrees upon arrival was nothing short of shocking. The first order of business was shedding my winter coat. The cast members retrieved their luggage from the conveyor belt, but my new suitcase remained conspicuously absent. A single forlorn suitcase circled the belt, but it clearly wasn't mine. After confirming the luggage tag, I reported the issue to airport officials. They gathered my information, promising to locate and deliver my suitcase as soon as possible. Since it was out of my control, I decided to get some rest and pray the airlines might have delivered it during the night.

The following morning, we ventured to the Van Wezel Performing Arts Hall. I grew increasingly nervous as my dance belt, tights, ballet slippers, and specialized makeup for my role were all packed in my missing suitcase. We were summoned to the stage for spatial orientation and a sound check. The theater was immense, and the stage seemed even larger than Radio City Music Hall's. The floor was unforgiving cement, devoid of any springiness. With the curtain about to rise in twenty minutes, a fellow cast member lent me a dance belt, and we found a pair of beige tights that clashed with my white costume, making me appear unclothed from the waist down. But, as the saying goes in show business, "The show must go on!" As pre-show anxiety crept in, a brisk knock on my dressing room door jolted me—it was my suitcase, finally delivered by the airline. Apparently, a man had grabbed it by mistake, never bothering to check the tag, and stashed it in the trunk of his car. Only upon attempting to unpack did he realize his error. The airline staff extended their apologies, and I expressed profuse gratitude while hurriedly changing into my own attire and made it to the stage just in the nick of time.

I marveled at how the orchestra seamlessly synchronized with the production cues despite the lack of a full run-through. The tempos were consistent, and despite having to adjust my choreography for the expansive stage during entrances and exits, the performance went remarkably well.

The next day presented an unexpected challenge. Upon arriving at the theater, I warmed up and ventured onstage to review some choreography. As I began executing a ballonné, searing pain shot through the front of my shin, from just below the kneecap to the top of my foot. It was excruciating, and I felt panic rising. I sought advice from fellow cast members, but none offered any helpful insights. So, I called Sandra and described my condition hoping that her years of dance experience would have a remedy.

"Oh, yes, you have shin splints. The muscle is pulling away from the bone, causing that pain," she explained.

While it was reassuring to have a diagnosis, I wondered if there was a remedy.

"You need to do lots of pliés and tendus," she advised.

Easier said than done, given the excruciating pain I was in. However, her recommendation proved effective in alleviating the discomfort, and I managed to get through the performance. Fortunately, I had a couple of days to recuperate before our next show in Miami.

Our journey continued with a three-week stay at the Parker Playhouse in Fort Lauderdale. We were informed that we'd be sharing the theater with another touring production, but I had no inkling that it was David Bowie and Juliet Mills starring in "The Elephant Man." While I wasn't particularly a Bowie music fan, I held immense admiration for his acting abilities, and the chemistry between him and Ms. Mills was undeniably electrifying. After witnessing their first show, I approached the stage manager to identify myself.

"Hi, I'm Ron Boucher and I am performing in Alice." Is there any possibility that I can be a fly in the wing and observe the show from backstage?" He kindly obliged, and I situated myself on stage right where there were the fewest entrances and exits.

After a couple of shows, curiosity finally got the better of Ms. Mills, who approached me to inquire about my presence backstage. I explained my background, where I had performed, and how I had positioned myself as a drama student, keen to absorb the nuances of their acting. Ms. Mills was deeply impressed by my dedication and attended one of our performances. The experience of learning through observation from both Mr. Bowie and Ms. Mills was invaluable, akin to a masterclass in acting.

Living out of a suitcase was far from enjoyable, particularly when paired with a roommate whose schedule didn't align with mine. At one point, in pursuit of a good night's sleep, I moved out of the hotel and stayed with relatives. By the tour's conclusion, I was eagerly anticipating my return to the bustling streets of New York City. Oh, and the entire time we were in Fort Lauderdale, it was freezing. A cold front from the north had dipped so low that the orange groves had suffered. The day before we left, desperate for some sun, most of the cast headed to the beach. We dug holes in the sand to shield ourselves from the chilly breeze off the water, making it just tolerable enough to bask in our bathing suits in the sun.

Return from the Rabbit Hole: A Divo's Réquiem

The day after my return from Florida, Aida was the first performance on the schedule. As was customary, I disrobed and awaited the application of makeup to my body before slipping into my costume. However, an odd atmosphere prevailed, my fellow performers were staring at me, their usual camaraderie silenced. Just before body makeup application, a manager entered the dressing room. Seeing me, his brows frowned as he stopped abruptly in his tracks.

"Didn't you receive the message? You've been replaced! Dress up and come to my office," he ordered.

I slipped on my clothes, gathered my belongings, and hastened to the manager's office. I sat there waiting for him to end his call, a nervous ball of uncertainty.

The manager hung up and shot a piercing question my way,

"Just who the hell do you think you are?"

Stumbling to respond, I offered, "I'm sorry, I'm not sure what you mean." I was completely perplexed as to where this was coming from.

He extracted a newspaper clipping from his drawer, a piece from the Standard Times, my home town newspaper from New Bedford. The article featuring a headline boasting "City Tenor Fills Bill at Met," embellished with a sizable image of me in the role of the Saint of Bleeker Street from the New York City Opera. The manager's tone shifted as he interrogated me further.

"Who do you think you are? Placido Domingo? And what about this, you, being James Levine's protégé?

It turned out that the article had been published while I was on tour, and, consequently, I hadn't seen it yet. The conversation shifted as he tossed the article my way. Quickly grabbing the paper, I perused the article to understand what was so offensive. Despite its complimented tone, I clarified.

"Oh sir, I never claimed to be Mr. Levine's protégé."

Doubt lingering, he dialed the newspaper, asking to speak with the woman who wrote the article, Marian Mitchell. She was was not in the office.

Angrily slamming the receiver in the cradle, he looked up at me and said, " In any case, there was a mix-up in calling you in. We thought you were another young man, an actual protégé of Mr. Levine. You're let go, especially since you're not scheduled for any spring season productions."

Not able to validate my honesty, he dismissed me with a swift brushstroke signaling me to leave his office.

While I wasn't overly concerned, assuming I could return to the New York City Opera, I learned they weren't offering seasonal contracts to most soloists anymore, and the young artists program didn't involve performing.

In New York City, survival takes precedence. Now that I found myself unemployed and in need of quick financial stability, it became imperative to rethink my strategy. Luckily, I had been able to save most of my income while on tour. Sandra had prepped me on how to be very frugal through her own multiple touring experiences. My plan was multifaceted: secure employment, resume auditions, continue vocal lessons and coaching, and maintain my dance classes.

In addition, there were only a few weeks left to complete the course at the hair institute. I returned just in time for the review for the NY State Board Exam. Fortunately, most of what would be on the exam was covered during the first part of the course with hands-on procedures that I had already learned before I had begun at the opera house. A few weeks later I took the exam and received my cosmetology license.

Armed with my new-found credentials, I sought employment at Harvey's Bazar, a hair salon nestled on 72nd Street between Broadway and Columbus Avenue. The salon's owner's name was indeed Harvey. As we began the interview, his eyes twinkled with fond memories of days lost.

"Young man, you must be a performer?"

The cat was out of the bag, my cover was broken, my disguise tossed, as he swiftly discerned my performer's aura during the interview, steering our conversation towards my artistic accomplishments.

"I recognize that sparkle in your eyes! I used to have the same sparkle and many similar dreams. Ok, here's the deal!"

He assured me a job, provided I stayed true to my purpose in the city. Harvey also generously allowed me to create my own schedule, granting me the opportunity to work with walk-in clients while I built my clientele.

One particular day, as I was wrapping up with a client, the bell rang signaling someone had entered the salon. A brief glance over to the door, a French beret caught my eye. Then the sound of broken English.

He assertively declared, "I vant haircut."

Harvey explained that all stylists were currently occupied, but the man, growing more impatient, insisted.

"I don't have time to vait, I want haircut now!"

I was just concluding with my client so I volunteered to assist him. I swiftly tidied up my station and approached the waiting area to escort him to my station.

"Okay, sir, I can take... Oh my God! Mr. Nureyev!"

Clad in a peasant-style shirt with long sleeves, snug knit tights, and conspicuous absence of a dance belt, making his appendage obvious, Rudolf Nureyev stood before me, looking as if he had just left a dance class. Completing the ensemble were tall brown leather boots not quite touching his knees. He sat down in the chair.

"How do you know who I am?"

Believing he was jesting, I responded, "Mr. Nureyev, everyone knows who you are. We also crossed paths a few years ago, although I doubt you remember."

Trying to be entertaining, I shared with him our encounter that happened one early Sunday morning in October of '76, when I was on my way to rehearsal at the State Theater.

"Mr. Nureyev, you were sitting on the fountain. As I crossed, you asked me where I was going. I clarified that I was an opera singer en route to rehearsal, and you attempted to dissuade me from attending, suggesting I accompany you to your apartment instead."

He was not amused, offering no comment to my anecdote and remaining unresponsive. After the haircut was complete, he paid at the register and departed without a word of thanks or a tip.

As summer approached, I found myself deeply entrenched in my routine. Bill, my vocal coach, encouraged me to dedicate this time to honing my vocal technique. He initially referred me to John Alexander, a tenor I had admired from the New York City Opera's production of "Manon" with Beverly Sills. However, his approach to singing did not resonate with me, as it clashed with the technique that I had already received.

It was about that time that I received an enticing phone call from Robert Fiance Hair Institute.

"Ron, this is Robert. I have a job opportunity for you if you're interested," he said.

He proceeded to inform me that Pierre Michel Hair Salon was seeking an individual who could converse in French. When he learned that I wasn't performing at the moment, there was nothing on the immediate horizon, and that I was already working in a hair salon, he suggested I'd be a better fit for this upscale 5th Avenue salon, offering considerably higher income. The prospect of "a lot more money" was alluring.

Pierre Michel, situated at the corner of 57th Street and 5th Avenue, was a salon co-owned by Pierre and Michelle. My interview with Pierre was conducted in French. He opened with a question designed to be intimidating.

He asked, "What is your weakest area in hair?"

I responded promptly: hair coloring. Satisfied with my candid response, Pierre assigned me to work under Robert Renn, the salon's premier colorist renowned for his innovative highlighting technique, emphasized in his recently published book. Robert was a flamboyant and openly gay

RON BOUCHER of St. Anthony of Padua parish, New Bedford, is a licensed hair stylist as well as an aspiring singer with the Metropolitan Opera. Obviously a shoo-in for the role of the Barber of Seville. (Rosa Photo)

Cutting Hair

individual who enjoyed sharing stories of his adventures on Fire Island with clients. He relished being the center of attention, and the salon served as his stage. Since I didn't consider the salon my primary career, I was content to allow him the limelight. Initially, I was tasked with washing and rinsing clients' hair, discovering that the addition of a head massage boosted my tips. However, this reduction in Robert's gratuities led to me being reassigned as Robert's personal assistant. My responsibilities included mixing color formulas or bleach and providing foil squares while he conducted his high-volume highlighting appointments. It seemed like everyone in New York City was going blonde. After approximately three weeks, my friend, an actor, reached out to request highlights. I approached Pierre, inquiring if I could perform the highlights at the salon, but it turned out my friend couldn't afford it.

Unbeknownst to me, Mr. Renn was soon departing, and this was Pierre's way of evaluating my readiness. It became evident that he was satisfied because soon he announced that starting the following Tuesday, I was on my own because Robert would be away for a week.

That Tuesday, Mr. Renn had a steady flow of clients and juggled them simultaneously. Three hours passed without a client for me and I grew disheartened. It felt like a significant departure from the norm. Then

Pierre approached, informing me of a VIP client in need of a color reversal. Panic seized me as I had never performed such a procedure.

" I don't know how to do a reversal!" I said, expressing my concern to Pierre.

"It's easy. You do the same thing as when you do highlights, just using color. You've got this!"

As I waited at my station, gathering a few materials for the procedure, Robert said, "Ms. John, this is our colorist Ron and he will be taking care of you today!"

Ms. John stood in front of me at about 5' 6" tall, slim body and a remarkable smile. So concerned about the task at hand, I completely focused on her over-bleached, almost white hair. As she began to speak with an adorable Australian accent, she quickly informed me that the reason her hair was almost white was because they kept adding highlights during her recent filming *Xanadu* and she desired a return to a more natural look. At that moment I realized I was attending to Olivia Newton-John.

As I wove each section of hair, covered it in color, then wrapped it in foil, she asked how long I had been with the salon. Presenting the perfect opportunity, I explained that this was a temporary endeavor while on season break from Lincoln Center. These words worked like magic, immediately finding a shared topic for discussion. She relaxed into my chair, and our conversation flowed naturally as we discussed the challenges of our respective careers and her journey as a singer/actress. We shared the singers who had an influence on us, mine being Mario Lanza, and hers, Petula Clark. When the procedure was finished, she seemed very pleased, she wished me the best of luck with my career, and I wished her continued success with hers. Her departure hug and kiss left the other stylists with the impression we were best of friends.

That week was enough to raise my position with Pierre, and he appointed an assistant to support me. When Robert returned the following week, I found myself working side by side with him, as equals. This transition wasn't easy for Mr. Renn, who was unaccustomed to sharing the spotlight. He was the salon's diva, and the situation didn't sit well with him. To compound matters, whenever new celebrity clients arrived, they were often assigned to me when I was available. These clients included individuals from NBC, various news anchors, and talk show hosts.

Of all the celebrities I worked with that summer, one stood out distinctly in my memory. A woman who appeared to be in her fifties occupied my chair for a hair coloring session. She exuded elegance with her simple jacket and blouse that had that classic Chanel look, and she soft-spoken grace, reminiscent of Sandra's disposition.

Robert recognized her immediately and tried to insert himself into our conversation while tending to his client. It was apparent that she was a famous personality, yet her identity eluded me, and I was reluctant to reveal my ignorance to either her or Robert. Even when he addressed her by name, my memory failed me. She refrained from discussing her career and exhibited a keen interest in mine by asking me questions about what brought me to NYC.

That evening, after returning home, I phoned my mother and asked, "Do you know an actress named Hedy Lamarr?"

Her gasp of recognition implied they had been close friends.

"Of course, I know who Hedy Lamarr is! Oh my God, she was breathtakingly beautiful. Why do you ask?" My mother spent the evening contacting her friends to share the news that I had styled Hedy Lamarr's hair.

Ultimately, I began earning enough in tips to cover my lesson expenses, while my salary helped manage basic living costs like rent, phone bills, and food. However, my tenure at the salon was destined to be short-lived, as by the arrival of autumn, I was prepared to return to my true calling: singing.

Reflecting on my encounters with Mr. Nureyev, Ms. John, and Ms. Lamar, I realized that when I was not Ron Boucher, the opera singer, I was treated as subservient. But as the opera singer, even when engaged in hairstyling, people regarded me differently. Their tone shifted, and they seemed fascinated by my dual roles.

Drifting Away: The Driftwood Duet

My relationship with Sandra underwent a transformation when she began dancing alongside a Russian dancer named Misha Korogodsky. He was a striking, dark-haired figure who possessed immense strength. He had a history with the Bolshoi Ballet before his defection. My understanding was that life for him as a Russian Jew had become increasingly difficult in Russia. When given the opportunity to leave, he seized it and brought his wife and son to NYC.

Initially, Sandra exhibited hesitance regarding Misha, often requesting my presence when they rehearsed together. Misha was on the hunt for a partner capable of executing extraordinary adagio work. Sandra, fearless and unwavering, allowed herself to be tossed and flipped during their rehearsals. Their collaboration yielded a particular lift where he would balance her in the palm of his outstretched hand while she posed on pointe gracefully in an arabesque position. This breathtaking feat made its debut in a New York City Opera production called "La Belle Hélène" during the spring of 1977. The two dancers posed on pedestals, resplendent in all-white attire, resembling statues. With a simple clap from one of the principal singers, they sprang to life, dancing into this lift that would forever immortalize Sandra in the world of dance.

Misha harbored desires beyond their professional partnership, although Sandra resisted. However, everything changed in November of '77 when they were performing together in Los Angeles at the Dorothy Chandler Pavilion, during a production of "Die Fledermaus." As soon as they returned to NYC, I visited and sensed something was amiss as I watched him walk around the apartment with comfort and familiarity. He left for an appointment and as the door to the apartment closed, I turned to Sandra.

"You didn't! Please tell me you're not involved with him!" I said.

Sandra reluctantly admitted the truth. I felt a profound sense of betrayal. I had harbored hope that she wouldn't succumb because she had given every indication that she disliked him. Now that they were embroiled in an affair, he became insistent on keeping me at a distance, delighting in flaunting his conquest.

Apart from a single opportunity to showcase his skills in the production, *La Belle Helene*, it seemed that Misha's dancing was limited, and the company was disinclined to center productions around him.

During the second half of the season, the company performed *Carmina Burana*. Although it is an opera, this production was done as a full ballet with chorus and soloists acting more like instruments in the orchestra. The focus was on the choreography set by John Butler. Sandra was the sole dancer chosen from the NYC Opera Ballet Company to be one of the four main dancers, marking a significant achievement for her. The production isolated Sandra from Misha, and in turn, it seemed he developed an obsession to separate Sandra from her friends, family, and, especially me.

My meetings with Sandra became clandestine, restricted to late-night encounters in the laundry room or discreet rendezvous in the grocery store's back aisle. Misha persuaded her to leave the opera company, leading to her permanent departure from Lincoln Center, her artistic home for twenty-five years.

Subsequently, they accepted a position as guest artists in Newport News, Virginia, which eventually led to a brief stint as artistic directors for the Virginia State Ballet. They often returned to NYC for business and for lack of reason, I would sense their visits. Sandra and I would find ways to meet in secret. Each time we met, she seemed happy to see me. I always sensed her circumstances were not her choice which caused me to worry.

Though I perceived that something was amiss, it appeared as if she had resigned herself to the situation, leaving me helpless to do anything about it. She was at her thinnest, weighing a mere ninety-two pounds, but she remained radiantly beautiful on stage. Regrettably, aside from sporadic performances at Radio City Music Hall, Misha and Sandra mostly engaged in guest appearances with regional opera companies, master classes, and work with Dance Caravan, a national dance competition organization. By their fifth year, performance opportunities had dwindled, and Sandra, almost relieved, had come to terms with the twilight of her career.

In September 1982, she decided to break free from her personal and professional ties with Misha. However, Misha was determined to prevent her from dancing again. According to Sandra's recollection, during an argument while he was trying to persuade her not to leave, he took matters into his own hands. He brutally injured her little toe by crushing it in a way that necessitated surgery to remove the bone from the toe, effectively destroying her desire to dance on pointe ever again.

Sandra reached out to Ms. Cheryl and her husband Mike to help her move her things from Virginia back to her apartment in NYC. The entire move was done under concealment and secrecy so that Misha would be unaware.

They had just completed depositing the last of Sandra's belongings in her apartment from the rented U-haul and were heading back out, waiting for the elevator. Simultaneously, I was leaving my apartment from the 28th floor. There was never a time when the elevator door stopped on the 17th floor that I didn't anticipate Sandra stepping in. This time was no different. When the elevator stopped on seventeen, my heart began to race with anticipation.

The door opened and there was Sandra, Cheryl and Mike. Cheryl drew back while uttering "Oh Jesus!" and Sandra calmly said, "Well hello!" with a sense of déjà vu as we embraced. Although my exterior exuded calmness, my emotions were running in all directions. After Cheryl and Mike left to return to New Bedford, Sandra and I spent all evening together as she explained the entire ordeal that lead her to that point.

My hopes were reignited. We resumed our friendship as if time had stood still. For Sandra, healing would take some time both physically and emotionally. She was wounded and sullen. She was missing that spark she had once exuded, and was instead withdrawn, quietly nurturing her slowly mending foot.

During a lunch at O'Neil's Balloon restaurant on 72nd and Columbus Avenue, engaged in pleasant conversation with Sandra, I suddenly saw her eyes widen with fear, and her body recoiled into the seat. I followed the direction of her gaze and saw Misha glaring at her from the window. He rushed for the entrance. I stood, my adrenaline surging. I was determined to protect her. He approached and as his eyes met mine, he turned and left.

I assured Sandra he was gone, and her nerves began to calm. I had hoped that Sandra would now view me as her protector, her hero, a role any genuine man would undertake for a damsel in distress.

Although her foot had healed and she could dance en pointe again, Sandra had lost her passion for classical ballet and sought more contemporary work. In her vulnerable state, she fell prey to another individual seeking to advance in the dance world, Juan. He came with an embellished résumé that included choreographic credits with the Dance Theater of Harlem and a Gold Medal from the 1984 Olympics. He believed that through Sandra's connections he could advance his aspirations to become a choreographer like George Balanchine or Robert Joffrey.

I later learned that Sandra and Misha had hired him and others for a ballet production in Virginia. During this period, Sandra was steadfast in her determination to remain free from Misha's control, and this particular dancer provided her with much-needed support. Coincidentally, he used her fame to be invited to choreograph for the National Ballet de Peru under the condition that Sandra would serve as a guest artist on a nationwide tour sponsored by Coca-Cola. It was an opportunity too significant for Sandra to decline.

Artistically, the tour was successful. The performances in an outdoor stadium were sold out. People had come to see the American ballerina.

When Sandra returned from the tour, she told me how sick she had become from food poisoning and was left alone to be cared for by nuns in a convent. However, when she threatened to leave, Juan would suddenly be warm, caring, and affectionate. But once the tour was over and she was back in NYC, so was her relationship.

A few months later Sandra revealed a troubling secret over dinner: she was pregnant. My assumption was that she would opt for an abortion, given that the child was likely his. To my astonishment, she emphatically declined.

"Does the father know?" I asked, expecting an affirmative response.

She confirmed that he did but added that he was disinterested in the child and wanted her to terminate the pregnancy. Despite the less-than-ideal circumstances, I offered to marry her and vowed to raise the child as my own. She declined, explaining that she couldn't burden me with her mess.

Shortly afterward, Sandra received a call from a woman who owned a studio in Williamsburg, Virginia, where Sandra and Misha had previously taught. The studio was vacant, and she wondered if Sandra or someone she could recommend might be interested in taking it over. For Sandra, it was a lifeline, a chance to escape quietly to Williamsburg and fade into obscurity and a means to support herself and her child.

Weeks later, Juan visited her, and she disclosed her intentions. Another week passed before he showed up unannounced at her apartment, bypassing the doorman. He professed his love for her, his foolishness, and his willingness to sacrifice his career to move to Williamsburg with her and establish a school (and of course, a company).

They were married in a modest ceremony at Rutgers Presbyterian Church, and I reluctantly agreed to serve as his best man. When the minister inquired if anyone had objections, I hesitated, raising my hand briefly before Sandra scowled at me, prompting my silence.

A few weeks after the wedding, Juan and Sandra moved to Williamsburg to begin their new life. Sandra, resigned to her fate, left me in charge of her apartment and its safe keeping. Her self-confidence and resolve were at their lowest. She felt defeated and helpless. Although we said our goodbyes, I don't think either of us believed we would not find our way back.

The apartment was our conduit for continued communication. I could tell during our talks that there was excitement for the new studio. However, I also sensed her trepidations with her marriage. Sandra, in her sixth month of pregnancy, confirmed her suspicions that her new husband was involved with other women. Alone in Williamsburg, she succumbed to depression and the patterns of an emotionally

Connecticut Grand Opera
Formal Headshot

abusive relationship, which pained me deeply every time I saw her, either when she came to NYC to hold auditions for the company or my occasional visits to Williamsburg.

I had finally come to terms with the fact that Sandra and I would never be together; but that we would remain distant friends. I had rationalized her previous relationship with Misha. He had possessed charisma. He was striking, ambitious, well-dressed, and, of course, tall. This justified in my head why she hadn't chosen me, a man, 5 feet 8 inches with short legs. But to marry this 5-foot 6-inch man who wasn't even particularly attractive! What kind of failure did that make me? There was a period when I wanted to punish myself, spiraling into a deep depression, questioning my self-worth and identity. The complexities of human relationships and the unforeseen turns they take left me pondering the weight of our decisions and the unpredictable paths they can set us on.

The Connecticut Grand Opera: The Overture

My two-year hiatus came to an abrupt halt when my agent called bringing news that Menotti was set to stage Bleeker Street with the Connecticut

Grand Opera. He had been in direct contact with Menotti, inquiring if he'd be interested in having me reprise my role in the New York City Opera production. Unfortunately, Menotti had declined, suggesting that six years might have rendered me too old for the part. Fueled by determination, I dialed Menotti's number and pleaded for another chance. He agreed to meet me for lunch and to his surprise, my physical appearance showed little change. He reconsidered and decided to bring back the magic by casting me once more. The production premiered on Saturday, November 20th, 1982, at the Klein Memorial Auditorium in Bridgeport. Lorenzo Muti of Spoleto, Menotti's protégé, conducted the production, featuring soloists from esteemed opera companies including the Metropolitan Opera, the New York City Opera, and the National Opera. The cast principals comprised Elizabeth Volkman, Melvyn Poll, Rosemarie Freni, Irwin Densen, Donna Casella, and me.

As I commuted to rehearsals from NYC, John Hiddlestone, the general manager, asked if I could bring Menotti along. Amidst our many conversations, one stands out in my memory. But before I share that, I must provide you with some background information.

During my college years, I bought a Datsun B-210, an unassuming box-like vehicle. After I moved to NYC, my sister Renee inherited it. The car eventually returned to me, in its faded army green hue and like my VW with its floorboard rotting, but it was my symbol of progress. Lincoln Towers boasted its own underground parking garage, a luxury that came at less than $100 a month, offering valet parking and the convenience of owning a car in the city. Owning a garaged car in New York was a sign of status, even if it was a worn-out Datsun B-210. It symbolized upward mobility.

During one of our shared commutes to Bridgeport, Menotti made an observation that stuck with me. He spoke with a blend of gratitude and humor. "Please don't take this the wrong way, as I am very appreciative of the ride and your company, but it's quite remarkable how circumstances change. Not too long ago, I had a Rolls-Royce picking me up at Heathrow airport for a command performance before the Queen. And now, here I am, riding in a Datsun. How things have changed, indeed!"

It was a poignant reminder that one's career trajectory can fluctuate wildly, taking even the most prominent to unanticipated heights or plunging them into obscurity.

Vocal Recovery: The Choral Rhapsody

Refocused on my singing career, I began coaching lessons more regularly. But while working with my vocal coach, Bill (maestro William Hicks), he saw the need for some work on my technique. He suggested that I study with Clarice Carson, a distinguished Canadian soprano, and celebrated Metropolitan Opera performer renowned for her commanding vocal prowess in roles such as the Lady-in-Waiting in *Macbeth* and Desdemona in *Otello*. After listening to me sing, she accepted me as her student.

Clarice resided at 10 West 66th Street and enjoyed one of the few duplex apartments—the other half of which was occupied by the renowned soprano, Marilyn Horne. A significant hurdle, though, was that I was no longer part of the young artists program, which meant I had to pay for my lessons. Clarice charged $120 per hour and expected cash upon arrival. Nonpayment or failure to provide a 24-hour cancellation notice resulted in a compulsory payment for the lesson. I needed to draft a weekly schedule encompassing jogging around Central Park, voice lessons, coaching sessions, ballet and jazz classes, and gym workouts, all woven around my work schedule. Luckily, Bill graciously reduced his fee, and Mme. Darvash didn't charge for my ballet classes. I became a member of the West Side YMCA due to its affordability and proximity to my apartment. The harsh reality, however, was that my earnings at Harvey's Bazar were insufficient to sustain this regimen.

Our professional relationship was unique. Clarice's teaching style was nothing if not bold—unapologetically candid, brash, and almost shockingly blunt. She never hesitated to express her displeasure, often with language that could rival a seasoned truck driver's. I couldn't help but find her colorful critiques amusing, even when she quipped, "They hired you to sing this? What is the opera world coming to?"

Her approach was as unorthodox as it was unforgettable. However, for some reason, I was not intimidated and found her amusing, which seemed to entertain her and strengthened the mentorship that we had developed. After a few months, she graciously invited me to attend her own coaching sessions with Joan Dornemann from the Met.

One of the first directives Clarice issued was for me to join a gym. She attributed my occasional bodily tremors during powerful vocal deliveries to the incongruity between my prodigious voice and my slender physique. Another intriguing task involved jogging around the Central Park reservoir while singing my arias—an exercise that simultaneously challenged my stamina and vocal control. However, the most profound lesson I gleaned from Clarice was the essence of true vocal support—a technique that I later incorporated into my own teaching career with remarkable success.

Admittedly, while Clarice's teaching methods resonated deeply with me, they did not prove effective for everyone. Much like the way John Alexander's vocal approach failed to resonate with me, Clarice's unconventional style did not yield favorable results for a select few of her students, some of them professional Met singers. Nevertheless, her unorthodox wisdom left an indelible mark on my journey as a singer and educator.

A series of events transpired involving several of Clarice's students, where she wielded her influence in ways that undermined their self-esteem and inflicted vocal suffering. One of her students from the Met brought these issues to light. This paralleled my own experience under John Alexander's methodology, due to his high lyric tenor approach. Clarice's technique catered more to the dramatic or Helden Tenor category, which I was identified with – possessing both baritone qualities and a tenor range.

Among those affected was a strikingly handsome tenor whose once-beautiful high lyric voice had deteriorated. He had chosen the aria "Una

Furtiva Lagrima" from *Elixir of Love*. Before even uttering a word, he appeared on the verge of bursting. With a deep inhalation, he held his breath, pressurized his chest, and seemed poised to unleash the aria "Di quella pira," a brief tenor piece (more precisely, a cabaletta) sung by Manrico in Act 3, Scene 2 of Giuseppe Verdi's opera Il *Trovatore*. This aria was traditionally reserved for the most seasoned of tenors. As he parted his lips to sing, the sound erupted with fervor, his body trembled, and his face mirrored the vivid hue of a summer sunset. The instructor intervened, halting his performance and instructing him to recline on the floor. The rest of us circled around, kneeling and placing our hands gently on his body, rocking him back and forth.

She then leaned in, placing her ear near his mouth, and said, "Alright, I want you to try this again. But this time, imagine you're singing a lullaby to a baby you're trying to soothe to sleep, not attempting to raise the dead."

After several cycles of controlled inhalations and releases, she guided him to continue to the next breath and sing upon its release. The ensuing sound that graced our ears was that of a finely executed lyric tenor, with each note surpassing the last. Halfway through the aria, she halted him, instructing us to return to our seats.

"Now, do it again, and don't change a thing," she urged.

As the saying goes, old habits die hard, and it took him several attempts to recapture the effortless ease with which he had first produced his graceful sound—a hallmark of a high lyric tenor.

Next up was another tenor, Leslie Harrington, who had not been one of Clarice's students, but rather a friend of the instructor. Leslie made an immediate impression. He stood tall, had broad shoulders, exuded a radiant smile, and possessed charisma that overflowed. To say he was larger than life would be an understatement, and his voice matched his commanding presence. With the elegance and skill reminiscent of Pavarotti, Leslie graced us with a beautifully executed *Cielo e Mar* from *La Gioconda*.

Finally, it was my turn. After Leslie's formidable performance, I felt humbled and considered refraining from singing. Refusing to allow me to resign, I opted for "E la storia del pastore" from *L'Arlèsianna*. My approach to this aria had turned laborious; however, the essence of the aria persisted. For whatever reason, it took everything I had to get through that piece. I was physically, vocally, and emotionally spent. Recognizing this, Leslie, rose and came to embrace me tightly, a momentary balm for my aching soul, reminiscent of the fatherly reassurance I yearned for.

Leslie swiftly became a surrogate big brother, and his girlfriend, Jacqueline, a Parisian with an uncanny resemblance to Susan Sarandon, entered my life. Leslie frequently performed at the Maestro Restaurant on West 66th street, the opera bar of Lincoln Center. A white grand piano graced the center, and opera singers took the stage throughout the evening. I bonded with Jackie while Leslie sang. Jackie's empathy led her to recognize there was a loss, something tormenting me. Although it was still unclear what that was, I quickly developed a profound connection to her. After a few months of friendship and confiding in her about my relationship to Sandra, Jackie recommended I see her therapist, Una.

Reluctantly, I embarked in therapy, cynically expecting no tangible change. Una's initial focus was restoring my self-esteem by identifying my patterns and suggesting ways to break free. My discourse frequently revolved around Sandra – my dreams, the towering heights of potential, and the subsequent plummet to reality. Therapy kindled hope in me, hinting at the possibility of worthiness, a sentiment that pivoted my attention to Jackie. Our bond was genuine, muddling my relationship boundaries, yet her allegiance to Leslie remained steadfast, a reality I grudgingly had come to accept.

The Debutante and Codependency: The Quickstep Dance

In the summer of '83, I decided to stay in the city. As I skimmed through the audition section of *Backstage*, I spotted a casting call for an obscure Victor Herbert operetta, *The Debutante*, and successfully landed the role of Lt. George Grimston. This production reignited my passion for performing, helping me to refocus on my career.

During this time, I befriended another performer, Hugh, who after missing a train, needed a place to crash. Ordinarily, this would have been simple, except I already had a roommate who was sharing my studio apartment.

My roommate situation was ideal. David, a retired car salesman from Cape Cod, had

The Debutante

long dreamed of acting and was now free with both time and money. He decided to give it a shot in New York. He would arrive at the beginning of each month, flying in from Cape Cod to LaGuardia on Sunday evening. Typically, he spent his mornings rehearsing lines for a potential guest spot on one of New York's many soap operas or calling his agents to let them know he was available for work. By Wednesday, if nothing had come through (which was usually the case), he'd head back to Cape Cod. Since he spent most of his summer on his boat, David was rarely around, making it easy for my friend to stay over occasionally.

But Hugh's stays became more frequent, his belongings gradually encroaching on my space—or rather, David's. He even pushed David's clothes to the end of the closet to make room for his own. After *The*

Debutante wrapped, my friend's stay somehow became indefinite, and, caught up in my work, I didn't fully register the subtle takeover happening in the apartment.

When September arrived, David returned to find the new arrangement. He wasn't having it. After asking me directly whether Hugh was paying rent (he wasn't), David issued an ultimatum.

"He leaves, or I do," he said.

With no real alternative, David left, and I found myself with a new, unplanned roommate.

Subsequently, my new roommate's presence became increasingly intrusive, encroaching on my privacy, friendships, and personal life. Without a clear understanding of what was happening, I allowed the rest of my social circle to follow suit .

It wasn't long before my studio apartment proved inadequate, prompting me to seek a one-bedroom unit. The process was more arduous this time. The landlord, a Chicago-based company, held vacant apartments, oblivious to the impending real estate market shift towards apartment-to-co-op conversions. Vacant units were designated for maximum sale prices, leaving renters with little inventory to choose from. Amid persistent phone calls, I secured an available and affordable apartment just two floors above mine, apartment 30S.

Yet, the new space didn't alleviate my predicament. My new roommate continued to infiltrate my life, enrolling in vocal lessons under my instructors. His ambiguous funding for these lessons raised eyebrows. Without a job, he began neglecting his rent responsibilities and, in his view, compensated by bringing groceries from his father's health food store which carried organic meats and vegetables.

Despite my requests, his promises of change proved inconsistent.

Finally, an opportunity arose during a visit with his family to discuss my concerns. To my surprise, the family seemed to be aware of a pattern he had with other roommates, and they advised me to evict him.

Connecticut Grand Opera: The Operatic Encore

That same summer, the Connecticut Grand Opera reached out to my agent to extend an invitation for me to return for a production of *Don Pasquale*, slated to premiere on November 9. This event stirred something within my new roommate, who began to display signs of envy and jealousy. Armed with a music degree, he considered himself vocally superior and physically more imposing, heightening his insecurities. Because the new production took me away from the city, he had time to entrench himself deeper into my realm.

The production had my complete attention and dedication. It was a new opera to add to my repertoire and boasted a star-studded cast featuring Colette Boky, Richard McKee, Ezio Di Cesare, Cliff Williams, and myself. Christopher Renshaw, recruited from Covent Gardens, directed the show, marking the celebration of the renovated Palace Theater

Don Pasquale: me and Cliff Williams

in Stanford, Connecticut. The opening was accompanied by a Gala on December 14, featuring luminaries like pianist Claudio Arrau, Metropolitan Opera's Grace Bumbry; Russian prima ballerina, Natalia Makarova; American Ballet Theatre's Principal dancer, Sean Lavery;

Hungarian internationally acclaimed cellist, Janos Starker; and The American Symphony Orchestra under Italy's Gabriele Bellini's baton. It was hosted by Jerome Hines a bass-baritone who had sung at the Metropolitan Opera for over 45 years.

During this period, a conversation with Maestro Arrau left a profound impression on me. I mused about the maturation of opera singers around age fifty and inquired when pianists peak. His response, as an eighty-year-old, was simple yet impactful.

"My dear young man, I do not know the answer to this, because I haven't peaked yet!"

These words became the bedrock of my artistic journey, inspiring me to continually hone my craft in pursuit of new heights.

Once more, I was asked to chauffeur. This time it was Mr. Renshaw. Abandoning the Datsun, I purchased a brand-new Nissan Sentra hatchback.

Christopher seemed far more mature than I, exuding confidence in his abilities. To discover he was only three years my senior was shocking. We forged a strong connection. He said he found me amusing, bright, and talented. Our camaraderie grew during rehearsal process, ultimately blossoming into a lasting friendship. During one rehearsal, I found myself in an absurdly oversized hat and suit, a comedic mishap that became a cornerstone of the production's humor. Christopher embraced this whimsical approach, with Norina singing in the shower and Ernesto mimicking trumpet playing. The opera triumphed, receiving rave reviews, including a personal note of appreciation from John Hiddlestone.

Before returning to London, Christopher arranged a lunch meeting and confidently suggested that I belonged on Broadway. He believed my dramatic conviction, comedic timing, vocal versatility, and dance ability were better suited for musical theater.

Yet, in the same breath, he proposed a potential role in *L'elisir d'amore* at Covent Garden. "Ron, I think Nemorino would be perfect for you!"

Meanwhile, my roommate's behavior deteriorated rapidly. Post-Christmas, I encountered an unsettling scene arriving back at my apartment after being away for a week: dishes piled high, roaches scurrying, and my clothes strewn carelessly. Most shocking was the intrusion into my locked bedroom. The door had been busted open, my bed was unmade with food crumbs and dirty plates all over the black sheets. My closet doors were open, my dress shoes in front of my bed, and my dress pants in a pile on the floor. As I examined the pants, I saw that the hem had been undone to accommodate our height difference.

Despite my anger and insistence that he leave, he ignored my request and his audacious actions persisted. It was then that I realized a change was necessary, but I needed help on how to make that happen. Seeking counsel from my therapist, I formulated a plan to extricate myself from my roommate's manipulative grip.

With newfound resolve, I issued him a 30-day eviction notice. Despite his disregard for the ultimatum, I was determined to reclaim my space. My friends including Leslie and Jackie offered their apartment during their absence, allowing me space for myself. This helped me to finally gain a better perspective on the situation and the person I had become. Looking in the mirror I saw a young man who had lost that confidence, questioned career decisions, and allowed a festering of self-doubt regarding my talent and ability to sing. Armed with therapist-guided insights, I managed to take charge of my situation.

First, I waited for him to be at work before entering my apartment. Second, I had all my mail held at the post office in order to insure I was receiving them.

The long-anticipated 30-day deadline had finally arrived. Armed with boxes, I packed his belongings and had the locks changed. My confrontation with him was firm. I phoned him at work and told him all his belongings had been placed in the lobby and I could not guarantee their safety. I also informed him that the locks had been changed and the doorman had been told he was not allowed in the building. Cutting all ties and asserting my independence gave me a sense of accomplishment that was profound.

Jackie guided me in revamping my apartment, personalizing the space through thoughtful decoration. Realizing my financial position was comfortable, I transformed my bedroom into a masculine, yet inviting, sanctuary which included custom-made black lacquered furniture, a pearl grey carpet, and carefully chosen wallpaper that brought harmony and comfort to the space.

I meticulously transformed the kitchen as well, with every dish and utensil polished. The once-cluttered walk-in closet now served as a space where I could reorganize my belongings. I bid adieu to the past and embraced the solitary independence I had longed for.

Back to Hell: The Inferno Harmony

At the singing workshop where I met Leslie and Jackie, another acquaintance named Kristine entered my life, and a friendship blossomed between us. Married and a mother of two, she resided on 67th Street between Broadway and Amsterdam. Kristine suggested that I study with her teacher, someone she had turned to after parting ways with Clarice. With Clarice away on a performance engagement, I decided to give this new opportunity a chance. The maestro, Carlo, a short and eccentric man who fancied himself as such, greeted me. Although his appearance was comical, he was a skilled pianist and offered promising students a chance to perform at his Italy-based festival. His disregard for time boundaries and his penchant for extending lessons made him a preferred mentor.

My initial encounter with him proved to be truly enchanting. He lavished praise upon my vocal resonance, musicality, and rich tonal quality. As we explored various arias spanning diverse styles, he gained a deeper understanding of the nuances in my voice.

"Young man, we need to get you back on the bandwagon!" he said gleefully, sparking my enthusiasm.

Upon my return for the second lesson, I found myself immersed in an aria when he abruptly interrupted to elucidate the source of vocal support. Familiar with this concept, I complied when he suggested loosening my belt, a practice I had encountered with Clarice and previous instructors. However, Carlo's perspective on support delved much lower. I hesitated, drawing back as he pulled me towards him.

"Stop being ridiculous, I'm trying to show you something about support!"

He was assertive, attempting to justify his actions. Resuming my position, I stood before him, my pants still unzipped, granting him the benefit of the doubt.

"Now, support begins from here," he declared, pressing just above my pubic bone, and then lifting my shirt to reveal my stomach. As I sang a phrase, he exclaimed,

"Yes, there it is, now you are supporting."

Another musical phrase followed, but midway through, he stopped me.

"You are all tense, you need to relax. Now, turn around."

Instructing me to remove my shirt, he proceeded to massage my shoulders, intermittently pausing for me to sing. During this, he began to expound on the connection between the voice and sexuality, jesting about how the finest singers were also the most adept lovers. Pressing on my lower back, his hands then attempted to lower my underpants. Startled, I recoiled and gathered my belongings.

"If you can't be professional, then I don't want to study with you!" I told him as I left.

Immediately, I contacted Kristine to recount the unsettling incident. Her response was not one of indignation towards Carlo but rather directed at me, accusing me of fabricating such a tale about a supposedly kind and generous individual. She insisted that I had misinterpreted his actions.

Carlo called me to reschedule my lessons, a gesture I attributed to Kristine's intervention. Over the next month, he heeded my boundaries, and I believed he had understood my message. Gradually, my apprehension eased, and I began to relax in his presence. As we plunged into a new aria, I shifted to stand closer to him at the piano. But as I leaned in, his actions took a predatory turn. His hand cupped me inappropriately, crossing all boundaries. Reacting with a blend of force and repulsion, I pushed him away sending him to the floor. The lesson ended abruptly, with me leaving, hurling a prewritten check at him as I departed, signaling my disgust.

My parents had just arrived to visit for the weekend when my doorbell rang. The doorman hadn't rung me, so I assumed it was someone within the building. I found myself grappling with a subpoena from a city official. Carlo had sought legal recourse, suing me for my actions. Overwhelmed and broken by the situation, I begged my parents to let me return home. The city that had once held such promise now seemed to have defeated me. My mother was receptive to the idea of me returning home, but my father's response was unexpected. He encouraged me not to give up, reminding me that I was a fighter, not a quitter. Although I was torn, my father's words resonated deeply.

In the middle of this turmoil, Leslie and Jackie arrived to have dinner with me and my parents. Seeing the state I was in, they asked me to recount the events, sharing how Carlo's actions had led to a lawsuit. Jackie disclosed a similar experience involving Carlo, whereas Leslie's vigilance had thwarted his advances. An attorney friend of Leslie's helped ensure that the case was dropped. This news, along with the unwavering support of Jackie and Leslie, spurred me to continue my pursuits in New York.

Putting all the pieces back together was a challenge. My confidence in my vocal ability had been shattered, first by incident at the Met, and now with Carlo. I tried to throw myself into my singing but, not working with a teacher, I quickly developed some problems trying to make my voice bigger and more mature sounding. I had abandoned all technique, and I realized I needed to get back with Clarice.

During my first lesson back, she shared with me that my ex-roommate tried to use manipulation to alienate me from her. She was glad to see that I had triumphed, which inspired her to have me sing the aria "Di Quella Pira." The previous technique I could rely on had been skewed, and I was manipulating the sound rather than effortlessly producing a pure tone. An embarrassing moment occurred when Maryln Horne opened Clarice's apartment door and yelled up the stair. "Clarice! You're squeezing his balls too tight!"

Clarice sensed that there might be something clinically wrong with my voice and asked Dr. Grobchide, a Met-appointed voice doctor, to attend one of my lessons. After observing, he insisted I visit him at his office the next morning, where I endured his scrutinizing gaze. Dr. Grobchide resembled a small version of Alfred Hitchcock with a thick German accent in a white lab coat accentuated by an old-fashioned light reflector on his forehead.

"Hmm… Ya! Oooooh, and tsk tsk," he muttered.

He then directed me to stick out my tongue, an action that led to intense pain as he manipulated it.

With a solemn tone, he revealed his diagnosis. "Ok, Mr. Boucher, I have a recommendation for you if you wish to continue to sing and have a career. You need to take a year off and rest."

Was he serious? A year's hiatus felt like an eternity to any singer.

Clarice called me to find out what Dr. Grobchide said. She told me to heed his words and with that, she cancelled all the lessons I had pre-scheduled. She told me that she once had to stop singing as well. This didn't make me feel any better. There was one small saving grace to this, Dr. Grobchide also told me that after six months I could start vocal technique lessons with Clarice.

The Foot Fetish Fandango

It was the evening after receiving the news that I was to remain vocally silent for one year. In my misery, I joined Leslie and Jackie at the Maestro restaurant, where Leslie was performing. On a rare occasion, Larry, the restaurant's renown house accompanist, would invite me to sing. Always honored when asked to sing, this particular evening my performance felt like my swan song. After my song, a gentleman approached Leslie and me. He introduced himself as Stan, the newly appointed Executive Director of the New York State Podiatric Medical Association. He was intrigued by my voice but had noticed my lack of enthusiasm.

Leslie asked me to share my predicament with him. "So, what are you going to do to pay the bills?" he asked.

I told him about my idea to reach out to some of my clients to see if they had short- or long-term projects they wanted me to manage. Stan listened as I spoke about the past projects I had worked on.

"I may have something you might be interested in," he said. As he spoke of his offer, I listened intently. Stan proposed we meet the next day at his office on 31st and 6th Avenue. Intrigued, and open to a new possibility, I agreed to the meeting.

Situated in a rundown building, the office lacked employees, and urgently needed repairs. Stan, a Californian executive recently divorced with three children, was now openly gay. His aim was to modernize podiatry practices. He tasked me with observing the association's operations, particularly the conference division. His authoritative demeanor and level of expectations rubbed some old staff members the wrong way, which made him recognize the need for change in personnel. I was adamant with Stan that I was only committing to working for him for one year. I began my new job as his secretary for three months, then assumed the role of conference director.

As I immersed myself in my work, Stan orchestrated a full overhaul of the organization's staff. He introduced his ex-wife, Gina, into the mix. He also hired a receptionist, Jackie, to add professionalism to the reception area. Stan's strategic maneuvers transformed the association's trajectory, including relocating the office to a prime Manhattan address on Fifth Avenue.

Under Stan's guidance, I evolved as a writer and speaker, honing my creative writing skills for business. My involvement expanded as I proposed changes for the annual conference and prepared a meeting for the House of Delegates. Stan became a mentor, shaping my business acumen and expanding my knowledge base.

Late nights, often followed by dinners where I learned about wines, became the norm. (You know where this is going don't you?) Sure enough, rumors began circulating about our relationship, culminating in a board member's bold question about our romantic involvement. Stan neither confirmed nor denied, leaving me bewildered. Confronting him, I demanded clarity, and he confessed his feelings. Furious, I rejected his advances and left the office.

The following morning, I found myself awake early, torn about whether to go to work. My job was something I genuinely cherished; it had provided me with a sense of challenge and fulfillment, giving me a focus during this singing hiatus. Stan shared my passion for opera and classical music, often enjoying my vocal performances alongside the tunes playing on NPR. Finally, I had a stable income covering all my expenses with a surplus. Why did he have to complicate things?

Amidst these thoughts, the intercom buzzed.

"Mr. Ron, there's a Mr. Stan here to see you," the doorman said.

Damn! I thought. *Now what was the right course of action?*

"Karl, please tell him to wait for me in the lobby. I'll be down shortly."

When I reached the lobby, I saw Stan sitting contemplatively in one of the chairs, gesturing for me to take a seat beside him.

"Just listen," he began, his tone earnest. "I made a mistake, and I apologize. I allowed irrational fantasies to cloud my judgment and put our working relationship at risk. I sincerely apologize and ask you to consider returning to work. But the choice is yours."

Then he left.

I didn't return to work immediately. Instead, I scheduled a session with Una, my therapist, who helped me gain perspective on the situation. For sixty minutes we focused on my concerns, and the conclusion was clear. I would go back to work. I called Stan to convey my decision but requested the remainder of the day off. He accepted, expressing his gratitude. I feared that this incident might alter the dynamics of our working relationship, but to my surprise, after a few days, things seemed to return to normal.

La Bella Donna: The Temp Interlude

During conference season, we brought on board many temporary staff, many of whom, like me, were performing artists. These individuals weren't just grateful for the work; they also reflected dedication, charm, and a unique understanding of the flexibility required to accommodate auditions, rehearsals, and lessons. My primary stipulation to the temp staff whom we hired was that tasks needed to be completed on time.

Stan frequently expressed his admiration for the caliber of people I managed to recruit, and their consistent desire to return for future opportunities spoke volumes about their positive experiences. Among the first artists I hired, one person, Bob, stood out., Bob crafted exquisite papier mâché dolls resembling well-known figures. We were fortunate to attend his debut gallery showing in SoHo. Another notable hire was a young man brimming with Broadway aspirations. During a conference, he received a call for his fifth callback audition for a Broadway show. Although Stan was initially hesitant to grant him leave, I managed to convince him of the importance of pursuing one's dreams. Within months, we were rejoicing in his well-deserved success. Witnessing the genuine gratitude of this aspiring actor warmed my heart, knowing that our support had played a part in making his dreams come true.

Yet, one temporary worker would leave an indelible mark on my life. Her name was Donna, a twenty-one-year-old with impeccable organizational and secretarial skills. Beyond her professionalism, she radiated beauty and possessed a distinct fashion sense. With porcelain-white skin and a slightly varied bob haircut accenting her jet-black hair, she stood at an elegant 5 feet 8 inches, making her appear stunning in anything she wore.

My awareness of her charms wasn't unique; even Stan's 18-year-old son was captivated. Seeking my counsel on whether to ask Donna out, his infatuation mirrored my own. However, my attention was primarily on my impending Caribbean vacation with friends from school. American Airlines once offered what they dubbed the "Beach, Bar, Car Package," a deal that bundled airfare, accommodations, assorted liquor bottles, and a rental car into an irresistible ensemble. It remains one of the most compelling combination offerings I've encountered. Our chosen retreat was a cozy waterfront hotel. I had placed the deposit for a suite using my credit card.

Regrettably, my plans took an unexpected turn when my travel companions backed out, leaving me with non-refundable reservations. My attempt to secure a refund yielded a surprising offer from the hotel manager: a bungalow studio suite on the waterfront, fully covered by my existing deposit. Facing the prospect of a solo trip, I humorously mentioned my situation to Donna during a conversation. Unexpectedly, she expressed interest in joining me, prompting a more serious discussion over drinks.

Meeting at a bar in the Empire State Building, I delicately inquired about her relationship status, considering her known involvement with Stan's son. Her explanation made it clear that there wasn't a romantic involvement, and I mulled over the possibilities. Evaluating the arrangement, I stipulated a 50/50 partnership and requested a deposit of $250.

Over the next five days, Donna and I spent every moment together, both at the office and after work until it was time to go home. With each passing day, I experienced an unfamiliar yet exhilarating sensation. Donna seamlessly blended into my world, embracing my activities and my thoughts. Our communication flowed effortlessly, fostering an openness and connection that felt extraordinary.

At one point, Donna candidly shared a poignant chapter of her past to me, revealing how she became pregnant at seventeen. Constrained by her strict Catholic upbringing, her family concealed the pregnancy, even from close relatives.

During her pregnancy, she was forced into isolation until her seventh month when she was transferred to a home for unwed mothers. After giving birth to a baby girl, the child was immediately taken away for adoption, leaving Donna devastated. The emotional trauma was overwhelming, but after a brief period of grieving, her parents enrolled her in a nine-month secretarial school program. Upon completing the course, her father mandated that she leave the family home. His harsh words and actions compounded the wrenching loss of her baby.

Without a roof over her head, she sought refuge on a sofa in the basement of a friend's residence. At the tender age of 19, she crossed paths with a man named James, who may have worked at a gay bar but identified as straight. Their whirlwind romance swiftly escalated, culminating in a drunken decision to marry. The relationship quickly soured, spiraling into a cycle of abuse perpetuated by James. His aggression escalated to the point of physically assaulting her and then imprisoning her in the bathroom. Salvation came in the form of her steadfast friend who rescued her.

However, Donna's trials were far from over. She discovered that she was pregnant once more. Faced with the grim prospect of reliving the traumatic past, she made the painful decision to terminate the pregnancy.

Seeking a solution, she connected with a Haitian doctor in the distant outskirts of Manhattan who performed the procedure.

Unfortunately, what transpired was far from what Donna had anticipated. The doctor failed to disclose that she was well into her second trimester, and the operation went awry, leaving fetal bones embedded within her uterus. This tragic oversight led to severe hemorrhaging a couple of months later, necessitating an emergency Dilation and Curettage (D&C) procedure to extract the remnants. As Donna navigated through this nightmare, medical professionals warned her of the scarring that had occurred, possibly compromising her ability to conceive in the future. The hopes of future motherhood now seemed precarious.

Feeling the urgent need for escape, she discovered solace in a "Born-again" Christian community, or commune, nestled in Chapel Hill, North Carolina. Initially, the group provided the nurturing support she craved. Yet, as her strength and independence resurfaced, the group's benevolence morphed into control, at times even crossing the line into surveillance. The situation reached an unsettling apex when she realized she was being shadowed.

She ultimately left, making her way back to New York City. Accompanied by her faithful feline companion, Paisley, she found refuge with a friend. Leveraging her adept secretarial skills, she secured a position through a temp agency, thus setting the stage for her entrance into our office.

The memory of our first week together remains vivid in my mind. We opted to catch a movie, *The Color Purple*, in the vibrant heart of the Village. Little did I anticipate that this outing would reveal yet another layer of Donna's talents, her captivating singing voice. She aspired to make her mark on Broadway and recounted another heartrending tale.

Earlier, she had surreptitiously auditioned for a role in a new musical and happened to secure the part. Her parents, alerted to her audacious endeavor, vehemently declined to sign her contract, and promptly pulled her from the production. While aspects of her story seemed enigmatic to me, our burgeoning musical connection superseded any questions that might have arisen.

As the days crept closer to our long-awaited Caribbean getaway, our conversations flowed with ease, and our laughter felt genuine, unforced. Yet, an important matter needed addressing—our lodgings were for a single person and included only one bed. As we headed toward her train returning to her apartment in Brooklyn, I seized the moment

"Do you want to spend the night?" I asked.

Her reaction marked the initiation of our intimate journey, a scene that could have been extracted from the pages of a romance novel. Layers of clothing gently peeled away, revealing delicate porcelain skin and lithe contours that radiated an innate femininity. The canvas of her breasts and belly bore the bittersweet imprint of stretch marks, poignant reminders of the life-altering events that had indelibly marked her. In harmonious unity, we moved through motions that seemed orchestrated by destiny, a synchronicity that resonated with substantial intensity. Guided by her humor and a shared exhilaration, our initial encounter flowed seamlessly, leaving me, for one, unequivocally satisfied. Our imminent Caribbean adventure was poised to be a period of blissful enchantment.

Stan, ever gracious, coordinated the perfect send-off by arranging for his personal chauffeur to usher us to the airport. Donna appeared resplendent in her attire—a form-fitting skirt, a midriff-baring white tank top, blue denim high heels, and an elegant wide-brimmed black hat. We elected to savor a leisurely breakfast in the airport as we continued to absorb as much about each other as possible. Time eluded us, and only the announcement of our boarding call snapped us out of our reverie. Her stylish heels slightly hampered our mad dash to the terminal, but we reached our gate just in time.

Our arrival was just right for a swift room check-in followed by a change into more suitable beach attire. The rendezvous point for guests was the outdoor Tikki bar, where we swiftly learned that our chosen abode was notably "gay friendly."

Wondering if Donna felt comfortable in this environment, I presented the possibility of seeking an alternative lodging option. Her response? She threw her arms into the air reclining back in her chair, her grin stretching wide. "This is perfectly fine with me, your choice!" she exclaimed. She felt at ease amidst the ambiance. Another couple, senior in years and slightly more conservative in outlook, was initially taken aback by the open atmosphere of the resort. However, observing our decision to remain, they decided to do likewise.

By the second day, we were swapping stories over shared meals, laughing at inside jokes that seemed to spring up out of nowhere. Handshakes turned into pats on the back, and even the quietest among us joined in the lively conversations, any initial awkwardness having been left behind entirely.

What does one do on a beautiful tropical island, where crystal-clear, tranquil waters beckon at your doorstep, the weather hovers perfectly in the mid-80s to 90s, and a car awaits to explore hidden beaches and island treasures and with a beautiful woman you have already fallen in love with because you are an incurable romantic? Add the allure of wonderful local restaurants recommended by the resort and the possibilities feel endless. Yes, of course, we did it all!

As the week progressed, I came to a conclusion. Donna was the woman I wanted to spend my life with. This realization was so profound that I was spurred into action. During our final cocktail hour, someone asked if I planned to return.

"I'll be back next year for my honeymoon!"

Donna on the other hand agreed to return to the island with a different vision—her next visit wouldn't be for a honeymoon.

Upon returning to the bustling streets of NYC, the idea of resuming our former separate lives felt impossible. At the time, I had a new roommate, a frequently traveling Associated Press editor. The day we arrived home, however, Sandra called asking if I could help find someone to sublet her apartment. It felt like a sign, meant to be. Sandra's rent was slightly higher than the AP editor was paying me, but he would have the apartment to himself. He accepted. Now to pose that risky question.

"Donna, would you like to move in with me?" I asked.

Her immediate concern was financial; with only a temp job, she worried about affording rent and other costs. I reassured her, explaining that I wasn't asking her to split expenses but to take the time she needed to relax, heal, and rebuild her life after the hardships of the past four years.

I felt the depth of our connection had already surpassed the casual work interactions and sporadic dinners we'd once shared, but the question lingered—did she feel the same? When she agreed and began packing her belongings from her Brooklyn apartment, it felt like the start of something transformative.

In the months that followed, our bond only grew stronger. Day by day, the affection between us deepened, mirroring my own emotions and solidifying the sense that we were exactly where we were meant to be—together.

For some time, our relationship had remained cocooned within its own little universe. My family and friends, bewildered by my uncharacteristic reclusiveness, clamored for introductions. Leslie and Jackie were the first couple to meet my new girlfriend. We planned a gathering at a Japanese restaurant on the Lower East Side, with Donna adopting the role of a vivacious, slightly ditzy girlfriend—similar to the character Adelaide from *Guys and Dolls*.

The introduction unfolded in sitcom fashion; Donna's portrayal notably convincing as I introduced her to Leslie and Jackie. Donna snapped her gum and spoke in a high pitch voice much like Carol Burnett's character as Ms. Wiggins. While Leslie was charmed and captivated by her beauty, Jackie, assuming a protective stance, remained skeptical, failing to comprehend what I saw in her. Amidst the awkward dinner conversation, I attempted to shift the spotlight to Leslie's opera career, hoping he would divert the discussion.

Donna, quick on her feet, responded with feigned innocence and in a voice mimicking the character "Edith" on the sitcom "All in the Family" squeaked, "I'm a singer too! Wanna hear?"

Leslie and Jackie both quickly and politely declined, signaling the end of the evening. As they prepared to depart, I said, "Leslie, Jackie, allow me to introduce you to my girlfriend, the real Donna."

Speaking in a much softer voice, Donna laughed and said, "It was all his idea—please don't think poorly of me." Her polite, well-mannered demeanor shone through in both her words and actions, marking the shift from her theatrical guise to her authentic self. The rest of the evening continued with ease, punctuated by Jackie's admission that Donna's performance had been remarkably convincing.

Next up were my parents. My mother harbored suspicions about the relationship, puzzled by the extended duration before any introduction took place. Reluctantly, Donna agreed to make the trip to meet them. The drive to my hometown of Mattapoisett stretched endlessly, the leg from Providence to our destination marked by Donna's frequent reapplication of face powder.

We arrived well past midnight, and I had hoped, perhaps naively, that we might simply greet my parents in the morning. However, as we entered my mother suddenly appeared from her bedroom like a lively jack-in-the-box, her voluminous hair resembling the Bride of Frankenstein.

Donna stood wearing her signature black felt wide-brimmed hat, accompanied by large silver hooped earrings with airplanes in the center. My mother's greeting was spirited and animated, her curiosity and warmth as genuine as ever.

At first, Donna sat stiffly, offering polite smiles as my mother launched into her sharp, quick-witted stories. But then, a spark—Donna caught onto the punchline of a particularly cheeky remark and let out a laugh that lit up the room. My mother's eyes twinkled, sensing a kindred spirit, and soon the two of them were trading quips like old friends. By the end of the weekend, Donna was seated comfortably between my father and sister, sharing stories of her own, while my mother beamed and passed her another drink. It was as if she had always been part of the family.

In the weeks that followed, it was my turn to meet Donna's family. She had warned me about her mother, Mary, who was often likened to the Pope. She was a staunch conservative Catholic, living with a steadfast 1950's ethos, reflected even in the house's decor. With Scottish roots and an assertive demeanor, she held sway as a potent force. Donna's father, once a Wall Street executive for an oil company, had been compelled to retire early due to health concerns.

This visit marked my first visit to Floral Park, Long Island. It had been a long time since Donna had seen her parents. She had hoped that meeting me could bridge the gap between them.

Donna's descriptions of her family and her home proved to be accurate. Although I initially suspected she might be exaggerating, my assumption was dashed when I experienced her family's atmosphere firsthand. Even a character like a "Leave It to Beaver" mother would have updated her hairstyle from slightly teased hair with the side flip, or at least her fashion choices and furniture. Even the culinary offerings that evening were dated and transported us back to an era of casseroles and overcooked meats.

Donna's family home, with its charmingly outdated aesthetic and nostalgic menu, gave me a glimpse into her roots—simple, unpretentious, and deeply grounded. It was a stark contrast to the vibrant, modern woman I had come to know. Yet, in that juxtaposition, I found a new appreciation for Donna's ability to balance the values of her upbringing with the dynamism of her present. This authenticity, paired with her unwavering efforts to nurture and uplift me, became the foundation of something extraordinary between us.

Our relationship stood apart from my previous experiences in a significant way. Donna consistently went out of her way to surprise and please me, conveying a deep sense of my importance to her, and, above all, her love for me. She dismantled the barriers of hurt, insecurity, and feelings of unworthiness that I carried, becoming an unwavering partner in every aspect. With her by my side, I felt truly secure, secure enough that after six months of being together, I made a decision.

Just Get Her To The Church: The Ring Cycle

It had been four blissful months of living together. We were deeply in love and basking in shared happiness. Over time, our candid conversations often wandered into the territory of marriage. We had been so open and honest about our pasts that I felt no hesitation—each day only reinforced my first impression and gut instinct that this was meant to be. Sure, it was a short time to make such a life-altering decision, but logic and love aren't always on the same timeline. Donna, for her part, had given me no reason to think she wasn't on the same page.

One evening as we were sitting quietly on the couch, Donna reading a book, the moment seemed right. But I didn't have an engagement ring. Subtlety isn't always my strong suit, so I went with what I had: my grandmother's heirloom diamond that I wore as a pinky ring. I decided to seize the moment. There was no grand gesture, no swooping down on one knee with a string quartet playing in the background.

"Donna?" I asked.

She looked up, shifting her eyes from her book to me. Pulling the make-shift ring from my pocket, I asked, "Will you marry me?"

She blissfully accepted my proposal and just like that, we were engaged. I assured her that the ring was temporary and she would have her own heirloom to hand down. Then, still snuggled on the sofa, we tossed around wedding ideas.

Donna seemed happy with the heirloom ring, but I wanted her to have something uniquely ours. A summer trip to Massachusetts presented the perfect opportunity. Enlisting the help of a jeweler my parents trusted, we designed matching sets of rings. Donna's engagement ring featured two dazzling bands, each set with ten baguette-cut diamonds. The engagement ring featured a prominent center stone. My wedding band mirrored hers with two bands of baguette-cut diamonds merged into a single piece.

Now, all I needed was a proper moment to redo the proposal, in Ron's true style. I had to come up with an element of surprise—and a cruise over Labor Day weekend delivered just that. One evening, under a sky sprinkled with stars, we found ourselves alone on the ship's deck. I saw my opportunity.

Trying to keep my voice casual, I said, "Donna, do me a favor and take off my grandmother's ring." She gave me a look that clearly said, *What on earth for?* But after a little coaxing and mild confusion on her part, she reluctantly handed it over.

Channeling my inner Houdini, I swapped the rings, and, with an uncharacteristic touch of drama, dropped to one knee. I slipped the new engagement ring onto her finger and asked her to marry me. It was September 7, 1986—an unforgettable moment that officially set the wheels in motion for the next chapter of our lives.

The wedding date was set for March 28, 1987. However, an obstacle surfaced—Donna's mother wasn't on board, not in disapproval of me, but due to a moral conflict created by our living arrangement. As a devout Catholic, she believed we were living in contradiction to the Church's position. She believed that a Catholic wedding would be impossible as no priest would perform the ceremony.

Meanwhile, my mother was busy compiling a guest list that had already crossed the one-hundred mark, with numbers still climbing. With only six months remaining until the big day, my mother was eager to ascertain the extent of Donna's parents' contribution. I soon confronted the matter head-on. My soon-to-be mother-in-law, Mary, reiterated her firm stance: unless it was a Catholic wedding, she would not be contributing to the festivities. She was happily surprised when I revealed that not only had I found a priest willing to officiate, but I had two—both of whom had been my high-school teachers at Bishop Stang: Fathers William Norton and

Calistus Bamberg. Furthermore, she was astonished to learn that our wedding was scheduled to take place at St. Francis of Assisi church on 31st Street just a few doors down from my office building.

Mary now eagerly joined in the preparations, making strategic recommendations about both the venue for the reception and the guest list. My choice was to opt for the renowned Plaza Hotel at the corner of Fifth Avenue and Central Park South. Leveraging my expertise as a convention and meeting planner, I had hoped to secure a significant discount and utilize personal favors to make it affordable. Mary humored me and set a date and time to meet. She agreed that the ballroom at the Plaza would be quite impressive, but so was the cost, even with a discount. Now it was her turn to present her recommendation. It was the Union League Club, a private establishment on Park Avenue South and 37th Street where her brother Paul, an attorney, was a member. If we had the reception there, the dinner would be a reasonable $25 per person, with no facility rental costs attached. If we agreed, Mary arranged for us to have the honeymoon suite at the Plaza on the evening of the wedding as an incentive.

In addition, there was one notable condition regarding the number of guests. There was only to be one hundred guests, which included the wedding party, priests, singers and guest musicians. My parents were limited to inviting fifty guests, ten of which were included in the wedding party. We chose the Union League Club, and my mother found herself in quite a dilemma, as her list extended well beyond one hundred names, prompting her to grapple with the arduous task of elimination.

With the reception venue decided upon, we delved into the details of the ceremony. Donna entrusted me with selecting the music. Naturally, I approached Leslie, not only to be my best man but also to lend his exceptional vocal talents. Another friend, Cheryl, a gifted opera singer who had recently returned from a four-year tenure at the Vienna State Opera, joined our musical ensemble.

However, the excitement of these selections hit a roadblock when the minister of music rejected all my choices, vehemently asserting that none of them were permissible. To make matters more challenging, both the

"Ave Maria" and the "Panis Angelicus" had been removed from the church's new music repertoire. Undeterred, I promptly sought the approval of Father Callistus. Showing a keen interest in the prospect of renowned singers and a violinist performing at the ceremony, he granted his endorsement for the music I had selected.

In a generous gesture, my friend Tracy, who was head of food and beverage for the St. Moritz hotel when I first began with the Association, had transitioned over to the Omni Hotel across from Carnegie Hall. As a wedding present she gifted us the infamous "Jackie Gleason" suite to host my parents and sisters, for three nights. She also offered a special rate for any of my out-of-town guests.

Next on the agenda was to find Donna a wedding dress. Having purchased a few dozen wedding magazines, we leafed through each one. Although there were several she liked, only one stood out. It was an off-white, silk, fitted dress with the signature big, puffy sleeves of the 80's, and designed by Milady. A bridal salon in Floral Park only blocks from her parents' home carried the dress.

Six weeks before the wedding the dress arrived, and Donna was scheduled for her first fitting. The Saturday before her appointment, the phone rang. It was 7 a.m. in the morning — I answered.

"Ron, this is Mary, please do not respond, I don't want Donna to know I am speaking with you." Mary implored me not to react hastily to the news she was about to convey. "The bridal shop caught fire last night and burned to the ground. Nothing was salvaged including Donna's gown."

Then she requested that I tell Donna that the shop had promised to do the best they could at locating another Milady dress, and with time on our side, there was still hope.

With that, she hung up, leaving me with the difficult task of delivering this unfortunate news. I climbed back into bed, spooning with Donna, and shared the news gently while assuring her that I would do everything possible to find the Milady wedding dress. What followed were screams, panic, and a call to her mother. The first thing on Monday morning, I contacted the Milady company and explained the predicament. They were understanding and promised to search their sales records to find a store that still had the gown in stock. In less than twenty-four hours, they had located the dress and arranged for its transfer to a temporary store set up by the bridal shop in Floral Park. At Donna's first fitting, she had initially measured to be a size 6-8. The dress that arrived, however, was size 14, and, instead of silk, it was made with white taffeta. The saving grace was that Donna was now a size 10 or 12 which meant there was less tailoring to do. The crucial point was that she had the Milady dress she desired.

There were no other catastrophes, and the well anticipated day had arrived. The night before, Donna stayed at the apartment with her maid of honor and I stayed at the Omni Hotel, with a high school friend, who was in the wedding party. The wedding ceremony was set for 1 p.m. and everyone arrived on schedule. I stood alone in the church's vestibule, awaiting my best man, who was going through his music with the organist up in the loft.

Attempting to fully grasp the weight of my emotions in that moment is nearly impossible. I stood on the precipice of a life-altering commitment, a sacred vow binding two lives as *husband and wife.* As I reflected on everything that had led me here, one memory crystallized with startling clarity.

Alone in the vestibule, lost in thought, a sudden premonition flickered through my mind—brief yet piercing. It was not fear or nerves but something deeper, an unspoken knowing that my marriage might not endure. For the smallest fraction of time, I saw an alternate path, a chance to step away, to acknowledge a truth I hadn't dared to name. Was I about to make the same mistake Sandra had made with Juan? Or were my doubts rooted in something even more unsettling—was I unconsciously clinging to the hope of a future with Sandra? Had I been holding onto a fantasy, or was *this* the fantasy?

The answer was simple—just call off the wedding. If Sandra had been sitting in that church, maybe I would have. But she wasn't. She was in

Williamsburg, immersed in her production of *Snow White*, a world away from this moment.

And so, I couldn't do it. I silenced the voice whispering doubts and dismissed the premonition as nothing more than the usual bridegroom nerves. After all, I believed I loved Donna—with a passion that ran deep, that touched the very core of my soul. Didn't I?

The ceremony was accompanied by impressive pomp and circumstance, enjoyed not only by the attending guests but also by the homeless individuals who had gathered at the back of the church. The bridal march evoked memories of Maria's graceful walk down the aisle in the classic film "The Sound of Music." Fathers Norton and Callistus, knowing my character, shared their thoughts on my potential as a husband, provider, and future father.

As we exchanged vows, another friend, Bob, a professional violinist, graced us with the ethereal strains of the Meditation Theme from the opera *Thais*. I had been introduced to this piece during a Metropolitan Opera performance featuring Beverly Sills, and the experience left an indelible mark on me. During the offertory, Leslie sang the "Ave Maria," set to the melody of the Intermezzo from *Cavalleria Rusticana* by Mascagni. This piece held special significance as a tribute to my early mentor, Mrs. Emilie Gregoire Taubman, who had shared that Toscanini had orchestrated and conducted the piece for her to perform on the Bromo Seltzer Hour, a radio show in the 1950s. Leslie's voice echoed throughout the church, bringing a sense of reverence.

At communion, Cheryl performed the "Panis Angelicus", a piece I selected to honor my grandmother's memory and one that I had sung many times. To conclude the ceremony, Leslie and Maria sang the duet "Nuit d'hymenée" from Gounod's opera *Romeo and Juliette*.

The exchanged vows, the affirmative "I do's," and the concluding "We did!" marked the momentous occasion.

The Union League Club's grandeur was undeniable, featuring an elegant marble split-heart staircase leading to a balcony, adorned with mahogany wall panels. The in-laws had arranged for the cocktail reception in the Club's stately library, a room graced with a cathedral ceiling with a striking chandelier suspended at its center. The melodies from a string quartet filled the air as guests indulged in hors d'oeuvres while awaiting the opening of the ballroom doors. Attendees found their places behind monogrammed place cards that bore their individual names. A procession of white-gloved waiters entered the room, evoking imagery of a White House Dinner.

The celebration included two notable toasts. First, my boss and friend Stan shared words of wisdom that went beyond the typical sentiments of everlasting happiness. Leaving an indelible impact, his eloquent speech bestowed upon us the strength to confront adversity and surmount life's challenges. The second toast, a rendition of the "**Libiamo**" duet from *La Traviata*, was delivered by Leslie and Cheryl and accompanied by Elaine Chelton. Their lively and entertaining performance brought everyone to their feet, and was the pinnacle moment of the reception.

And, of course, no wedding would be complete without a cake. Our cake was indeed unique—a three-layer Italian cappuccino mousse cake, a favorite dessert from our treasured Italian neighborhood eatery, Il D'Uomo. Ciro, the restaurant's owner, crafted this masterpiece for our wedding, and it served as the dessert of the evening. The top layer was preserved for our first-year anniversary, while the middle layer was sent to the Omni's Jackie Gleason suite where my parents were staying. The festivities ended at the Union League Club around 8 p.m., but my parents had no intentions of not partying into the night. In true Yvette fashion, my mother invited her guests, complete with laughter, jokes, and abundant spirits to the suite at the Omni. Not wanting to miss the fun, we joined them.

As the clock struck midnight, Donna and I retired to the Plaza's honeymoon suite, as had been arranged by Mary, my newly ordained mother-in-law. The bridal suite overlooked Central Park South. The room's ambiance and decor was befitting the hotel's storied reputation.

Though our immediate desire was to cast aside our formal attire and sink into the inviting four-poster bed, Donna felt compelled to don her bridal peignoir, gliding around the room as the chiffon robe trailed behind her like an ethereal veil. Thus, the final pre-sleep ritual was fulfilled, leaving only one task remaining—to consummate our marriage with just enough vigor before surrendering to a well-deserved, deep slumber.

As Mr. and Mrs. Boucher, we awoke to the captivating sight of Central Park and the urban symphony of traffic sounds emanating from Central Park South, also known as 59th Street. Although there was no pressing need to hurry, our desire was to return to our apartment. A finishing touch to the festivities remained: a horse and buggy ride through Central Park, which I had arranged. Our out-of-town guests, in no rush to leave New York, took the opportunity to either attend the Sunday matinee Broadway musical *Nunsense* or indulge in some afternoon shopping. It was around 7 p.m. when we finally found ourselves alone, embracing this new life as Mr. and Mrs. We contemplated the changes, pondering whether we felt any different, and considering what it all meant for our future.

Our honeymoon began four days later and marked a return to St. Croix, as promised. Recreating the magic of the previous year was an impossibility. The faces around us had changed, with the exception for one couple who had joined us once again. Our quaint bungalow, nestled away from the main hotel, had succumbed to a hurricane, so we found ourselves in the main hotel this time. We arrived at the hotel, just in time to change, settle in, and join all the guests at the tiki bar for happy hour before using our rented car to venture into town for dinner.

On the second day, we stumbled upon a movie being filmed. As we joined the crowd of onlookers, a member of the crew approached me and inquired if I'd consider a paid role to be in the movie. I explained that I was on my honeymoon and, if they wanted me, they'd have to include my wife. To my surprise, they agreed. The shoot lasted two days, leaving us with the rest of our stay to savor.

The island was as intoxicating as the piña coladas. The guests were observant that this was a special time for us and gave us distance. We filled the week with excursions to private beaches, snorkeling in remote areas rich with sea life, shopping in the village market area, and, of course, romantic dinners for two. Before we had realized, the week had come to its conclusion, and we were on our way home.

Upon our return, a call from my agent reminded me that it was time to resume vocal work, as the year-long hiatus from singing had ended. With my upcoming commitment to the Connecticut Grand Opera, I resumed vocal lessons and coaching sessions after my regular work hours. The nine-to-five grind before each lesson proved taxing on my energy, making these sessions particularly challenging. This compelled me to concentrate and employ the techniques I had learned.

In addition, my day job quickly began to demand far more attention than I had anticipated. My focus shifted to organizing the annual House of Delegates conference, which I had chosen to host at the PGA Sheraton in West Palm Beach, Florida. This selection was based on lessons learned from my previous Association conferences.

During my training at my first conference, I noticed something problematic. The Nevele—a classic Jewish resort in the Catskill Mountains —served family-style meals, with their endless platters of replenished food, had an unintended effect: delegates grew sluggish, disgruntled, and combative, making it nearly impossible to meet the agenda's demands. Determined to shake things up, I selected "The Sagamore" in upstate New York for the following year's event.

The Sagamore boasted a renowned golf course and upscale amenities, making it an appealing choice on paper. However, its "nouvelle cuisine" proved to be a culinary culture shock for the delegates. Elegant presentations of filet of beef or fish with a modest arrangement of provincial vegetables, each served on an expanse of white porcelain dishes —were met with indignation. The backlash was so intense that a few delegates even demanded my dismissal. Stan, my boss, however, couldn't help but appreciate the ambition behind my choices and took pride in how well he had trained me to make bold decisions.

Determined to recover from the second year's debacle, I selected the PGA Sheraton for the third conference that I directed. During a pre-conference meeting with the head of food and beverage, I relayed the delegates' culinary grievances and was assured that meals would be served buffet-style, ensuring plenty of food to satisfy even the heartiest appetites.

As the conference date approached in May, the workload intensified. Both my secretary and I clocked countless hours of overtime, buried under an avalanche of last-minute details. Donna, by now well-versed in her role as the "conference widow," playfully resigned herself to watching her husband disappear into the vortex of conference directorship.

It was "Showtime," and the conference at the Sheraton was an undeniable hit with the delegates. The buffet setup was a triumph, with endless options and ample servings keeping everyone content. The resort's head of food and beverage, however, was less enthused. Despite planning ahead, they were forced to tap into every food reserve they had to meet the demand. It was clear we wouldn't be welcomed back the following year—but for that moment, I reveled in the success of an event well-executed.

In a twist of fate, Donna had started her own new direction, finding employment as the personal secretary to Bruce Friedlich, the CEO of a prominent advertising company, Henderson Friedlich Graf & Doyle. Bruce swiftly recognized Donna's talents, marveling at her creative prowess and innate flair for the world of advertising. Characteristic of Donna's approach to life, she threw herself wholeheartedly into this new position, determined to excel.

Amidst this whirlwind of activity, an additional commitment materialized on the horizon: a concert back in New Bedford for a church fundraiser. This prompted me to enlist the help of my friend and collaborator, Elaine, who now plied her talents as a rehearsal and concert pianist with the New York City Ballet. Donna, too, was invited to partake, her voice possessing a deep, rich quality that echoed the smoothness of Ella Fitzgerald and at times even the smoky allure of Peggy Lee. Donna's vocal prowess was a treasure I held dear, and any chance to harmonize with her was a welcome prospect. Yet, it was clear that our vocal styles belonged to disparate realms, a fact that didn't make us vocal partners, despite our shared love for singing. Embracing the spirit of the fundraiser, I intentionally selected songs that would highlight Donna's artistry, adhering to the unwritten rule that a gentleman should never outshine a lady, unless, of course, one bore the mantle of Luciano Pavarotti.

Respite Over: A Lieder

In November 1987, I stepped back into the world of opera, rejoining the cast of *Don Pasquale* alongside Janice Hall, Mario Bertolini, Louis Otey, and Juan Luque Carmona. This time, the dynamics felt different. The director, who had previously served as the stage manager for the original production under Christopher Renshaw, struggled to capture the same spontaneity and slapstick humor that the first cast had effortlessly embodied.

Opening night was an affair of elegance and grandeur, marked by guests in gowns and tuxedos and capped with a lavish reception following the performance. I had Donna select a cocktail dress befitting the evening's splendor. A natural beauty, Donna transformed into a top runway model the moment she donned a black, form-fitting Christian Dior dress from Lord & Taylor, complete with a taffeta bubble peplum. A small pillbox hat adorned her head, accompanied by a face netting, black gloves, and heels that granted her three extra inches of height compared to me. Her ability to apply makeup flawlessly further heightened her allure. She turned heads as she entered the theater. Even the conductor couldn't resist complimenting her exquisite appearance after the opera.

I playfully quipped, "Be careful! She might bite if you get too close!"

Amidst the preparations in my dressing room, an AGMA representative arrived to deliver my paycheck. A sense of bewilderment washed over me as I questioned why John Hiddlestone, the General Director, wasn't distributing the paychecks as customary. Opening the envelope, I scrutinized the check, only to discover that the amount fell short of my contractual agreement.

"Hold on!" I called out to the representative, who was already on her way out.

"Where's the rest of my money?" I demanded, certain that there had been some mistake.

She calmly explained, "Oh, I apologize for not mentioning it earlier. We deducted the dues you haven't paid since you stopped singing. Since you never requested a suspension, you are still considered an active member. But now you're fully paid up."

Her tone carried a faint note of satisfaction, as if she had caught me in a scheme.

On November 19th, the curtain ascended once more. The orchestra filled the air with music, and the glaring stage lights obscured my view of the audience. But this time, as I stood there, I felt a disconnection from the passion that once had consumed me. I was bewildered, desperately searching for that rush of adrenaline that had always ignited my performances.

As I breathed life into my character with my voice and expressed the artistry through the skills I had honed, a profound, persistent ache settled within me, shrouding my thoughts in doubt.

For the first time, I found myself questioning the very reasons I pursued this path. Was it the feeling that a world devoid of Sandra within the realm of the arts held no allure? Or had I grown complacent, settling for a steady job, a beautiful and loving wife, and feeling of contentment?

With favorable reviews under my belt, my manager and I agreed that it was time to refocus on meeting the expectations of my vocal repertoire. However, he admitted that there wasn't a substantial amount of work available for me in the United States, which was crucial for both employment and ongoing training needed to advance from *comprimario* (second character) roles to principal ones.

Instead, he presented an intriguing opportunity for me to relocate temporarily to Cologne, Germany, where young artists like me were welcomed. I couldn't muster much enthusiasm for the idea of relocating to Germany, especially considering my aversion to singing in the German language. The guttural articulation of German stood in stark contrast to the lyrical flow of Italian and French, presenting a challenge I was hesitant to embrace.

In the midst of these considerations, I found myself summoned to Stan's office on a Monday morning. Closing the door behind me, he wasted no time getting to the point.

"Ron, you've proven yourself to be excellent both on stage and in your role here, as I suspected you would be when I hired you."

A pause lingered in the air as he settled into his seat behind the desk.

"You fulfilled your commitment to me, and the performance world has opened its doors to you once more. Now, what's your choice going to be?"

"I'm not going back," I declared, pondering whether this decision would ultimately leave me with deep regrets.

With those words, my operatic career ended.

The reasons behind this shift remained elusive, but the satisfaction and elation I once derived from performing on stage seemed to have waned. I had grown comfortable with the predictable salary that exceeded my expenses, the security of a routine, and most significantly, the investment I wished to make in my relationship.

With the upcoming annual conference on the horizon, there was little time to dwell on my choice. The relentless pace of work consumed my days, punctuated only by a brief holiday respite that welcomed the dawn of 1987.

Love, Marriage, and Then Reality: A Marital Minuet

As Donna's husband and someone a decade her senior, my intent was to provide support without impeding her personal growth during the transformative years between twenty-one and thirty. I encouraged her to maintain her independent friendships and to explore her passions and creativity while seeking stability and comfort.

The marriage acted as a balm, healing many of the rifts that had existed between Donna and her family. They seemed fully supportive and enamored of me. We formed harmonious bonds. Yet, beneath the surface, I detected a subtle rivalry between Donna and my sister Carol, who was only two years younger. Donna effortlessly commanded attention whenever she entered a room, sharing the spotlight with my mother. Her sharp, dry humor lifted conversations with a swift and witty delivery.

The "Co-op Boom" of the 1980s was a time during which many existing rental apartment buildings converted into co-ops. The housing complex where I had been living since 1976 was not spared. I had to decide whether to purchase my apartment at the insider's price of $70K or remain a renter. Despite advice from Donna's family attorney, I chose to postpone the decision.

Over the months, the pressure to buy the apartment mounted steadily. A neighbor, a fellow performer recognizable from his appearances on TV shows like "The Adams Family," approached us one evening. He had a peculiar request. He asked that we consider buying his apartment at the insider price. He would continue to live in his apartment and pay the mortgage payments until he passed. However, for us to do this, we would have to sell our apartment and then find a place to live until he died. His proposition took us by surprise. Then he disclosed that he was living with AIDS and had limited time left.

Overwhelmed by shock and uncertainty, we left his apartment but ultimately decided to purchase my apartment to secure stability amid the unpredictability of leasing arrangements. Donna, influenced by advice from her parents, was already inclined to explore housing outside the city within a sixty-mile radius. If we were to have a child, raising a little one in the city wasn't our preference, prompting us to search for houses with a reasonable commute time.

Donna favored Victorian-style houses and initially considered one in Newburgh. However, both our parents and friends, Leslie and Jackie, advised us against it, suggesting it would be better to build a new home rather than renovate the existing dwelling. Then Donna came across real estate listings in Lambertville, NJ, situated across the Delaware River from New Hope, PA. The commute, about an hour and a half on a good day, required careful consideration due to my late hours. I contemplated the neighbor's proposition again, given his deteriorating health and our housing search. But we were still faced with the prospect of finding temporary housing until his passing raising more complexities.

One afternoon, Donna called to inform me that her real estate agent found the perfect house in New Jersey. I had previously dismissed the idea of moving to NJ, but I agreed to be open-minded and see the property.

John, the real estate agent, picked us up at our apartment building and drove us to Jersey City. He showed us a row of townhomes near Lincoln Park. The property for sale had a second-floor entrance opening to a Victorian-style living room with oak floors, a slate fireplace, and an elegant U-shaped staircase. The family room, also on this floor, could serve as a sitting or TV room. Upstairs, two bedrooms flanked a connecting hall with the bathroom in between. The bath featured a unique pull-chain oak tank and matching seat and vanity. The first floor held a smaller dining room with exposed brick walls, leading to a kitchen that needed renovation. The price was $155K and within our means. The commute was a one mile walk to Journal Square or a bus ride with a stop at the corner of our street. At Journal Square we could pick up the Path Train right into the station under the World Trade Center and catch the subway to any destination in the city.

It all happened so fast. By July 1988, we became the proud owners of a townhome at 199 Belmont Avenue.

Decorating the house proved enjoyable, as our preferences aligned, leaving little room for disagreement. We purchased a moiré-covered, deep plum-colored sectional couch that spanned two walls of the family room, its chaise placed in the living room. Donna ingeniously added beaded fringe to transform the chaise's contemporary style into a Victorian piece, complementing my grandmother's oriental rug. A used black baby grand piano graced the first landing of the staircase. Our formal dining room featured a Chinese-style black layered oval table with walnut inlays and matching chairs, alongside a glass and mirrored wall unit. Closets were modified to create a new laundry space, and a stacking washer and dryer were installed. Our bedroom was furnished with a 1940s mahogany bed and his-and-her dressers. The guest bedroom housed my NYC bedroom set, completing the interior transformation. By September's end, we could finally unwind and embrace the serene ambiance we had crafted.

Yet, as with all older properties, issues arose. One morning as I was getting dressed, I heard a loud crash followed by a scream. Bursting into the bedroom, I found Donna covered in white plaster, the ceiling above her having collapsed. Instantly, we thought of the movie "The Money Pit" and burst into laughter, realizing we were living our own version of it. Thankfully, the homeowner's insurance covered the repairs, and we resumed our daily lives.

Donna had discovered a newfound passion for crafting jewelry, and she exhibited remarkable skill in this creative pursuit. Our weekends were transformed into treasure hunts at flea markets, where we scoured vintage costume jewelry. Donna would expertly disassemble these pieces and then reassemble them into unique earrings, necklaces, and brooches. Transforming a corner of our dining room, she fashioned a workshop, using my grandmother's sewing cabinet as a table for her creative space. At a certain point, she even managed to secure an account representative, though that person's usefulness turned out to be quite limited.

Meanwhile, Mr. Friedlich, her boss at the advertising agency, embarked on selling his business and relocating to a new spot in the southern part of the West Village. It soon became evident that Bruce was struggling with Alzheimer's disease, which meant that he increasingly leaned on Donna to maintain his business affairs and accounts. Alongside his city residence, he also owned a house in Block Island, which he generously offered to us to enjoy on weekends, along with the use of his Mercedes, which he seldom drove. Life that summer was splendid, our romantic connection thrived, and our intimate life was both vibrant and fulfilling. What more could a man wish for?

A point of concern yet lingered. Since the start of our relationship in 1986, Donna and I had forgone using contraception. Worries arose after so much time passing and no conception. At this juncture, my friend Jackie proposed that we consult her gynecologist, Dr. Rubel—yes, the brother of the renowned Stephen Rubel, who owned Studio 54. Following a thorough examination, Dr. Rubel conveyed to us that he did not detect any concerns and advised that we continue trying, assuring us that conception would likely occur in due course.

The Art of Deception: The Veiled Aria

Donna always mentioned her membership in MENSA, a society that welcomes individuals with an IQ in the top 2% of the population. The Society fosters camaraderie and engagement in a variety of social and cultural activities, including people from diverse backgrounds. My wife was a genius! Yet, whenever I mentioned this topic with her mother, she would deflect the conversation. Surprisingly, there were no certificates or trophies adorning her bedroom walls at her parents' home, a peculiar absence given her mother's profession as a schoolteacher. Not that I particularly cared about Donna's intelligence, but these circumstances did plant seeds of doubt.

Unsettling nightmares began to torment Donna. In the dead of night, her restless tossing and turning would wake me from my sleep. A recurring dream involved someone snatching her baby away from her. As time went on, these episodes increased in frequency. I confided in Stan, who theorized that despite her current life's comfort and stability, a lingering fear of losing everything might be surfacing in her subconscious. He believed her mind was coping with this fear by manifesting the act of her child being taken from her in her dreams. On one particularly distressing night, she even lashed out violently, striking me and jolting me awake. I instinctively clutched her tightly in attempt to calm her down. I made the suggestion that she might be able to influence her subconscious by trying to alter her dream. This was a hasty solution, but remarkably, it worked. The nightmares ceased, yet I sensed that the underlying ache for her lost child remained. Every year on August 25th, the anniversary of her daughter's birth, I noticed that she seemed to experience days of profound mourning.

When I suggested she attempt to find her child, she said that she was already registered on the adoption registry, a platform allowing parents and children to reconnect, that is, if both parties were registered. I learned that the adoption had been handled by an uncle. Nevertheless, all records were sealed, including the adoptive identity of the child and her whereabouts.

However, August 25th of 1988 triggered a new turn of events. Donna reached out to the baby's father and met with him. I was already in bed when she returned home and briefly discussed their conversation about the baby. The next day, I received a call from her explaining that she'd be coming home later because she was going out for drinks with friends after leaving work early. There was an inexplicable tone in her voice that signaled something was different. Could she be lying to me? Upon her return, I could sense her every word was a fabrication, an intentional lie. I probed her about her whereabouts, to which she responded, "shopping." Prodding further, I confronted her with my suspicion.

"You were with him, weren't you?"

After a few teary moments of denial and my persistent inquiries, she eventually admitted the truth.

"I needed to see him last night because he asked me to marry him, and I had to give him an answer tonight."

My mind was spinning with questions. How was this even possible, let alone under consideration? I was certain we had a happy marriage, a stable bond, and a life filled with everything we could wish for. Why hadn't she immediately responded to his proposal with a firm, "I'm happily married!" Why did she need to wait until the following night to give him an answer? Was our marriage on the verge of unraveling? And the sheer audacity of that man—knowing she was married yet still daring to make such a proposal!

In the weeks that followed, I desperately tried to make sense of our conversation while avoiding the painful reality of what had happened. Our busy lifestyle—filled with work and social engagements—allowed the weeks to pass quickly, carrying us into the holiday season. Thanksgiving was spent at her parents' house in Floral Park, and Christmas in Massachusetts with my family. The festive ambiance was infectious, nudging us into a more romantic and harmonious disposition.

By January, we seemed to be back on track, and the incident with Stephen was forgiven—or at least it appeared that way. For me, however, it was not entirely forgotten.

The Miracle of Birth: The Elixir of Love

"You will never have children in this lifetime!" were the stark words of a fortune teller who, for a mere dollar, answered my question from her Tarot cards. It was 1985, and she was seated in front of Lincoln Center with a small table. I had posed the question, "Am I ever going to have children?" Indeed, a strange question for someone who wasn't in a relationship. But my thoughts were that if the answer was yes that my loneliness would be over. Her response only deepened my depression. My Catholic "mea culpa" had me feeling unworthy of such a precious blessing. This fate, it seemed, was one I had to come to terms with.

Fast forward two years. I was married to Donna, opening up the possibility of having a child, as per Dr. Rubell. Around mid-February, Donna began experiencing bouts of nausea. Though she brushed them aside initially, they persisted over the next few days. On the third day of these episodes, I boldly declared, "Donna, you're pregnant!"

She insisted she wasn't, citing her prior pregnancies as evidence that she would recognize the signs. Nevertheless, we made a quick trip to the drug store, and indeed, the test confirmed that she was pregnant.

The months leading up to the birth of our daughter were some of the most joyful in our relationship. Other than when we were working, we were inseparable. Dr. Robinson, Donna's obstetrician, projected a due date of September 19th—ironically, the same day as Sandra's birthday.

In May, I received a call from Christopher, inviting me to audition for the role of Nemorino. Christopher was back directing at Covent Garden in England, and the performer in me couldn't resist the allure of this opportunity. So, I plunged into practice, reacquainting myself with the required arias. Surprisingly, my voice handled the tessitura more easily, with greater agility, likely due to the hiatus in singing. I was averse to leaving Donna at home, so we decided she would accompany me to London for the audition. To avoid stirring any feathers at work, I submitted a request for two weeks' vacation in June.

I contacted a British banker, Alexander, who worked for Chase Manhattan Bank. I had met him during one of my previous vacations to St. Barts. He graciously extended an open invitation to stay with him if I ever found myself in London.

Not only was he generously willing to accommodate us, but he also insisted on picking us up a Heathrow Airport. We were warmly greeted, and he seemed delighted to meet my pregnant wife. Alexander's flat was just a few blocks from Buckingham Palace and in walking distance to many of the museums. As we settled in, I brought Alex up to speed of all that happened since we had last seen one another. Donna shared some of her high points about our relationship. Mostly, Alex was genuinely thrilled about my upcoming audition and eager to hear all about it.

The next morning, I left Christopher a message confirming our safe arrival and my readiness for the audition. I awaited his return call. When he finally reached out from Sydney, Australia, his news left me devastated. Due to political issues, they could only audition and hire British nationals or those with prior performances in the British Commonwealth. I was crushed and sunk into depression. I yearned for a quick return to New York and the comfort of the predictable.

Alex, though, took charge. "Give me your money!" he said insistently.

We handed him the roughly two-thousand US dollars we'd brought along. The next morning, we found British currency and a schedule of activities on the kitchen table. It was a structured plan allocating precisely enough funds for transportation, lunch, and an adventure.

By noon time, Donna couldn't take another step. Her back and feet were aching. We abandoned Alex's list and returned to his flat. That evening when Alex returned from work, he expressed understanding, however, we could sense he was disappointed that we had not completed the excursion.

Alex decided to take a new course of action. "We are going to Paris for the weekend!" he said. With Alex in control of our finances, he assured me that everything was within my budget.

As dawn broke the following morning, we found ourselves greeted by Alex and his companion, Trevor, a quintessentially British fellow and proprietor of a Piccadilly Circle shop, specializing in his own line of neckties. Upon meeting, Donna and Trevor ignited an instant connection, leading to animated dialogues that seemed to flow endlessly.

For the first leg of our journey, we hopped into Alex's Mercedes and headed toward the Cliffs of Dover, where we boarded a Hovercraft that ferried us across the English Channel. Throughout the voyage, our unborn child channeled the legendary swimmer, Gertrude Ederle, the first woman to swim the Channel in 1926, as her lively movements in Donna's abdomen provided us with a comical aquatic performance.

Upon reaching land in Calais, we next experienced the thrill of France's high-speed A-26 highway, cruising at 125 mph through the countryside. After a mere two hours, we set foot in Paris, a city that was full of allure.

Our lodgings, strategically located opposite the Notre Dame Cathedral and framed by the Seine River, was a charming early 1900's hotel resonating with quintessential French character of high ceiling, fireplace, herringbone wood floors and decorative plaster moldings. Our room, replete with lofty ceilings and grand windows, gained our admiration, although our tight schedule allowed little time for appreciating such luxuries.

Pressing forward, lunch beckoned, leading us to a cozy bistro nearby. The menu included items like steak frites, boeuf bourguignon, and my favorite, mousse au chocolat. A request to use the facilities revealed an unconventional French design. A door labeled "Les Hommes" led me into a stark white space with a porcelain-lined floor hole, a peculiar experience that welcomed me to France's bathroom culture.

Back at the hotel, a brief respite followed, during which Donna indulged in a quick nap, while Alex and I coordinated plans for the evening. I wished to fulfill my mother's dream of attending the *Folie Bergère* or the *Lido Show*, but they were closed for the summer season. Undeterred, we embraced the unknown and selected a show foreign to us that included dinner.

Our taxi ride transported us to a slightly questionable part of Paris, triggering momentary doubt, which soon faded as a stream of elegant cars and well-dressed individuals converged upon the building. Our dinner theater experience began with an unconventional seating arrangement of tightly packed rows of tables, which sparked both intrigue and amusement among the attendees. The evening took an unexpectedly humorous turn when the French patrons seated next to us, in their attempts to figure out who was with whom, sparked a series of chuckles. Because we could understand French, their assumptions added an unexpected layer of fun to the night, enhancing the overall experience.

Then came the moment when they started teasing us, insinuating that being English, we were perhaps unaware that we were attending a French drag revue. However, they did not realize that Alex and I comprehended their remarks. Eventually, I responded in French, shocking them into embarrassment and shifting the dynamic toward friendliness. Although the show was entertaining, it was quite different from the anticipated *Folie Bergère* or *Lido* performances, which promised stages filled with beautiful women adorned in feathers and rhinestone-glittered costumes, their movements artfully choreographed and complemented by a featured singer and a master of ceremonies. Instead, this show was dominated by stand-up comedy, a raspy drag singer, and a dozen drag showgirls. As the night wore on, we retreated to our hotel, ready to rejuvenate for the sightseeing extravaganza that awaited us the next day.

Before turning in for the night, I playfully teased Donna about my eager anticipation of a charming maid, adorned in the classic black and white uniform, complete with fishnet stockings and a suggestive bustier, who would come in the morning to serve us breakfast in bed. My ego briefly let its imagination run wild, entertaining the notion of a ménage-à-trois, only to be promptly reined in by my more sensible side.

The following morning, as if on cue, there was a polite knock on our hotel room door. Donna and I lay beneath the sheets, both unclothed. I swiftly perked up, arranging the sheets just enough to pique the maid's curiosity and convey a hint of provocation. In my best French accent, complete with the requisite rolling of the "R" as Parisians do, I chimed, "Rrrrrrentier."

The door swung open abruptly, revealing an older woman, perhaps in her sixties. Her weathered complexion suggested she might have fought in the French Revolution and indulged in a few too many French pastries over the years. Without hesitation, she marched into the room. In a low and gruff voice, she greeted us with a simple, "Bonjour monsieur…madame."

My immediate reaction was to clutch the sheet and hastily lift it to my chin, an instinctual act of modesty.

With little regard for our presence, she unceremoniously deposited the tray at the foot of the bed. Then, without uttering another word, she strode over to the window and flung open the wooden shutters. Her actions spoke volumes. As she prepared to exit, I mustered a faint "merci." The door slammed behind her. Donna, now in fits of laughter, vividly reenacted my expression, the reality starkly contrasting with my earlier expectations.

At 9 a.m., we met in the hotel lobby. Alex's well-prepared itinerary propelled us into a day of exploration. First stop: the Louvre, where we marveled at renowned works, including the *Mona Lisa* and the on-loan *Pietà*. The pace was brisk, and the experiences left indelible memories. A swift lunch preceded visits to the Eiffel Tower and Notre Dame Cathedral. A personal request from me was to see the Paris Opera House and the splendor of its Couloire de l'Opera. It surpassed my wildest imaginings, I focused on the grand staircase, adorned with numerous balconies. Looking up, I beheld a dazzling ceiling, adorned with four allegories representing *The Triumph of Apollo*, *Minerva Battling Brutal Force Before the Assembled Olympians*, *The Charm of Music*, and *The City of Paris Receiving the Plan for the New Opera*—classic paintings by Isidore Pils.

That evening, Donna and I went to Montmartre, which offered the quintessential romanticism that saturates French-themed movies. The evening was fittingly romantic and left an enchanting impression that lingered in our hearts.

Alex's query about my desires before returning to London led to an unforgettable adventure the next day. We boarded the Paris Métro and arrived at a bustling flea market. Among the myriad treasures, a tarnished brass candelabra beckoned. I wondered how to transport it back to the States, and Alex's pragmatic advice—to disassemble and pack it—proved instrumental, making it a cherished item that continues to adorn my piano.

Returning across the English Channel on a more turbulent Hovercraft, our acrobatic baby once again entertained us, her spirited movements bridging the gap between countries. Nonetheless, as we reached firm land, her energetic displays ceased.

Back in London, our reunion with the city was marked by a classic meal of fish and chips. Soon after Donna suddenly became ill. Because of the pregnancy we were considerably concerned, so Alex arranged for medical attention at a nearby hospital to ensure our baby's safety and wellbeing. An ultrasound was performed revealing that the fetus was thriving and it seemed after some anti-nausea medicine, mother was doing much better as well. After a few hours Donna was released, and we returned to the flat. Despite the unexpected detour, we cherished the sight of our unborn child.

Our stay in London concluded with an impromptu party, a true testament to Alex's hospitality and the friendships we had formed. The casual gathering captured the essence of our time in London, with Alex's friends contributing to lively conversations and adding an air of intrigue about my career.

From the onset of the pregnancy, Donna held a firm belief that our forthcoming child would be a boy, even though the ultrasound had not confirmed the baby's gender. Donna's conviction was shaped by her experiences with previous pregnancies. This sense of certainty added a deeper emotional layer to the moment, as we decided on the name Alexander Thomas Boucher. The name not only reflected my own unflattering view of my first name but also carried a profound connection to our French heritage, making the choice all the more meaningful.

However, the next ultrasound done in NYC revealed the gender of a baby girl. Donna's reaction left me with the impression that she was shattered. Nevertheless, the quest for a new name ensued. We each established an office-wide polling system to decide. This process eventually led to the name; Kathryn.

As autumn neared, we eagerly anticipated our baby's arrival. The due date came and went, and medical intervention loomed as a possibility. Finally, Kathryn's entrance into the world was made possible by a mix of medical assistance, unexpected rapidity, and a father's hands guiding her journey.

The profound realization of parenthood struck me after we welcomed our daughter into the world. Suddenly, the enormity of my responsibility as a husband and father became real. As we left the hospital, I understood that life would never be the same again, and the journey of nurturing, guiding, and protecting our family had just begun.

The Sky Is Falling: Singing in the Rain

Expectations accompany parenthood, as does the reality of daily care for a newborn. However, the maternal behavior I observed in Donna did not seem to align with the warmth and joy often associated with welcoming a beautiful new baby that I had anticipated. Initially, I attributed this to postpartum depression or something similar.

As the months passed and we entered our third month of parenthood, it was time for the annual conference. For the conference weekend, we relocated to the Marriott Marquis—Donna, Katie, and I—adding to my already exhaustive 6 a.m. to midnight responsibilities. Nonetheless, I was bursting with pride as I paraded around with our little one whenever possible. During our stay at the hotel, Donna seemed more herself. However, once the conference was over and we returned home, her behavior seemed once again unsettling. I discussed my concerns with our pediatrician, Dr. Rocchio, and his nurse, Stephanie. Their recommendation was to find a specialist who dealt with postpartum depression.

Our third anniversary prompted a getaway to Orlando—a five-day vacation for the three of us. I hoped the trip would restore some semblance of normalcy and reignite the passionate intimacy we had shared before Katie's birth, an aspect of our relationship that had been incredibly fulfilling. It was evident that the trip couldn't fix what was amiss.

Frequently, Donna complained about her inability to handle the baby. To accommodate, I started bringing Katie to the office. She turned out to be an absolute angel. My office was isolated in the very back of the building, separated by a long hallway, boardroom and another long pathway where all the other offices were located. With the door closed, the sounds of a crying baby were nonexistent, ensuring no disturbance. My work often involved telecommunication, and my office setup included a headset connected to my phone.

When Katie was awake, I would secure her in her carrier against my chest, facing outward. She reveled in this position, constantly reaching for anything within her grasp. My desk became a hub of activity as I frequently rose to attend to her needs, which kept her content and engaged. While this arrangement appeared to work well, Stan later asked me to stop bringing her to the office as a certain colleague was uncomfortable with the fact that Donna wasn't working while I managed childcare.

Given our frequent travel and the added necessities of a baby, our compact two-door Nissan hatchback was proving inadequate. It became clear that we needed a larger vehicle, so we decided to purchase a new Oldsmobile Silhouette. Stan's generosity extended to providing a bonus for the down payment on the van. With considerable amount of travel planned that month we were very appreciative of the new spacious vehicle. We visited the Concord Resort, another Catskills destination like the Nevele; spent time with my parents in Massachusetts, including dinner with Fr. Norton; and even made a stop to see my in-laws in Floral Park.

With no improvement on the home-front, we finally enlisted the help of a therapist, Gretchen Viterman, at Spence Chapin—the same institution where Donna had placed her first child for adoption when she was seventeen. Donna remembered the counseling services they had provided her. We both believed that her current state of mind was somehow linked to her previous pregnancy and the emotional impact of being forced to give up the baby for adoption.

The initial joint therapy session did not proceed as expected. After 45 minutes of Donna sharing her feelings or lack thereof, followed by my observations, I detected what seemed to me, an undercurrent of hostility from Gretchen.

She said, "Well, maybe Donna just doesn't want to be married anymore!"

That stunned us into silence and our defense mechanism united us momentarily, prompting us to reevaluate the problems. We decided therapy with this individual was not the answer.

After much discussion of how Donna was feeling, the loss of self, and other issues that arose after Katie was born, we concluded that it might be helpful if Donna returned to work. Unfortunately, Bruce's early-onset Alzheimer's disease had necessitated his complete retirement. Donna reluctantly joined a temp agency, eventually landing a full-time position with the prominent Wall Street law firm, Sullivan & Cromwell. The fresh environment and added responsibilities appeared to serve as the catalyst Donna needed to reclaim her sense of self.

Realizing we needed help with Katie, my father, newly retired, moved in with us. He must have had serious concerns about Katie's well-being to leave my mother and take on this responsibility. I could sense his trepidation about our situation, and I saw his unwavering devotion to our daughter. His presence allowed Donna and me to focus on our jobs and each other.

Donna often worked late, sometimes returning home around 8 or 9 p.m., just in time to kiss Katie goodnight before I put her to sleep. The weekends were dedicated to assisting my dad with a kitchen remodeling project that had not yet been completed. On Sunday mornings, while Donna slept in, my father, Katie, and I attended church. My father, a man of few words, subtly conveyed his observation that Donna's interaction with Katie resembled that of an older sister engaging with a younger sibling. He remarked that while the playtime was enjoyable, she seemed quick to transfer the responsibility to any adult present. On the surface, our life seemed relatively ordinary—peaceful, free from arguments, and content. After all, my dad was up at the crack of dawn, taking care of all our daughter's needs: feeding, bathing, putting her down for naps, taking her for walks, and the occasional ice cream run to the mall. Dinner was always ready when we got home. Forget a nanny—we had a full-time granddaddy!

However, one aspect that hadn't yet resumed was our sexual life. We attempted to rekindle it, but I felt that Donna's body language conveyed a lack of enthusiasm, which instantly dampened my own interest. Despite this, my love for her remained strong, and I was willing to exercise patience.

Transitioning: The Evolution Overture

After four months with us, it was time for Dad to return to his life in Massachusetts. His departure left us facing a new dilemma: how to manage without his help. Thankfully, my boss, Stan, proposed a solution. He suggested that I work remotely from home and provided me with a computer and all the necessary tools to make it possible. With my office computer left on by my secretary, I could seamlessly connect and complete my tasks.

Impressed by my productivity while working remotely, Stan left for an extended trip to Europe. However, his departure instigated changes in the workplace. Within weeks, his ex-wife—who had assumed more decision-making responsibilities in his absence—informed me she was uncomfortable with my remote arrangement and rescinded Stan's approval.

As Stan's absence stretched on, I felt that his ex-wife became increasingly involved in the organization and that her decisions sometimes conflicted with mine. An unsettling feeling began to grow that my job might be in jeopardy. This was reinforced when she hired a young man, gave him an unusual title, and assigned him to my former office, which was conveniently located right next to hers. The newcomer was sharp, intelligent, impeccably dressed, and exuded ambition. He quickly developed a close working relationship with her, and when Stan finally returned from Europe, he, too, appeared to be captivated by the young man's abilities.

Over time, I noticed Stan's health seemed to deteriorate, and I felt that my professional dynamic with his ex-wife became increasingly strained. I wondered if she knew she was undermining my work as she continued to collaborate closely with the new hire. Feeling uneasy about the situation, I decided to keep detailed records for my own peace of mind.

One afternoon, she entered the office visibly upset, directing strong words toward me in front of others. This was perplexing and left me momentarily taken aback. Recognizing the need to address the growing tensions, I approached Stan to share my concerns about the workplace dynamics and his ex-wife's close collaboration with the new hire. I expressed the importance of resolving the matter and made it clear that it was impacting my ability to continue in my role. My conversation with Stan prompted him to take immediate action, and he addressed the issue directly with her. For a brief period, the situation seemed to stabilize. She reverted to her usual pleasant demeanor, acting as though nothing had happened, leaving both my secretary and me bewildered.

It wasn't long after that Stan disclosed the truth about his deteriorating health: he had AIDS. This revelation explained his recent struggles. Although the Association's Board of Directors was aware of his illness, Stan had never officially disclosed this information. Stan was no longer at the helm, and I felt that his ex-wife's animosity toward me made my job precarious. With the presence of the new colleague, I was now dispensable.

I panicked and confided to a board member (with whom I had developed a friendship) about the issues I was facing at the office and included a bit too many details. My intention was to secure my position. Unfortunately, the plan didn't unfold as expected.

Stan learned about my conversation and he called me into his office. We had a calm conversation during which he explained that he needed his ex-wife at that time and that I had reached the limits of what the Association could offer me. He presented a solution: my own business. I could retain all the equipment at home, including the computer and copy/fax machine. He would support me in launching "Event Planners International," focusing on medical conferences.

The endeavor proved to be initially successful. My first client happened to be Our Lady of Mercy Hospital, which provided me with steady employment until May of '91. Afterwards, however, securing new clients proved elusive, and my savings began to dwindle at a rapid pace. Fortunately, unemployment benefits came to our rescue, and by working at home I eliminated $300 per week in childcare, commuting expenses, and meals while on the road, putting ourselves in a more stable financial position.

While I cherished being a stay-at-home father, by August, I began to miss the daily interactions with adults in a professional setting. I longed for the banter between Stan and me. I yearned for the city's vibrancy, my apartment in Lincoln Center, and the array of wonderful restaurants within easy reach—quite the contrast to our money-draining home, which had been vandalized three times, while we were inside. One of those incidents occurred when my father was living with us.

As we were enjoying dinner in the kitchen on the ground floor and Katie was upstairs asleep, I heard what seemed like footsteps above me. I dismissed it at first, but upon hearing it again, I hastened to the second level and discovered a man at the door.

Politely, I inquired if I could help him.

He stammered, "Oh, excuse me! Is dis da Jones residence?" then promptly fled down the street.

We all rushed to the third floor to check on Katie, who was sound asleep. After I searched the baby's room and found everything in order, I crossed over to our bedroom. There, Donna stood staring at our bureau's drawers strewn across our mattress. Upon closer inspection, I realized the intruder had taken a few pieces of jewelry, including a ruby ring of mine. My father reported that the man had also taken his watch from the side table in the family room. Nothing of significant value was lost, and no one was harmed. Nevertheless, the feeling of violation was overwhelming, leaving me with a sense of disdain for our home and Jersey City. Remarkably, I had experienced no such incidents during my years living in NYC, sometimes even with my apartment door, left unlocked during the day.

As unemployment benefits approached their end, and our finances became more strained, it was time to consider a full-time position instead of continuing with my business, which wasn't gaining much traction. On a Monday evening, while perusing the New York Times help-wanted section, I stumbled upon an ad for a conference director position at Chemical Week Magazine, complete with a contact number—unusual for a job posting. I called the number, and a man who answered introduced himself as Michael, the magazine's editor-in-chief. Michael wasted no time and asked about my experience. He provided me with a number to fax him my resume immediately and called back about 15 minutes later to schedule an in-person interview.

During the interview, I learned that the magazine already had a conference director, but the company needed a second conference manager. Hoping to keep my business active, I proposed that Chemical Week become one of my clients. Michael agreed to the arrangement. The other conference director, being more experienced than I with foreign conferences, took the lead. We divided the list of conferences—Russia for him, Houston, and Poland for me, with both of us working on Hong Kong.

Only weeks after my start, Michael and the other director had a major confrontation, resulting in his abrupt dismissal. He was given just five minutes to pack his belongings under Michael's watchful eye before being escorted out. Michael then said if I wanted to continue with Chemical Week, I had to become a full-time employee. I agreed and after visiting HR, I moved into other director's former office.

A month later, Chemical Week moved to 7th Avenue and 57th Street. My new office faced a luxury residential high-rise. Outside my office was a row of cubicles for secretarial and support staff. Additionally, I had access to the graphic design department to help execute my marketing and promotion concepts.

It was common to see guys going over to someone's office with their morning coffee to talk about the upcoming game or the one played the night before. But coming to my office to chit-chat soon raised an eyebrow. Three colleagues seemed unusually engrossed by something outside the window behind me. Turning around, I discovered the source of their fascination—a couple in a neighboring high-rise apartment engaged in an intimate moment in their shower. It was clear that the designer or installer of these three-quarter-length windows had made a mistake. While the occupant couldn't see outside, anyone from the exterior had an unobstructed view inside.

Like clockwork, every morning around 9:15 a.m., a young woman, fit and athletic, would step into the shower. As she stood under the streaming water, her drenched dark hair cascaded down her back, creating a mesmerizing scene. Then another lean and athletic figure, reminiscent of a cyclist, stepped into the shower to join her. Together, they shared tender moments, lathering soap across each other's skin with care. Her leg rested on the ledge as their hands explored the closeness between them. Their kisses were deep and unhurried. Moving in harmony, they embraced fully, their intimacy a quiet, passionate rhythm. In just ten to fifteen minutes, it was over.

Unfortunately, Michael caught wind of the situation and promptly put an end to this unintentional spectacle, restricting everyone from visiting my office. Camaraderie had its limits!

Michael and I appeared to have a good working relationship, although it was notably different from my rapport with Stan. I couldn't help but notice that he consistently arrived early in the morning and regardless of how late I worked, he was still present when I left.

One November evening, around 7 p.m., as I was preparing to depart, he intercepted me and in an inquisitive tone asked, "Where are you going?"

I explained that I needed to head home to pick up my daughter from our caregiver.

In response, he uttered, "That's what your wife should be doing. Your primary focus should be on your job."

Michael was neither married nor a parent. Did this statement reveal a bit of a Napoleon complex? He had just made a grave error. He asked me to prioritize my job over my daughter, and that was out of the question. I attempted to explain the situation but quickly realized that it was falling on deaf ears and left for home.

Soon after, Michael recruited a new employee, Judy, a shrewd and accomplished business sales associate. Judy assumed control of the conference finances, including income and expenses. My responsibilities were reduced to conference logistics. Thankfully, Michael consulted her daily on financial matters, which freed me to do my primary work.

Judy insisted on having her own office, and because we needed to collaborate closely, I had to be nearby. Michael initially proposed that I give up my office to her and relocate to a cubicle outside her office. Having enjoyed my own office for the past eight years, the idea of moving into a cubicle didn't sit well with me. So, I devised an alternative solution. I approached one of the sales team members, who was stationed on the graphic design side, and suggested that he switch to my office—specifically, the one with the morning peep show, a proposition he eagerly accepted. Judy was then accommodated in the freshly vacated office.

Adjacent to it was an open area nestled between two pillars. It resembled an open floor plan and offered a splendid view of southern Manhattan through large windows. Although it lacked privacy, it was far superior to the confines of a cubicle or a cramped office. In fact, it was so spacious and appealing that it gave the impression that Judy was my personal secretary.

Meanwhile Donna was increasingly engrossed in her job and worked considerable amounts of overtime. Katie spent from early morning until late in the evening often until 8 p.m. under the care of Raquel, a Filipino woman. Raquel's husband was understandably displeased when his wife was still looking after Katie upon his return home, neglecting her own family responsibilities. Raquel told us that we needed to pick up Katie no later than 7 p.m., which added more pressure to my already demanding situation. Stress took its toll on me, affecting both my work performance and my emotional well-being.

I began to experience panic attacks, prompting me to seek therapy from a counselor named Stephen. His therapeutic approach incorporated aspects of Freudian and Jungian methods, and I found it easy to open up to him. He encouraged me to explore new job opportunities and to take actions that would alleviate sources of stress, such as cleaning our home, which led me to hire a house cleaner for the second time.

Donna's behavior seemed to be a study in contrasts, depending on whether we were in public, with family, or alone. For example, during Thanksgiving at my in-laws', Donna exuded positivity, affection, and engagement with Katie. However, upon returning home, I noticed a change in her demeanor; she seemed more withdrawn and less engaged with both Katie and me. A similar pattern seem to play out during our Christmas trip to Massachusetts. My emotions felt like a pendulum, oscillating between hope and despair. My therapist ultimately suggested that we seek couples counseling and referred us to Suzanne, a counselor in his building.

February 12th marked my departure for Hong Kong. It was my first trip away from Donna and Katie, and I felt deeply concerned about leaving my daughter's well-being in someone else's hands, even if they were her mother's. My departure was two days before Valentine's Day. In a romantic gesture, I arranged for flowers to be delivered.

Judy and I boarded a flight from Kennedy Airport to Hong Kong, with a layover in Japan. The plane was a double decker, with first class on the upper level. There were maybe a half a dozen people with us in first-class. The flight was twenty hours, during which my body struggled to find rest, leading to frustration because I was unable to sleep sitting only slightly reclined in my seat. To find some semblance of comfort, I removed the seat cushions from a few seats and laid them on the aisle floor, allowing me a few hours of sleep. The flight from Japan to Hong Kong presented a different scenario—no first-class section, and the majority of passengers disregarded the "no smoking" rule. Judy, a smoker, was content, but I found myself concerned about my health due to the smoke-filled cabin.

At long last, we reached Hong Kong, landing in Kowloon. The city was vibrantly electrifying, resembling New York City on steroids. We settled into the Grand Hyatt hotel. The lobby was filled with elegant black marble, accented with Caribbean blue lighting. My room boasted a stunning view of the harbor. I had just enough time to put down my luggage when Judy and I had to meet with the hotel's conference staff to discuss logistics.

During the meeting I suddenly felt unwell—shaky, nauseous, and clammy. I excused myself and returned to my room. Shortly after, there was a knock on the door. It was the hotel's Director of Conference Services. He recognized my discomfort as jet lag and insisted on guiding me to the hotel spa. There, I was introduced to the spa manager, who prescribed a regimen to alleviate my symptoms. I was asked to undress, then led to a sauna, instructed to sit for twenty minutes while drinking several bottles of water. Afterward, I was then directed to take a cold shower. Following these steps, I returned to my room and slept soundly until 6 a.m. the next day. When I woke, I felt completely reinvigorated and ready for the day, even before my first cup of coffee.

Our makeshift office was conveniently situated right in front of the main conference room on the hotel's mezzanine. However, it was also adjacent to one of the kitchens, which emitted strong fish odors that made eating unappealing. The second night of the conference marked a significant event: a dinner at the Aberdeen Marina Club, featuring a traditional Chinese junk boat ride up the river. These boats, primarily used for tourism, departed from the hotel marina at 6 p.m. Cocktails and hors d'oeuvres were served during the cruise. After an hour, we reached our destination. The guests were led to an exquisitely decorated banquet room adorned in beige and gold. Crystal chandeliers sparkled overhead, and arched windows overlooked the harbor. The dinner was a culinary delight, followed by a delectable dessert.

As the evening wound down, it was time to settle the bill with the Club manager. Michael pulled out a credit card, the only authorized credit card.

"I don't think we should pay for all 150 meals. Only 147 guests showed up," he said.

"Michael, we contracted for and they prepared 150 meals. We have an obligation to pay for all of them." I said. Even Judith chimed in, agreeing. Before I could stop him, Michael snatched the invoice from my hands and said, "I'll show you how to do your job!"

He marched to the Maître D. We watched as he was escorted to the club manager.

For thirty minutes, as we waited and the temperature dropped precipitously, I could hear the heated voices of my boss and the club manager. The guests grew restless and cold. Some opted to take taxis back to the hotel. I, however, had to remain.

Eventually, Michael reemerged, sauntering across the room. He thrust a paid invoice at me. Judy and I looked at the invoice clearly marked with its revision. "What? Only one meal deducted?" I asked. "Really?" I rolled my eyes and together we returned to the junk, chilled to the bone.

It seemed to me that Michael's behavior continued to deteriorate, solidifying my decision to resign once the trip was over. He departed early on the last morning of the conference leaving Judy and me to finalize things. With our flights scheduled for the following day, I decided to take advantage of a rare free afternoon and evening.

I engaged a driver arranged by the concierge to explore Hong Kong's shopping scene. My first stop was a men's clothing store in a modern high-rise building. The exorbitant prices quickly put things into perspective – I was out of my element. Undeterred, I continued exploring and stumbled upon an alley side street filled with fair-like outdoor booths selling affordable knockoffs. I indulged myself with purchases, including a jade green silk bomber jacket for myself. I hunted for something special for Donna. Eventually, I found a jewelry store where a unique necklace caught my eye. To my surprise, the price was affordable at $150. With Donna's fondness for handmade jewelry, it was the perfect gift.

For my final meal in Hong Kong, I wanted a change from Asian cuisine. I asked the concierge to find me an Italian restaurant and was directed to the hotel's penthouse floor, where the finest Italian dining awaited. Despite initial sticker shock, I embraced the indulgence, knowing it would be charged to my room and paid by Chemical Week. The meal left me content and relaxed, and I returned to my room for a restful sleep.

Returning home, I felt the weight of uncertainty pressing down on me. How would Donna react? Would her mood swing toward warmth or frost? My suitcase seemed heavier than usual, burdened with the anxiety of what awaited me on the other side of the door.

As I climbed the stairs and stepped inside, I was met with a sight I hadn't expected: Donna, her face lit up with a smile I hadn't seen in ages. Before I could speak, she wrapped her arms around me, her kiss a familiar melody I'd nearly forgotten. Behind her, on the couch, was Katie nestled in her carrier, framed by a sparkling banner Donna had crafted. "Welcome Home Daddy," it proclaimed in glittering letters, the warmth of those words thawing my apprehension.

Eagerly, I reached for Katie, expecting her tiny arms to reach back. Instead, she turned her face away with the exaggerated defiance only a baby could muster. It was her way of saying; *How dare you leave me?* Still, her pout brought a smile to my face.

I was itching to unpack, to share the treasures I'd brought back from Hong Kong. Donna's eyes lit up as I pulled out the his-and-her silk bomber jackets, their vibrant embroidery shimmering under the light. I handed over gifts for other family members before saving the best for last. Donna watched me with anticipation as I placed a black velvet pouch in her hands.

Inside was an intricate necklace: graded onyx beads, delicate glass monkey charms, and ancient empress silver nail guards. Her breath caught as she lifted it into the light, the piece a perfect blend of history and artistry. "It's stunning," she whispered, her voice thick with emotion. She kissed me again, her gratitude unmistakable. For a fleeting moment, it felt like I'd bridged a gap between us.

That night, as Donna drifted into sleep, I lay beside her, longing for the intimacy we once shared. The house was quiet, but its walls seemed to echo with the promise of something mending. Comforted by the knowledge that I was home, I, too, surrendered to sleep.

The next morning, over coffee, I announced with resolution, "Donna, I've decided not to return to Chemical Week,"

She looked at me, unperturbed, as if she'd seen this coming. "Good," she said, setting her mug down. "Now you can stay home with Katie, take care of the house, and we'll save on childcare and commuting costs."

Her practicality was expected, her reaction indifferent. Still, a part of me had hoped for something more—some acknowledgment of what the decision meant. But as the morning light streamed in, illuminating the remnants of the previous night's warmth, I resolved to let her response settle. After all, I was home, and for now, that was enough.

Our first couple's counseling session was six days after my return from Hong Kong. The typical therapist scene played out—a couple sitting awkwardly on a couch while the therapist took notes. Suzanne, a middle-aged professional, listened to our recollections and agreed that our love was evident, expressing optimism that the issues could be resolved swiftly. This was exactly what I wanted to hear, as I was determined to fix things. Donna, however, expressed skepticism, believing that Suzanne underestimated the gravity of our problems, and that resolution wouldn't come quickly or easily.

Over the following months, my world narrowed to the dimly lit rooms of therapy sessions. Twice a week, I poured myself into individual sessions with Stephen, dissecting my failures, fears, and hopes. The rest of the time, Donna and I sat across from Suzanne in joint sessions, our words like fragile threads trying to stitch together something broken. Fixing our relationship consumed me, a relentless obsession that left little room for anything else.

Then came the day before our fifth wedding anniversary. In Suzanne's office, the air felt heavy, thick with unspoken truths. Donna sat aside from me, her hands clasped tightly in her lap, a faint shimmer in her eyes. Suzanne's voice cut through the silence, calm but pointed. "Donna, can you tell Ron how you're feeling about your marriage and your feelings for him?"

Donna turned to me, her gaze chilling. I braced myself, gripping the edge of the couch as her words struck like a hammer. As I remember, she said "Ron, our marriage is over. I don't have any feelings for you anymore. Actually, the thought of you touching me is repulsive."

The room seemed to tilt, and I fought to keep my composure as a flood of mortification, anger, and despair washed over me. Her words replayed in my mind, sharp and unforgiving. She wasn't just giving up—she was obliterating any hope I had left.

After the session, Donna went home. I, on the other hand, needed an outlet for the storm raging inside me. At the gym, I attacked the weights with a ferocity I didn't know I possessed, each rep fueled by anger and heartbreak. When my muscles screamed for relief, I retreated to the sauna, the heat searing away the edges of my pain as I tried to collect myself.

By the time I got home, the sun had dipped low, painting the yard in a soft, golden light. Donna was outside, laughing softly as she played with Katie, music drifting from speakers. The sight tugged at something deep inside me, but I couldn't bring myself to join them. Instead, I retreated to the family room and impulsively slid our wedding video into the player. The scenes flickered to life, but I'd forgotten one key detail: the sound was linked to the outdoor speakers.

The vows we'd exchanged five years ago spilled into the yard, mingling with the music. Moments later, Donna appeared at the doorway, Katie on her hip. She sat down beside me, her eyes expressing a mix of anger, sadness, and something softer I couldn't quite name. I reached for her, and to my surprise, she didn't pull away. Instead, she leaned into me.

For over an hour, we sat there on the couch, holding each other and crying silently. The weight of her earlier words still lingered, but in that moment, the tears felt like a release, a fragile bridge over the chasm between us. Even Katie seemed bewildered by our tears, her tiny hands patting our faces in an attempt to console us.

Finally, I stood, wiping my face. "Come on," I said, my voice rough but resolute. "Get dressed. I'm taking my family out to dinner."

Donna blinked at me, then nodded. The simplicity of the gesture felt monumental. Minutes later, we were in the car, heading to the Marriott Marquis in the city. The dinner was elegant, the food exquisite, and for a fleeting moment, the dark cloud that had hovered over us seemed to lift. We laughed, talked, and clung to the fragile hope that maybe, just maybe, there was still something worth saving.

Kindred Spirits: The Harmony of Souls

Upon returning home, the weight of reality hit me hard. My sessions with Stephen and counseling with Suzanne had led to the acceptance that my marriage was beyond repair. As weeks went by, Donna and I maintained our distance—it was my understanding that she spent late nights working while I focused on preparing for the upcoming conference in Poland.

Not soon after, I got a phone call. Sandra's voice crackled through the line, strained but steady.

"I need your help," she said, her words tumbling out in a rush.

Her company was in chaos—budgets rejected, meetings held without her, accusations of overspending flying thick and fast. Her voice wavered, tinged with a vulnerability I hadn't heard in years. The memories of our shared past stirred, and before I fully processed the weight of her plea, I found myself agreeing to fly to Williamsburg around the 22nd.

When I landed at the Norfolk airport, a familiar figure, Sandra, stood by the arrivals gate. She waved, her smile warm but tinged with weariness. As we settled into the car and began the drive to Williamsburg, the hum of the tires on asphalt filled the silence. Finally, I broke it, recounting the fragile state of my marriage. My words spilled out haltingly, a mix of hope and resignation. I spoke of Donna, of the flicker of hope I clung to despite the mounting evidence of our impending end. Sandra listened, her hands gripping the wheel tightly, her occasional nods encouraging me to continue.

The drive felt both endless and fleeting. It had been years since we'd spent time like this, our connection reduced to sporadic updates after I married Donna. Yet here we were, the years peeling away with each mile, the familiar rhythm of our conversations rekindling something long dormant. As we approached Williamsburg, I couldn't help but wonder what challenges awaited—not just in Sandra's world, but in mine.

As we drove, Sandra's voice wavered between calm and candid as she spoke about her life. She mentioned, almost offhandedly, that she and her husband had been living apart for four years. The conversation paused as we turned into her townhome development, "Jamestown 1607," a cluster of neatly arranged townhouses with identical brick facades. Children's laughter echoed faintly from the direction of the community pool, a central feature of this suburban enclave catering to single mothers and middle-class families alike.

Inside, the scent of fresh laundry and faint traces of lemon cleaner greeted us. Her townhome, modest but carefully maintained, revealed much about Sandra's personality. The eat-in kitchen, a sea of white and blue, displayed a mix of practicality and charm. White Ikea furniture, neatly arranged, caught the midday sunlight streaming through the window, and a cork board cluttered with family photos and school reminders hung by the fridge. Upstairs, the soft thudding of footsteps hinted at Marco, her energetic eight-year-old son, who soon appeared, a whirl of motion and questions, his toy airplane clutched tightly in one hand.

Sandra didn't linger on small talk. She gathered papers from the coffee table and spread them out in front of me, the frustration in her movements betraying the composure in her voice. "Here's the situation," she began, tapping her finger on a financial report. "Mansur, the Russian teacher I hired, is trying to undermine the company. I'm sure of it. He's been rallying board members and parents against me."

Her words hung in the air as she reached for another stack of documents. "The board is divided. Some back him, others are on my side, and then there are a few who... well, they're just waiting to see how this plays out."

She slid a detailed ledger toward me, the faint crinkle of paper punctuating her explanation. "Take a look at this. Our Cinderella production went over budget, or so our Treasurer claims. But I went through everything—receipts, deposits—and we're actually in the black." Her blue pen scrawled circles and underlines over specific numbers, the precision of her work evident in every mark.

Saturday arrived, and Sandra was scheduled to teach. Meanwhile, back at the house, I sat at the kitchen table, the company's by-laws spread before me, their legalistic language offering clues and potential solutions to a dilemma more fraught than she dared to say aloud.

Observing Sandra during this time, I couldn't help but notice the transformation within her. The elegance and beauty that had once entranced men were now overshadowed by weariness, concern, fear, and exhaustion. Previously a whirlwind of Italian energy, Sandra now moved through her routines robotically. Her teaching style had evolved, deviating from her New York methods. Even her attire had shifted dramatically from the New York artist in high-heeled boots (or stylish shoes), Ann Taylor skirts and blouses, to earth shoes, floor-length peasant skirts, and leotard tops. Her hair had been cropped short, very different from the silky chestnut waves that once cascaded down her back. Her posture of confidence had been replaced by an air of vulnerability. Even her dance studio seemed devoid of the NY sophistication. The lobby of the studio displayed no trace of Sandra's presence or mention of her illustrious past —not even the iconic image of her performing an "arabesque en pointe."

Yet, the unwavering love and respect her students held for her remained unchanged.

One afternoon, I leaned back in my chair, watching Sandra's tired movements as she flipped through her phone. "Pick your favorite restaurant," I suggested, hoping to lift her spirits.

Her lips curved into a faint smile. "Giuseppe's."

That evening, as she stepped out of her room, she wore the same bohemian style she always defaulted to—flowing fabrics and muted colors that seemed to mirror her mood. An idea struck me, a memory of her in a different time and place. "Hang on," I said, motioning her back. "Let's try something else tonight."

Digging through her closet, I unearthed a forgotten collection of sleek, tailored clothing from her New York days—pieces she hadn't worn since her time with Misha. A black blazer, a satin blouse, and a pair of fitted trousers emerged from the depths, still carrying the faint scent of ambition and dinners in the city.

"Put these on," I insisted, holding them up. She hesitated, her hand brushing the fabric like it held a memory she wasn't ready to face. But she took them, and when she returned, the transformation was undeniable. The sharp lines of the blazer accentuated her posture; the shimmer of the blouse caught the light, illuminating her face. Her hair, combed back with care, framed her features in a way that felt both nostalgic and new.

At Giuseppe's, heads turned as we walked in. A waiter paused mid-step, and a couple at a nearby table glanced over with approving smiles. Sandra's cheeks flushed, but a spark lit her eyes. As the evening unfolded, I reminded her of the stories behind the clothes—the stages she had conquered, the rooms she had commanded, the dreams she had chased. Each word seemed to draw her shoulders back a little more, the flicker of confidence growing brighter.

By the time dessert arrived, she laughed more easily, her gestures animated in the way I remembered. The dim glow of the restaurant lights caught the gleam in her eyes, and for a moment, it was as if the weight she'd been carrying had lifted, replaced by a glimmer of the woman she used to be.

The next day, I met with board members, probing for information. Positioned as a consultant, I addressed the challenges facing the company's summer program and upcoming productions. Gathering as much insight as possible, I returned to New York to analyze the information and come up with some recommendations. However, my upcoming trip to Poland put my plans to help with her studio on pause.

Ritorna Vincitor: A Polish March

My resignation from Chemical Week caused complications. A few weeks after I left, Judy had difficulty finalizing our contracts with the Polish conference, because none of her calls were being returned. While at Chemical Week, I however, had had no trouble establishing contact. As it happened, our London office learned that I was a former opera singer who could speak French. Our contacts in Poland spoke French and my language fluency turned out to be a key diplomatic asset for doing business with them. Doors that had been previously closed swung open.

When Judy attempted to take over after my resignation, the Polish representatives cut off communication once more. Reluctantly, Michael was forced to make a call to me himself. "Ron, this is Michael. Could you come to the office tomorrow? I really need to speak with you." His tone was uncharacteristically measured, almost pleading, and I couldn't help but feel intrigued.

Truthfully, I needed a distraction. The weight of my domestic troubles felt suffocating, consuming my thoughts. That evening, I took a long walk with Stan by the Westside Pier, the Hudson River reflecting the soft glimmer of city lights.

"Ron," Stan began, his voice steady yet pointed, "Do you realize how much you've sacrificed because of other's poor decisions? It's time to recognize your value. Let's head back and draft what you need—what's acceptable to you—in writing." His words rang with clarity, cutting through my inner turmoil like a beacon.

The following morning, I arrived at the office early. Judy intercepted me, her expression fraught with worry. "Ron, the Warsaw people have completely stopped communication, and we can't—" She was cut off as Michael appeared, ushering me into his office.

Moments later, Louis, the CEO, joined us. "Ron, we need you to resolve the Polish situation. The conference is sold out, flights are booked, but we still don't have accommodations. Please work something out with Michael." He left abruptly, leaving Michael and me to negotiate.

Michael wasted no time. "I want you to come back to work," he said, leaning forward.

This was my opportunity to reclaim some dignity. "Michael," I began, my voice steady, "first, I want the bonuses I earned from previous conferences. Second, moving forward, I want to be paid the same salary as my predecessor. Third, I want the paid vacation I've accrued. Finally, I want three months' compensation after I leave Chemical Week. And one more thing—don't ever put me in a position where I have to choose between my family and this job again."

Michael nodded hesitantly but faltered when I presented the contract Stan and I had prepared. Just then, The CEO, Louis, reappeared. "Have you reached an agreement?" he asked. Under Louis's watchful gaze, Michael hastily signed.

Returning to work brought a surprising sense of relief. Judy and I developed a much more amicable relationship, and I found solace in focusing on professional challenges rather than personal strife.

With the Polish business resolved, I departed from Kennedy Airport on June 7, 1992, boarding a direct flight to Warsaw, equipped with my portable Sony CD player and the album, *The Domingo Songbook*, by

Placido Domingo. His song, *He Couldn't Love You More*, echoed my sentiments. I played it on repeat, reaffirming my belief that no woman would forsake a man who loved her with such intensity without finding another to replace that love. Donna's incessant talk about her boss, a tall, blonde, accomplished lawyer from Park Slope, Brooklyn, and her recurrent mention of wanting to reside there, fueled my suspicions of their involvement. In my mind, they were likely to replay the story I had lived.

When I arrived in Poland, there was a message from Donna's mother waiting for me at the front desk. I called her at once.

 "Ron, Donna has come down with pneumonia, and she is staying with me. Your parents have Katie with them," she said.

My parents were in the midst of their own upheaval, relocating from Florida to Massachusetts for the summer, and yet they graciously offered to take Katie for a couple of weeks.

The conference was held at the Victoria Inter-Continental Hotel in Warsaw, a relic of the 1950s with its garish orange and green décor. Upon arrival, we were greeted in the lobby by politicians, dignitaries, and key hotel personnel. Krystyna, our contact, had arranged a small reception with hors d'oeuvres and champagne. As conversations ebbed and flowed, she leaned toward me and muttered in French, "Look at them. They're all pompous assholes." Her candor startled a laugh out of me, but she quickly stood, raising her glass to propose a toast in halting English. "We welcome you all to Poland and Warsaw. We hope you enjoy your stay and have a successful conference."

Later that evening, seeking respite from the day's tensions, I made my way to the hotel spa. In the sauna, there were two other gentlemen lying on their towels, completely nude. Following suit, I unwrapped myself, placed my towel down and reclined. Slipping in and out of consciousness, I heard the two men leave and was grateful for the solitude. That peace was short-lived. Moments later, two women entered, completely naked, their laughter echoing softly. Embarrassed, I quickly sat up and wrapped my towel over me and apologized in French explaining I wasn't aware that the sauna was co-ed. They laughed at my awkwardness.

"You're from the U.S., aren't you?" one of the women asked. Flustered, I left the sauna and retreated to my room.

Over the next few days, Krystyna and I developed a strong working relationship. One afternoon, she approached me with a smile. "Mr. Boucher, we'd like to invite you and fifty of your guests to a special surprise dinner. A bus will pick you up at 6:30 p.m."

The following evening, the group assembled, and we boarded the bus. As we left Warsaw, traveling down increasingly rural roads, Michael grew visibly uneasy. "Ron, do you have any idea where we're going?" he asked. His agitation grew with each passing mile, and he muttered darkly about the dangers of being Jewish in a formerly communist country. Just as he approached me for the third time, the bus came to a stop in a wooded area.

"Why are we stopping?" Michael demanded.

Krystyna stepped forward, her calm demeanor easing the tension.

"Please follow me," she said.

Beyond a row of trees, the soft glow of lights revealed a small, white stucco cottage. Inside, a grand piano, tables, and French doors leading to a candlelit patio awaited us.

As champagne flutes were distributed, Krystyna raised her glass. "Ladies and gentlemen, on behalf of my government, I welcome you to Żelazowa Wola, Chopin's birthplace."

Gasps rippled through the group, and my heart swelled. To be here, in the presence of Chopin's legacy, was a profound honor.

Dinner was a five-course masterpiece, each paired with exquisite wine. As the pianist played Chopin's compositions, the music seemed to float through the trees.

Then, as dessert was served, Krystyna stood again. "Ladies and gentlemen, our pianist tonight is renowned for his Chopin interpretations but is also an esteemed opera accompanist. Mr. Boucher, would you honor us with an aria?"

Michael grabbed my arm. "You're a conference manager, not an opera singer," he hissed.

I leaned in, my voice low but firm. "If I don't sing, your worst nightmare might come true on the way home." Pulling away, I approached the piano and whispered to the accompanist, who smiled and nodded.

As the first notes of "E lucevan le stelle" from *Tosca* filled the air, I poured my heart into every word. The final notes hung, the crowd erupting into thunderous applause.

The next day, Judy and I dined together in town. Over dinner, she confessed, "Michael hired me to make your life miserable, hoping you'd quit. But after last night, I realize how much you've endured."

With that, we forged an alliance, transforming our working relationship into a partnership.

On the conference's final day, Krystyna invited Judy and me to a private screening at City Hall. The Mayor turned to his interpreter, who conveyed in French that we were about to witness a special film reserved exclusively for distinguished guests. We were guided to plush, burgundy velvet chairs, their arms wide and inviting. As we took our seats, we were informed that the film would proceed in three parts: the history of Warsaw before the war; actual World War II footage of the city's devastation by Hitler's army; and Warsaw's post-war reconstruction, aided significantly by the French, who repurposed bricks salvaged from the rubble.

The second segment of the film gripped us with unrelenting emotion. The harrowing images of a city reduced to ashes, its soul laid bare, were almost too much. Judy and I instinctively reached for the tissues thoughtfully placed beside our chairs. Silent tears traced paths down our cheeks as we absorbed the anguish and resilience etched into every frame. Our visible reaction seemed to resonate with our host, who was observing us. He later noted that he had hoped we would appreciate the gravity of the documentary.

As the final frames faded and the lights gradually grew brighter, we composed ourselves, disposed the multiple tissues we had used and offered our heartfelt thanks to the Mayor. Before we departed, he presented each of us with a beautifully crafted coffee table book on Warsaw, a gift that I treasure to this day, its pages a poignant reminder of the city's indomitable spirit.

British Color: A National Anthem

With Katie with my parents and Donna with her mom, I realized I had a few free days left. After phoning my friend, Alexander, and rescheduling my flights, I was all set to spend the weekend in London. Alex greeted me at Heathrow Airport. It was late but we shared a cognac before retiring for the night.

A sharp knock on my door jolted me from sleep. I groaned, squinting at the clock on the bedside table. 7 a.m. The door creaked open, and Alex's eager face appeared.

"Get up! You're going to the 'Trooping the Colour'," he announced, his voice bubbling with excitement.

"Trooping the what?" I mumbled, still tangled in the haze of sleep. Alex's expression turned to one of exaggerated disbelief.

"You don't know what 'Trooping the Colour' is?" he exclaimed, as though I had just confessed to not knowing the Queen herself.

Before I could respond, he launched into an animated explanation. "It's only one of the most spectacular events in Britain! A grand military ceremony to celebrate the monarch's official birthday." His words spilled out in a rush, painting vivid pictures in my mind. "There'll be over 1,400 soldiers, 200 horses, and 400 musicians all parading at Horse Guards Parade. The Queen inspects the troops, and then there's a fly-past by the Royal Air Force. You can't miss it."

His enthusiasm was infectious, and soon with my handwritten directions. "What are these for?" I asked. "Oh! I have seen this many times before, But this is a most likely once in a lifetime for you to witness." Moments later I was weaving through the bustling crowds that lined the streets of London. The air buzzed with anticipation. Children perched on their parents' shoulders, Union Jack flags fluttered in the breeze, and the faint strains of military bands drifted over the sea of spectators.

I found a spot near the barricades, and the rhythmic beat of drums grew louder. The first regiments came into view, their scarlet uniforms blazing in the sunlight, brass buttons glinting with each precise step. Horses adorned with elaborate bridles trotted past, their riders sitting tall.

Then came the fly-past. The roar of engines filled the sky as planes soared overhead in intricate formations, trailing red, white, and blue smoke. The crowd gasped and clapped, faces turned skyward, captivated by the spectacle.

Random people in the crowd speculated whether the Queen would ride a horse or choose a carriage because of her age. I was positioned between two men, a curmudgeonly older Englishman on the left and a flamboyant man on the right who was obsessed with Lady Diana.

As the procession commenced with the Royal family, my eyes darted between Prince Phillip and Prince Charles on their stallions and the Queen Mother in her adorned carriage. A crescendo of cheers erupted when Princess Di's carriage came into view. The flamboyant man nearly fainted from excitement. Just as the procession concluded, the man on my left leaned forward and, addressing both of us, proclaimed, "Well, it was my good fortune to have seen two queens in one day." His tone was serious but his eyes were twinkling.

For a moment, I forgot my grogginess and the early wake-up call. Caught up in the vibrancy of the ceremony, I found myself swept into a world where history and tradition collided with modern celebration, leaving an indelible impression.

―

True to my word, I returned to Williamsburg on July 20th, this time accompanied by Katie. Unknowingly, this visit set in motion a new course of events that would shape my future. Sandra and I, we quickly settled into a comfortable rhythm. Sandra taught during her summer intensive ballet program, and I undertook the role of child-minder. Katie and Marco's harmonious interactions were evident.

Observing Katie's response to this low-stress environment, I noticed a transformation in this environment: she was more receptive, markedly happier and increasingly independent. She thoroughly enjoyed Marco's vibrant company. My familiarity with Marco provided a smooth integration into his life for me, and his affection for me spurred a subtle competition for my attention. The ease of being around Sandra returned, reminiscent of our time together in New York. She exuded simplicity and realism, approaching life one day at a time.

Throughout the ten-day stay, I collaborated with the ballet company's Board of Directors to identify gaps in fulfilling fiduciary responsibilities and to proactively address potential legal challenges.

This candid discussion galvanized change, leading to resignations and restructuring. The visit concluded with so much uncertainty that I was asked to return as soon as possible.

In August, I returned to deal with the unresolved matter with the Board. During meetings with the remaining board members, we executed changes to the company's structure. We named Sandra as Artistic Director and made her a voting member of the Board. In the midst of these discussions, the new Board President offered me a position as Executive Director, which would require me to move permanently to Williamsburg. This was not a possibility at that time.

My domestic dance with Sandra continued harmoniously, offering moments of ease and natural alignment as we flowed through our daily routines calmly, with affection and lots of laughter. The children relished a carefree final stretch of summer before school beckoned. Before leaving, I agreed to return for a September 24th board meeting and to render a decision regarding the position. There was still so much uncertainty with unresolved matters with my marriage, parenting after a divorce, and employment. With that consideration, I did urge them to consider other candidates.

Turning Point: The Turning Toccata Revisited

Just before my final days at Chemical Week, I found myself walking back from Michael's office after bidding him goodnight, intending to head home myself. It was past 8 p.m., and the office was deserted, except for a striking redhead sales associate who had been recently assigned to my former office. Our interactions had been minimal; we had merely crossed paths. As I stepped into her office, she sat on the edge of her desk, her short skirt and slightly undone blouse hinting at her cleavage, while she inquired about the Warsaw conference. In a flash, memories of the infamous couple engaging in shower escapades in that office rushed back. My eyes involuntarily wandered to the window, where they were at it again, under the glow of the bathroom light. Trying to regain focus on her face, I noticed her following my gaze.

In a sultry tone she remarked, *"Oh, so that's what the talk was all about. I heard about that couple but have never seen them in action."*

She sauntered closer to the window, leaning forward with her hands on the ledge. *"Oh, wow, they're really going at it."*

Mirroring her position, I stood behind her. In an instant, the charged scene, her intoxicating perfume, and her proximity stirred a deep arousal within me. The room buzzed with electricity, and my control wavered as I subtly pressed my pelvis forward, met by her gentle push backward—a teasing brush of contact. She sensed my desire, leaning harder against me, her head arching back onto my chest, her ear against my lips and breath.

"*Lock the door*," she whispered urgently.

Swiftly, I secured the door and returned to our position. We embraced with urgency, our longing evident in every touch and glance. The scene being played out from the shower heightened the atmosphere, and the unspoken connection between us grew stronger.

Months of suppressed emotions culminated in this moment, a blend of passion and vulnerability. We moved in sync, the energy between us mirroring the fervor we had witnessed. Every sensation was intensified by the anticipation that had built over time.

As the crescendo of our connection was reached, the world outside seemed to pause, leaving only the rhythm of our shared experience. The moment lingered, but reality soon intruded as voices from the hallway reminded us of the world beyond.

With a quiet understanding, we composed ourselves, exchanged a few soft words, and parted ways. That night marked the end of one chapter, leaving its memory etched in time, never to be revisited.

On the last day, Judy and I had our last lunch together. She handed me a gift box containing a necktie from Bergdorf Goodman. The tie was mix of royal blues, purple, and golds with imprinted logos of famous hotels around the world, along with a card that said. "Dear Ron, To one of the best hotel negotiators in the business! Thank you for the months we have worked together. If we survived Warsaw, I'm certain our paths will cross again! I wish you all the good things in life you deserve. Love, Judith."

The following day was a counseling session with Stephen. His amused smile hinted that he had noticed something about me had changed since our last meeting.

"You seem quite different from the last time we walked," he commented, his expression sly.

I had no shame; there was no sense of violating any sacred tenets. Guilt had no place here. In fact, I found the experience liberating, cathartic, more satisfying than any massage. I relayed the events without divulging intimate details.

"So, how did it make you feel?" He wore a constant grin throughout our conversation and said, "Ron, I think you're on the right track,"

Scotland: A Misty Aire

I believe it was the result of an article that appeared in a trade magazine, listing me as the up-and-coming conference director, that earned me an invitation to Scotland's prestigious St. Andrews Resort. The excursion also included trips to Glasgow and Edinburgh and a dinner at a nearby castle. The trip included two free round-trip tickets from American Airlines, and I decided to take Donna along. For four days, we would be pampered and indulged. While I viewed this as a final attempt to find common ground and begin our path to recovery, I also felt perturbed, thinking that Donna didn't deserve to share something I had earned.

Within hours of our arrival, Donna's laughter rang out across the garden, drawing the attention of an eager 18-year-old who hovered close by, his gaze fixed on her every move. She leaned in, her hand brushing his arm as she spoke, her expression a mix of playful mischief and focused intent. I lingered nearby, watching their interaction unfold, a tightening in my chest reminding me of the connection I once shared with her—a connection now veiled by her easy charm with strangers.

The young man's father approached, his eyes carrying the shadows of recent hardships. "Divorce," he confided as we exchanged polite pleasantries. The conversation flowed naturally, and before long, I found myself speaking with uncharacteristic frankness about my marriage, the words tumbling out as if searching for solid ground.

At dinner, Donna's energy filled the room. Her animated gestures and sparkling eyes contrasted sharply with my quiet observations. By the time the meal ended, exhaustion nudged me toward bed. Morning brought an early breakfast—a blur of clinking plates and muted conversation—before we set off with the other guests for Glasgow and the promise of adventure.

The rugged and inviting countryside unfolded before us, as we mounted dirt bikes. Donna revved her engine with a determined grin, challenging the young man to match her speed. Mud sprayed from their tires as they raced ahead, their shouts of exhilaration blending with the hum of motors. I trailed behind, the distance between us not merely physical but tangible in every way. She hardly glanced back.

The pattern became an unspoken truth. On every excursion, Donna's attention was elsewhere—on the thrill of competition, on the company of others. I remained present, a shadow tethered to the edges of her vibrant world, silently yearning for a place in her gaze.

One of our evening dinners took place at Blenheim Palace, owned and occupied by the Duke and Duchess of Marlborough. As we disembarked from the chartered bus, we stood in front of a magnificent stone castle that transported our minds to a bygone era depicted in historical films. The grounds were a marvel, featuring elegant English landscaping and a multitude of peacocks displaying their splendid plumage.

Inside the castle's dark foyer, a table was set for fifty people. I vividly remember the appetizer—haggis, a traditional Scottish dish containing sheep's or calf's offal mixed with suet, oatmeal, and seasoning, boiled in an animal's stomach. Most guests shied away from this infamous dish, but I found it unexpectedly delicious, happily accepting the extra portions that others rejected.

The highlight of the evening came after dessert, when our host led us to the castle's entrance doors. Upon their opening, darkness lay ahead. We gathered cautiously beyond the front steps, and a spotlight illuminated a circle of grass before us. From the distance, bagpipe music gradually approached. Stepping into the light, a group of men dressed in traditional Scottish kilts stood before us, each holding bagpipes with plumes resembling peacock feathers.

As the music played, I was momentarily transported back to the world of Brigadoon. The performer in me was itching to step forward and deliver an encore of my famed dance. However, my hesitation was interrupted when an authentic sword dancer stepped forward, his steel swords reflecting the spotlight's glow. After around twenty minutes of extraordinary bagpipe artistry, the men slowly turned and disappeared into the darkness, their music fading away—an ideal ending to a magical evening.

We traveled to Edinburgh the following day, where Donna and I spent most of our time shopping for souvenirs. Donna was in high spirits, a side of her I hadn't witnessed in a long time. We wandered along cobblestone streets lined with thatched-roof homes and quaint shops. After a quick hour-and-a-half trip, we returned to the resort to rest before dinner. This final dinner was to be held in the main dining hall. Kilted men served us a meal of pheasant followed by after-dinner drinks and cigars in the green room. A group of us proceeded to one of the ballrooms, where we continued sharing drinks, jokes, and camaraderie.

The chatter of the group filled the air, glasses clinking and laughter rising as the evening unfolded. Then, a voice cut through the noise, a suggestion tossed out like a dare: "Why don't you sing for us?"

All heads turned to me, their faces alight with anticipation. I hesitated, glancing at Donna, who'd stopped mid-conversation to look my way, her expression unreadable. The chorus of encouragement grew louder, wrapping around me until resistance felt futile. With a tight smile, I nodded.

"Alright," I said, rising to my feet. "But no piano, so bear with me."

A ripple of excitement passed through the room as I cleared my throat, their expectation weighing on my shoulders. My mind settled on a piece: "E lucevan le stelle" from *Tosca*. The opening notes lingered in my memory as I began, the first lines escaping my lips in a quiet but deliberate tone.

The room hushed. Each word, each note hung in the air, carried by nothing but my voice. I poured every ounce of discipline and passion into the performance, navigating the intricate runs and soaring high notes with precision. My gaze, however, betrayed me, seeking Donna across the room. She sat motionless, her eyes locked on me, an intensity in her expression I hadn't seen in years. Admiration? Longing? The question burned within me as I sang.

The aria ended in a quiet crescendo, the final note dissipating into silence. For a heartbeat, the room remained still, then erupted into applause. Donna rose, moving toward me with a deliberate grace. Before I could fully process her intent, she wrapped her arms around me, her kiss warm and lingering.

"You were incredible," she whispered, her voice tinged with emotion. For a fleeting moment, it felt like the connection we'd lost had returned, rekindled in the glow of shared admiration.

The evening wound down, laughter fading as we retreated to our suite. Donna, still flushed from the wine and the night's revelry, leaned into me with an intensity that caught me off guard. Her playful remarks danced on the edge of suggestiveness, her fingers brushing my arm as she spoke. My pulse quickened, but so did my unease.

Her gaze locked onto mine, a smirk playing on her lips as she leaned closer. "Do you know how irresistible you are when you sing?"

I hesitated, searching her face. The wine had loosened her inhibitions, and though her words were what I'd longed to hear, the shadow of her earlier flirtations with the young man lingered in my mind.

"Donna," I said, my voice steady despite the turmoil within. "I... I can't. Not like this. You've had too much to drink. Let's talk in the morning, when we're both clear-headed."

Her smile faltered, replaced by a flicker of hurt. She stepped back, her arms crossing protectively over her chest. "You're unbelievable," she muttered before turning away and slipping into bed without another word.

I stood there for a moment, the echo of her words cut deeper than I cared to admit. The night's triumph now felt hollow, weighed down by the complexities of what had unfolded.

There were two beds in the room: Donna slept in one, and I slept in the other. The next morning, we didn't address the events of the previous night. We packed our suitcases and descended to the lobby. The shuttle to the airport awaited. After bidding our farewells to the others and expressing gratitude to our hosts, we headed home. This trip became the last romantic chapter of my marriage to Donna.

A Month of Reckoning: The Foxtrot

It was only a few days after I had returned to New Jersey that I received a response to the resumé I had submitted to Symedco Corporation, a pharmaceutical marketing firm focused on new drugs entering the market. Located in Princeton, New Jersey, I had a promising initial interview on September 11th for the position of international conference director. The positive impression from my second interview on the 17th translated into a concrete job offer with a salary reaching six figures. I was scheduled to begin working on October 5th, a decision that ensured I stay in New Jersey.

Fulfilling my commitment, I returned to Williamsburg to meet with Sandra's Board of Directors, inform them of my employment offer with Symedco and presented my recommendations for moving the company forward.

Upon my arrival, I was informed of new setbacks suffered by Sandra's ballet school. Her top ten senior dancers had been drawn away to a new studio by promises of greater opportunities, which greatly impacted the studio. Sandra's formerly top supporter financed the new studio with a commitment to support it for nine months, after which it would be solely responsible for its expenses. This precarious situation required immediate attention to prevent further losses.

My first task was to stem the tide of departing students and restore confidence in her studio. While maintaining business as usual, Sandra and I began crafting the season's performance schedule. Since a full ballet production wasn't feasible for the spring, we decided to focus on smaller events, such as fundraising weekends with the New York City Ballet, a showcase at the Generic Theater in Norfolk, and a collaborative effort with the Gainesville Ballet in Florida. Evaluating the company's repertoire, I recognized that the contemporary ballet choreography, set to classical baroque music, garnered noticeable local acclaim which, in turn, manifested some additional financial support. Williamsburg's appreciation for early music combined with a modern dance approach attracted community recognition and bolstered the company's financial standing.

Regrettably, I had to convey to the board and Sandra that I couldn't accept the role of Executive Director. Instead, I'd remain available as a consultant when necessary. Upon returning to New Jersey, I promptly enrolled Katie in a nearby preschool close to our home. In preparation for my upcoming job with Symedco, I had all my suits dry cleaned and acquired a couple of fresh white shirts. I also made arrangements for Raquel to pick up Katie from school every day.

Everything was finally set to begin my new position the following Monday morning, but Donna was nowhere to be found. In those days before cell phones, we were reliant on our landline for communication. It was around 9 p.m. on a Sunday evening when the phone finally rang. In anticipation of Donna's call, I answered it, only to discover that it was the woman from Symedco who had hired me. "Ron, I have some unfortunate news."

She went on to explain that they had recently lost two major European accounts, which I was supposed to oversee. Consequently, the partners had decided to postpone my start date. While I still had a job, it wasn't commencing immediately. This was a bit disappointing, but I could see a silver lining in the delay, as it would allow me to continue working on some of the projects I had initiated for Sandra's ballet school and company.

I lay awake, listening to every creak in the house and the hum of cars passing beneath the bedroom window. At 3 a.m., when a car stopped in front of our house, my heart skipped. I leapt out of bed, straining to hear what was happening. The front and back passenger doors swung open, followed by the driver's side rear door, setting the scene like an old circus clown stunt where everyone piles out, runs around, and jumps back in.

Donna emerged from the car first, followed by three men, all exchanging flamboyant kisses and hugs as they said their goodbyes. I watched quietly, then returned to bed, my mind still racing. Donna crept up the stairs moments later and slipped into Katie's room, settling on the daybed we had bought for Katie when she outgrew her crib.

Shortly afterwards, I began the process of seeking a divorce, preparing for life without her.

Meanwhile, it was October 20, Katie's birthday. The customary practice as dictated by the school was for parents to provide treats for the classmates. With Donna still not awake by mid-morning, I took charge, arranging pizza and donuts, and decorating the school lunchroom. Even as the party's start time approached, Donna had yet to appear, adding to my growing frustration. By the time she finally arrived, the party was nearly over. She was apologetic, but offered no excuses. For Katie's sake, I played along with the charade. Afterward I took Katie home in silence.

With still no word from Symedco, I seized the opportunity for a long weekend trip with Katie to visit my parents. We returned home to an unexpected scene: an uncorked wine bottle, unwashed dishes, including two of our finest wine glasses, and an unmistakable indication that our bed had been shared by two. A bouquet of flowers on the baby grand piano stood as an emblem of the insult added to my injury. Her explanation—that the flowers were a birthday gift from someone at work—was not only irritating but also heightened my growing suspicions that she was having an affair.

During what would be my final therapy session with Suzanne, she declared with conviction that the marriage was over and urged me to leave immediately. Departing her office, I was shattered but I knew her words were rooted in truth.

At 4 p.m., I walked briskly toward the Path Station on Christopher Street, my thoughts scattering like leaves in the wind. The sun bathed the city in an unusually warm glow, drawing crowds to the sidewalks. I passed the Duplex, a gay friendly bar known for showcasing up-and-coming musical and vocal talents. It's doors were thrown wide open. A flash of familiarity caught my eye. I froze. Sitting at the bar, relaxed and smiling, was Donna.

A jolt of disbelief coursed through me. My steps faltered, confusion twisting quickly into anger. What was she doing here? I crossed 7th Avenue, my heart pounding, but halfway across, I stopped. My anger demanded answers. Turning sharply, I retraced my steps, my resolve hardening with each stride.

As I entered, the bartender's voice reached my ears: "Hey, Donna, looks like someone's coming for you—cute guy."

She glanced up, her expression barely flickering as she turned back to him with a casual laugh. "Oh, that's my husband!"

The words hit me like a slap. The ease, the apparent nonchalance in her tone only fueled the fire simmering inside me. I closed the distance between us, my voice low and steady despite the storm brewing within.

"Donna, can we talk outside?"

Her eyes flickered with something—hesitation, annoyance—before she followed me out into the afternoon light. I didn't waste time.

"Why aren't you at work? And why are you here, at a gay bar, in the middle of the afternoon?"

Her response was as stunning as it was baffling. "I am loved here!"

The absurdity of her words left me momentarily speechless. Loved? What about the love waiting for her at home? My voice tightened as I reminded her of the love she had from Katie and me, emphasizing the impact of her choices on our daughter. Each word was a lifeline thrown into the widening chasm between us, but her demeanor remained maddeningly detached.

Realizing I was teetering on the edge of losing control, I took a measured step back. "Donna, this isn't something we can ignore anymore," I said firmly. "Katie's been asking for you. She needs her mother. And so do I."

The weight of my words hung in the air, but I saw no shift in her expression. Resentment clawed at my chest, and I knew I couldn't stay.

"I'm staying with Tristan tonight," I added, my voice cool and deliberate. "You can reach me if there's an emergency. But don't expect me home."

Without waiting for a reply, I turned and walked away, the hum of the city enveloping me. Each step felt heavier than the last, but this time, I wasn't looking back.

Symedco remained apologetic that they could not commit to a starting date. They appreciated that I was still interested.

No longer able to tolerate my marital state of limbo, I met with my attorney to determine what I needed to do to move to Virginia. I left her office with a "Separation Agreement" that Donna and I had to sign. As soon as we officiated the document, I was free to leave with Katie.

I had anticipated that Donna would reject the terms outlined in the agreement as she wanted one of the lawyers at her office to go over it. Not long afterwards, to my surprise, I found the document on the piano, signed.

I returned to Williamsburg on November 2nd and finalized my commitment by signing a contract to assume the role of Executive Director for the Contemporary Ballet Theater.

I was staying at Sandra's townhouse as per usual. It was a late evening; Marco was already asleep upstairs, and Katie was visiting my parents in Florida. Sandra stood in the doorway of the half bath, and I indulged in my customary flirting, not anticipating any reciprocation. It had always been subtle, but this time, she responded in a way that seemed to dissolve the barrier between us. The chemistry and electricity still shimmered in the air. A simple kiss paved the way for a cascade of emotions, momentarily giving rise to self-doubt about my values and commitments. Yet, these concerns were fleeting, overshadowed by the passion of the moment. Our kisses grew more fervent as I guided her to the couch. Slowly, we shed clothing, my lips tracing the contours of her body. Each touch was a symphony, each movement a dance, as we merged in a sensual pas-de-deux. For me, it was the realization of a dream. Hours passed, and only the impending dawn reminded us of time's passage. Though brief, the sleep that followed was the most restful I had experienced in years.

A few weeks later, I found myself back in New Jersey with Katie, preparing for the ballet company's highly anticipated excursion to New York City that had been in the works. I took the opportunity to pack more of our belongings for the move to Williamsburg.

During my time at the house, a card protruding from Donna's purse caught my attention. Succumbing to curiosity, I slipped the card from its envelope and read, "Darling, you are the best thing that ever happened to me." This deepened my suspicions about her loyalty, though I never confirmed the nature of her relationships. With Sandra, I was able to fully let go of the past and the hope that it could somehow be reclaimed.

I had to agree to allow Donna to take Katie to her grandparents' house in Long Island during the Thanksgiving weekend. I met them at Penn Station, where I bid farewell to Katie.

Simultaneously, Sandra and I transitioned to the St. Moritz Hotel, as I had arranged an exceptional weekend for a select group of dancers and their family members.

For the New York City excursion, I arranged a bus for fifty people to depart Williamsburg at 7 a.m. the day after Thanksgiving. The journey took around seven hours. Upon arrival, I coordinated everyone's check-in at the St. Moritz on Central Park South, which offered stunning views of the park. A special dinner awaited at "Il D'uomo," one of my favorite Italian restaurants, followed by an enchanting Christmas show at Radio City Music Hall. After a short walk back to the hotel, I was certain that everyone was ready to retire for the night.

Sandra and I found ourselves in bed by 10:30 p.m. and we realized that it was rather absurd given that we were in New York City—our familiar territory. I promptly got out of bed, insisting we seize the opportunity to do something. Dressed and ready within fifteen minutes, we headed east on 59th Street to the Palm Court Room at the Plaza Hotel, a famed establishment, the atmosphere was as delightful as the dessert, champagne and chocolate-covered strawberries.

During our romantic interlude, an elderly lady dressed in all black, accompanied by a group of young men entered and immediately became the center of attention. Dubbed the "black widow" due to her attire and age, she ignited curiosity and conversation. Adding to the charm of the evening, a trio of musicians began playing, with a solo violinist taking requests. I asked for the "Intermezzo" from the opera *Thais*. Yes, it was the same piece that was played at my wedding to Donna, but the beauty of Massenet's composition overshadowed any sentiment.

As Sandra and I walked back to our hotel, we contemplated how our home had been mere blocks away not long ago. We reflected on the impact our decisions had made on our lives: Sandra with her marriage and move to Williamsburg and me with my marriage and move to New Jersey. We also took comfort in the promising stage of our transformed relationship— shifting from platonic to romantic—bringing both excitement and caution, as we had both been wounded before. Our night ended in each other's arms, making love before drifting into a peaceful slumber.

Following breakfast the next morning, the dancers from the Williamsburg group congregated at Lincoln Center for a master class led by principal dancer Debbie Wingert of the New York City Ballet. The event took place in the Rose Hall, offering a rare opportunity for the subset of students we had brought to the city.

After the class, a few chose to watch Debbie rehearse her Arabian dance for her upcoming performance in the Nutcracker Ballet. Others opted for a Broadway matinee or shopping excursion. Dinner was individual choices, followed by a captivating performance of the Nutcracker by the NYC Ballet. Post-show, we gathered at Café Mozart for dessert before returning to the hotel.

The following day, Sunday, featured a private tour of Lincoln Center. Sandra guided the group through the New York State Theater while I showcased the Metropolitan Opera House, revealing dressing rooms and behind-the-scenes views.

Once everyone had boarded the bus for the return trip to Williamsburg, Sandra and I headed to the house in New Jersey to pick up Katie. When we arrived, Donna was alone, her expression calm but distant.

"Where is Katie?" I asked, a knot of unease tightening in my chest.

"Darlene took her for a walk," Donna replied nonchalantly.

"Darlene? Who's Darlene?" I inquired.

"She's a friend who needed a place to stay. I thought it would be nice to have someone else here and help with expenses. She's staying in Katie's room."

Sandra nudged me, gesturing toward a pair of men's shoes by the front door—shoes that didn't belong to me. My mind raced, the questions multiplying. Was Donna seeing someone? Was he upstairs in the bedroom while we stood here? The thought burned in my mind, and before I could stop myself, I asked, "Why are there men's shoes at the door?"

Donna didn't flinch. Her reply was almost too casual: "Oh, those are Darlene's."

The explanation didn't sit right, but before I could press further, the front door swung open. Darlene and Katie stepped inside. All my doubts and questions dissolved the instant I saw Katie's bright, welcoming smile.

At that moment, nothing else mattered. Donna, the shoes, the unease—none of it could hold me. My focus narrowed to Katie and the urgent need to get her out of that house. It was as though a door had closed behind me, shutting out the life I'd known with Donna, while the life ahead with Sandra and Katie beckoned.

There was only one trip left. I returned to New Jersey to pack the last of Katie's and my belongings, closing the door on our lives there. It was December 8th, the Feast of the Immaculate Conception—a day steeped in significance for Catholics. The symbolism of the day wasn't lost on me. It was a time to reflect on grace, renewal, and beginnings that emerge even from painful transitions. As I sorted through the remnants of our old life, I couldn't help but wonder if this move, however uncertain, was part of a larger plan—one that might lead Katie and me to something purer, something new.

When it was finally time to leave, I braced myself for a dramatic farewell, half-expecting Donna to seize Katie in a fit of regret, crying, "I can't let you go!" But the only tears shed were ours—Katie's and mine. Donna stood frozen, her cold, distant stare cutting deeper than words ever could. It was over, clean and absolute.

As I started the car, the silence between Katie and me felt heavier than the boxes piled in the back. I wiped my eyes, forced a smile, and whispered, "Everything will be all right, Katie. You'll see."

But as the wheels rolled forward, and we crossed the threshold into the unknown, my conviction faltered. Would everything truly be all right?

Katie and Me

Each mile south felt like stepping further into a dense fog, the road ahead a void filled with uncertainty. And yet, deep within, a flicker of hope refused to be snuffed out.

This wasn't just a journey to Williamsburg; it was a step into the unknown —a pilgrimage not of miles but of the soul. Katie and I couldn't foresee what lay beyond the horizon, but an unshakable sense stirred within me: this wasn't the end of our story. It was the threshold of something entirely new: a beginning veiled in shadows, waiting for the moment when the darkness would finally give way to light.

To be continued.

ABOUT THE AUTHOR

Ron Boucher has spent a lifetime bringing stories to life—on stage, in the studio, and now, on the page. A classically trained singer and dancer, Ron began performing at age 15 and went on to appear with the New York City Opera, the Metropolitan Opera, and with the Emmy Award winning, Prince Street Players.

But his greatest role has been behind the scenes— teaching, directing, and nurturing young talent. As founder of the Community Alliance for the Performing Arts (CAPA) Fund and co-creator of the Eastern Virginia School of the Performing Arts, Ron has dedicated over two decades to helping children and teens find their voices—literally and artistically.

From the footlights of opera houses to the joy of watching students shine in their first stage roles, Ron's journey is a celebration of passion, perseverance, and the transformative power of the arts.

www.ingramcontent.com/pod-product-compliance
Lightning Source LLC
Chambersburg PA
CBHW051257120626
46547CB00015B/1977

* 9 7 8 1 9 6 0 8 0 8 1 5 8 *